D1744333

BMW
MOTORCYCLES
Gold Portfolio
<u>1950-1971</u>

Compiled by
R.M.Clarke

ISBN 1 85520 3774

 BROOKLANDS BOOKS LTD.
P.O. BOX 146, COBHAM,
SURREY, KT11 1LG. UK

A -BM50BGP

ACKNOWLEDGEMENTS

Now well established in their own right, Brooklands Books Gold Portfolio series of motorcycle titles has proved a popular addition to the original car series and the information contained in each title is widely recognised by enthusiasts as an authoritative source of both factual and comprehensive data about various makes and models. Our objective is to collect interesting stories and road tests on a marque and present them in a compact form so that owners and others interested in the subject will not have to search through back issues of old magazines to trace an elusive feature.

This title, which covers BMW singles and twins, will appeal to those of a more discerning nature who appreciate the high quality of the many different models produced by this Munich-based manufacturer. Here we bring together within one cover a collation of the more significant magazine features published between 1950 to 1971.

The generous assistance given so readily by the world's leading publishers has made this in-depth collection of information possible. Brooklands Books are greatly indebted to the publishers of each of the following magazines for permission to reproduce their copyright material: *Cycle, Cycle Guide, Cycle World, Motor Cycle, Motorcycle Mechanics, Motor Cycling, Motorcyclist Illustrated* and *Motorcycle Sport*.

Our thanks also go to The Classic Motorcycle for allowing us to use Martyn Barnwells photograph of Phillip Tooth riding a 1956 BMW R26 on our front cover.

R.M. Clarke

BMW were latecomers to motorcycling as they did not manufacture their first complete motorcycle under their own name until 1923. They had made aircraft engines during the 1914-18 war, as instanced by their logo which depicts an aircraft propeller spinning against a blue sky. The Treaty of Versailles meant they could no longer make them and so, after a brief diversion producing office furniture and agricultural machinery, started making motorcycle engines instead.

Their first twin cylinder model was based on the British-made Douglas but they then saw advantages in following the engine layout of the ABC, in which the horizontally-opposed engine was mounted transversely in the frame. Thereafter their twin cylinder models followed a similar arrangement, building the engine in unit with the gearbox and adding the sophistication of shaft final drive. Most manufacturers also had at least one cheaper model in their range and, to achieve this objective, they introduced a single cylinder machine in 1929. It was claimed to be the first ohv single cylinder engine to have its valve gear fully enclosed. Like its larger brothers it was not particularly cheap but the quality was certainly there.

It was not until 1948 that BMW were permitted to again resume the production of motorcycles and initially were restricted to a capacity of 250cc. After a couple of years the familiar black and white twins reappeared and by 1960, the first of their memorable R50S and R59S models made their debut, with their distinctive Earles-type front fork. Today they have acquired a collectors' value and good examples will realise high prices at motorcycle auctions. The late sixties saw the birth of a new generation of twins, the /5 series, the larger capacity examples of which coincided with the superbike era. They added a new dimension to BMW ownership with their refined handling and outstanding mechanical quietness.

Jeff Clew

CONTENTS

494 c.c. Transverse-twin

A Quality German Machine with an Appeal Alike to the Touri;

WHEN the production of civilian motor cycles restarted after the war years, no machine emerged in its post-war guise with higher goodwill based on earlier products than the R51/2 B.M.W. The pre-war production machines had earned praise throughout the world, a B.M.W. had won the 1939 Senior T.T., and a B.M.W. still holds the maximum speed record.

Nowadays only one horizontally opposed B.M.W twin is in production. The machine is basically similar to the R/51 of 1939, but incorporates a few modifications, the most interesting of which is the redesigned cylinder heads and overhead rocker

The R51/2 B.M.W. has an unobtrusive appearance which belies its high performance

gear. The pre-war five-hundred was marketed as a sports model, but no such claim is made for the current machine; indeed, it has a general appearance which suggests a touring roadster of demure performance. Therein lies one of its attractions, because while the R51/2 is well mannered and pleasurable to ride at medium speeds, it has a top-end performance that puts it in the sports category and encourages the appellation " Jekyll and Hyde."

Coil ignition is employed and is switched on by depressing the body of the lighting switch fitted in the head-lamp shell. Each cylinder has its own carburettor fed through intake pipes

connected to a single air filter sunk in the top of the crankcase-cum-gear box casing. The carburettors have no air slides; instead, there is an intake shutter at the mouth of the filter.

For cold starting it was found that an adequately rich mixture was given by flooding the carburettors; the shutter was not employed. The kick-starter crank is on the left side and has its axis in line with the machine; the most convenient way to depress the pedal is with the right foot while the machine is on its central stand. By British habits this might seem to be an inconvenient necessity, but two factors lessen any criticism that might be applied to this kick-starter layout. First, the engine started readily whether it was hot or cold; secondly, the tick-over was absolutely reliable, so that the chance of the engine's stalling was remote. Moreover, the engine idled so quietly and, with the ignition retarded, so slowly that one felt almost encouraged to keep the engine running for lengthy periods, when in similar circumstances with many machines there would have been the inclination to stop the engine and to restart it when ready to move off.

Mixture strength to each cylinder, as supplied by the separate carburettors, was correctly balanced for idling and low speeds and indeed, as far as could be judged, for all speeds. Pick-up of the engine as the twistgrip was turned was clean throughout the range. The twistgrip has a longer travel—a slower action—than usual on British machines and was perhaps slightly heavy in operation. The operation of all controls was inclined to be heavy and the foot-change pedal sufficiently stiff in movement to become tiring at the end of a long day's run.

With the machine stationary and the engine idling, the clutch freed satisfactorily so that bottom gear could be engaged without noise; one could not feel the operation of the gear-change mechanism through the pedal, which sometimes resulted in doubt as to whether the gear had been selected. The clutch took up the drive smoothly, though rather quickly. The

machine as a whole is nicely balanced and could be ridden at very low speeds and manœuvred slowly in confined spaces feet-up without any special skill. In such circumstances the steering was light and entirely free from roll—as it was throughout the speed range.

The transverse disposition of the cylinders makes it necessary for the footrests to be slightly farther back than on the majority of machines. Handlebar width is above average—30in direct from tip-to-tip. At first, the riding position felt slightly unconventional, but after a few miles' experience was considered to have its merits, especially for the ease with which the footrests could be used for support. This is not to imply that the saddle was not up to its work—it was, in fact, commendably comfortable. Footrests, saddle and handlebar are adjustable.

The B.M.W. is quiet mechanically, and the silencers give an admirably subdued exhaust note. There is something more than absence of mechanical clatter. What noise does

Power unit is of attractively neat design and is beautifully finished. Throughout the test no oil leaks occurred

B.M.W.

and the Sportsman

Handlebar controls are neatly grouped. Lid of the tool-box in a tank recess has a lock

emanate from the engine is dull and as if insulated by, say, very heavy oil. At town speeds the B.M.W. is pleasurable to ride. It encourages one to be in gentlemanly mood by reason of its quietness and easy acceleration. The engine pulls well and incites ambling in a highish gear in relation to road speed though there was the objection that there is a hardness in power delivery that can, indeed, be felt at speeds as high as nearly 40 m.p.h. when accelerating in top gear. Each power stroke can be felt.

The "Jekyll and Hyde" characteristic of the machine is soon apparent when open roads are encountered. There is a complete absence of high-frequency vibration, and as the revolutions mount the engine has the smooth, noiseless power flow of a turbine. Performance is zestful, and, because of the smoothness, quietness and effortlessness of the engine, speeds achieved can be deceptive. When driven as hard as open road conditions permitted, the engine proved tireless and remained unusually cool, as might be expected with the light-alloy cylinder heads so fully exposed to the air stream. Any top-gear speed above 40 m.p.h. to the maximum could be regarded as a comfortable cruising speed so far as the engine was concerned.

To avoid clashing, gear changes had to be leisurely. When obtaining the quarter-mile acceleration figures it was found that third gear, if engaged as rapidly as possible irrespective of the clashing of pinions, slipped out of mesh. Perforce, therefore, gear changing had to be slow for this type of performance data, and the hindrance is reflected in the time and speed figures recorded.

Both front and rear suspensions are inclined to be hard by modern British standards. For example, at dawdling speeds—say, 10 m.p.h.—over cobbles and tram-track inspection covers, the amount of front fork and rear plunger movement was negligible so that suspension was largely provided by the tyres. Under average conditions, the suspensions have a well-controlled movement, the slight hardness perhaps contributing to the marked degree of stability of the machine especially apparent during high-speed cornering. The steering was pluperfect (the damper was never brought into use) and the machine handled in the most confidence-inspiring manner without the lightest signs of drift or chopping-out when cornering fast on indifferent surfaces. Stability was also of a high order under wet road conditions; skidding was never experienced.

The brakes of the machine tested did not match the perform-

ance, largely because the front brake lacked real power, no matter how much effort was given to applying the lever.

Throughout the test the engine remained free from oil leaks; the degree of cleanliness was outstanding, with the crankcase retaining a "just-from-the-showroom" appearance. Mudguarding was above average in effectiveness. The beam from the head lamp gave a wide spread of light of higher-than-average intensity, and the dipped beam, while adequate for the rider, had a clean cut-off that ensured oncoming drivers were not dazzled.

Many detail features of the B.M.W. appeal to the experienced rider. Both wheels are quickly detachable; the tools are carried in a tank recess provided with a lock; a locking bar is supplied which fits into mating fork and frame lugs and, when in position, ensures that it would be impracticable for the machine to be wheeled or ridden away.

It is understood that modifications which are being introduced for the R51/2 will include the fitting of a prop-stand, and a narrower handlebar; on the new bar the clutch and brake levers will require a smaller hand span, and the operation of horn and dipper controls will be more convenient.

Information Panel

R51/2 494 c.c. B.M.W.

SPECIFICATION

ENGINE : 494 c.c. (68 x 68 mm) o.h.v. horizontally opposed twin. Fully enclosed valve-gear operated by push-rods and twin chain-driven camshafts. Light-alloy cylinder heads and cast-iron barrels. Light-alloy pistons. Crankshaft supported by two ball bearings. Oil-pump in crankcase reservoir driven by skew gear and shaft from offside camshaft ; reservoir capacity, 3½ pints. Compression ratio, 6.3 to 1.
CARBURETTOR : Bing-Spezial 1/22/29 and 1/22/30 ; twistgrip throttle control, air shutter on intake cleaner in upper gear-box cover.
IGNITION and LIGHTING : Bosch coil, with manual advance by handlebar lever. Bosch 70-watt dynamo ; 7in head lamp.
TRANSMISSION : B.M.W. four-speed gear box with positive-stop foot control and hand lever. Gear ratios : Bottom, 11.8 to 1. Second, 8.87 to 1. Third, 6 61 to 1. Top, 4.85 to 1. Single-plate clutch in flywheel. Shaft secondary drive with flexible coupling at front and universal joint at rear. Spiral-bevel final drive gears in oil bath ; reduction ratio, 3.89 to 1. R.p.m. at 30 m.p.h. in top gear, approx. 1,900.
FUEL CAPACITY : 3 gallons.
TYRES : Metzeler, 3.50 x 19in studded, front and rear.
BRAKES : 7.87in dia front and rear.
SUSPENSION : B.M.W. telescopic front fork with hydraulic damping ; plunger-type rear-springing, with coil compression springs and rubber deflection stops.
WHEELBASE : 55in.
SADDLE : Pagusa, rubber pan-type, with tension spring anchored to nose pivot. Unladen height, 29in.
WEIGHT : 396lb, with approximately 2 gallons of fuel.
PRICE Not yet available in Great Britain.
ROAD TAX · £3 15s 6d a year ; £1 0s 8d a quarter.
MAKERS : Bayerische Motoren Werke A/G., Munchen 13, Germany. Concessionaires : A.F.N., Ltd., Isleworth, Middlesex.

PERFORMANCE DATA

MEAN MAXIMUM SPEED : Bottom : 38 m.p.h
Second : 56 m.p.h.
Third : 75 m.p.h.
Top : 88 m.p.h.

MEAN ACCELERATION				10-30 m.p.h.	20-40 m.p.h.	30-50 m.p.h.
Bottom	...	...	...	2 4 secs	—	—
Second	...	...	...	3.4 secs	4.0 secs	3.8 secs
Third	...	...	...	5.6 secs	5 4 secs	5.6 secs
Top ...	...	...	...	—	9.2 secs	9.0 secs

Mean speed at end of quarter-mile from rest : 65 m.p.h.
Mean time to cover standing quarter-mile : 19.8 secs.
PETROL CONSUMPTION : At 30 m.p.h. 94 m.p.g. At 40 m.p.h., 72 m.p.g. At 50 m.p.h., 61 m.p.g. At 60 m.p.h., 48 m.p.g.
BRAKING : From 30 m.p.h. to rest, 31ft (surface, damp tar-macadam).
TURNING CIRCLE 16ft.
MINIMUM NON-SNATCH SPEED : 16 m.p.h. in top gear.
WEIGHT PER C.C. : 0.89 lb.

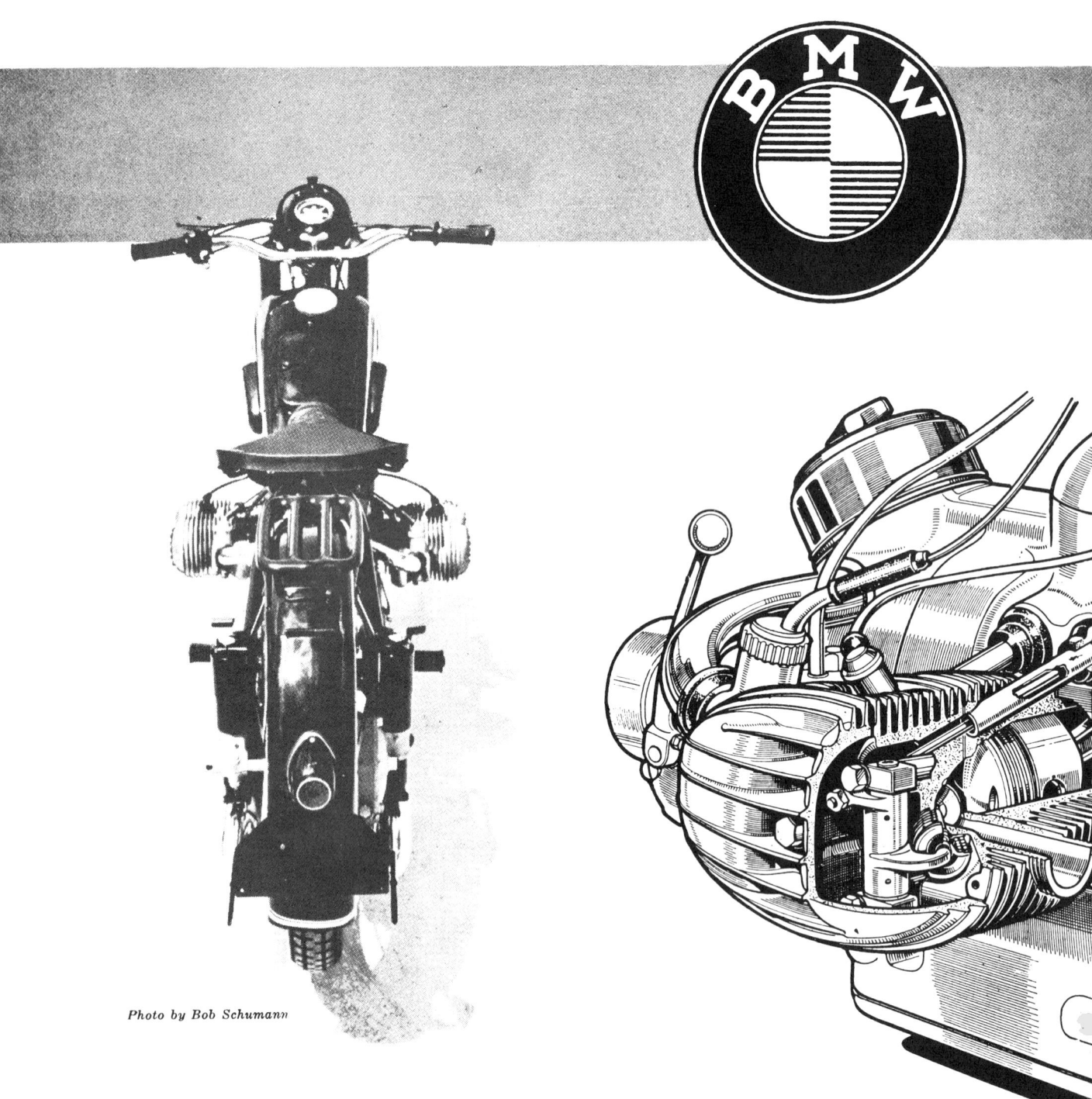

Photo by Bob Schumann

ABOVE, Culmination of 25 years' labor—appears sleek and powerful from any angle. From the beginning, the Bayerisch Motoren Werke of Germany has pioneered in reliability and the application of advanced mechanical refinements. The R 51/3 and R67 models are identical except that the R 51/3 contains a 500 cc displacement, while the R67 is of 600 cc. The 67 was primarily introduced for sidecar work and has a 1 to 5.6 compression ratio, not susceptible to octane fluctuations. The 500 cc unit has a higher ratio of 1 to 6.3. Basic appearance over previous year's models is barely discernible, but upon going inside, you will find many advancements

ABOVE, Chains of '51 have been shed in favor of gear drive from main shaft. Camshaft, ignition, magneto, and oil pump are now all driven by helically toothed spur gears (compare with cutaway shown in BMW road test—CYCLE, July, 1951). Sectional steel crankshaft runs on hardened journals in two ball-bearings. Hardened connecting rods run on roller bearings, and along with pistons, piston pins, cams, pushrods, rocker arms and valves, are splash lubricated. The splash system is motivated by a pump that sends oil under pressure through a passage-way in crankshaft housing to two splash lubricating rings on the crank-shaft, to an injector nozzle on front crankshaft bearing cover for the spur gear drives, and to left cylinder for additional oil to that barrel

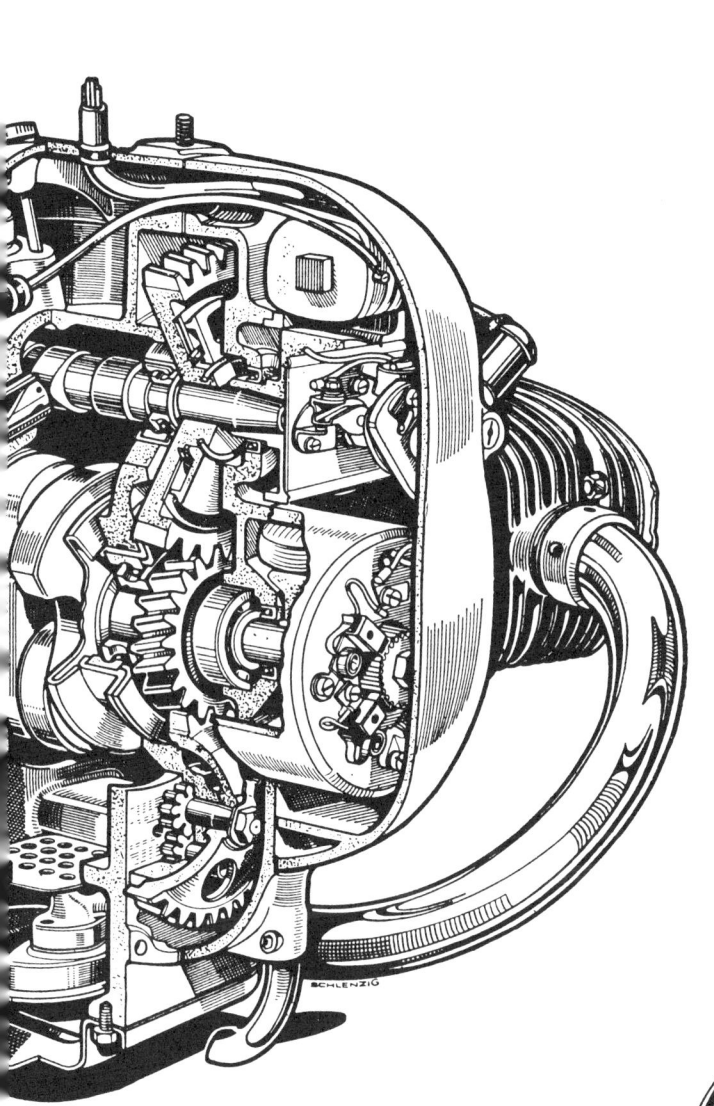

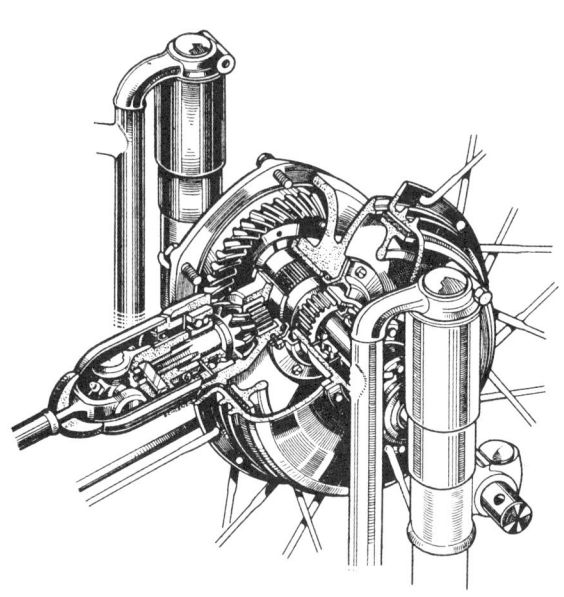

ABOVE, The famous BMW shaft-drive rear spring unit. Propeller shaft running from transmission to rear wheel has elastic rubber coupling to reduce power impulse vibrations and compensate for change in length of shaft during operation. Rear end of shaft terminates in universal joint with easily removable dust-proof cover. Driving pinion and disc gear are helically toothed, running silently in oil bath. Disk gear runs on needle bearings in rear wheel drive unit, on ball-bearings in housing. Gearing can be changed here

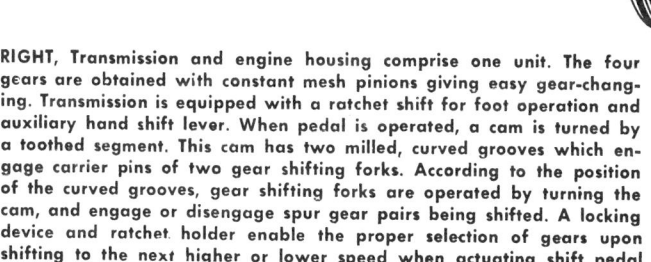

RIGHT, Transmission and engine housing comprise one unit. The four gears are obtained with constant mesh pinions giving easy gear-changing. Transmission is equipped with a ratchet shift for foot operation and auxiliary hand shift lever. When pedal is operated, a cam is turned by a toothed segment. This cam has two milled, curved grooves which engage carrier pins of two gear shifting forks. According to the position of the curved grooves, gear shifting forks are operated by turning the cam, and engage or disengage spur gear pairs being shifted. A locking device and ratchet holder enable the proper selection of gears upon shifting to the next higher or lower speed when actuating shift pedal

The 590 c.c. o.h.v. Twin Model R 67/2 B.M.W. and STEIB Type S500L SIDECAR

A view of the outfit which shows the final drive shaft, the rear suspension and the tank-top tool box. Also seen is the large sidecar locker.

A German-built Sports Outfit with Shaft-drive and Many Unique Features

IT is almost inevitable that the name of Steib should be coupled with that of B.M.W. when sidecar outfits are under discussion, for in many years, this German-built motorcycle has been harnessed to this German-built sidecar so frequently that the immediate reaction on seeing another make of " chair " attached to the machine would be one of surprise.

By courtesy of Mr. B. G. North, a director of Kings of Oxford, Ltd., a model R 67/2 B.M.W., to which was attached a sports single-seater S500L Steib sidecar, was lent to " Motor Cycling " for an extended test. It had but 400 miles registered on the speedometer. During the three months the outfit was in our hands, it was used for routine " hack " journeys and, on several occasions, for " express " runs from London to Birmingham. " Express " is a suitable word to use for, from door to door, the motorcycle proved to be a faster means of transport than the train.

" Dream " Features

As most people know, the B.M.W. is a unique motorcycle; it possesses many of the features that appear in specifications " dreamed up " by an enthusiast in his search for the ideal model. Neat in appearance, the transverse, h.o.-twin engine, with car-type clutch, a unit gearbox and shaft drive, looks compact. Few external auxiliaries live outside the light-alloy castings which form so much of the engine and in fact, they number but two—the pair of German Bing carburetters.

Basically simple in conception, the main casting is virtually a box into which the crankshaft is inserted at approximately mid-height. Above the crankshaft—which runs on ball bearings—is a single camshaft driven by helical gears. On to the sides of the

Head-on, the B.M.W. presents a very neat aspect, the transverse cylinders deriving the maximum benefit from the air-stream while the sidecar body is well protected by the surrounding chassis members.

box are bolted the cylinder barrels of cast iron with light-alloy heads. Push-rod operated, the rockers pivot in pedestals bolted to the cylinder heads and the push-rod seat, at the centres, in flat-base, large-diameter tappets. Light-alloy covers enclose the inlet and exhaust valves and also the rocker gear.

The magneto, with stationary windings, and the 60-watt dynamo, are driven respectively by extensions of the camshaft and the crankshaft. Thus there are three compartments within the outer skin; a central area in which crankshaft and cams work, a forward annexe for the camshaft and oil-pump drives and, at the extreme front of the engine, a third compartment in which are located the electrical components. The base of the central compartment forms the oil sump, closed by a simple, shallow, pressing.

The drive is taken through a single-plate clutch to an " all indirect " gearbox and finally to a helically toothed crown-wheel and pinion via a shaft which has a rubber coupling at its forward end and a mechanical universal joint immediately in front of the bevel housing.

A duplex tube, welded frame carries the engine-gearbox unit and has undamped plunger suspension at the rear; the telescopic front forks have double-acting hydraulic damping. An important and, to-day, unusual virtue is that all three wheels are not only quickly detachable, but interchangeable as well.

Several features are unusual to British eyes. Positive-stop gear changes are made with a short pedal on the left-hand side and the kickstarter, also on the left-hand side, works transversely.

On the machine in question, integral lugs for the sidecar were fitted to the off side and the Steib had, therefore, to be attached to " made-up " fittings. After an initial settling down period, these, once re-adjusted, gave no trouble and the outfit proved rigid enough. A simple suspension, involving a trailing arm and coil spring, is fitted to the sidecar wheel and the outfit is therefore fully sprung.

A " flash-back " to the impressions received when the tester first drove the combination may be of help.

Initially, certain details had to be memorized: foot brake on the right; gear change on the left; ignition switch combined with light switch—push in to turn on the " sparks " when red indicator light goes on together with a green " neutral " gear indicator light. Turning this switch to the right brought in the tail and " dim " lights;

became apparent and it was considered inadvisable to hold 60-plus for any length of time. Gearchanges were made early, without any attempt to let the engine revs. rise, for results were as good, if not better, if " top " was engaged at just over 40 m.p.h.

Although the footrests can be moved vertically, the riding position cannot be varied much and those with long legs may find the pipes from the carburetters to the in-built air-cleaner rather too close to the shins. The locations of neither gear-change pedal nor brake pedal can be altered. The general degree of comfort is augmented by the use of a front-pivoted saddle with adjustable spring tension.

" Firm " Suspension

At first the suspension was thought to be a trifle " firm " although, as the mileage increased, the ride softened. High-frequency bumps were unsettling, particularly to the sidecar passenger, for whom the " chair " springing, on cobbles and uneven stone setts, did not always absorb the bumps.

No doubt this firm riding was responsible for the taut feel of the outfit as a whole and, if the passenger did not always enjoy the

turning to left produced the full driving light. The dip switch, combined with the horn button, was found on the left-hand bar.

Fitted on the left, the sidecar chassis rail is apt to be knocked and scraped when the kick-start lever is pushed down and this prevents full use of the starter which could, with advantage, be geared higher. For some reason, the machine did not always react to well-established routine when starting from cold. In nine attempts out of ten, immediate response was forthcoming when the carburetters were flooded and the air-control, on the gearbox casing, was closed; the tenth attempt finished with a " wet " engine and almost full throttle opening had to be given. When warm, a push with the hand on the pedal was sufficient and, indeed, used frequently for demonstration purposes.

Gear Changing

With first gear engaged—silently if the very light clutch was withdrawn quite fully —the green indicator light goes out. The drive is taken up quickly but smoothly once the short movement of the clutch had been appreciated. At no time during the test was there any sign of clutch slip whatsoever.

Considerable experimentation was necessary before silent upward gearchanges could be made. Without due deliberation —and always if the rider was in a hurry —a tell-tale " clonk " resulted. Downward changes were invariably accompanied by some noise; in this case, the quicker they were made, the quieter they proved to be. This noise appears to be inseparable from units with an engine-speed clutch-to-gearbox mainshaft. It is thought also, that a twist-grip with a quicker action and less backlash would assist materially on downward changes.

Perhaps insufficient time was allowed for the engine to settle itself for, when cold, slight piston slap noise came from one cylinder. This disappeared when the engine warmed up, returning if the unit was run slowly for any length of time. A tight gudgeon pin was the snap diagnosis but it interfered little with the performance of the

(Above) The tester was most impressed with the handling of the outfit on the road. It revealed a quality of " tautness " despite the fact that all wheels are sprung.

(Right) A " close-up " of the near side of the B.M.W. engine. The unusual, transverse kick-starter, the fulcrum of the gear-change pedal and the battery mounting will be seen.

machine and was outstanding only because of the lack of noise generally.

This general mechanical silence was undoubtedly one of the most endearing features of the B.M.W. Other than for the exhaust burble—a reasonably subdued note—milestones passed in silence, for valve-gear, gearbox and transmission were quite inaudible.

With the ability to rev. freely and with a comparatively low compression ratio, the performance characteristics were unusual. It was quite possible to force a long pull in top gear without sign of distress and yet the engine would turn smoothly in " third " at over 50 m.p.h. Although the machine was almost devoid of vibration, there was one small period which made itself felt, however, and this was on the over-run at approximately 40 m.p.h. in top gear, equalling about 3,000 r.p.m. When driving through this speed, the tremor was almost indistinguishable.

Many miles were covered at a cruising speed of between 55-60 m.p.h. In fact, this proved to be the gait at which the machine was usually driven, for it seemed effortless. Above 60 m.p.h., a certain fussiness

vigorous manner in which the outfit could be handled, it was a delight to the driver. In spite of a body that appears slim, the width of the outfit, owing to the protruding off-side cylinder, seems wider than most. Violent cornering methods would not induce the sidecar wheel to lift—in fact, all three wheels slid before this would occur when a passenger occupied the sidecar seat.

Both brakes were excellent, particularly with respect to their continued efficiency. Little adjustment was necessary and throughout the period of test the only non-standard feature was a squeak from the front drum on a wet day. Later this disappeared and left brakes which could hardly be faulted.

Lights were quite adequate for the machine, the dynamo serving to keep the battery well charged.

Maintenance of the B.M.W. is absurdly simple. Ignition and lighting machinery are both housed beneath a light-alloy cover secured by two screws and are easily approached, while tappet adjustment, at the rockers, is but a matter of minutes. Both gearbox and bevel casing were checked for lubricant by removing the easily reached

Engine: Horizontally opposed, o.h.v. twin set transversely in frame; bore 72 mm., stroke 73 mm. = 590 c.c.; C.R. 5.6 to 1; cast-iron cylinder barrels, light-alloy cylinder heads; built-up crankshaft mounted on ball bearings; steel connecting rods with roller bearings; single central camshaft gear driven; gear-type oil pump feeding to collector rings on crankshaft for big-ends, to helical gear drives and to left cylinder barrel; camshaft and tappets lubricated by splash; two 24 mm. Bing 1/24/15/6 carburetters; ignition by Noris stationary coil magneto with automatic spark control.

Transmission: Gearbox bolted up to form unit with engine; single-plate dry clutch interposed between engine and four-speed gearbox; gear-change mechanism foot operated with auxiliary hand lever, neutral indicating lamp on headlamp shell; ratios 5.69, 7.45, 10.42 and 17.52 to 1; top ratio has spring cushioned drive on layshaft; final drive by shaft to crownwheel and pinion on rear hub, rubber coupling at front of shaft, universal joint at rear.

Lighting: Noris 6-volt 60-watt dynamo to battery mounted behind gearbox; Bosch headlight with integral ignition switch, ignition warning light and neutral indicator.

Frame: Welded duplex tube frame with undamped coil-spring plunger rear suspension; telescopic hydraulically damped B M W front forks with thief-proof lock.

Wheels: Quickly detachable and interchangeable; 3.50-in by 19-in. tyres, front and rear.

Brakes: B.M.W. internal-expanding brakes 7¾-in. diameter front and rear with finger adjustment.

Tanks: Welded steel petrol tank, capacity 4½ gallons; oil container integral with crankcase, capacity 4 pints.

Finish: Black enamel with white line on petrol tank.

Equipment: 120 m.p.h. speedometer, internally illuminated; electric horn; tool kit in tank-top built-in box.

Price: £354 plus £98 6s. 8d. P.T. = £452 6s. 8d.

Makers: Bayerische Motoren Werke, A.G., Munich 13, Germany.

Agents in Great Britain: A.F.N., Ltd., Falcon Works, Isleworth, Middlesex.

The Sidecar

Chassis: Steib single-loop of steel tube; body suspended on two coil springs in tension with adjustable attachment.

Wheel: Mounted on coil spring suspended trailing arm; quickly detachable; 3.25-in.

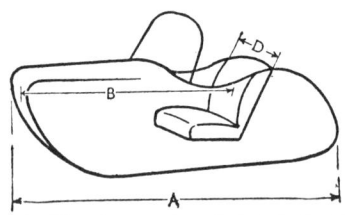

by 19-in. tyre; mudguard pivoted at rear to facilitate wheel removal.

Body: Steib sports single-seater panelled in steel; hammock-type seat upholstered in blue plastic cloth, rear luggage compartment fitted with coach lock.

Dimensions: A = 72 ins.; B = 47 ins.; D = 18 ins.

Finish: Exterior finished in black; fold-down hood with stowage bag in waterproof cloth.

Price: £95 plus £25 6s. 8d. P.T. = £120 6s. 8d.

Extras: Hood £9, tonneau cover £3 10s.

Makers: Spezialfabrik Fuer Seitenwagen, Nürnberg, Germany.

Agents in Great Britain: A.F.N., Ltd.

---

hexagonal caps, but required none. Perhaps some improvement is possible where the engine is concerned, for the oil-filler orifice is rather small.

Other than for the specific conditions mentioned earlier, the Steib sidecar is comfortable and the luggage space good. On one particular trip, using unconventional stowing methods, a vast amount of luggage and stores were carried, only an army pack, strapped to the locker lid, looked unusual. The windscreen deflected air effectively, and although the hood took some minutes to erect, it remained watertight. As a sporting single-seater, this sidecar is admirable.

Traditionally an oil-tight machine, the R67/2 maintained this tradition throughout our temporary ownership, and was displaying only two smears of lubricant when the machine was returned. These occurred at the off-side (right) gearbox cover-plate and at the juncture of the first and second main engine castings. The exhaust pipes, each blued at the sharp bend in front of the port, were the only other disfigurements to a clean and remarkably handsome machine.

Above:
Family party. The Steib sidecar offers considerable comfort and is well weather proofed. The domestic dachshund fits appropriately into this product of the Fatherland.

On the left appears an epitome of the results of our test also indicated on the right in the form of a graph.

TESTER'S ROAD REPORT

MODEL 1952 590 c.c. R67/2 B.M.W.
S 500 L STEIB SIDECAR

Maximum Speeds in:—

Time from Standing Start

Top Gear (Ratio 5·69 to 1) 68 m.p.h. = 4975 r.p.m. 51 secs.

Third Gear (Ratio 7·45 to 1) 58 m.p.h. = 5648 r.p.m. 23⅕ secs.

Second Gear (Ratio 10·42 to 1) 42 m.p.h. = 5745 r.p.m. 8⅘ secs.

Speeds over measured Quarter Mile:—

Flying Start 66·7 m.p.h. Standing Start 42·45 m.p.h.

Braking Figures On TARRED GRAVEL **Surface, from 30 m.p.h.:—**

Both Brakes 38 ft. Front Brake 60 ft. Rear Brake 72 ft.

Fuel Consumption:—

30 m.p.h.—68 m.p.g. 50 m.p.h.—44 m.p.g.

Oil Consumption:— 2200 m.p.g.

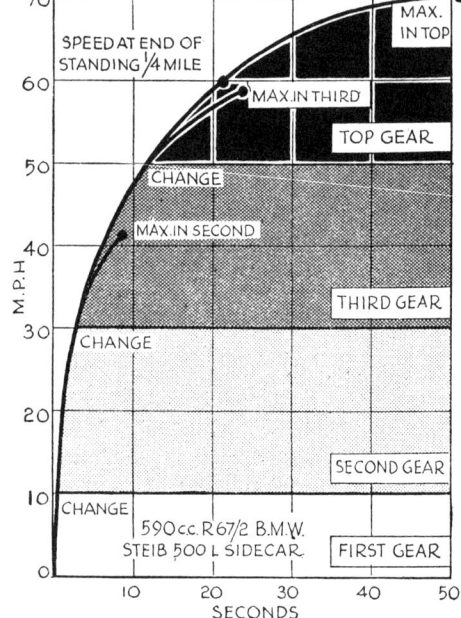

100 YARDS ABOVE NIAGARA

R25 model BMW was fully chromed for Kamillo artists. Modifications were few; weight equals stock models. Air tires were exchanged for solid rubber tires with steel wire inserts, and a ½-inch groove in the middle where rope will later guide wheels. Two eyes mounted on the front forks (above the dust guards) house a steel spike which blocks the front wheel during their special acts

MUNICH'S SCHORSCH MEIER, internationally known as BMW's best racing and Trial driver, who also is the main BMW dealer for Munich, displayed a fully chromed R25 during the past week to the astonished youngsters of Munich. Many guessed that perhaps an East Indian maharajah had ordered the gleaming cycle to round up the members of his harem—but not so.

Actually a group of high wire artists had the cycle altered to order. The suspension has been removed (that is the springs replaced by stiff tubing) both front and rear. The tires were taken off and full-rubber tires with steel stands and a ½-inch groove installed. A ring was mounted over the headlight to permit one of the "Kamillo" artists to stand on his head during the act, while a foot-brake lock mechanism holds the cycle at any point.

What's all that for, you ask? Well, here is the answer: The Kamillo artists, a group of four, are specialists on the slack rope. They have marched over a rope stretched between two mountain peaks at the Zugspitze (6,000 feet peak above sea level) and have marched and bicycled up and down the rope during a wind of 40 mph, and a temperature below 10° F.

To not only keep in shape, but also in business, the Kamillos have decided to travel the easy way over the Niagara Falls—on a tight or a slack rope (whatever the police permit), not on a bicycle, but on this 25R model BMW Schorsch Meier sold them for 3,000 Deutsche Marks —or about $750, as against the list price of 2,400 Deutsche Marks, or somewhat over 600 bucks. They're coming soon, so watch 'em ride over a course none of us would probably care to take.

Ring on top of headlight is base for second man's head. While one drives, holding a 30-foot pole to keep balance, the other juggles with feet and arms, standing on his head, mind you, 100 feet above Niagara Falls. Last year these "thrill merchants" cycled over a slack rope slung between two peaks on Germany's highest mountain—the Zugspitze.

To keep rear wheels blocked, BMW has special ratchet-type foot brake which locks in down position: release is effected by a hand lever

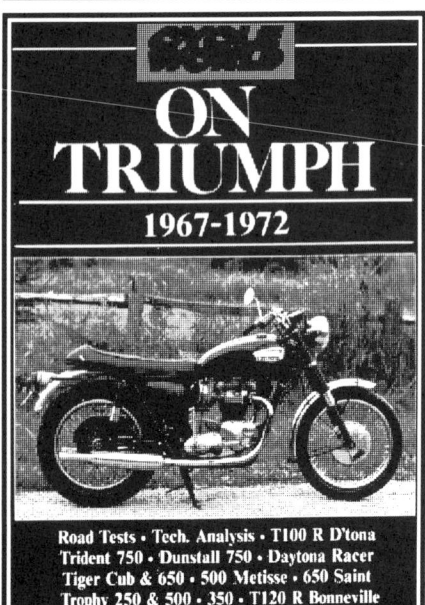

1953 BMW racing model has shorter, streamlined engine to reach speeds above 120 mph. For the first time torque shaft is covered for better aerodynamic design, has larger oil pan, and new brake system with dual action in the front

GERMANY'S SUPER THREAT

by F. H. Baer

TO BE TRIED out first at the Hockenheim race of 1953, the new BMW 500 cc racer is a successful combination of three main desires: it has boosted engine output, bettered driving characteristics, and lowered weight. Since it is not possible to develop one of the characteristics alone—this would mean lowering of efficiency of the other two desired features—the BMW people have compromised to produce a cycle which drives faster than a commercial airplane of the years before World War II, has more power output than a standard US automobile (at least the smaller 6-cylinder jobs).

To reach these records, BMW's engineers have stuck to the use of serial parts, or have designed parts which later may be used in the serial cycles. For that reason, BMW remained with the traditional 2-cylinder pancake system, with torque shaft instead of a secondary chain. The engine is shorter, more compact, and better streamlined than the serial R68; it also turns higher than the R68: about 8,000 rpm. The actual power output, though secret, is estimated 85 to 115 hp.

To arrive at this output, BMW engineers have ported and relieved the intake manifold and the valve arrangements. A tower shaft transmits the power for the two overhead camshafts from the crankshaft. Weight reduction is achieved by use of light alloys, which are, however, for rigidity's sake armed with steel inserts.

Use of dural sprockets for the drive of the magneto, etc. is to balance and eliminate changes in clearances caused by heat. The electron casting expands under heat, mind you, in a different ratio than the steel or aluminum engine parts. Dural is best to counterbalance the expansion variation during warm-up and racing.

A special feature is the both-sides foot shift, permitting the driver to shift either with the right or the left foot, a feature necessary on tight curves. Also for longer races is an enlarged oil pan which, armed with deep aluminum fins for better cooling, holds more oil to keep the temperature down.

The rear drive, built into the brake drum of the highly polished full-width brake, was streamlined, and the torque shaft covered with tubing to permit aerodynamically better shaping. A nylon disk replaces the former mechanical universal joint, for smoother absorption of shocks and more flexible operation.

The front and rear suspension has been changed to the now stylish swing-arm suspension, temporarily replacing the telescoping suspension system. BMW engineers, however, pointed out that the reason for adoption of the swing-arm suspension is the drive to reduce the "nodding" of the cycle while changes in the speed occur, and to prevent the cycle from "dipping" while operating the front brake. The riding characteristics are thus considerably bettered.

The telescopic suspension is not out of production and will probably remain. BMW engineers' intention was to find—for racing's sake—a new concept to halt the undesired motions of the cycle. Tests and calculations with the cycle's wheelbase and its center of gravity led to the correct angle and the stiffness and the detail construction of the swing-arms.

The front and rear suspension may have their stiffness altered by conical roller bearings which, on the one hand, guarantee a clearance-free fitting of all suspension parts and, on the other hand, permit the quickest change according to the driver's weight and course characteristics.

The BMW 500 cc racing models come in three different frames of the "cradle"

Close-up shows new cylinder head, foot-gearshift and crankhousing breathing vent on top of bell housing. Output of engine per cubic inch displacement is in upper international quality class

type. The frames differ in the wheelbase only, because of the different lengths (height) of the drivers. Divided into "A," "B," and "C" type frame, the tallest and the shortest of the 6-man BMW factory team finds "his" made-to-order machine. This was done to permit a driving position (crouching, or sitting) best for the course's and race's necessary driving technique. Imagine such detail!

I don't know whether it may be said in public, but tests are on the way at BMW's to find out the characteristics of fuel injection in the 2-cylinder pancake type. I hope that Mr. Hoepner of BMW isn't too annoyed, but this fuel injection test is the first conducted in Germany, and for that reason alone, would create

attention. Maybe he won't be too mad, and will let me look at the testing cycle for a good report to CYCLE.

The third feature of the BMW 500 cc racing cycle is that it is lighter in weight than the 340 lbs. serial R25-2 model. This, in conjunction with the enormous engine output, makes it a bomb on two wheels, and combined with its good riding abilities, one of the foremost predestined winners of Germany's 1953 racing season.

Front brake system features two levers to operate on one cable; each lever is progressively agitating one of the two brake shoes. Design might enter production. Note that short fender is so mounted that even distance from tire—regardless of suspension action—is insured

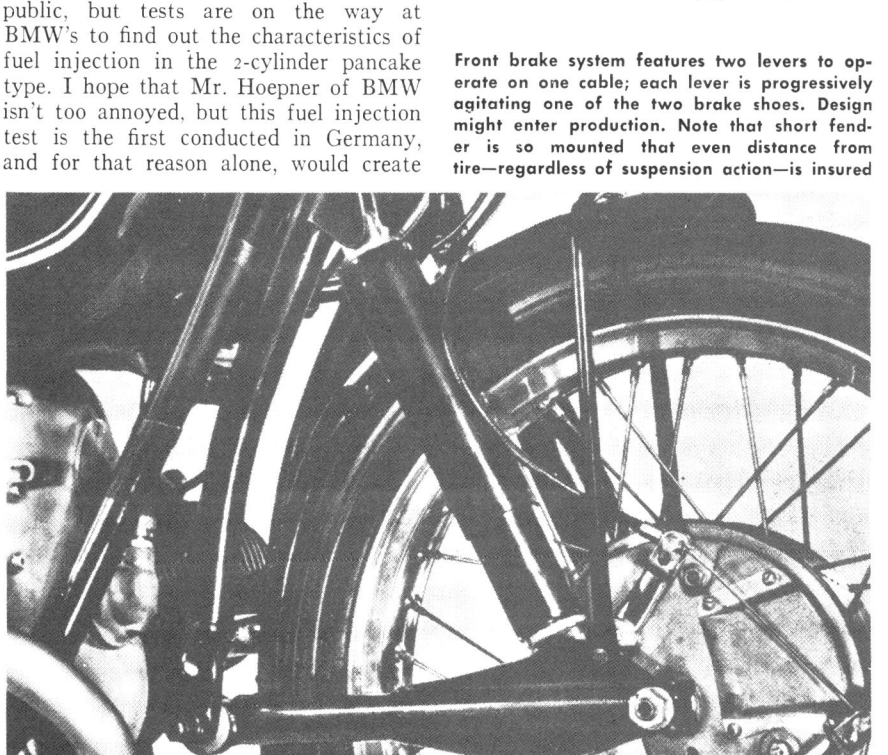

One way to see a new and strange country is to cross it on a motorcycle, best way say the Robberts.

BMW HONEYMOON

By Lois McNab

FEW AMERICANS would consider a motorcycle, even with seats built for two, as ideal honeymoon transportation. But take a pair of young Swedes, newly married, fresh off the S.S. Stockholm and with few American dollars in their possession—to them a motorcycle seems like an ideal honeymoon ticket—coast to coast!

Such was the case with John Scott Robbert and his bride Gunvor, who recently arrived in New York from Sweden with plans for a tour of the United States. To carry out this tour, they brought with them the rarely seen 1953 model BMW R/68 machine which turns 7000 rpm on a compression ratio of 8:1. An economical way to travel? On a tour up and down the Atlantic seaboard, thence across the continent to Los Angeles, the Robberts maintained an average speed of 60 and averaged gasoline mileage of 60 the entire 7000 miles!

"We probably could have gone much faster," said young Robbert, who plans on making America his permanent home, "but we were trying to stay within the law all of the way." As it was, their most striking impression of the trip was the frequent roadside accidents. In the Smokey Mountains of Tennessee, particularly, they passed a number of wrecked cars.

The couple, who sailed for America aboard the Stockholm three weeks after their wedding, visited relatives in Connecticut, Virginia and North Carolina before setting out across the continent. They shipped their luggage and carried with them only raincloths, toilet articles, sweaters for night riding and a rifle. The latter in response to relatives who described the horrors of the open American road!

Leaving the Southern states, the Robberts went through Rock Island, Ill., and then across the corn belt and through Colorado. John was most pleased with his bride who "uttered not one word of complaint on the entire trip."

They had a small feud with a Cadillac in Iowa—"the car was filled with prosperous farmers, who were trying their best to pass. The road was under repair, and covered with gravel. Finally the Cadillac found an opening and rammed by us, perilously close, shooting gravel into my legs," said John. "We bided our time and got revenge. Climbing through the hills, the BMW was able to maintain a much better speed than the heavy Cadillac and we were able to pass, first slowing slightly and digging our wheels, sending a fine return spray of mud and rock back into the Cadillac grille!"

Other experiences with their new countrymen were more pleasant, the couple related. They were unable to understand why "everyone we talked to was so extraordinarily kind and wanted to know all about us." Many Swedes came up to say hello at their stops along the way, the Robberts' homeland being identified by the large "S" on their license plate. John speaks English fluently, he spent the war years here with his mother and twin brother. Gunvor, or "Gunnie," as she is called by her American friends, is able to converse in her new tongue, but only a little slower than her husband.

The BMW proved to be an excellent road companion for the Robberts—no significant repairs were needed, and it took them only 10 days to travel from Charlotte, N.C., to Los Angeles. Their first and last days on the road they gave the cycle an extra "push"—spending 24 hours on the road without stopping their first day, and driving well over 500 miles on their last day. "It was the last day going through the Mojave desert that we suffered most," said John, "continuing hour after hour through the 120 degree heat."

They found during their long drive that they easily out-distanced mere automobiles — "sometimes cars would pass us on a flat, open stretch, but sooner or later we always caught up with them and went on ahead and never saw those cars again."

The couple gained much assistance from the service of policemen all along the way, who helped them keep their BMW wheels pointed along the proper highway. In a gas station in a small town in Iowa they found company in the person of an Englishman, who was waiting for them on a Vincent. The three of them joined forces and completed the journey west together.

The Robberts have now hung their cycling gear in a small cottage in Northern California where John is learning the lumber business at a sawmill.

Robberts found trim R-68 BMW an ideal means of highway transportation; had power, economy.

They wouldn't trade the memories of the BMW trip for anything—"in no other way could we have met so many different types of Americans or seen so much of the country," the Robberts agree. ★

14

The 600 cc R-69 has new swing-arm suspension all around. The drive shaft passes through one of the suspension arms. 35 hp motor gives a top speed of more than 100 mph.

THE BMW Company always has been famous for their sound approach to the problem as to how a motorcycle should be designed and built.

Shaft-drive and telescopic suspension were the trademark of BMW mo-

models. Suspension travel at the rear has been increased from 3 in. (on the older models) to almost 4 in. in the latest design.

With an eye to sidecar operation, special efforts have been made to make the BMW frame as sturdy as possible

mands reduced caster).

For the 1955 models, the fuel tank is slightly narrower but a little higher, giving the same fuel capacity (4.5 gallons). The toolbox is now located at the left side of the tank.

Handlebars measure 25.5 in. in width and are adjustable to accommodate build of riders as well as a variety of riding positions.

Throttle action on the new models is quick and provides precision adjustment.

Large alloy finned brake drums are fitted and the Duplex brakes on both the R-50 and F-69 have increased braking area.

Wheelsize has been reduced from 19 in. to 18 in. Standard models are normally equipped with a rubber saddle, but a dual seat is available as optional equipment.

The proven 500 cc and 600 cc engines are of the same construction as previously, but the power output of the BMW R-50 has been increased from 24 to 26 hp. Carburetors are repositioned for more foot room.

The new four-speed transmission with three shafts has been developed from the design of the R-25-3 models. The final-drive-shaft is now completely enclosed in the right swing arm mem-

New BMW Features Include New Suspension Front and Rear

torcycles in the days when most motorcycles were fitted with girder forks and rigid frames.

In 1952-53, the BMW racing models and record machines were equipped with full swing-arm-suspension for both the solo and sidecar machines, and the 1955 BMW Twins, the new 500 cc Sport R-50 and the fast regular production motorcycle, the 600 cc R-69 Super Sport are equipped with a similar design front and rear. These models have been designed for the connoisseur for whom its performance, sound and purposeful design should have a strong appeal. The R-69 has a top speed of more than 100 mph.

For 1955, the BMW front and rear suspension arms are pivoted in tapered roller bearings. This system eliminates bearing play and adjustment is easy.

The suspension has been designed for long spring-travel and the initial deflection movement is soft to enable the suspension to absorb the slightest road irregularities, while the correct progressiveness of the spring rate prevents bottoming on rough surfaces.

The length of the front swing-arm has been determined after exhaustive research and road testing to minimize "dive" when the brakes are applied and "rise" when accelerating.

The new front suspension has a travel of 4.3 in. (1.8 in. in the upper range with 2.5 in. in the opposite direction) as compared to 2.3 in. on the previous

to prevent flexing. Many valuable lessons were learned from the factory's competition experience (Last year BMW captured the world championship in the sidecar class).

Provision is made to stiffen the suspension on the new machines for pillion riding, simply by turning a lever on the swing arm.

The new models, despite the number of improvements, still are within the weight limit of the older models. An interesting feature is that front wheel caster is easily adjustable for either solo or side car use (side car use de-

ber. Clutch operation is made easier by the use of a new design disc-like springs.

The R-67-3, the robust 600 cc touring model is again being manufactured, retaining the telescopic front and rear suspension.

The R-25/3, the 250 cc single cylinder model remains unchanged and will continue to be produced with telescopic front and rear suspension.

BMW export statistics show that the majority of BMW export machines to countries all over the world, are BMW R-25's.

A fast combination. The 50 cc R-50 with the BMW "Special" side car. The R-50 engine develops 26 hp.

15

494 c.c. B.M.W. R50

Vibrationless Flat Twin with Shaft Drive : Exceptional Comfort, Quietness and Cleanliness : Outstanding Braking, Steering and Roadholding

FOR more than 30 years B.M.W.s have pinned their faith to the flat-twin engine with its almost perfect balance and its excellent cooling when transversely mounted. During that period the famous German marque has also earned renown for allegiance to shaft transmission, cleanliness of power units and high quality of workmanship. On a number of occasions B.M.W.s have been among the pioneers of new trends in design. Specific instances include the adoption of welded frame construction and hydraulically damped, telescopic front forks. The latest R50, a high-performance touring five-hundred, introduced at the 1955 Brussels Show, abundantly maintains the makers' reputation for up-to-date design, first-class engineering and outstanding all-round performance.

The new model features pivoted-fork springing at front and rear, and the transmission shaft is enclosed in the right-hand member of the rear fork. Road behaviour of the R50 is extremely gentlemanly. Indeed, it is difficult to visualize a machine of conventional conception being more smooth, quiet, comfortable and clean to ride. Except during inclement weather, the machine could be ridden in ordinary walking clothes without any fear of their becoming soiled.

At all speeds from normal tickover to valve float the engine was turbine-smooth in operation. Only when the unit was idling extremely slowly was there a trace of lateral judder. Flywheel inertia is high and contributes to the exceptional sweetness of the transmission. On its low bottom-gear ratio of 16.95 to 1, the R50 would trickle along at moderate walking speed with the clutch fully engaged and would accelerate smoothly from that speed merely as the result of the twistgrip being opened.

An ingenious twistgrip design gives a graduated rate of opening of the two throttles. A bevel gear on the twistgrip sleeve actuates a similar gear which operates both throttle wires through a cam device. As a result, twistgrip action is slow in the lower ranges of throttle opening and becomes progressively more rapid as the degree of opening is increased. The delicacy of throttle control thus afforded enhanced the smooth operation of engine and transmission and removed much of the irritation from negotiation of heavy traffic.

Engine starting was effortless and certain. Preliminary requirements were merely to close the strangler, momentarily depress each float tickler and switch on the ignition. With the twistgrip set for a fast tickover, the engine invariably came to life at the first depression of the kick-starter. The starter pedal moves in a transverse plane and it was a simple matter for the rider to operate it with his right foot while standing on the left of the machine.

When the strangler is closed the carburettors are fed with filtered air from inside the crankcase casting. During the moderately warm weather which prevailed for the test period, the strangler was opened as soon as the engine fired. Idling was slow and reliable whether the engine was hot or cold.

One of the most outstanding characteristics of the power unit was its quietness of operation. The level of mechanical noise was probably as low as that of any air-cooled, poppet-valve engine. There was never more than the subdued rustle of well-oiled machinery. The pleasant hum from the interconnected exhausts reflected the fact that exhaust noise is controlled by legislation in Germany. Indicative of the unusually high standard of mechanical and exhaust quietness achieved by the B.M.W. engineers is that the noise which was most perceptible to the

When the air strangler is closed, the twin carburettors are fed with filtered air from inside the crankcase casting

Sleek and businesslike, the R50 B.M.W. is finished in black and chromium. The pivoted front fork has provision for adjustment of trail. The front brake is of twin-leading-shoe design

The driving shaft is enclosed in the right-hand pivoted-rear-fork member. Shock-absorber top mounting is unorthodox

Fitted with a lock, the left-side kneegrip hinges down to reveal a capacious tool box let into the tank

rider at a level-road speed of 40 m.p.h. in top gear was that made by the front tyre on the road.

Acceleration was zestful without being tigerish, but was chiefly notable for its sweetness whether the engine speed was high or low. When ridden in built-up areas, the R50 provided silky, unobtrusive travel at 30 m.p.h. in top gear. On the open road there was no mechanical consideration such as engine vibration, noise or lack of riding comfort to influence the rider's choice of cruising speed. With the rider normally seated, any indicated speed from 11 to 90 m.p.h. was equally pleasant and comfortable, except that there was an almost-imperceptible "hardness" in power delivery at about 57 m.p.h. in top gear.

The transverse disposition of the engine results in most efficient air cooling of the cylinders and cylinder heads, and sustained cruising at about 80 m.p.h. failed to evoke the slightest sign of distress from the power unit. When checked for accuracy, the speedometer proved to read fast by approximately 10 per cent at all speeds.

Wide spacing of the gear ratios and a relatively heavy engine-speed clutch combined to make clean gear changes difficult. For upward changes the technique which was most effective in mini-mizing clashing of the dogs was to apply firm upward pressure to the gear pedal before the clutch and throttle controls were operated, so that the gears were shifted as soon as the clutch was slipped and the twistgrip eased. Because of high flywheel inertia it was necessary to re-engage the clutch gently if a slight lurch of the machine was to be avoided. Downward changes were best effected with a firm, quick pedal movement and an appreciable increase in engine speed.

Engagement of bottom gear with the engine idling slowly was usually quiet and neutral was easily located from bottom or second gears. A green light in the headlamp shell indicates that neutral is selected. Take-up of the drive was confined to a relatively small range of movement of the clutch lever but it was by no means difficult to ensure a smooth getaway.

Slightly heavy at ultra-low speeds, the steering was otherwise superb. Though the steering damper was never brought into play, straight-ahead steering was rock steady. For test purposes the rider's hands were removed from the handlebar at maximum speed with complete confidence. Bend swinging and cornering were equally delightful. The machine could be heeled over stylishly on slow or fast curves in the sure knowledge that it

Information Panel — 494 c.c. R50 B.M.W.

SPECIFICATION

ENGINE: 494 c.c. (68 x 68mm) overhead-valve, horizontally opposed twin. Fully enclosed valve gear, magneto and dynamo. Aluminium-alloy cylinder heads. Crankshaft supported in ball bearings. Roller big-end bearings. Compression ratio, 6.8 to 1. Semi-dry-sump lubrication; oil capacity, 4 pints.

CARBURETTORS: Bing, with twistgrip throttle control. Air filter incorporating strangler.

IGNITION and LIGHTING: Noris magneto with auto-advance. Separate Noris 60/90-watt dynamo with automatic voltage control. Varta 6-volt, 8-ampere-hour battery. Bosch 6½in-diameter headlamp with pre-focus light unit and 35/35-watt main bulb.

TRANSMISSION: B.M.W. four-speed gear box in unit with engine; positive-stop foot control. Gear ratios: bottom, 16.95 to 1; second, 9.6 to 1; third, 6.49 to 1; top, 4.9 to 1. Single-plate dry clutch incorporated in engine flywheel; fabric friction linings. Final drive by enclosed shaft and helical bevel gears. Engine r.p.m. at 30 m.p.h. in top gear, 1,965.

FUEL CAPACITY: 3¾ gallons.

TYRES: Firestone Phoenix, 3.50 x 18in front and rear.

BRAKES: 8in diameter; twin-leading-shoe front and single-leading-shoe rear; finger adjusters.

SUSPENSION: B.M.W. pivoted-fork front and rear springing employing multi-rate coil springs and hydraulic damping. Two-position adjustment for load on rear shock-absorbers. Two-position trail adjustment at front-fork pivot.

WHEELBASE: 56in unladen. Ground clearance, 6½in unladen.

SADDLE: Cantilever type, pivoted at nose; rubber top. Unladen height, 30½in.

WEIGHT: 413 lb fully equipped and with full oil sump and one gallon of petrol.

PRICE: £305. With purchase tax (in Great Britain only), £366.

ROAD TAX: £3 15s a year; £1 0s 8d a quarter.

MAKERS: Bayerische Motoren Werke A.G., Munich, Germany.

BRITISH CONCESSIONAIRES: A.F.N., Ltd., Falcon Works, London Road, Isleworth, Middlesex.

PERFORMANCE DATA

MEAN MAXIMUM SPEED: Bottom:* 29 m.p.h.
Second:* 52 m.p.h.
Third:* 76 m.p.h.
Top: 90 m.p.h.
* Valve float occurring.

HIGHEST ONE-WAY SPEED: 94 m.p.h. (conditions: moderate tail wind and rain; rider wearing two-piece riding suit and overboots).

MEAN ACCELERATION:

	10–30 m.p.h.	20–40 m.p.h.	30–50 m.p.h
Second	3.6 sec	3.4 sec	3.3 sec
Third	5 sec	5 sec	5 sec
Top	—	8 sec	7.8 sec

Mean speed at end of quarter-mile from rest: 76 m.p.h.
Mean time to cover standing quarter-mile: 16.8sec.

PETROL CONSUMPTION: At 30 m.p.h., 95 m.p.g. At 40 m.p.h. 80 m.p.g. At 50 m.p.h., 65 m.p.g. At 60 m.p.h., 60 m.p.g.

BRAKING: From 30 m.p.h. to rest, 27ft (surface, dry concrete).

TURNING CIRCLE: 16ft.

MINIMUM NON-SNATCH SPEED: 11 m.p.h. in top gear.

WEIGHT PER C.C.: 0.83 lb.

Incorporated in the headlamp shell are the combined lighting and ignition switch, speedometer and ignition-warning and neutral-indicator lights

would follow the chosen line faithfully. No components fouled the road however steeply the R50 was banked. The centre-stand extension—on many machines an offender in this connection—is neatly recessed into the underside of the left-hand silencer. For all practical purposes the effects of torque reaction (during acceleration and deceleration) arising from the transverse mounting of the engine were unnoticeable.

With a comparatively rearward footrest setting, the riding position is such as to render long periods of high-speed riding untiring to the rider. The slight forward crouch involved did not prove to be uncomfortable for low-speed work in town. To match the offset of the cylinders, the B.M.W.'s footrests are staggered slightly, but the effect ceased to be noticeable after the first few moments spent in the saddle. Though the gear pedal is not adjustable for position and the handlebar grips, complete with their built-in control clusters, can be rotated only on the bar, the siting of every control was just about perfect.

Front and rear pivoted-fork springing combined to furnish leech-like roadholding at all speeds and a high degree of insulation from bumps. The action of the front fork was rather firm at low speeds but was ideally suited to fast riding. Pivoted at its nose, the pan-type saddle further enhanced the rider's comfort.

High road performance necessitates good brakes. Those fitted to the R50 (both are of 8in diameter and the front has two leading shoes) were not only uncommonly powerful but they

also matched the behaviour of the remainder of the machine in their smoothness of operation. The strength of the return springs in the front-brake mechanism made initial operation a trifle heavy, but the brake was delightfully controllable except on its first application in humid weather, when it had a tendency to grab. Because front-brake torque is transmitted through the fork arm, application of the brake raises the front of the machine and stiffens the fork action. The efficiency of both brakes was unimpaired by hours of rain and no brake adjustments were required during a test of nearly 1,000 miles.

The electrical equipment of the B.M.W. functioned most efficiently. The horn was clearly audible to other drivers at all speeds. The rubber-mounted headlamp threw a wide, flat beam which illuminated both sides of the road for a sufficient distance ahead to permit speeds up to 80 m.p.h. to be used on unlit main roads in perfect safety after dark.

Not a smear of oil appeared on the outside of the power unit although the R50 was ridden hard for many hundreds of miles. In filthy weather, the mudguarding was found to furnish above-average protection.

Maintenance requirements have been reduced to a minimum on the R50; those which remain can be carried out with great ease. Valve-clearance adjustments are extremely accessible after removal of the rocker covers, each of which is retained by three nuts. Two captive nuts secure the cast-aluminium front cover to the crankcase. Removal of the cover exposes the contact breaker and dynamo brush gear.

From stem to stern, the R50 is endowed with features which indicate that it was designed by knowledgeable motor cyclists for connoisseurs. Both wheels are quickly detachable and both have polished, light-alloy rims, straight spokes, full-width hubs and chromium-plated balance weights attached to appropriate spoke nipples. Front-fork trail and shock-absorber mountings are readily adjustable for sidecar work. Two-position preloading of the rear shock-absorber springs for pillion work is effected by hand.

The key which operates the steering lock fits the tool box which is concealed behind the left kneegrip. A quick-release rubber strap secures the battery on its platform, while rubber grommets prevent the ingress of water to the carburettors at the points of entry of the throttle cables. Firmly mounted in a reasonably clean position, the tyre pump is fitted with a rubber cap to exclude grit. In the modern continental trend, knurled clutch and front-brake cable adjusters are incorporated in the handlebar pivot lugs.

Finish of the R50 is in serviceable black and white enamel, with a generous use of chromium plating and many light-alloy parts highly polished. In short, the latest R50 is one of the most outstanding contemporary models, combining to an admirable degree high performance, silky running, quietness, comfort, cleanliness and ease of maintenance. Its high engineering quality gives real pleasure to the knowledgeable and should add appreciably to pride of ownership.

By contemporary standards the rear frame is of unusual design, but permits an extremely rigid sidecar mounting

B M W
SETS 8 WORLD RECORDS

The 500cc B M W, the World's Fastest Sidecar Machine

On October 4, 1955 BMW 500 cc. machines established 8 WORLD SPEED RECORDS. Six in the Sidecar Class, two in the Solo Class, also an absolute WORLD SPEED RECORD in the Sidecar Class at 177 miles per hour . .

Records established by William Noll on BMW with sidecar:

1 kilometer,	flying start	174	miles per hour
1 mile,	flying start	174	''	''	''
1 kilometer,	standing start	86.4	''	''	''
1 mile,	standing start	103	''	''	''
5 kilometers,	flying start	168.4	''	''	''
5 miles,	flying start	171.5	''	''	''

Records established by Walter Zeller on BMW solo:

10 kilometers	standing start	144.8	miles per hour
10 miles,	standing start	150.4	''	''	''

These records with the 500 cc BMW WITHOUT SUPERCHARGER are subject to approval by the FIM and are for the 500cc, 750cc and 1000cc classes.

BMW is YOUR kind of motorcycle
See the NEW BMW's, the world's most MODERN motorcycles . . .
Reliability backed by 6000 mile guarantee
Superb roadholding ability
BMW's are fast and quiet
BMW's are easy starting
BMW's are 100% oil-tight
BMW's have classy appearance
BMW part service is quick and sure
**ALL BMW MODELS
HAVE SHAFTDRIVE**
All BMW Twins have Magneto Ignition.

Model R-50, 500 cc, Twin
Model R-69, 600 cc, Supersport have the NEW SWINGARM SUSPENSION and the NEW EARLES-TYPE FRONT FORK

Model R-25-3, 250 cc, Single, OHV
Model R-67-3, 600 cc, 28 HP Twin have hydraulic front fork and rear suspension.

For Free Information Write!

In the East:
BUTLER & SMITH
160 West 83rd Street
New York 24, N. Y.

In the West:
FLANDERS COMPANY
200 W. Walnut Street
Pasadena 3, California

The 492 c.c. B.M.W. Flat Twin

Full Details of a Highly Successful Horizontally Opposed

Twin-cylinder o.h.c. Power Unit Incorporating Fuel Injection

Exclusive Description by ALAN BAKER, B.Sc., A.M.I.Mech.E.

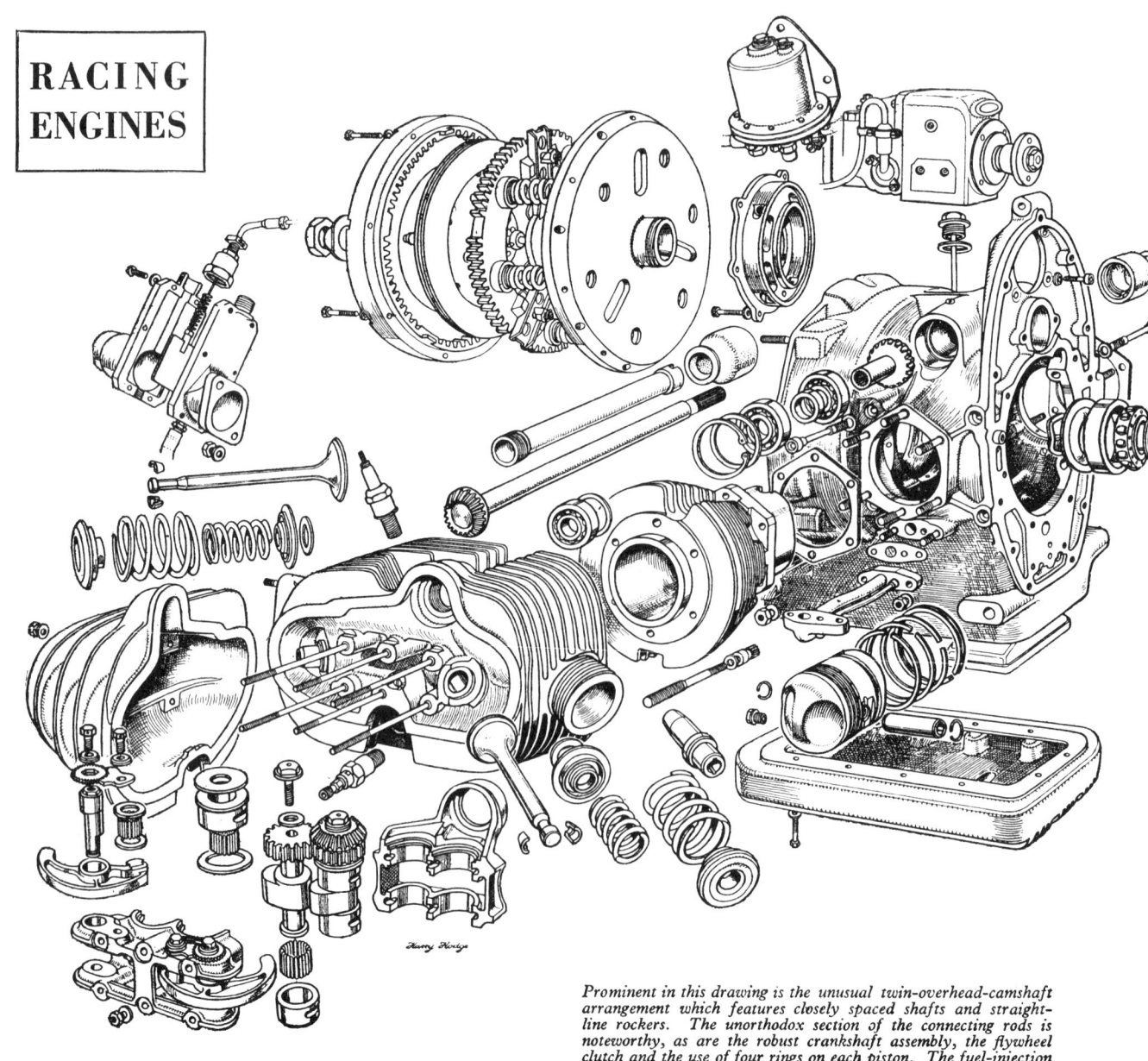

Prominent in this drawing is the unusual twin-overhead-camshaft arrangement which features closely spaced shafts and straight-line rockers. The unorthodox section of the connecting rods is noteworthy, as are the robust crankshaft assembly, the flywheel clutch and the use of four rings on each piston. The fuel-injection pump is located on the front cover, and the injector nozzles screw directly into the cylinder heads, below the cam gear

IN 1939, B.M.W.s made Isle of Man history by becoming the first German firm to win the Senior T.T.; Georg Meier, on the supercharged flat twin, won the race at record speed and Jock West, on a similar machine, was second. Since the war, B.M.W. racing interest has gradually shifted from solos to sidecars and, in 1954, the Noll-Cron team secured the World's Championship in the sidecar class with a B.M.W. outfit. Had Eric Oliver not been eliminated by a mid-season crash, the Championship result might have been different, but the German twin was undoubtedly extremely fast and utterly reliable.

The five-hundred B.M.W. has a lengthy genealogy extending back to 1923, when the first flat twin was built and raced; this ancestor had a side-valve

engine. Two years later the overhead-valve engine appeared, to continue with progressive development until 1935, when the supercharged double-overhead-camshaft unit was introduced. It made its début in the Island in 1937, the year in which Ernst Henne regained the world's

maximum speed record on a streamlined version.

Apart from the absence of a supercharger, the 1954 racing engines are fundamentally very similar to the pre-war units. To that generalization, however, must be made a very notable qualification, namely, fuel injection, which first appeared early in the 1953 racing season and was employed by Walter Zeller in that year's Senior T.T. Zeller lay ninth after the first lap but then came off, damaging his machine too seriously to continue.

There have been three stages in the development of the fuel injection: in the case of each cylinder head, at first the injector nozzle was mounted between the throttle slide and inlet port, spraying into the induction tract at an angle. Then came the layout used in the I.o.M. in 1953 in which the injector was mounted in the induction bellmouth, upstream of the throttles and injecting axially. Finally —last season—the nozzle was transferred to the cylinder head opposite the sparking plug. Removal of obstruction from

the inlet system improved the cylinder charging appreciably and thus resulted in increased power output.

At first sight, the dismantled 1954 B.M.W. factory engine gives the impression of sturdy orthodoxy. While closer study confirms the impression in many respects, it also reveals a number of unexpected features, both of detail and of basic design.

The crankshaft, with its 180-degree throws and 72mm stroke (bore is 66mm), is of built-up construction embodying no threads. Mainshafts are hollow and are integral with their crank cheeks which embody balance weights. Each crankpin hole in the elliptical medial web of the shaft has a shallow counterbore on the side of the web adjacent to the respective big end. Radius of the counterbore is greater than that of the end of the web and of the big-end eye, so that the shaft overall length is kept to minimum.

Like the mainshafts, the hollow crankpins are of 35mm diameter; one end of each is pressed into the medial web and locked in position by a solid, forced-in expander plug. After the big-end bearings and connecting rods have been assembled on the pins, the cheeks are pressed on and further expander plugs driven in. The plugs at the outer end of the pins differ from those at the inner end in having a small longitudinal hole for big-end lubrication.

The crankshaft runs in three bearings: at the rear is a self-aligning bearing embodying rollers shaped like shortened rugby balls; there is a ball bearing at the front of the crankshaft and another, of smaller diameter, in the front cover as outboard support for the timing pinion.

The one-piece crankcase is an Elektron casting. To obviate any chance of their loosening when hot, the two 35mm main bearings are pressed into housings separate from the case. Cast iron is used for the forward bearing housing and steel for the rear housing; both have a shallow spigot which is a press fit in the case, and both are secured by longitudinal bolts through the flange and also by four transverse bolts. The transverse bolts screw in from each side of the crankcase, one co-axial pair above and one below the crank axis.

Embodied in the forward main-bearing housing is the rear wall of the oil pump; the light-alloy body carrying the gears fits into a recess in the housing to which it is bolted. The pump is of the duplex gear type, one section of which feeds the main and big-end bearings while the other supplies the cam gear. Oil (S.A.E.40 viscosity) is taken through a gauze suction filter from a 2.8-litre sump, also of Elektron, bolted to the base of the crankcase and well finned for cooling.

Lubricant for the cam gear flows from the pump through oilways in the crankcase to external pipes which lie below the cylinder barrels; the pipes are flanked by larger-diameter pipes through which oil returns to the sump.

Oil from the other pump emerges from each main-bearing housing into a trap secured by screws to the adjacent face of each crank cheek. The trap is basically of disc form but has the periphery turned inward through 180 degrees to form an annular channel. Oil from the bearing housing is centrifuged into the channel; thence it reaches the big end through a hole in the trap wall communicating with the previously mentioned hole in the crankpin plug. Each of the crankpins has twin radial holes and, since they are directed outward, the oil flow has the maximum centrifugal assistance.

The layout minimizes internal oilways which could weaken the crankshaft assembly. It also simplifies building up the shaft because no holes have to be aligned. Furthermore, the traps act as very efficient centrifugal filters, which is

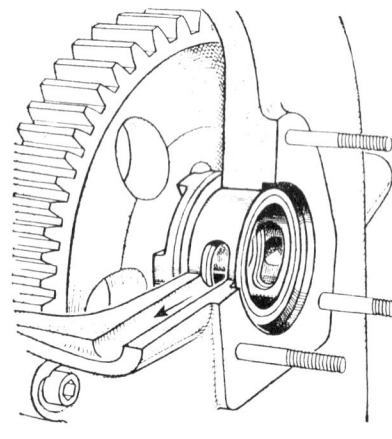

sary to embody a cush-drive in the steel gear to avoid tooth breakage of the light-alloy gear from the loading produced by violent acceleration or deceleration of the crankshaft.

A steel gear on the half-speed shaft meshes with the light-alloy magneto gear; this last has slotted fixing holes for timing adjustment. In front of the half-speed gear and driven therefrom by two pegs is a ported sleeve which runs in the Elektron front cover and serves as a timed breather; at the appropriate time the sleeve ports align with holes in the cover which lead to atmosphere.

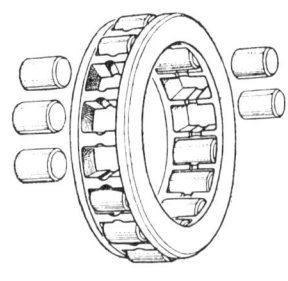

Three interesting internal details: (left) the engine breather, driven from the half-speed timing gear; (above) the single-row roller big-end bearing cage, the bars of which are relieved for lubrication purposes; and (below right) thickened-up gudgeon-pin bosses and oil-return slots in the full-skirt piston. Four rings are fitted

counter-bores in the crankcase casting.

An unusual double-o.h.c. arrangement is employed. In the case of each cylinder head the two camshafts lie close together within the split housing and each operates its respective valve through a short, straight rocker. The scheme is a compromise between the single-o.h.c. and the conventional double-cam layouts because, although the reciprocating weight with the rockers is higher than with direct-operated valves, there is less power loss since two spur gears replace the usual five. Certainly the reciprocating-weight aspect cannot be serious since the engines can run up to 9,500 r.p.m.

The B.M.W. layout is, in fact, well adapted to a horizontally opposed engine. In the normal manner for a 180-degree twin, the cylinder axes are staggered in plan view (the left cylinder is the farther forward) and, as mentioned earlier, the camshaft drive shafts are in line. Thus the right shaft drives the forward camshaft and the left shaft drives the rearward camshaft.

Camshafts and rockers run on needle rollers; the outer races of the camshaft bearings are suitably grooved so that the camshaft-housing holding-down studs form cotters to prevent rotation of the races. In each case the camshaft bevel is integral with the coupling gear, and its end thrust is taken by flanged bronze collars. The rocker spindles are carried in the camshaft housings and have eccentric ends for valve-clearance adjustment.

The method of locking the rocker

why only the gauze suction strainer is needed.

Highly unorthodox is the use of a flat section instead of an I section for the connecting-rod body between the big and small ends. The rod is relatively short—about 180 per cent of the stroke—and the B.M.W. technicians are unperturbed by any possibility of whip resulting from the absence of flanges. I-section rods have been tried but have been found more prone to failure, from fatigue cracks starting at the radius between flange and web. The flat section, which is about ⅛in thick, has proved entirely satisfactory and is, of course, very easy to polish.

Each big-end bearing comprises 14 rollers of 10×7mm running directly on the crankpin and in the big-end eye; both pin and eye have hardened surfaces. Guiding the rollers is a Duralumin cage, the periphery of which is relieved slightly for the whole width of the roller track. In the bore of the cage the bars are relieved over part of their length to assist the spread of oil, an action which is aided by shallow, radial grooves midway along each side of each bar. The oil holes in the crankpin are so spaced that lubricant is fed to the rubbing faces of the cage bore before reaching the rollers.

Within the gear case on the front of the engine are three pairs of spur gears. A steel gear on the crankshaft drives a light-alloy half-speed gear immediately above it; the gears are lubricated by jet from the front main-bearing housing. Also on the crankshaft is a steel gear meshing with the light-alloy oil-pump driving gear. It has been found neces-

Within the breather sleeve, and a push fit in the gear centre, lies the coupling for the fuel-injection pump drive. The coupling has holes with which engage three pegs projecting from the end of the half-speed shaft and is internally splined at its forward end to receive male splines on the pump-unit shaft. The pump unit is bolted to the outside of the front cover.

At the rearward end of the half-speed shaft, which is carried in two ball bearings in a Duralumin housing, is a bevel gear; with it mesh two bevel gears embodying short, hollow shafts which transmit the drive via solid shafts to the camshafts. The axes of the pair of bevels just described coincide in plan view but are inclined slightly downward in front elevation. Two closely spaced ball bearings support each bevel hollow shaft, the outboard end of which is internally splined. Lubrication of the gears is by splash from the big ends.

Engaging with the splines of the hollow shafts are male splines at the inboard end of the solid drive shafts. Each of the solid shafts has an integral bevel gear at its outer end and runs in a ball bearing pressed into the inboard half of a cast-iron housing. Split longitudinally in the vertical plane, the housing is held to the cylinder head by three pairs of studs; the two outer pairs also serve to retain the Elektron cam-box covers.

The camshaft drive-shaft cover tubes screw into the cylinder heads; their inboard ends have no positive location and are sealed by internally spring-loaded grommets, of synthetic rubber, fitting into

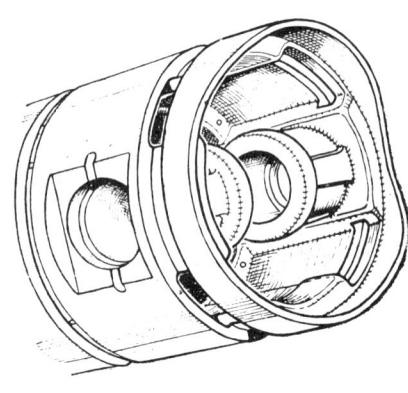

spindles is simple and ingenious: on one end of each spindle is a serrated washer which is located on the spindle by flats. With the serrations engage similar serrations on a short arm, the other end of which is bolted to the housing. If the bolt is slackened and the serrations are disengaged, the spindle can be turned by one serration or more and the serrations then re-engaged. For valve timing there is the usual vernier coupling between each camshaft and its driving gear. Valve overlap is equally disposed on each side of top dead centre and totals 120 degrees; the cams provide an opening of 320 degrees.

The rockers are I-section steel forgings, hardened in the bores, and are unorthodox in having cam-follower pads of chilled cast iron, a material which has proved exceedingly durable. A shrunk-in, dovetailed fit is employed for the pads, and the rockers are lightly peened over them on each side for security.

Owing to the close spacing of the cam-shafts, lubrication at each cylinder head is reduced to a single metering jet which sprays oil copiously on to the rubbing faces of cams and followers. The bevels and coupling gears are lubricated partly by splash and partly by oil from the crank-case which flows along the downwardly inclined camshaft-drive cover tubes.

Each cylinder head contains a part-spherical combustion space giving a fairly wide valve included angle of 82 degrees. The valve-seat inserts are shrunk in; manganese steel is the material of the inlet seat, and bronze is used for the exhaust seat. Both valve guides are of bronze which has a fairly high tin content.

Diameter of the tulip head of the inlet valve is 40mm and that of the stem is $8\frac{1}{2}$mm; sodium cooled, the exhaust valve has a convex head of 36mm diameter and its stem diameter is 11mm. Duplex coil springs exert a load of 97 lb with the valves on their seats. To reduce overall engine width, a stepped form of split collet retains the light-alloy spring collars.

Downdraught angle of the inlet ports is 15 degrees and their bore at the flange is 32 mm. Mounted directly to each port is a flat box containing a guillotine-type throttle which gives an unobstructed inlet when fully open. The throttles are con-trolled by a double-drum twistgrip and are individually adjustable for synchroni-zation. Air reaches the throttles by two long, tapering bellmouths attached to the throttle-box stubs by rubber hose and clips. From trumpet extremity to throttle measures approximately 8in, and from throttle to valve centre is about $4\frac{1}{2}$in.

Sparking plugs (one per cylinder) are located above the cylinder axes and the fuel-injector nozzles below; their respec-tive holes emerge into the combustion space on a common diameter between the valves, but the plug holes are canted to enable the plugs to clear the camshaft drive shafts. One plug thus points for-ward and the other rearward. Like the fuel pump, magneto and sparking plugs, the injector nozzles are of Bosch manu-facture and have a minimum delivery pressure of about 570 lb sq in.

Fuel is gravity fed from the tank to a paper-cartridge filter mounted on the right of the crankcase above the cylinder. From the filter, petrol passes to the pump, which is of plunger pattern—very similar to the type used on compression-ignition engines. There is no direct, rider control of pump delivery.

In the pump body is a diaphragm which is subjected on one side to induction-pipe depression by means of a balance-pipe system connected to the two throttle boxes. Attached to the diaphragm is a rack-rod engaging with a gear on each of the two plungers. Movement of the diaphragm caused by opening or closing of the throttle thus rotates the plungers; such rotation varies the internal porting and with it the amount of fuel delivered by the plungers. Surplus fuel is pumped back to the tank. An adjusting screw permits basic setting of the mixture strength. Lubrication of the pump is effected by engine oil from a separate half-litre container.

To give plenty of time for the mixing of fuel and air, injection of petrol occurs appreciably before the end of the inlet stroke but the timing is not critical to within 10 degrees and is adjusted by means of slotted attachment-bolt holes in the pump body. Ignition timing is fixed

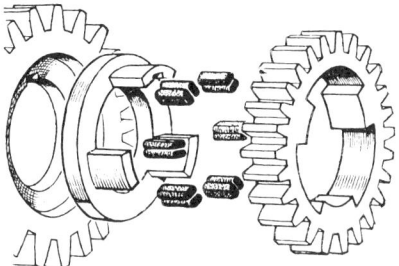

To avoid tooth overloading, the oil-pump driving gear embodies a simple shock-absorber

and is the same with fuel injection as it was when carburettors were employed (incidentally, the same applies to the compression ratio, which is 10.2 to 1).

Apart from providing a worthwhile gain in power—owing to the unobstructed induction system and the thorough atom-ization of fuel which occurs in the cylinder—fuel injection is stated to have given an improvement in specific fuel consumption of about 15 per cent; the consumption now obtainable on full load is 0.44 lb/b.h.p./hour—an extremely low figure.

Almost full skirted, the pistons have a scraper ring below the bosses for the taper-bored gudgeon pin. Three com-pression rings are fitted and the lowest has a taper face, with drainage holes to assist oil control. The piston crown is of nearly pent-roof shape and fits closely into the head space at each side to promote squish. To accommodate the contour of

the valve heads, the valve cutaways are convex and concave respectively under the inlet and exhaust valves.

In each case a ground joint is employed between cyinder head and barrel; after the grinding-in is completed, six studs are screwed into the head. The head is then fitted to the barrel, the studs pass through bosses in the barrel, and on to them are screwed sleeve nuts having splined instead of hexagonal ends.

Owing to their advantageous cooling location, the B.M.W. cylinder barrels have very modest finning by current standards. Die-cast in light alloy, they normally have shrunk-in liners, but chromium-plated bores—plating direct on the aluminium—have been alternatively employed with complete satisfaction. The engine examined had liners; they have a spigot which enters about $1\frac{1}{2}$in into the crank-case and is cut away fore and aft for connecting-rod clearance. Six studs secure each barrel to the crankcase.

A taper on the rear of the crankshaft accommodates a $22\frac{1}{2}$cm-diameter flywheel clutch. The clutch body is in two halves which are held together by a ring of eight bolts; the inner face of the rear half forms one of the driving surfaces. Sandwiched between that face and the pressure plate is a single, fabric-faced driven plate; the plate has a splined centre which transmits the drive to the gear-box mainshaft.

The rear half of the clutch body has internal peripheral teeth with which en-gage similar external teeth on the pressure plate. Actuating force for the pressure plate is supplied by six non-adjust-able springs seating in the front half of the clutch body. Clutch withdrawal is by means of a thrust rod passing through the hollow gear-box mainshaft; a hemispheri-cal pad, jointed to the end of the rod, seats on a cup in the centre of the pressure plate.

Forward half of the clutch body has a spigot fitting into a bore in the back of the rear main-bearing housing. There is a leather oil-sealing ring within the bore, and the spigot has a spiral groove to assist in preventing oil from entering the clutch housing. Clutch cooling is effected by a series of concentric ribs on the back of the clutch body and by air ducts in the housing.

Of conventional, all-indirect design, the gear box has a top-gear reduction of 1.3 to 1 and normally has five ratios, although four have been used on certain circuits. The complete engine-gear unit is sup-ported at three points in the frame: one each at front and rear of the lower por-tion of the crankcase, and a steady point above cylinder level in the crankcase half of the gear case.

The engine starts to run smoothly at about 4,000 r.p.m., begins to produce real power in the region of 6,500 r.p.m. and peaks at 9,000 r.p.m., at which speed it is stated to have an output of 58 b.h.p.

Below: The rockers are fitted with dovetailed-in, chilled-cast-iron pads. Right: Camshaft drive-shaft cover tubes are connected to the crankcase by spring-loaded, synthetic-rubber grommets

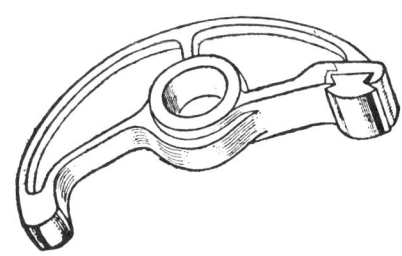

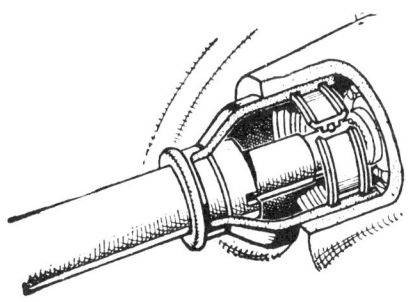

BMW R 69

THE BMW R69

To MANY the name BMW stands for the pinnacle in motorcycle engineering; this not surprising because although the BMW is unconventional, its basic design is obviously right and the attention to detail and finish are superb.

Shaft drive and the opposed twin design have been the hallmark of BMW motorcycles for many years. Basically nothing would seem more logical than placing a motorcycle engine square in the frame; that is to say with the engine crankshaft in the longitudinal axis of the machine. This enables the drive to be taken directly from the engine flywheel through the single plate clutch to the four-speed gearbox and from here via the drive shaft to the bevel gear drive of the rear wheel. Nothing could be more straight forward. The similarity to generally accepted automotive design practice is immediately apparent. Engine and transmission are built in unit and engine torque is transmitted through a car-type single plate clutch.

Because of the fact that the clutch is positioned between the engine and the transmission it only has to transmit engine torque. The final drive be-

Left to right: Charles Galbreath, owner of the test machine, and Earl Flanders, distributor, check the carburetor jets after speed run of 100 mph.

ing of the spiral bevel variety also is reminiscent of automotive practice. The drive shaft is rubber-cushioned to even out the torque pulsations and to safeguard the transmission elements against extreme peak loads.

New in the R 69 design is the drive-shaft construction enclosed in a tube which also serves as one of the rear wheel suspension swinging arms. All the drive-elements are neatly enclosed and protected against dust and water. They require no maintenance other than an occasional check and replenishment of the lubricant.

Left to right: Charles Galbreath, Clemens Weibel, Earl Flanders, and editor, Don Brown.

The only disadvantage of shaft drive in connection with the competition scene seems to be that an alteration in the gear ratio is not as easily effected as if the bike were fitted with chains and sprockets.

There is no doubt whatsoever that the BMW is easily controlled at high speeds. Perfect balance, unusual flexibility and a most reassuring feeling of safety are the foremost factors which give the rider of the BMW the utmost confidence in his machine, especially at high speeds.

There appears to be some confusion

on the often mentioned phenomenon of "torque reaction" in transverse engines. It is true that in the case of the BMW a slight rocking motion is felt when the throttle is opened and shut with the engine stationary. This motion however has nothing to do with the reaction of the "drive" torque, because with the machine stationary no drive torque is transmitted. Any engine that delivers torque — whether placed cross-wise in the frame or otherwise—tends to rotate with the same torque in the opposite direction.

It will be clear that the engine cannot do this on account of it being fixed in the frame. In other words, all the drive torque effects are canceled out in the frame and it is impossible for the rider to notice any effects of this drive torque reaction even if the engine is pulling hard. What then causes this rocking motion in the BMW when the throttle is blipped? This is caused by the "inertia" torque reaction of the revolving masses in the engine, such as the flywheel, crankshaft, part of the connecting rods etc., and this only occurs when the engine is accelerated or decelerated, but it

in motion.

During our speed testing at Rosamond, California, on the dry lakes, the wind was gusty and would in fact change direction frequently. The trouble with this, apart from the danger factor was that no matter how we set up the speed traps, the wind direction would change, ruining our most carefully planned approach angle. The wind was running across the desert at an approximate 28 to 30 miles per hour.

When doing speed tests under these conditions one has to bear in mind that a motorcycle, or any other vehicle for that matter, does not increase its top speed in direct proportion to the magnitude of the tail wind. In other words, just because there is a tail wind of say 30 mph, the motorcycle will not gain exactly 30 mph in top speed; nor will it slow down the same amount when running against it.

We ran the R 69 in both directions —one down wind run resulted in a speed of 112 mph and the return run against the wind clocked 98 mph. The mean speed according to these figures consequently averaged out at 105 mph.

that it would fire on the first kick. In fact editor Don Brown took him up on it and lost. The R 69 fired on the very first kick after a cold ride to the test grounds in an open pick-up truck. The engine idles very smoothly and faultlessly with an exhaust beat characteristic of this type engine. Very impressive also is the almost complete lack of vibration and mechanical quietness at all speeds.

The front suspension earned high marks. It is of the leading link type and in the static position the rear pivot point is slightly higher than the front wheel spindle. This means that there is a lever action (when the front wheel is braked) of the spindle with respect to the suspension arm pivot and this action just about cancels out the nose-diving tendency normally experienced with telescopic or girder forks, resulting in the bike remaining on a fairly even keel when both brakes are applied. And this is just as well as the stoppers on this machine are among the most powerful and smoothest we have ever tested, and this is especially true of the front brake which is of the two-leading shoe type with com-

ROAD TEST

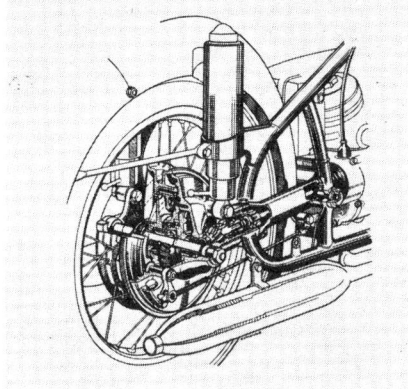

The rear suspension of the R69 BMW. Note enclosed drive shaft and spiral bevel gears and position of the suspension strut.

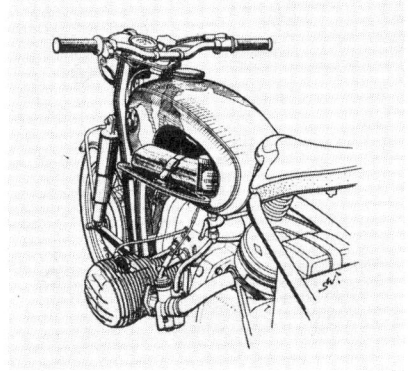

Note clever arrangement of the tool box which extends out from the gasoline tank.

Here the test crew checks the carburetor adjustments prior to the acceleration trials.

has nothing to do with drive torque. In other words if we open the throttle, the "reaction" of the engine torque necessary to speed up the revolving components is noticed and the machine can be felt heeling over against the direction of engine rotation. Conversely if the throttle is suddenly closed the kinetic energy of the rotating masses tends to drive the engine, which in turn causes an inertia reaction in the other direction. However, although this inertia torque reaction theoretically exists, its practical effect is so slight that it is not noticeable with the bike

While this figure does not necessarily indicate the exact top speed of the R 6 9 we do feel that on a normal day the machine should be capable of a top speed well in excess of 100 mph without unduly straining the engine.

Upon checking the acceleration we noticed that at very high rpm the valves could be made to float causing a distinctly audible clatter.

A very pleasant surprise is in store for anyone about to start the BMW for the first time. Earl Flanders briefly explained the correct starting procedure, offering to bet the test crew

pensated control.

The rear suspension also is most satisfactory; it has plenty of travel and the construction and mounting of the swing arm is very rigid. An easily operated control on the suspension struts stiffens the spring rate for pillion riding.

The clutch mechanism works faultlessly, the single plate clutch releases entirely under all circumstances and at no time was gearclashing experienced when engaging low gear from neutral. Earl Flanders pointed out that some experienced riders prefer to only partially release the clutch when shifting gears so that the rider can actually feel the gears meshing.

Our test machine was fitted with the Continental type flat handlebars and a very comfortable dual seat. For the speed runs this arrangement was most satisfactory for it allowed the rider to assume the "flat out" position with a minimum of fuss. However, for around town riding a Western type bar can be fitted if so desired. Like most German made machines the gear change lever is positioned on the left side and the rear brake lever on the right (DIN Standards). Sometimes this is confusing, especially when one is used to the opposite arrangement. Nevertheless, in the case of the R 69 both controls were very easy to operate and ideally arranged in respect to the rider's seating position.

As far as external appearance is concerned there is little doubt about it

Closeup of driveshaft and damping arrangement.

that the BMW never fails to impress the true motorcycle enthusiast. The light alloy castings and general finish are superb and the logical and orderly arrangement of the various components clearly indicates that this machine was designed and built by craftsmen who take a pride in their job. Even after the extensive test procedure the machine remained practically oil tight, only the slightest trace of oil could be detected.

Summarizing, we found the R 69 to be a highly desirable motorcycle. It is spirited in performance and equally matched with perfection in workmanship and obvious lasting qualities.

Because of its price (approximately $1,400) it is obviously aimed at the connoisseur desirous of obtaining only the very best. The BMW test machine was furnished by Mr. Charles Galbreath in cooperation with Earl Flanders, Western distributor. ●

Performance Summary

MAXIMUM SPEEDS

1st gear	32 mph
2nd gear	54 mph
3rd gear	85 mph
4th gear	105 mph (approximate)

ACCELERATION

¼ mile drag	15.5 sec.
1/10 mile drag	8.5 sec.

BRAKING DISTANCES

from indicated 20 mph to full stop—

Front brake only	17′
Rear brake only	38′
Both brakes	12′

GASOLINE MILEAGE

average (on road only) ....55 mpg appr.

SLOW RUNNING

High (4th) gear without lugging....................15 mph

Specifications

ENGINE: Opposed twin, push-rod operated overhead valves by central camshaft. Bore and stroke 72 x 73 mm (2.83 x 2.87 in.). Cubic capacity 590 cc. Compression ratio 8.0:1. Output 35 bhp at 6800 rpm. Wet sump lubrication. Two Bing carburetors.

ELECTRICAL EQUIPMENT: 6 Volt, 90 Watt generator. Headlight, stop-and tail light. Magneto ignition. Manual ignition advance in addition to automatic advance. Completely enclosed magneto and generator.

TRANSMISSION: BMW four speed gearbox built in unit with engine with positive foot-control. Gearbox ratios: First: 5.33.1; second: 3.02:1; third: 2.04:1; top: 1.54:1; Final drive bevel gear ratio: 3.18:1 (4.25 for sidecar). Large single dry plate clutch. Shaft drive to rear wheel with completely enclosed rubber cushioned propellershaft. Pinion and ring gear final drive.

FRAME: Special design with welded duplex tubes. Central stand. Leading arm front suspension with hydraulic damping. Swinging arm rear suspension with hydraulic damping, and quick spring rate adjustment for pillion riding.

TIRES: front: 3.50 x 18; rear: 3.50 x 18. Polished 18 in. light alloy wheel rims. Wheels are interchangeable.

BRAKES: Large diameter brakes in full width hubs, mechanically operated. Two-leading shoe type front brake with compensated control.

FUEL TANK CAPACITY: 4.4 gallons

OVERALL LENGTH: 83½ in.

SEAT HEIGHT: 29 in.

WEIGHT AS TESTED: 455 lbs

MANUFACTURERS: Bayerische Motoren Werke, Munchen 13, Germany.

DISTRIBUTOR: East, Butler and Smith Trading Corp., New York; West, Earl Flanders Co., Pasadena, Calif.

245 c.c. B.M.W.

Sports Single with Pivoted Suspension Systems

AN attractive new 245 c.c. overhead-valve sports model is added to the B.M.W. range. A typical product of the famous Munich factory, the newcomer is designated R26 and clearly owes its ancestry to the touring R25/3 which, incidentally, is continued unchanged. Most obvious difference from the R25 series is the adoption of

pivoted-fork suspension of both wheels; this form of suspension first appeared on the R50 and R69 models which were initially exhibited at last year's Brussels Show.

The front fork has single-tube stanchions with a bend below the headlamp brackets, and unusual rigidity is afforded by a bridge tube just above the pivot-spindle support lugs. Alternative positions giving solo and sidecar trail are provided for the pivot spindle. Both front and rear forks are supported on taper roller bearings and the shock absorbers have coil springs and hydraulic damping; those at the rear incorporate the familiar, manually operated, two-position adjustment for load.

Other characteristics of the larger B.M.W.s

which are repeated on the R26 are incorporation of lugs on the rear-frame loops to take pillion footrests, silencer fitting and sidecar connection; attachment of the shock-absorber upper ends to a reinforced mudguard; enclosure of the drive shaft in the right-hand arm of the rear fork; and a twistgrip providing variable-rate action. Fuel-tank capacity is 15 litres (about 3⅓ gallons). A large tool box is inset into the tank top. The handlebar is 25½in wide.

Bore and stroke of the new engine are 68mm, and the compression ratio is 7.5 to 1. The manufacturers claim a sustained power output of 15 b.h.p. at 6,400 r.p.m. As compared with the R25/3 model the R26 has larger finning on the cylinder head, to give improved cooling, and the carburettor choke diameter is larger at 26mm. In a box under the saddle are housed a large air filter and the battery. A pancake-type, 60-watt generator is driven directly off the front of the crankshaft. Ignition is by coil. An exhaust silencer of large but shapely proportions is fitted.

The four-speed three-shaft gear box gives overall solo ratios of 6.4, 8.48, 12.54 and 22.15 to 1; a transmission shock absorber is embodied and the clutch has a sprung centre. Full-width, light-alloy hubs containing brakes of 6.3in diameter and 1.4in width are specified. The wheels are equipped with 18in-diameter light-alloy rims shod with 3.25in-section tyres. Dry weight of the machine is said to be a little under 350 lb. Price in Germany is DM.2,150 (about £183 at the current rate of exchange).

The R26 looks bigger than a two-fifty

The 600 c.c. Horizontally-opposed o.h.v. Twin

B.M.W. R69

The Fatherland's Biggest and Most Up-to-date Production Machine Tested by " Motor Cycling "

OF all German machines, the undoubted leader in both technical design and detail finish is the B.M.W. R 69 which, being a 590 c.c. o.h.v. twin, is one of the few Continental designs which can provide a direct comparison with the many big British models. However, though the B.M.W. may therefore be considered as probably the nearest equivalent to our popular 600 and 650 c.c. vertical twins, several reservations should be entered. One is that it is designed as a luxury tourer, not as a sports machine. Such features as the now almost traditional h.o. engine and shaft drive make exact analogy with chain-drive vertical twins almost impossible, the design philosophy underlying the two schools of thought being entirely different, while one could buy two British twins for the price of one B.M.W., and still have the price of a puncture outfit to spare!

The safest ground from which a tester can judge the latest in a long line of Munich-built flat twins is in comparison with earlier models of the same marque. There can be no doubt that, with its swinging-fork front and rear suspension and fully enclosed transmission, the new B.M.W. is a vast improvement over its predecessors, which themselves held an enviable reputation. The rear suspension system is, of course, unconventional, the spring units being clamped into position

at about their half-way point; and angular movement accommodated within the unit itself. The frame, too, more nearly resembles an old-type " loop " structure, but it offers great rigidity, and a solid anchorage for a sidecar.

On taking over the test R 69—kindly loaned for the occasion by private owner Bill Potter, of Thornton Heath, Surrey—our man's first mental note was that the 600 c.c. engine was slightly noisier, mechanically, than had been the previous 500 c.c. job. That is to say one could, by listening real hard, just hear the valve gear in action! That frou-frou rustle apart, there was not a single mechanical sound audible.

Clutch action was smooth and sweet, the gear change—provided the rider's tactics were adapted to suit an engine-speed clutch —positive and easy. At first, the riding position gave signs of being just a little

different from that to which a British rider would normally be accustomed. One is seated a little more to the rear—a result of the transverse engine. It took only a few miles, however, to become enthusiastic over the natural attitude provided by the B.M.W., and it was with amazement that a tester normally finicky over control co-relationships discovered, after nearly 1,000 miles of riding, that the footrests were staggered by a couple of inches to suit the equivalent arrangement of the two big " pots."

The riding comfort provided by a combination of sprung saddle and suspension impossible to fault was a revelation. With one possible exception, the R 69 is the best-sprung machine in the rider's longish experience. Since the front end is made under Earles' licence, part of the credit obviously belongs to Birmingham! Readily adjustable by means of a built-in tommy bar

---

TESTER'S ROAD REPORT

Maximum Speeds in :—

Time from Standing Start

Top Gear (Ratio _4·9_ to 1) _102_ m.p.h. 6,760 r.p.m. 26·6 secs.

Third Gear (Ratio _7·8_ to 1) _81_ m.p.h. 8,300 r.p.m. 15·2 secs.

Second Gear (Ratio _9·6_ to 1) _54_ m.p.h. 7,020 r.p.m. _7_ secs.

Speeds over measured Quarter Mile :—

Flying Start _100_ m.p.h. Standing Start _61_ m.p.h.

Braking Figures On DRY TARMACADAM **Surface, from 30 m.p.h. :—**

Both Brakes _20_ ft. Front Brake _26_ ft. Rear Brake _64_ ft.

Fuel Consumption :—

30 m.p.h. 90 m.p.g. 40 m.p.h. 76 m.p.g. 50 m.p.h. 68 m.p.g.

(*Above*) *This view of the very clean engine unit shows the built-in air filter and the accessibility of the carburetter and rocker-box cover.*

(*Right*) *The Earles-type front forks and the extremely powerful twin-leading-shoe front brake.*

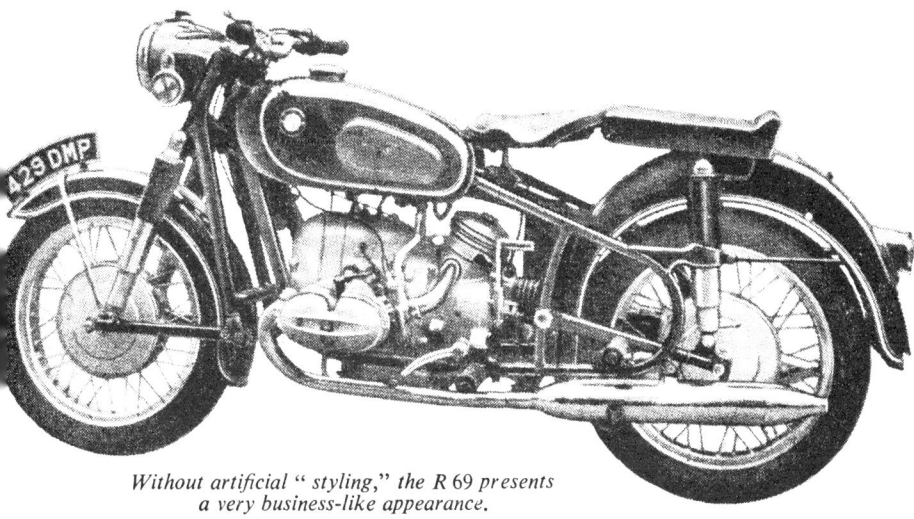

*Without artificial " styling," the R 69 presents
a very business-like appearance.*

on each leg, the rear springing harmonized well with the front, giving superb road-holding under all conditions.

Though flexible enough to allow of 20 m.p.h. traffic negotiation in top gear, the big engine really revelled under open road conditions. There seemed no limit on one's cruising speed. " Poodling " at a touring 40 m.p.h., or hurtling along the highway at over " 90 per "—it was all the same to the R 69. Seldom has the tester straddled a machine which made high-speed cruising so ridiculously easy! At 85-90 m.p.h., with the suspension smoothing out the bumps, the engine vibrationless, and the exhaust note a steady drone, nothing but the whistling of the wind and the needle of the speedo-meter indicated one's speed. It was just like riding in a big, comfortable car.

Acceleration—though not startling—was more than adequate for all practical purposes, the power coming in smoothly, without a flat spot, all the way up the range. Once the knack had been learned, quick gear changes could be made in either direction.

Steering was also first rate. Thanks to a low centre of gravity, the R 69 could be put into corners on any line the rider cared to choose, and it would hold to it tenaciously. It could be rapidly warped over from side to side—thanks in no small measure to an ideal riding position which enabled full knee pressure to be brought to bear—and was as handy as a lightweight when it came to manœuvring through traffic.

With such attributes, it was not surprising that the tester came to regard it as an ideal machine for putting up averages. On one memorable morning, when Press schedules were tight and time short, the R 69 conveyed a staffman from mid-Sussex to the New Forest and back between breakfast-time and lunch, with an hour or so's work thrown in! Over this tricky cross-country journey, measuring just over 90 miles on each stretch, the R 69 responded nobly, doing what had to be done in the minimum time, but also with the maximum safety. Naturally, this required the best use to be made of the model's ability to cruise well up the scale, and it was frequently held with the needle at around the 90 m.p.h. mark, with occasional downhill sprints bringing it near to 100 m.p.h. Under such conditions, fuel consumption naturally rose, but normally an overall 70 m.p.g. could be expected on give-and-take going.

No small contribution to the R 69's appeal was made by its excellent brakes. That at the front was of two-leading-shoe design. When the test figures were being carried out, the first two stops were both made in the allegedly " can't be done " distance of 26 ft *using the front brake alone!* For fear of causing apoplexy amongst readers, attempts were thereupon discontinued. With both brakes in action, the best figure ever obtained in a *Motor Cycling* test—20 ft. from a corrected 30 m.p.h. (the speedo. was 10% fast)—was obtained on the two first tries. No more were made.

On other points, too, the machine earned full marks. The lighting was first-rate; oil-tightness as near absolute as made no difference; the silencing effective; subsidiary design neat; mudguarding good. A hyper-critical tester might have complained that the dipswitch was a little too far from the left hand for comfort; that the otherwise neat toolbox, with Yale-type lock, concealed behind the left knee-rest was the Devil's own delight to repack; and that no adjustment appeared to be provided for a gear pedal which—to be honest—didn't in this case need readjustment, anyway.

But beyond those minor points of detail design, nothing adverse could be said—and certainly they count for little compared with the overall excellence of the layout, handling, performance and finish of this "100 m.p.h.-plus " scion of a long line of foreign aristo-crats. For a price of nearly £500 one expects a motorcycle of nearly Rolls-Royce quality. It is to its manufacturer's credit the the B.M.W. R 69 provides it.

The new swinging fork rear suspension, with enclosed drive shaft and adjustable spring unit.

....**BRIEF SPECIFICATION**....

Engine: 590 c.c. B.M.W. horizontally-opposed o.h.v. twin four-stroke; bore 72 mm. by stroke 73 mm. = 590 c.c.; cast iron cylinders; light alloy heads; valves push-rod operated; C.R. 6.5 to 1; Claimed b.h.p. 35/7,800 r.p.m.; Bing carburetters.

Transmission: Four-speed gearbox bolted-up to engine; car-type clutch; ratios 4.9, 7.8, 9.6 and 16.95 to 1; direct primary drive; final drive by enclosed shaft to hypoid gears.

Frame: Of welded tubular construction; duplex main frame, with extended loop-type rear bearers.

Wheels: Light alloy rims carry Continental 3.50-in. by 18-in. tyres.

Brakes: 7.9-in. twin-leading-shoe front brake; 7.9-in. rear brake.

Lubrication: By gear pump submerged in engine sump.

Electrical Equipment: Noris 6-volt 60-watt generator, crankshaft driven, supplies current for Bosch battery; coil ignition; Bosch head lamp; Bosch tail lamp; Bosch horn; ignition and neutral warning lights; combined horn button and dip-switch control unit.

Suspension: B.M.W. front forks, built under Earles licence, with B.M.W. hydraulically-damped suspension units. Swinging-fork rear suspension with adjustable B.M.W. hydraulically-damped suspension units.

Tank: Of welded steel, 4 gallons capacity. Locking tool box hidden beneath left knee-grip.

Dimensions: Wheelbase, 55¾ in; ground clear-ance, 5 in.; unladen seat height, 28½ in.; dry weight, 445 lb.

Finish: Black enamel with white lining; B.M.W. motif in blue and white on tank; chromium-plated details.

General Equipment: Comprehensive tool kit; tyre inflator; puncture repair outfit; steer-ing head lock; tool box lock; 120 m.p.h. VDO speedometer mounted in head-lamp shell.

Price: £397, plus £95 5s. 7d. P.T = £492 5s. 7d.

Annual Tax: £3 15s.; quarterly £1 0s. 8d.

Makers: Bayerische Motoren Werke A G. Ler-chenauerstrasse 76, Munich, Germany.

Concessionnaires: A.F.N., Ltd., Falcon Works, London Road, Isleworth, Houn-slow, Middx.

247 c.c. B.M.W. Model R26

*A Quiet, Lively and Economical Roadster with First-class
Springing, Steering and Braking, and a High Standard of Finish*

INTRODUCED for 1956, the R26 B.M.W. model is fitted with a highly tuned version of the earlier R25 engine and pivoted-fork front and rear springing similar to that previously confined to the 494 c.c. R50 and the six-hundred R69. Outstanding characteristics of the two-fifty are its excellent riding comfort, superb steering, smooth, powerful braking, a remarkably high level of exhaust and mechanical quietness, good fuel economy and a fine standard of engineering, detail design and finish. And, as the data in the information panel show, the R26 possesses a high performance for a two-fifty.

On some modern machines a combination of a reasonably low seat and footrest setting with an ample range of wheel deflection results in a tendency for the footrests or other components to foul the road on corners. This is not so on the R26. The laden saddle height is low enough to permit a short rider to place his feet firmly on the ground when required and the footrests are sufficiently low to afford a comfortably wide knee angle; both front and rear springing systems allow ample wheel movement. Yet the model can be heeled over to an extreme degree when cornering without the footrests or other parts scraping the ground, for the width across the footrests is only 21in, while the silencer and centre stand are well tucked away.

Width of the tank between the rider's knees is also comparatively narrow (9½in), while handlebar width is only 25in. The resultant riding position proved extremely comfortable at all speeds within the model's compass, and many consecutive hours were spent awheel without a trace of fatigue. Another feature contributing to riding comfort is a four-position saddle-spring adjustment which caters for riders' weights from 132 to 220lb.

Grouped in two clusters clamped to the ends of the handlebar, the hand controls were all very conveniently sited and sweet in operation. Though not adjustable for position, the rear-brake and gear pedals were also ideally sited.

In both front and rear shock absorbers, spring and damper characteristics are extremely well blended. Both wheel suspensions responded remarkably well to all varieties of road shocks from small ripples to pot-holes, yet there was never any pitching. On full front-wheel deflection, caused by crossing a deep road hole at speed, the front number plate broke the headlamp glass. Mounting the plate an inch farther forward would preclude the possibility of its fouling the glass. (It should be remembered that front number plates are not used in Germany.)

Steering of the race-bred variety made cornering a sheer joy, whether the bend was fast or slow, smooth or bumpy. Unusually little effort was required to heel the model over. Indeed, once the banking was initiated the R26 seemed to take matters into its own hands with superlative results. Of an equally high standard was the braking. Used independently,

each brake could be made to evoke a protesting squeal from the tyre. Applied in unison, they would stop the model smoothly, safely and, if necessary, rapidly enough for any emergency. Although the brakes were intentionally not spared, no adjustment was needed during a test of just over 500 miles. Front-brake torque is transmitted through the pivoted fork so that brake operation tends to raise the front of the machine, but not unduly so, and certainly not enough to cause fork judder.

Whether the engine was cold or hot, a first-kick start could virtually be guaranteed provided the carburettor was not overflooded. If that was done the engine would fire readily if the kick-starter were operated with the throttle wide open. A

Final-drive unit with enclosed shaft. The levers protruding from the shock absorbers provide manual adjustment for load

throttle setting as for a fast tick-over was normally required for starting, in conjunction with momentary operation of the float tickler when the engine was cold or none at all when it was hot. Whatever the temperature of the engine, it would idle very slowly and reliably when the throttle was closed.

Incorporating bevel gears which actuate the throttle cable through the medium of a cam, the twistgrip has a differential action giving a slow rate of throttle opening in the lower ranges and a progressively faster rate as the grip is rotated farther. This delicate control, in effect, enhanced the natural docility of the engine for traffic work and, in conjunction with a low bottom-gear ratio, smooth transmission and high flywheel inertia, made it easy to ride the R26 at a slow walking pace with the clutch fully engaged, and to accelerate sweetly from that speed.

With the exception that slight vibration was perceptible between 44 and 48 m.p.h. in top gear, and again at an indicated 60 m.p.h., any speed between the minimum non-snatch figure and maximum was equally pleasant to use. On long mainroad trips 50 miles were often packed into each hour by cruising on half-throttle or just over. This setting gave an indicated

*In spite of the hardest riding the R26
remained clean externally*

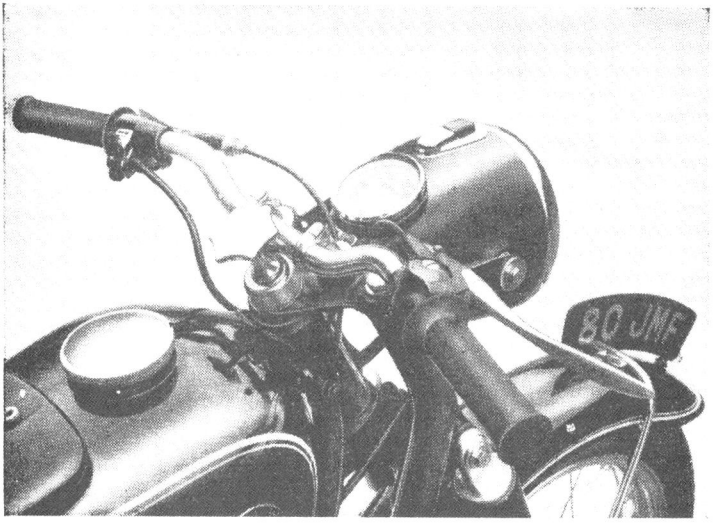
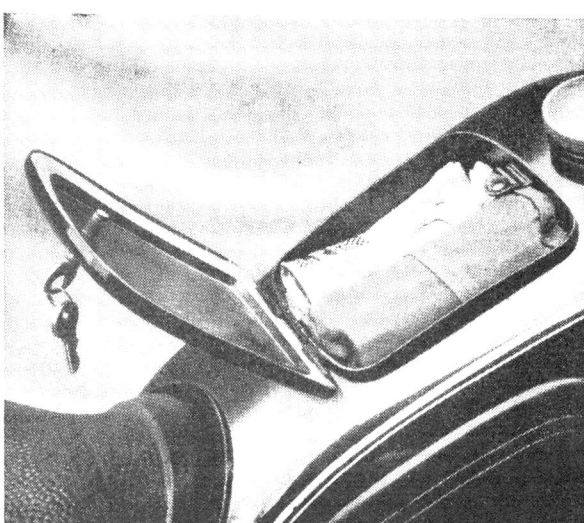

Left : The handlebar controls are neatly and conveniently grouped.   *Right : The tool compartment is waterproofed by a sponge-rubber strip in the lid*

speed of approximately 70 m.p.h. under windless conditions on level roads; but speedometer flattery was about 10 per cent throughout the B.M.W.'s speed range. When tested for stamina the R26 was ridden for several miles on end on full throttle without the least sign of distress. Hill climbing was excellent, thanks to the engine's high torque and flywheel inertia.

An engine-speed clutch and widely spaced gear ratios do not make for the best in gear changing. Upward changes on the R26 could be made with lightning speed provided some clashing of the dogs was tolerated. Alternatively, noiseless changes could be effected by means of a pause in pedal movement. A slight click accompanied all downward changes. Engagement of bottom gear with the engine idling was almost noiseless; neutral selection was child's play and was indicated by the illumination of a green light in the headlamp shell. Clutch engagement was smooth but because of the high flywheel

inertia, the lever was best released gently if a slight lurch was to be avoided.

A wide, powerful headlamp beam made daylight speeds safe on unlit roads after dark. Mudguarding efficiency was above average. At the conclusion of the test which included much hard riding, no oil had leaked from any part of the mechanism.

A fine-quality toolkit and good accessibility render maintenance easy. But it is necessary to remove the tank to gain access to the valve adjustments and this involves draining the fuel. However, adjustments are unlikely to be required except after decarbonizing the engine. The R26 bristles with attractive features such as quickly detachable, balanced wheels with polished, light-alloy rims, steering and toolbox locks and rubber sealing of the tool and battery containers. In its performance, unobtrusiveness, finish and detail design, the R26 cannot fail to engender great pride of ownership.

Information Panel

SPECIFICATION

ENGINE: B.M.W. 247 c.c. (68 × 68 mm) overhead-valve single with fully-enclosed valve gear, dynamo and ignition equipment. Aluminium-alloy cylinder head. Light-alloy connecting rod; plain big-end bearing. Crankshaft supported by three ball bearings. Compression ratio, 7.5 to 1. Pressure lubrication; oil compartment in crankcase, capacity 2¼ pints.

CARBURETTOR: Bing with twistgrip throttle control. Air filter.

IGNITION and LIGHTING: Coil ignition with auto-advance. Noris 60-watt dynamo with automatic voltage control. Bayern 6-volt, 9-ampere-hour battery. Bosch 6½in-diameter headlamp with pre-focus light unit and 35/35-watt main bulb.

TRANSMISSION: B.M.W. four-speed gear box in unit with engine; positive-stop foot control. Gear ratios: bottom, 22.17 to 1; second, 12.56 to 1; third, 8.49 to 1; top, 6.41 to 1. Single-plate dry clutch incorporated in engine flywheel; fabric friction material. Final drive by enclosed shaft and helical bevel gears. Engine r.p.m. at 30 m.p.h. in top gear, 2,630.

FUEL CAPACITY: 3¼ gallons.

TYRES: Metzeler 3.25 × 18in front and rear.

BRAKES: 6½in diameter × 1⅜in wide front and rear; finger adjusters.

SUSPENSION: B.M.W. pivoted-fork front and rear springing employing multi-rate coil springs and hydraulic damping. Two-position manual adjustment for load on rear shock absorbers. Two-position load and trail adjustments on front fork for sidecar duty.

WHEELBASE: 54½in unladen. Ground clearance, 6in unladen.

SADDLE: Pagusa cantilever type, pivoted at nose; rubber top. Four-position adjustment for rider's weight. Unladen height, 31in.

WEIGHT: 330 lb fully equipped and with full oil container and one gallon of petrol.

PRICE: £207. With purchase tax (in Great Britain only), £256 13s 7d.

ROAD TAX: £1 17s 6d. a year; 10s 4d a quarter.

MAKERS: Bayerische Motoren Werke A.G., Munich, Germany.

BRITISH CONCESSIONAIRES: A.F.N., Ltd., Falcon Works, London Road, Isleworth, Middlesex.

The 247 c.c. B.M.W. 26

PERFORMANCE DATA

MEAN MAXIMUM SPEED: Bottom: * 23 m.p.h.
Second: * 41 m.p.h.
Third: * 60 m.p.h.
Top: 72 m.p.h.
* Valve float occurring.

HIGHEST ONE-WAY SPEED: 73 m.p.h. (conditions: moderate side wind; rider wearing two-piece plastic suit and overboots).

MEAN ACCELERATION:

	10-30 m.p.h.	20-40 m.p.h	30-50 m.p.h
Second	5.2 sec	4.8 sec	—
Third	—	8.0 sec	7.6 sec
Top	—	11.5 sec	13.4 sec

Mean speed at end of quarter-mile from rest: 62 m.p.h
Mean time to cover standing quarter-mile: 20.5 sec.

PETROL CONSUMPTION: At 30 m.p.h., 120 m.p.g. At 40 m.p.h 100 m.p.g. At 50 m.p.h., 80 m.p.g. At 60 m.p.h., 67 m.p.g.

BRAKING: From 30 m.p.h. to rest, 29ft (surface, dry tarmac).

TURNING CIRCLE: 13ft 6in.

MINIMUM NON-SNATCH SPEED: 15 m.p.h. in top gear

WEIGHT PER C.C.: 1.34 lb.

BMW R60

Bayerische Motoren Werke — BMW for short—are the manufacturers of CYCLE's Road Test bike for this month. The BMW marque is also pretty well known to thousands of motorsport fans for its remarkable sports and family cars and aircraft engines.

However, either on two or four wheels, the common characteristic is unexcelled craftsmanship and astonishing mechanical precision. Throughout the different phases of the test, the bike lived up to its very fine ancestral reputation.

The model furnished was an R-60, 600 cc, with opposed twin OHV engine and was just out of the crate —only 8 miles on the odometer— when delivered to the CYCLE staff by its Western distributor, Earl Flanders, of Pasadena, Calif.

After a short briefing on starting technique by Mr. Flanders, the R-60 always was a "first-kick starter," even during the chilly Pasadena December mornings!

The R-60 engine features high torque at low RPM and comparatively low compression ratio.

It is specifically designed for side-car work. Nevertheless, this machine can also be considered a tough and absolutely reliable "90-plus" solo

The two levers, operating one independent cam each, are easily seen in the picture above. The result: two leading shoes in the front brake and extraordinary braking efficiency.

mount. Both brakes have full width and finned drums. The front one is equipped with twin cam operated shoes, which accounts for a maximum of braking efficiency with a minimum of pressure applied on the lever.

The leverage arrangement of the rear brake also provides an almost effortless operation.

CYCLE Publisher Clymer says BMW is one motorcycle that the rider dressed in normal clothing can feel comfortable on. BMW is silent and exceptionally clean. Ease of handling and perfect balance are BMW features.

All these details, plus a braking area of 28.2 sq. inches are the BMW's reply to the ever-increasing safety requirements of today's traffic conditions.

The binders are thoughtfully complemented with a race bred front and rear suspension. The front fork is of bottom link type and follows the Earles pattern, so successfully employed in the fabulous Italian 4-cylinder MV Agustas during recent European seasons.

The rear suspension may be instantly adjusted, via two handy little levers, to provide stiff or soft action which enables the machine to meet any load or road conditions.

Both fenders are deeply valanced to insure an adequate protection against splashing.

The tail section of the rear fender is hinged and can be raised to provide good access whenever the rear wheel has to be removed. The front fender brace is chromed. The oil-tight

engine is velvet smooth when pulling at any speed. It shows an almost unnoticeable tendency to rock when being accelerated or decelerated. This is due to the inertia developed by the revolving masses inside the engine, such as crankshaft, flywheel, etc. If the accelerator is twisted suddenly, with the machine stationary, it may be felt heeling over against the direction of engine rotation. On the contrary, when the throttle is suddenly shut off, an inertia reaction is caused in the other direction.

Of course, such reaction is so slight that it cannot be felt with the bike in motion.

The engine and the four-speed gear

The removable element of the air cleaner was easy to reach and caused no obstruction to the air flow entering the carburetors' funnels.

Clymer found cornering on BMW a real delight due to fine engineering design and excellent weight distribution.

Asst. Editor Carol Anderson approved the easy-to-get-at tool kit and the remarkable quality of its components.

box are of single unit construction and the smooth transmission of power is still further enhanced by the rubber-cushioned cardan shaft drive totally enclosed inside the right arm of the rear swinging suspension. At the end of the test a slight oil leak began to appear near the speedometer cable drive.

Although the catalogue states a 6.5:1 compression ratio, Mr. Flanders informed us that the models exported to the American market feature a somewhat higher figure of 7.2:1. Incidentally, the high torque at low RPM is not impaired at all by this circumstance. The two BING carburetors have a single air filter equipped with a strangler to help cold starts. The filter has a special element which should be changed every 7,500 miles.

The ignition advance control is automatic. There is a cap with integral dip stick on the left side of engine, to facilitate checking the crankcase oil level.

The generous dimensions of the mufflers in addition to their unobtrusive operation are clear evidence of the strictly enforced noise regulations prevailing in West Germany.

The unorthodox position and operation of the kickstarter lever takes a little time to get used to. However, once you become acquainted with its "kicking technique" it's for sure you'll never miss the conventionally located KS lever alongside the machine. The foot operated gearshift lever scored high for its effectiveness and neat location. There was no necessity to use the steering damper for the duration

of the test. The tail light has been specially redesigned and enlarged by the Factory in order to comply with the local State laws as far as the lens size is concerned.

The cushioned rubber saddle can be adjusted to suit the rider's weight. A luxurious twin seat and passenger pegs are available at extra cost. However, it is our impression that a machine which features the outstanding crafts-

Valve lash checking was a practical proposition! No gas tank to remove nor tricky separate rocker covers to deal with.

Engine flexibility and superb road holding ability were some of the many fine points of the BMW pointed out by Technical Editor Castro during the test.

Hot Rod expert, Rick Faucher, showed great interest and approved the front end treatment of the BMW. The Earles fork and the two leading shoes' front brake immediately caught his connoisseur's eye.

The large air cleaner and generous dimensions of the front shocks and the finned rocker cover make a gratifying view for both expert and beginner in the above photo. The glossy finish and shapely lines of the gas tank and frame are features.

The Flanders-made Western style handlebars help to enhance even more the excellent craftsmanship and design of the R-60.

manship and engineering quality of the R-60, should also be furnished with a twin seat and passenger pegs as standard equipment. The side stand and partial trip recorder are also available at extra cost.

The gas tank tap has a reserve position which allows for some 18 miles of extra riding. An antitheft device locks the steering head completely to the right hand position.

A good part of the road test was performed using the R-60 by day light and at dark, as a ride-to-work machine, and also some week-end trips were carried on. Night riding was simple and safe thanks to the perfect illumination furnished by the BMW lighting system and its 8 amp.-hour battery.

Due to the engine's tightness, no maximum speed runs were attempted. However the behavior of the "be-em" under normal road or freeway riding didn't impress the tester as a slow mount by any means! Furthermore, great care had to be exerted to maintain the speed under legal limits. Acceleration, though not startling, was

more than adequate for all practical purposes and the power came in smoothly all the way up the four gear ranges. Steering and road holding ability were well above any stock machine on the market today and if any comparison is to be drawn, it might be necessary to mention some racing thoroughbreds. These features, coupled with wonderful fade proof brakes, turned dense traffic riding into sheer pleasure. A speed of 18.5 mph was perfectly feasible in top gear without any lugging.

The test bike was equipped with western type handlebars manufactured by Flanders Company and allowed a very comfortable riding position either in stop-and-go commuting or definitely long trips.

Above the head lamp there is a red warning light to indicate the charge delivered to the battery by the generator. Another similar green light, close to it, glows when the trans is in neutral. The light and ignition switch is also located above the head lamp and is very easy to operate while riding. On the left side of the handlebar there is a combined horn and dimmer switch. The tool compartment is built-in on the left side of the gas tank and the knee grip on that side is also the compartment's door. There is a Yale-type key for it.

The tool kit includes a goodly number of high quality tools. Also a complete set for fixing flats and a handy rag are included.

The owner's Handbook is printed in English, French and Spanish and its 166 pages feature substantial literature, useful pictures and elaborated diagrams.

A business-like air pump is solidly attached on the right side of the machine.

Finally, may we add that the R-60 is one of the most versatile and reliable motorcycles we ever tested. Its superb craftsmanship and mechanical features make it a most coveted possession for anyone who enjoys motorcycling at its very best and, at the same time, whose pride of ownership leads him to choose only the finest.

Asst. Editor Carol Anderson and tester are amused at the unorthodox—but always effective—"kicking technique" required by the position of the KS lever.

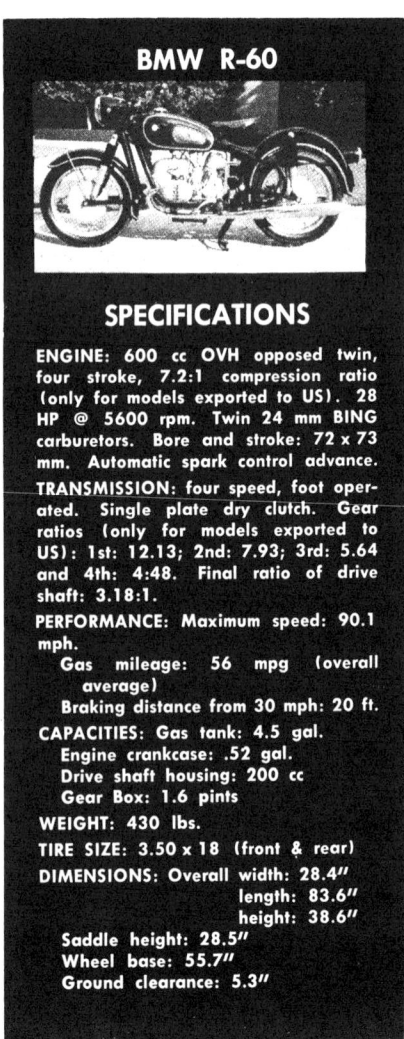

BMW R-60

SPECIFICATIONS

ENGINE: 600 cc OVH opposed twin, four stroke, 7.2:1 compression ratio (only for models exported to US). 28 HP @ 5600 rpm. Twin 24 mm BING carburetors. Bore and stroke: 72 x 73 mm. Automatic spark control advance.

TRANSMISSION: four speed, foot operated. Single plate dry clutch. Gear ratios (only for models exported to US): 1st: 12.13; 2nd: 7.93; 3rd: 5.64 and 4th: 4:48. Final ratio of drive shaft: 3.18:1.

PERFORMANCE: Maximum speed: 90.1 mph.
   Gas mileage: 56 mpg (overall average)
   Braking distance from 30 mph: 20 ft.

CAPACITIES: Gas tank: 4.5 gal.
   Engine crankcase: .52 gal.
   Drive shaft housing: 200 cc
   Gear Box: 1.6 pints

WEIGHT: 430 lbs.

TIRE SIZE: 3.50 x 18 (front & rear)

DIMENSIONS: Overall width: 28.4"
            length: 83.6"
            height: 38.6"

Saddle height: 28.5"
Wheel base: 55.7"
Ground clearance: 5.3"

Workmanship and Beauty —

...THE MARKS OF QUALITY!

FAMOUS BMW R-26 SINGLE 250cc

BMW R-26 features immaculate workmanship. 250cc 15HP engine has smooth, silent performance. Shaftdrive, Earles-type front fork, Swingarm Suspension, satin-smooth finish.

BMW TWINS — THE DREAM OF EVERY ENTHUSIAST

BMW MODEL R-69 SUPERSPORT TWIN

Here is the ultimate in performance from the 36 HP, OHV super-tuned engine. Quiet, surging power makes you the master of the highways. BMW R-69 — for those who want and take pride in owning the best.

BMW MODELS R-50, 500cc, and R-60, 600cc

Enjoy absolute reliability, outstanding performance and cleanliness as only a shaftdrive Twin can offer. BMW R-50 has 500cc, two cyl. OHV engine with 26 HP. BMW R-60 has 600cc, two cyl. OHV engine which develops 28 HP.

All BMW models are available with solo seats or dual seat.

All BMW Twins are equipped with high handlebars, trip speedometer, magneto ignition, new king-size tail-light.

SEE YOUR DEALER OR WRITE FOR INFORMATION

Across Europe and Asia on a BMW

by Jim Gilzean

Regardless of how big a suitcase one buys, there are always those last two or three articles which just won't fit in with the lid closed. This was the age-old problem that confronted me as I excitedly packed for my approaching tour.

I can already visualize the inquisitive wrinkles forming on the foreheads of those of you who have, at one time or another, gone on a lengthy motorcycle trip.

"Why is this fool babbling about suitcases, when saddlebags are used on motorcycles," you must be thinking. Well, in Germany where I was stationed with the Army, saddlebags just aren't used. They are replaced by a rack, behind the dual seat, upon which Germans have the knack of fastening everything but the kitchen sink.

Only after extensive unpacking, repacking, and unprintable language, was my suitcase finally packed with all my necessities, and balanced precariously on the rack, along with my bedroll and a rucksack full of food.

By the time all the aggravating, but essential, last minute details and checks had been taken care of, it was ten o'clock before I got under way, beneath brilliant Fall sunshine. The countryside was familiar as far as the Mohne Dam. Movie goers will know this as the first and largest of the three dams that were destroyed in "The Dam Busters." One can still see the huge patch of new concrete where it has since been repaired, and put back into operation. From here south, almost all the way to Frankfurt-on-Main, the road was a delightful roller-coaster track, through scenery beautifully like our own Laurentian Mountains.

Frankfurt is well into the American Zone of Germany, and, while exploring the wonders of this and the other southern German cities of Heidelberg, Stuttgart, and Munich, I was greeted by innumerable calls of "Hi Canada," and spent the time waiting at many a traffic light, in a friendly chat through the windows of the passing cars of some of our friendly neighbors in the United States Forces.

My method of seeing as much of a city as possible, in a short time, is to deliberately get lost and then spend an hour or two just driving aimlessly through the streets, taking in the sights, before trying to find an exit in the required direction. This helps greatly in holding my shattered nerves together as I would undoubtdly become lost in any case, and it gives me a great inner satisfaction to best myself to the punch and say that I did it on purpose.

From Frankfurt, I had the advantage of the fabulous Autobahn for the remainder of the day, except for sightseeing excursions through Heidelberg, the university city of "The Student Prince" movie fame, and Stuttgart, the Detroit of the German automotive world.

The lengthy dusk gave me plenty of warning to find a camping site, and the fall of darkness found me munching beans "a la can" beside my sleeping bag, in a small copse near Augsburg.

Disappointment reigned as I opened my eyes to find visibility limited to ten feet. Even after I had put my glasses on, I could still only see thirty feet, due to dense fog. Reluctantly I crawled out of the "sack" and was soon feeling my way along the Autobahn, with one hand constantly wiping the condensation from my bi-focals. After about two hours, however, the sun finally broke through, just as I was approaching Munich. Here, much to my dismay, I found that it was only a little after eight o'clock, and me with two hours behind me already. This disgusting "crack of dawn" habit continued for the entire trip. I guess it must be that darned fresh air—too much of it isn't good for a fellow.

Near the Austrian border, I spotted an interesting looking side road, leading off towards the mountains in the south. A quick check with the map showed me that this was an alternative route to my temporary destination, Salzburg, in Austria, so, off the beaten track I went. This decision proved itself as the colorful foothills of the Alps drew closer, and finally enveloped me in their patchwork design of autumn reds, yellows, and golds, under the dark green crown of the hardier pines on the higher slopes of the mountains.

Long before the city is reached, the horizon is broken by the battlements of the guardian castle of Salzburg, atop her rocky butte, keeping a protective eye on the ever-growing metropolis beneath her. Womanlike, probably reminiscing about her younger days and wishing, once again to hear the clamor of the battles of men, fighting for her possession.

South from this city the road gradually rose for a hundred scenic miles until at last I was confronted by the entrance to the Grossglockner Pass. Seeing those towering grey and brown monsters frowning down made me feel like the proverbial fly in the soup bowl, being scrutinized before removal. After a long first, second, and occasionally third gear climb, with many appreciative stops to enjoy the awe-inspiring Alpine beauty, I arrived at the souvenir shop on the highest point on the pass (approximately 8,500 feet). The sight that lay before me here is beyond verbal description, but I shall be brief, and do my best. From the nearest mountain peak, across

Highest section of the Gross Glockner pass in Austria.

the valley, all the way to the jagged horizon, the snow-topped crags grasped at the sky, each in a super effort to outgrow its neighbor. In the gap between the nearest peaks, the white caps gradually hazed into blue, and added even more majesty to the royal scene.

Before turning in for the night, I climbed down the last half of the pass, and set up shop near a fast flowing river.

Shortly after hitting the trail, I made a gas stop, and had my first encounter with fellow enthusiasts—two very pretty young Austrian girls en route to Denmark for a holiday, aboard a well-laden Vespa.

I was still up in the mountains when, after an invigorating morning's run, I passed through the Italian customs. At first there was little visible change, but soon the mountains were replaced by rolling hills, and these too finally disappeared behind me. The fact that I was in Italy now became apparent in the white-walled villas and the disciplined rows of olive trees. Every city, town or village here has its square in the center, complete with elaborate flower beds and fountains in the shade of stately palms.

The Adriatic coast highway to Trieste is something to be remembered as the road is, for most part, about two hundred feet above the sea, and sometimes nothing but a shear drop separates pavement from water. It was in Trieste that my already shaky nervous system had its first real test, which was to be continued in every city of considerable size in Italy. If you can imagine the sidewalks jam-packed with Italian women in light, scanty summer dresses, then you can imagine how much I was concentrating

on the road. Add to this, a host of tiny Fiats bearing down on me from every direction, with both the gas pedal and horn button fully depressed, and you have confusion at its peak.

Somehow I got through unscathed, and proceeded back alongside the Adriatic to Venice, where I parked the B.M.W. and took a well earned rest on—no, not a Gondola—but the Venetian counterpart of a streetcar, similar to the sight-seeing boats used at the Thousand Islands of the St. Lawrence, Lake of the Woods, or any other Canadian water resort. The traffic situation here varies from elsewhere in Italy only in speed, as the majority of the boats are fitted with horns, and all go as fast as possible, in true Italian tradition.

Since it was dark when I got back to the machine, I did not venture too far before settling down for the night, not a little shaken from my debut on Italian roads.

The countryside of "sunny" Italy apparently overslept until ten o'clock before shedding its heavy blanket of fog, and it was pretty chilly going until then. The rest of the day made up for it, however, as the Mediterranean sunshine soon cheered things up.

The highlight of the day was my visit to the minute (forty square miles) Republic of San Marino, about twenty miles inland from the sea port of Rimini. A relatively flat country, it is landmarked centrally by a very steep mountain bearing the burden of the capital city, after which the country is named. Actually it is little more than a small town and was protected in former years by what is now the major tourist attraction, its three fortresses. Due to the off-season timing of my visit, these were

Author Jim Gilzean's BMW just before departure.

unfortunately closed to the public but, nevertheless, for a short time they succeeded in taking my thoughts back four or five hundred years.

Proceeding south, I soon came upon another memorable scene, when I first saw Ancona. This city is situated on a hill at the far side of a bay, as approached from the north. The whitewashed buildings seem to rise right out of the sea, and accumulate one on top of the other, the whole pyramid of glistening white being surmounted by an ancient and equally beautiful cathedral.

I was caught unawares by nightfall, and inquired about camping from two policemen on their very interesting Moto-Guzzi 500 c.c. horizontal singles. When they had finished oohing and aaahing over the B.M.W., and I likewise over their machines, we all mounted up and they escorted me to a wonderful campsite complete with running water, sinks, and toilets. Nowadays, it's even hard to ''rough it'' when one goes camping.

Have you ever tried putting on a pair of trousers without getting out of a sleeping bag? Sounds tricky, doesn't it? Well, this was the problem that faced me as I awoke to find an exceptionally good looking young woman making herself busy tidying up the adjacent campsite. Eventually I got untangled, packed up, and hit the road once more.

Southern Italy, being fairly well poverty stricken, still relies mostly on the old horse and cart for transportation purposes. Since Italian roads are not the widest in the world, when I encountered a steady stream in each direction of these buggies laden with fruit, I felt grateful that I had only the width of a motorcycle to contend with, as cars were held to a crawl.

Early in the afternoon I reached the port of Brindisi, where I was to catch a ship to the Greek island of Corfu. While making arrangements at the shipping office I suffered the greatest setback of the whole tour. The return fare for the B.M.W. and myself was to cost $70 and this for a distance of only 75 - 80 miles one way. Bad as this may already sound, I must add that this is a twelve-hour overnight journey with no meals supplied, and I had to spread my sleeping bag on the hard open deck. Nevertheless, I had come this far and my stubborn streak wouldn't let me turn back.

Since the ship didn't leave until the following afternoon, I drove out of town for a ways to a quiet beach before bedding down.

With lots of time to spare I went for a run right to the top of the ''heel'' of Italy, and then turned back to Brindisi to sign some more papers for the shipping agent. Still with time on my hands, I headed for my little beach of the previous night, and spent a lazy afternoon sun bathing and swimming in the blue Mediterranean bay.

Back to town again, and this time straight through to the docks, where I cleared customs and looked around for the loading area for the machine. At this point I had a wonderful surprise when, after so many days of babbling foreigners and sign language, a young couple drove up on a Vespa, the man wearing an immense Stetson, buckskin jacket and blue jeans, asked in a real Yankee drawl ''Say, bud, where are we supposed to load these darned machines?''

They were a happy-go-lucky California man and wife who had been touring Europe for two years by hitch-hiking or any other means that they chanced upon, working with musical groups as they went. They had just bought the Vespa, and were going to see how the Greeks would receive a Western guitar and song.

Eventually we got the bikes on board and, picking out a good camping spot at the stern, we set out

Beach and small craft harbor near the town of Korfu, Greece.

to find some more English speakers. Our search was rewarded by a South African couple, on tour with a brand new M.G. ''A'' coupe, and an Australian couple, hitch-hiking home after an unsuccessful year in England. When the excitement of leaving port was over, we all settled down to a most enjoyable evening of singing and bull throwing, before turning in.

After considerable trouble with the local authorities over my having a N.A.T.O. armed forces pass instead of a passport, I was cleared into Greece. After saying farewell to my overnight friends, I was just in time to shove the bike aboard a small passenger ferry before it departed from Corfu to the mainland. Also on board, much to my surprise, was an identical B.M.W. twin to my own. The owner was a young Greek from Thessalonika, who had been attending university in Germany, and was now on his way home after completing his course. I was lucky in that, apart from Greek and German, he could also speak excellent English.

My original plan had been to travel south-east to Athens and then north to Thessalonika, but I accepted his kind invitation to become his travelling companion, spend a night at his home, and to visit Athens on my way back.

The mountains in the west of Greece are certainly very picturesque, but the roads are in a pitiful state of disrepair. A paradise for enduro enthusiasts is the wind up, over, and down each mountain, gravelled in places, but for the most part, just dust or plain earth surfaced. The only traffic in this part of the world consists of a few rickety old buses, which run what I would imagine to be a fairly unreliable service between the various towns and villages in the area.

The standard of living here is very low, and the main trend of life is sheep and goat herding. Quite often, we rounded one of the many corners and found the road blocked by a mass of milling woolen

backs, and had to apply the brakes hastily.

That night, I had the added luxury of my friend's tent and just as well, because it turned out that we picked a very windy camping spot. Here also, I discovered that the bumpy roads had taken their toll and burst a can of tomato juice, making quite a mess of the inside of my pack.

I guess the confidence of having a roof over my head once again made me sleep late for a change, and it was almost ten o'clock by the time both machines were packed up and ready to go. Under a cloudless sky the countryside was shown off to its best advantage. By a matter of general direction we followed a river. This was seen, sometimes as a tiny silver ribbon hundreds of feet below, sometimes as a raging torrent yards away, and still again as a quiet meandering mirror, leisurely winding towards the Mediterranean.

At a gas stop we were told of a short cut in our direction and decided to take it, since it cut our journey to the next town from fifty to thirty miles. Had we been driving cars this would have been our undoing, as the ruts were as deep as two feet at times from the gravel trucks that used this road. At it was we had a three foot strip between the ruts that was hard baked mud, almost as smooth as pavement. During this detour we had to cross the aforementioned river six times without the aid of bridges. Like I said, an enduro rider's heaven.

It was after dark when we finally arrived in Thessalonika, surprised at having found a little pavement for the last forty miles or so. We drove straight to his house, where his mother prepared us a meal fit for kings, after which I was shown to a bed with an unbelievably thick mattress and I was soon snoring between real sheets.

Another late morning, but, nevertheless, great. The first in over a week that I didn't have a stump or rock practically embedded between my ribs. Breakfast over, my friend took me on an interesting tour of the first and only truly modern city I was to see in Greece. He then took me to the eastern exit where we parted, and I struck out for Turkey. I didn't quite make my destination by nightfall, as I had a bit of trouble with the rear fender. It was beginning to crack under the strain of the heavy load on the luggage rack, and the adverse conditions of the so-called highways. I tried various new methods of suspending my packs without much success.

Another distraction was a very narrow escape when a donkey got panicky at the last minute as I was about to pass him, and dashed across the road in front of me. There are still a few donkey hairs to be found on my clutch lever to prove this.

Despite these setbacks I had a most interesting coastal drive along the shore of the Aegean Sea, on a quite smooth asphalt highway, no less. Nightfall found me still quite a few miles from the Turkish border.

Confusion and despair were the first orders of the day, as the engine could not be turned over by the kickstarter or any other means. The simplest of solutions was found, but only after desperate visions of engine and gearbox parts strewn all over the roadway, as I imagined myself doing an on-the-spot overhaul. Yours truly was to blame, naturally. I had left the fuel tap open, and the left-hand cylinder must have just been starting its power stroke when I switched the engine off the previous night. This left the intake valve just open enough to allow the gas to trickle in overnight and fill up the cylinder, so that the first kick in the morning completely closed the intake valve, sealing the cylinder, full of gas, with the piston at bottom dead center. All the mules in God's green earth couldn't have moved that piston. I finally discovered the cause when I removed the

Beyazit Square in the center of Istanbul.

ACROSS EUROPE . . . (Continued)

spark plug in a last despairing effort at trouble-shooting.

Troubles over, or, so I thought, I went merrily on my way, until I ran out of gas and had to push the cycle four miles to the next gas pump. It was a very disgruntled traveller who finally pulled into the Greek customs office that morning, and then passed on to the Turkish authorities.

Unaware that the Turkey-Syria crisis had arisen since I had last heard a news report in Germany, I was surprised to see armed soldiers on guard here and also at all strategic places, such as bridges, railroad crossings, etc., throughout Turkey. Inside the customs office was an American who taught at Istanbul University, and his wife, who were having trouble getting their newly acquired Volkswagen into the country without the necessary papers.

Turkish roads are paved, but have about five layers of asphalt and every few yards the surface of the road skips a few layers, putting any speed at all completely out of the question. Scenery tends to get boring since from the top of one hill the road goes down into the valley, and then straight up to the top of the next hill. Living conditions are little better than those in Greece, and I often saw, through the uncovered windows of brick shacks, that the inside decorations were bare bricks also.

Forty miles from Istanbul the poor road suddenly gave way to a wonderful super highway, as smooth as velvet. I had a companion for a few miles before he saw a camping place he liked. He was an Indian who, after attending university in England, was returning to India via Triumph Tiger Cub. The reason he camped so early was that he intended to stop near Istanbul for two or three days.

This great city is rightfully called "The Gateway to the East," as it is a wonderful specimen of the mingling of the old with the new. I was both awed and humbled by the immense size and brilliant colors of the fabulous Mosque of Sultan Ahmet.

While roving around this place of wonder I met a pleasant chap on an old '47 Ariel 350 c.c. We had supper together in one of the better class restaurants, after which he showed me some of the sights that I had previously missed. He then took me home where I met his family before driving to the outskirts of the city with him, where we bade each other farewell.

This had been a particularly interesting acquaintanceship, as he spoke just as much English as I did Turkish—not a word. We conversed the whole evening by means of sign language or by scribbling pictures on scraps of paper, to help put a point across.

Since I was quite far behind my schedule I decided to push on at least as far as Greece that night. The trip to the border was punctuated by stops to rearrange and readjust the load on my now badly sagging rear fender. The Turkish authorities were a little grumpy at being awakened at one o'clock in the morning, and when I got to the Greek office I found it closed down completely so I was stuck in No Man's Land for the night.

I returned the same way I had come, as far as Thessalonika, but with a little more trouble to add to my enjoyment, namely a leaking carburetor float. I minimized the spillage by partially blocking off the fuel line with a piece of paper, and this did the job as best as could be expected. I also solved the rear fender problem by removing the tail piece that hinges up to facilitate the removal of the wheel. It had become so bad that it had worn a deep groove in the rear tire.

I was lucky enough to find a B.M.W. dealer in Thessalonika, where I purchased a new float before heading west once again. Naturally, now that most of my rear fender was gone it started to rain and I got a steady stream of mud from the rear wheel right up my back. In the afternoon it stopped just raining and began to really pour, and so I decided not to take the shortcut I had taken a few days previous, as I would undoubtedly become bogged down miles from help, knowing my luck. The roads were by this time a sea of mud, and progress was made mostly in second and third gears. Every time I adjusted my packs now I had to kneel in two or three inches of mud and, despite a good coat of dubbin before I left Germany, my leather jacket became saturated and, consequently, very heavy. Altogether I was quite a mess as I rode into the town of Kalamata to look for a hotel. The only establishment of this type in town could offer me one bed in a room with three others at thirty-five cents for the night. Little as it was, at least it was dry and so, after a nourishing supper of (ugh!) cold corned beef hash and beans, I went to sleep early before the other tenants could come in and start asking foolish questions of the foreigner in their room.

After climbing into my still wet clothes I was pleased to find that I had accidentally stumbled on a place of interest I was sure I would miss—the Monasteries of Meteora, which I believe were featured in the movie "Boy On A Dolphin." These monasteries are perched on top of high, sheer edged rock formations on the outside of town. Seemingly, the monks still have to use rope ladders when leaving and returning from their few excursions to the outer world.

It was here that I finally devised a secure method of tying my packs on, and I was to use this for the duration of the trip. The food pack was nearly empty, so I put it and its contents in the suitcase, and placed this on the right dual footrest, securing it to the frame and to what was left of the rear fender. My bedroll I tied around the headlamp.

Naturally, it was still pouring all this time and when I started off it didn't take me too long to get used to the wet clothes.

I might add here that my original plan of visiting Athens was out, as I had already missed the mid-weekly boat that left for Italy and the next one, on Sunday, left me not enough time to get back to the base before my leave was finished. Oh well! Better late than never, I always say.

No sooner did I get rid of one problem, namely the load distribution, than another stepped up boldly to take its place. I went through one of the many huge puddles a little too fast and some water got inside one of my carbs, making it cut out. Oh! the joy of past remembrances; sitting in three inches of oozy mud, carefully stripping, drying and assembling a delicate little carburetor (where did all those darned parts come from?), in the midst of a Mediterranean rainstorm, proclaiming aloud my censored woes to the Gods. Don't go away yet, reader, the fun is just beginning. I dried all the little delicate parts all right, but my diminutive brain forgot all about the great big throttle slide. Result: the next corner I came to I shut off the throttle, but the slide was still wet and stuck inside the carb, so it had no effect on the engine at all, and I went shooting into the ditch at the far side of the corner with the engine still revving like crazy. Five minutes later I was once again upon my muddy throne with that carburetor strewn in front of me.

Road conditions were even worse than the day before. At one point where the road was being repaired I had to get off and push the cycle through about two feet of mud, and at another place I went over three miles just barely moving in second gear, with the wheel spinning wildly. Scenery was least on my mind, as apart from the fact that I was too busy concentrating on driving to bother about it, there was none to be seen anyway, for the low rain clouds. It finally stopped raining at dusk, and it was after dark when I arrived at the small town where I intended to spend the night, only to find that there was no hotel there. Of course, I thoroughly enjoyed driving outside of town, and looking for a campsite in the dark, but at last I found a place where I laid down my sleeping bag, after first wringing out most of the water.

No sir! The sport of motorcycling never came closer to losing a dedicated enthusiast than that black day in Greece.

I was disgusted to find that it was still foggy when I awoke, but once under way I found myself climbing out of the valley and through the mist into a glorious stream of sunlight. I continued on to the summit of the mountain, where I stopped to inhale the breath-taking view that was spread around me in all directions. The sea of cloud, glistening in the early morning sun, obliterated all but the green islands that were the tops of other mountains. The cloud looked solid enough to walk on, and, indeed, I could almost visualize the ancient Gods of Greece, each one seated on a mountain, engrossed in an argument as to which was the greatest.

Before long I was at the port and learned that I couldn't get transportation to the island of Corfu until that evening, so after giving the cycle a well earned wash I spent a lazy day, drying my belongings and just soaking up that long lost sunlight to the fullest.

Once aboard the boat, I met a German student who had just completed a tour of Greece and was now going to explore the wonders of Italy. He could speak quite good English, so we decided to get a hotel room together until the ship left for Italy in two days.

In Corfu a pleasant surprise awaited me. Three U. S. ships were in the harbor and the town was simply teeming with sailors and marines, so I spent an extremely interesting evening shooting the breeze with a couple of marines who were staying at the hotel.

Although no riding was done the next day I still had a pretty busy time as the groove that the ailing rear fender had worn in the tire had become so bad as to warrant a new tire, and putting this on took up most of the morning. Also, I had to send a telegram to my Army base in Germany, telling them that I would be a few days late. The remainder of the afternoon was spent souvenir hunting and sightseeing in general, to be followed by some more idle gabbing with marines before turning in.

Settling up with the hotel proprietor was followed by a hasty trip through customs, and then on to the loading area with the bike. Since the ship left at ten o'clock in the morning, we had daylight almost the entire trip and consequently had time enough to meet quite a few interesting people on board. My most talkative acquaintance was an elderly Irish journalist who takes his holidays on the continent every year, mostly in his favorite country, Italy. The meeting that proved to be the most lasting was with a German youth of my own age who had been assisting his father on a business trip to Athens and who was now returning to Germany by train. Being a staunch motorcycle enthusiast, owner of a Maico 400 c.c. Typhoon and possessor of a natural dislike for European train travel, he asked if he could accompany me as far as Munich, where he lived. On receiving his father's permission, I decided to brace up the fender a bit and take him along, as I would be glad of his company since he could speak excellent English.

The Mohne Dam in Germany was seen by U.S. audiences in the movie "Dam Busters."

Our arrival in Brindisi was a little too late to start messing around looking for a campsite, so we took a hotel room in town.

Our first chore was to find the railroad station and send my friend's suitcase on to Milano, where we would have to check in at the station again to pass it through customs before sending it across the border to Munich. On completing this, Tom (my friend) and I found a reputable garage where we had the rear fender reinforced to take Tom's weight. After obtaining satisfactory results we packed up, and headed west.

Soon the sea was far behind, and we were speeding through the white walled vineyards, so similar to those seen the previous week. Not for long, however, as, once across the "heel" of Italy we descended to Taranto and the sea again. From there we followed a wonderful climb into the mountains and at that height Taranto appeared as a tiny white haven, without the slightest hint as to the beehive of activity that it was.

The rest of the day until dark was spent almost entirely on top of a belt of mountains that span the country. As if the scenery was not beautiful enough on one side, and it most certainly was, the road quite often conveniently travelled the crest of a ridge, so that the grandeur of the wild Appenines could be appreciated in all directions at once.

The temperature dropped sharply after dark, so we decided to get a hotel again, as Tom had no blankets and mine were not enough to keep us both warm on such a night. Consequently we stopped early at a small town called Eboli, and after supper

ACROSS EUROPE . . .

we took in a movie before returning to the hotel.

The first place of interest we came upon the following day was Salerno. After leaving the city the road continues around the bay and up to the top of an overhanging cliff from where a superb view of the city is seen with its colorful sea-front drive.

Not too far from here we arrived at one of the major attractions of the entire tour—the ancient city of Pompeii. Historically minded readers will remember that this metropolis of times gone by was buried with ashes in the great eruption of the volcanic Mount Vesuvius in 79 A.D. In recent years archaeologists have, and still are, attempting to restore it to their conception of its original grandeur. It amazes me to think how ingenious those Romans were many years ago, as ancient counterparts of large water taps have been uncovered at certain street corners giving proof of a controlled underground water system.

The people's pastimes are pointed out in the large amphitheatre which has an unusually complicated labyrinth of dungeons and narrow passages beneath the tiered seats.

Another interesting point was the bodies of two of the original actors of "The Last Days of Pompeii," who had been chipped out of their stony graves. They were jet black, but proof of their reality was where some toes and fingers had become broken off during restoration. The white circles of the bones could still be seen.

It would certainly be a great experience for one's imagination to visit this place when it is completely restored; to feel the streets trembling under the wheels of speeding chariots, and to hear the sadistic cries of the people as the lions go to work on the Christians in the great amphitheatre.

Reluctantly we dragged ourselves away from this historical masterpiece and continued on our way. A few miles past Pompeii we came to the ocean again and there, covered with a haze from the heat of romance, the passionate Isle of Capri broke the horizon. Passing this we enjoyed an inspiring drive along the coast to Naples, and then on through some beautiful countryside, till that evening we arrived in Rome. Since it was too dark to see much that night, we drove to a camping grounds a few miles out of the city where the owners made us completely at home. Some Canadian Air Force boys had been there the previous year and had left a good impression, so the owner and his wife got out some musical instruments and we all had a sing-song for a couple of hours. We were each then given a mattress and told to sleep in their garage as it was too cold outside. A wonderful boost to international relations.

In the morning our first objective was, naturally, Rome. I have read much about it but seemingly it wasn't enough as even my wildest expectations were exceeded. Those travel magazines don't exaggerate a bit when they call Rome the "City of Fountains and Statues," as both of these abounded wherever I looked. The Fountain of Trevi, the Coliseum, the Forum, the Vittorio Emmanuel Monument, the Castle of San Angelo, and last, but by no means least, the Cathedral and Square of St. Peter, all passed before my wondering eyes. I found it hard to believe that all these famous places were actually there before me, even more spectacular in real life. I felt proud to see a 1957 Ford with an Ontario license plate in St. Peter's Square, but I failed to find the owners in the vicinity.

With a heavy heart and a badly shaken time schedule, I finally managed to turn my back on this haven of enchantment, only to be greeted at the outskirts of the city by yet another masterpiece in marble—a huge outdoor athletic stadium. This is entered under an arch, closely guarded by two, ten-feet tall, stony gladiators, armed to the teeth. Once inside the arena we found ourselves completely surrounded by gleaming white, equally tall and muscular specimens, each fully equipped for a different sport, from the ancient discus thrower crouched for the lunge right up to an honest-to-goodness baseball batter waiting for the next pitch, wearing nothing but a convenient oak leaf and a grimace of concentration.

Wonder at Italian beauty didn't leave us as we continued on our way, since the rolling hills near Rome really present a pretty picture with their luxurious villas and exotic gardens. This area, I would imagine, corresponds to Beverly Hills in California, in that it is a residential area for the wealthy.

Naturally, we took the wrong road out of the city, but after discovering our mistake a delightful drive across some picturesque mountains brought us back to the coastal route. Although very beautiful at first, this level, sandy beach type of maritime scenery became quite boring after a while, and the rest of the day as far as Pisa passed uneventfully, except for four aggravating delays where we waited at various railroad crossings for the same slow freight train to chug past. In my opinion, the Italians are a little too safety conscious where this problem is concerned, as they close the gates long before the train is even in sight.

Since it was dark when we arrived in Pisa we intended to stop overnight in order to see the famous Leaning Tower by daylight. A pleasant surprise was in store for us, however, as both the tower and the adjacent cathedral were brilliantly floodlit. Being a warmer night than usual, after thoroughly scrutinizing the tower, we drove on to La Spezia. It was just past here that our night journey gave its reward. After passing through a small coastal village on a bay, the road rose steeply to the top of one of the surrounding hills. From this peak the lights of the aforementioned village seemed to dance across the bay on the crest of a few ripples that made the reflection of the full moon seem irregular.

A few miles farther on we found what we thought to be a deserted barn and we laid out our blankets on top of huge heaps of straw inside the building.

We were rudely awakened by an old lady with a wicked looking pitchfork in her hands. Her face soon became even more wrinkled but with a friendly smile after we had proclaimed our peaceful intentions with elaborate sign language, and she went about her chores leaving us to pack up and leave when we were ready.

Genoa was our first goal, and due to my carelessness our stay here was prolonged more than we had intended. I picked a very inopportune time to make a detailed inspection of a particularly attractive feminine pedestrian. While I was so occupied, the car in front of me stopped for a red light and I stopped upon sudden contact with his rear bumper, denting it. Have you ever been called everything under the sun by an angry Italian in his native language? Believe me, he didn't take very long to give me an inferiority complex, even though I couldn't understand a word of it. By the time the police came, escorted us to the station, found an interpreter, and got everything straightened out, it was late in the afternoon and consequently we covered very little distance that day. After we were set free once again night soon fell, and with it came an extremely dense and cold fog, so we boarded for the night in a hotel in a small town about half way between Genoa and Milano.

Cloudy and cool was the weather condition for the whole day but, once again the mileage was limited so we didn't worry too much about the weather. We had a brisk drive to Milano where we had to stop at the railway station in order to pass Tom's suitcate through the customs and freight it on to Germany. Unfortunately, the customs office was closed when we arrived and wasn't due to open until two o'clock. To pass time we toured around the city until we chanced upon the local indoor swimming pool, and a swim was unanimously voted as the next activity. It turned out to be the largest indoor pool I had ever seen, and we really enjoyed our dip.

After dispatching Tom's suitcase, we continued north toward the Swiss border, through the really inspiring foothills of the Alps. As we gained altitude, the popularity of the Swiss chalet type of house in mountainous country became more apparent until no Italian villas could be seen anywhere. Since the sun had disappeared behind the mountains when we finally arrived at the border of Switzerland, we made camp by the roadside a few miles past the customs office.

Rain was once again the order of the day, and by the time we broke camp we were both already quite damp. We climbed steadily at first through a dreary looking forest that had long since lost its golden autumn coat of leaves to the bitter wind. The trees now shivered in their nakedness. Soon the rain stopped, and then the road leveled out and we were on a vast sort of shelf that continued almost as far as the Austrian border.

I was bitterly disappointed when, after reading about the beauty and majesty of the Swiss Alps for so long, my chance to see them in their real glory was wiped out by a low overcast sky which hid the tops of the mountains. Nevertheless, I shouldn't complain as I appreciated to a fuller extent the lovely mirror lakes, green fields and pines below level of the clouds.

When we stopped for a hot drink at St. Moritz I realized how selfish I was being. While I was bemoaning the fact that the snowy peaks were behind the clouds, poor Tom had been taking the full brunt of the spray from the rear wheel and he had no waterproofs to protect him. Before we started out again I unpacked the bedroll and Tom wrapped a blanket around himself, Indian style, to help keep out the wet.

Not far from St. Moritz we crossed a fast flowing river that was refreshingly sea green in color. The road followed its rugged course well into Austria before the two parted, and by that time we had come through many of the narrow-streeted villages that seem to be so typical of Switzerland. These helped me to understand why continental trips cost so much by car. Most of the expenses goes to various body shops for removing dents in the fenders, acquired by trying to maneuver through the slim, serpentine streets of the villages in almost every European country.

Soon after we crossed into Austria the rain started coming down again and we were so miserable that all interest was lost in the scenery. The historic city of Innsbruck came and went before my practically unseeing eyes, and after what seemed to be an age had gone by, we were stopped at the German customs. Before long the rain stopped again, but we didn't exactly jump for joy because it was replaced by a thick, cold fog just as darkness crept over the drenched countryside. Eventually we encountered the Autobahn and turned west towards Munich. We stopped on the outskirts of town to warm up my hands so that I wouldn't fumble with the controls in the busy traffic of the city, and I found that the front of the motorcycle and myself were covered with a thin sheet of ice where the fog had condensed and frozen. This was the main difference between rain in central Europe and Greece—the temperature.

It didn't take us too long to find Tom's house where we were greeted by his worrying father and given a delicious hot meal. After bidding farewell, I continued on a little farther before taking a bed at one of the cheap boarding houses to be found on the Autobahn.

In the morning my only objective was to get home just as soon as I could and to get rested up in order to be fit to start work the following day. (Some hopes! I'm never fit at the best of times, let alone after a three-week ordeal like this). The fog continued until about ten o'clock and then, just like magic, it disappeared and in its place was the sun in all its glory. After a while it even started to warm things up a bit and eventually my teeth stopped chattering.

My route home was identical to that of the outward trip, except that I made no small sight-seeing excursions on the way, excluding, of course, the time I came up to a corner too fast and had to take the convenient escape road that went straight on. The only other extraordinary event of the day was when the soggy remains of my well-beaten suitcase came loose on one end and swung right around, becoming jammed solidly between the frame and the rear wheel. Upon removal I found a large hole ripped in it but, nonchalantly, I was soon on my way again. When I finally made my triumphant entry into camp and untied my belongings, my case practically fell apart in my arms and I didn't even have to open the lock to get the contents out, but only had to shake it vigorously above my bed and watch whatever was inside it fall out of the holes.

Being four days late, my first job was to report in to the Orderly Officer, but my telegram had arrived on time and consequently nothing more was said. In true Army tradition, however, unable to tell me off for being late, he proceeded to blast me out for not shaving. Oh, well! Such is life.

To sum up: I shivered, sweated, cursed, got soaked, eaten alive by flies and screamed at by irate drivers in unknown languages. To complete the above list I had to think and think hard, because what comes to mind when my thoughts turn to my Turkey trot are not these dreary memories, but remembrances of the interesting people I met, the beautiful scenery I saw, the priceless education that is gained from travel, and the heaps and heaps of plain, good old-fashioned fun I had.

What did it cost? Well, I left with $230, and returned with 75c in my pocket. That's cutting it pretty close, eh? Don't forget, though, that that includes $70 for the boat fare from Italy to Greece and back, and those miles aren't included in the 4,700 that the odometer registered from the time I left camp. That leaves $150 for a three-week trip which I consider not too bad.

Was it worth it? I'll let you figure that one out for yourself when I say that a few of the small wheels at the back of my brain are turning with intentions of a six-months-to-one-year tour of South America. Whether or not I'll make it remains to be seen but, nevertheless, many an evening has been, and will be, spent hunched over maps of that continent, figuring out mileages, memorizing place names, and hoping, hoping, hoping.

Penton Sets New Coast-to-Coast Record On BMW R-69

How would you like to leave New York City at 5.59 A.M. on a Monday morning, and at 8:10 A.M. on the following Wednesday arrive in Los Angeles--just 52 hours, 11 minutes and 1 second total elapsed time—which includes time consumed for refueling, eating and sleep?

That's exactly what 33-year-old John Penton did on June 8, 9, 10, 1959, covering 3,051 miles from New York to Los Angeles.

We must give full credit to John's mount—a 600cc BMW R-69 model. Undoubtedly his selection was a wise one, and he rode one of the few machines that could have given such a fine performance and trouble-free ride.

The incredible John slept only 45 minutes enroute, ate two ham sandwiches, drank two cups of milk and a bowl of soup. He stopped only long enough to fill his tank with any brand of gasoline and averaged 40 - 45 mpg. He left several bewildered service station attendants in a daze enroute as, unlike most cyclists, he was not a bit conversational—for he had a job to do, and he did it.

He reported no trouble of any kind, not even a flat tire or a single spill. Across Oklahoma he rode 200 miles in a hard rain storm and encountered strong cross winds across parts of Texas and New Mexico.

Best of all, he kept within legal speed limits, which in some wide open spaces in the West are 70 mph and on the Western plains the towns are usually small and traffic not overcrowded.

Rotarian John Penton (wonder if he missed a meeting) is a modest, 145 lb. widower, with three sons, ages five, seven and nine. His past wins in the tough Jack Pine and Little Burr Enduros served him well as training practice. He is in perfect physical condition, probably because he was a physical education major at college. He knows how to conserve his energy and strength. His timing and judgment are exceptional. His fantastic ride was partly possible because he kept on going hour after hour at a steady pace. Frequent stops kill any average so he cut his stops to a minimum.

I met John for the first time 36 hours after his run ended at the Los Angeles Western Union office in downtown L.A. At that time he had slept, rested and was fresh and alert. I asked him many questions and his answers as he dictated them to me are given below. The following members of the CYCLE staff were present: Editor Carol Anderson, Technical Editor Erwin Tragatsch, Advertising Manager Americo Castro, with Secretary Zelda Buck who took the notes in shorthand.

That same evening he visited the half mile dirt track program

John Penton of Lorain, Ohio, WCC Member No. 572, is the new holder of the coast-to-coast motorcycle record—52 hours, 11 minutes, 1 second from New York City to Los Angeles, June 8 - 9 - 10, 1959. Photo shows him checking in at Western Union office in downtown Los Angeles. Attractive girl certifying time is Miss Jeanon Smith of Western Union. John rode a BMW R-69 model.—Photo by George O'Day, Los Angeles Herald-Express Staff Photographer.

at Ascot Stadium, sponsored by J. C. Agajanian. There he received a big ovation from the crowd after announcer Rocky Rockwood introduced him. He then led the single file parade of 60 riders before the official start of the races. Then in the Judges' stand he was congratulated by Rodger Ward, 1959 Indianapolis winner, and Mrs. Ward, who were guests at Ascot that night.

After the races, at 11:30 P.M., he rode to Riverside, 60 miles from Los Angeles (that guy really likes night riding), stayed over night with friends, and then returned to his home in Lorain, Ohio.

The first Coast-to-Coast record was by Volney Davis about 1907, on an Indian. He took about 45 days.

Later "Cannonball" Baker set many records—one in 1914 when he cut 9 days off the former record for a new time of 11 days, 12 hours and 10 minutes, on a 61-inch, 7 horsepower, Indian 2-speed model.

The last known record was made in 1935 by Earl Robinson of

Continued on page 46

CYCLE publisher, Floyd Clymer, interviews John Penton on the highlights of his run. At left is BMW Western Distributor, Earl Flanders. In background is the new home of the WORLDWIDE CYCLE CLUB, and John Penton, holder of WCC certificate #572, was the first member to visit this 21-room mansion—some call it "The Castle."

The R-69 engine was exceptionally clean, as Clymer found out when he rubbed his handkerchief over the case. The black mark on the muffler was caused, John said, by a plastic bag which blew against the muffler somewhere in the Midwest. The muffler heat caused the bag to disintegrate and badly burn the remains into the muffler shell. It was the same kind of a bag that has caused so much controversy lately as being responsible for the deaths of some children.

R-69 SETS A NEW
COAST TO COAST RECORD

**Total Elapsed Time:
52 hours — 11 min. — 1 second
as checked by Western Union
time clocks in N.Y.C. and L.A.**

CONGRATULATIONS
to John Penton for a wonderful performance!

● John Penton, our Lorain, Ohio dealer, set this fantastic record on his trouble-free BMW, leaving New York City on Monday a.m., June 8 and arriving downtown Los Angeles on Wednesday a.m., June 10th. Time includes all stops for fuel, rest and eating.

● John's success was due to his excellent physical condition (he slept only 45 minutes) and his *dependable BMW R-69.*

CONSISTENT PERFORMANCE

● This record was established by constant speeds—all within legal speed limits of every State enroute. No trouble of any kind, not even a flat tire was encountered. *And of course no chain adjustments were necessary.*

● Over fine highways, rough roads, up hill and down, over detours and hampered for 200 miles by hard midwest rain and high winds, then across the California desert and mountains John roared on hour after hour through days and nights.

Penton checking in at Western Union office in downtown Los Angeles. Certifying the time is Miss Jeanon Smith of Western Union. —Photo by George O'Day, Los Angeles Herald Express Staff Photographer.

For an effortless and enjoyable ride, be it across the U.S., around the world or for a Sunday spin with friends . . .

YOU ARE BETTER OFF WITH A BMW— THE WORLD'S BEST MOTORCYCLE AND THE CHOICE OF MEN WHO KNOW AND APPRECIATE THE FINEST DESIGN, WORKMANSHIP AND MATERIALS.

See your BMW dealer, or write for information

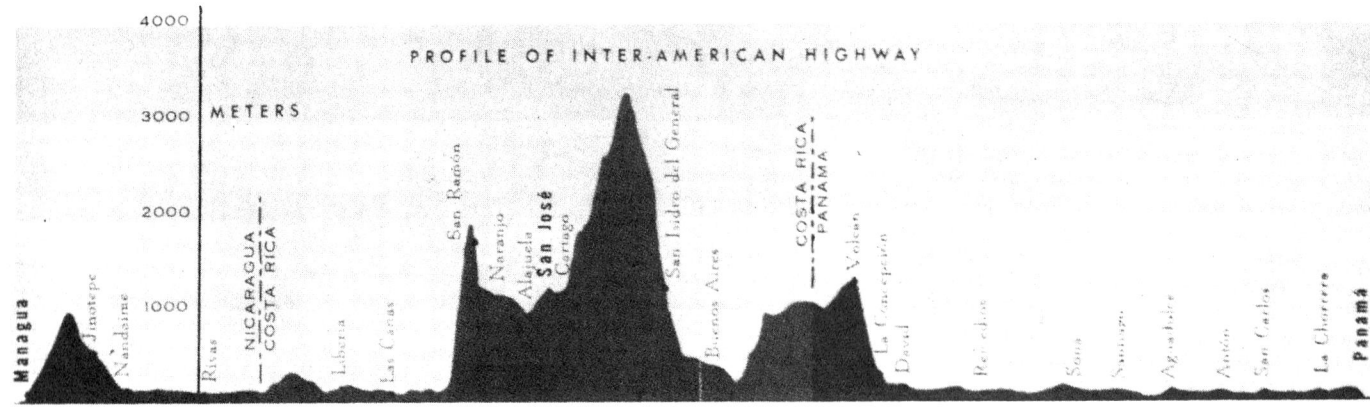

PROFILE OF INTER-AMERICAN HIGHWAY

TWO WHEELS ACROSS COSTA RICA

PART I
By PAUL E. WRIGHT

Picture, if you can, the unfinished part of the Pan-American Highway from the highlands of southern Costa Rica, through the steaming jungles and along tropical rivers and into the highlands along the Panamanian Border. It is only 90 miles long, but it took us two weeks to make it. Two weeks of hard work and heartbreak. Ninety miles of excitement and adventure.

In San Jose, the capitol of Costa Rica, two Australian fellows I met accidentally, had the same plan; a trip from the United States down the long slim highway to the South American continent. I really had to take my hat off to them as they were trying to do the trip on Lambrettas. I had a 600cc BMW with big wheels, lots of power and built as strong as a truck. At first it was sort of funny thinking of them making such a long trip on such little machines. But then they had come just as far as I had and were still going strong. Ahead, my AAA guide told me, the road went on a little further but then ended in the middle of nowhere. The road was non-existent from there to the Panamanian border.

The Costa Rican Moto Club and their president, don Rodrigo Araya Borge royally wined and dined us for our few days in San Jose in the true fashion of the fraternity of motorcyclists. When we needed some information or papers signed, one of their members was on the spot to give us a helping hand. We spent several enjoyable evenings at their clubhouse talking motorcycles and traveling. The popular bike in this Central American Republic was the big Harley-Davidson. They all talked H-D's and wanted to make the reverse trip that we had just completed. When we finally did leave San Jose, we left with a happy heart knowing we had made friends with a grand bunch of fellows in a wonderfully friendly country.

Questions about the road going south received a variety of answers. Some people told us that there was regular bus service every day. Others told us that the road did not even exist. Some told us we would be in Panama within two days; others said that if we tried to go south by land we would

most likely never get there. We polled all the information, took an analysis and decided that we would just have to go down to the end of the road and see what the real situation was. No one we talked to had ever been down there or made the trip himself. Everything was just hearsay. The Australian boys had their bikes all greased, oiled, and welded in a few places. The newspaper ran big articles about us on the front page telling how we were going to try and take our machines overland to Panama. All the time our little trip was taking on more and more the aspect of an expedition of jungle exploration. We had a large crowd of well-wishers to say goodbye by the time we topped off our tanks and headed south of the city.

Besides the supplies for the motorcycles of extra oil, tire patches, plugs, etc., we went to the central market to pick up some extra food. The storekeepers at the market had also read about our coming trip south and filled our bags with rice, beans, bread and catsup as if it were to be our last meal.

The road south started out over hard asphalt through rolling green coffee-covered hills. The noonday sun warmed our bodies even though it was January. People along the road waved as we passed.

Our route by-passed the volcano Irazu and we decided to cut over and climb to the top. The higher we climbed the colder it became. Late in the afternoon we were still climbing so we decided to stop at the top rather than try and make the descent after dark. Up and up we went. The Lambrettas started coughing a bit and their power dropped. I went on ahead as it was hard to slow my motor down enough for them to keep up. Just as the sun was setting I arrived at the rim of the volcano Irazu, 11,000 feet in the air. Out in the distance I could see the Caribbean on one side and the Pacific on the other. In the center was the gaping crater of the volcano. The insides looked something like a scene from a science fiction thriller, all desolation, no vegetation or sign of life. As the sun went down, the chill went right through my bones. Just a few hours before, we had been sizzling in the sun. The boys arrived and we all took shelter in a lookout house on the

brink of the chasm. This was a little house with a cement floor, a stone fireplace and one glassed wall that looked out over the crater. We collected as many dried pieces of wood as possible and took all our camping gear inside to try and warm up in front of the fireplace. When we left San Jose, we had planned on steaming hot jungles. On our first night out we almost froze to death. The sunrise was, however, well worth the discomforts of the cold night. We could see for miles in the crystal-clear morning air. From the Atlantic to the Pacific, the green countryside of Costa Rica was spread around us. To the north, there was one volcano peak after another sticking its cone into the air. To the south stretched a high range of mountains and then the green jungle, our next goal.

We were soon on the Talamanca range of mountains that we had seen from the top of Irazu. On the entire Pan-American Highway, this is one of the most scenic routes and was one of the most costly to build.

The road dwindled down to just two dried mud ruts as we descended into thicker jungle. Overhanging trees helped shade us from the burning sun.

The road passes along a skyline ridge for more than eighteen miles at altitudes of from 9,000 to 11,000 feet. In Costa Rica they call this "el paso de los muertos" or the pass of the dead. Thousands of workers died here during the construction due to exposure to the high altitudes, cold winds and rains. On the other side of the range, we arrived at San Isidro del General, 85 miles south of San Jose and supposedly the end of the Pan-American Highway, until Panama.

In San Isidro we asked the people about the road going south. We asked about the bus service and they thought we were crazy. Finally we did find out that there was construction on ahead and that a rickety old car made the journey every week to another village further south called Buenos Aires. We stocked up on food and gas and camped just outside of town. Our spirits were higher than kites with the news about the road. We had visions of being in Panama within a few days. By the time we had set up camp and cooked a hot meal, everyone in town knew what we were planning on doing. We had quite a large crowd around our camp. The town policeman showed up and took down our names, addresses and other information and said he would notify the embassy and our next of kin when we did not arrive at the southern border. The other people however, were more encouraging. One man told us he had personally made the trip from there to the Panama border but it had taken him about two weeks. Another man asked us to deliver a letter for him to his brother in Buenos Aires, so we felt as if we would make it that far anyway.

Early the next morning we did not even get out of sight of the town before the road dwindled down to just two dried mud ruts about a foot deep. We descended all the time into the thicker jungle. Every now and then a man would pass by with a heavy wooden ox cart with wheels about five feet in diameter. These are what had made the tracks we were following. The Lambrettas had a little trouble with the ruts as their wheels would drop into one of these deep cuts, the bike would fall until the frame hit and the wheel would not touch the bottom. The tires would just sit there and spin. We would have to get off and lift the machine out of the rut and try and travel in between the two gashes. After awhile we found it more advantageous to

ride alongside the track rather than on it. As the trees thickened overhead there was more shade from the burning sun. There were places where the trees were so thick that the sun never got through to dry the ground. At these places the trail was not dried mud but sticky, thick and deep. When we hit these spots we would either get stuck or slide into the ruts. When the sun did break through the trees, the mud was dried into hard clods like rocks. We did not know which we liked the best, to be jarred to death or slip all over the place. The few streams we had to cross the first day out were not too difficult. Across one stream there was a little bridge that we felt safer to go around rather than over. We camped the first night dead tired from pushing the bikes out of ruts, picking them up after slipping in the mud and from being out in the sun. We had not gone many miles but we were still making forward progress and would not turn back. The spot we chose for our camp was beside a little river with a deep dark pool. After a half hour's bath and swim to clean off the dirt and mud, plus a big dinner of rice, beans, fruit and catsup, we were ready to tackle anything the jungle had to offer. However, at the moment the only things we tackled were our sleeping bags and we slept until 10 o'clock the next morning.

Before we could leave in the morning we spent an hour or so tightening bolts and nuts. This we later found to be a daily necessity. Five miles of these roads put on 500 miles of wear. Our first big project of the day was to climb out of the little valley of the river by which we were camped. In the twilight of the evening before it had not looked like much of a hill but now in the full light of the sun we were not too sure. It looked more like a hill climbing course than a road. All loaded up I gave it the first try. The power of my BMW gave a good flying start. On the way up the overhanging trees made alternate hard and soft spots. Going from the brilliant sun to the dark shadow at this flying rate of speed did not give my eyes enough time to adjust. In one of the heavy shadows, I went into a hole, hit a rock and went off over the handlebars. My bike went one way, and my camera another and I kept on going ahead. The boys had a better method than mine, for the hills. They would get a real flying start, keep it wide open going uphill until just before the motor stalled, then jump off and run alongside with the motor pulling the

bike up the hill. They would have to keep running beside the bike until it developed enough power to pull both itself and the rider up. If the hill was real steep, one person would have to wait about half way up to run along behind, pushing. Hill climbing was never like this!

During the afternoon we came to the construction camp. The chief of the camp invited us to dinner but gave us a very discouraging picture of the road ahead. He said the road had been good up to the camp in comparison to further south. There were parts where his big four wheeled drive vehicles could not yet go. However, the thick steaks, mashed potatoes, and iced drinks brought us back to life. We thought the road ahead could not possibly be any worse than what we had already passed over, so we refused his offer to take our bikes back to San Isidro in a pickup and started out again. Saying goodbye to us, the camp chief told us he would keep some beds open for us and have a hot meal on the stove when we decided to come back.

Our friend from the camp was entirely correct. The road went from bad to worse to unbelievable. The road was still dropping down to lower land all the time. We would go up a little and then drop twice as much. The undergrowth was becoming thicker and thicker. The jungle closed in, around and over us. The next day we arrived at Buenos Aires.

The road going into town was not much more than a horse trail. The town itself was not much more than a one horse town. The wooden shacks, half fallen down, half rotted away, looked like a metropolis to us. The main street was a smooth place inbetween the buildings. The stores had a few little things with which we could replenish our supplies but were very expensive. About the only thing cheap was fresh baked bread with which we stuffed ourselves. The townspeople turned out en masse to look over our machines. They said jeeps got that far every now and then, but never such funny looking machines as we had. Airplanes were more common here than land vehicles. We delivered the letter we were carrying and got southerly directions out of town. The road went as far as the airstrip and then stopped. That was it, the real end of the Pan-American Highway until Panama, 90 miles to the South. Only a foot trail existed, leading through the thick jungle. Our adventure was only beginning.

The rough riding was hard on the machines and we spent an hour or so every morning tightening bolts and nuts. At this point the road was relatively good and can be seen leading through the jungle on the left.

This is the town of Buenos Aires, Costa Rica. It looked like a metropolis to us. The townspeople had never seen a motorcycle before, as airplanes were more common than land vehicles.

In last month's installment, Paul E. Wright on a BMW and his two Australian companions on Lambrettas journeyed from the Costa Rican capital of San Jose to the little town of Buenos Aires. Here, the Pan-American Highway which they had been following dwindled down to a foot path and finally stopped at the edge of an airstrip. There were now 90 miles of uncharted jungle to cross before the highway began again to the South, on the border of Panama.

TWO WHEELS ACROSS COSTA RICA

PART II

By PAUL E. WRIGHT

We had to circle the airstrip twice before we found a trail that seemed to be the most traveled and the widest. Many paths, in different stages of use, led only to an isolated house, and there ended. We followed a trail that was used only by horses and people walking, and it became wet and slippery as it descended into the moist jungle valley. Obstacles, such as fallen trees across our path, had to be cut through and moved. Most of these trees were rotten, so it was not a hard job to chop them through. Other obstacles, such as large rocks or deep gullies, caused constant detours. Our daily mileage got worse and worse as we ran into more of these obstacles.

Then there was rain. It was not a rain like we knew back in the States, but more as if you were standing under Niagara Falls. As we got lower into the dense tropical country, the more it seemed to rain. Every day we had rain at one time or another. The sky would be perfectly clear blue, the sun blazing down, when suddenly the air would start to haze over, black clouds would fill the entire sky, and buckets of water would pour on us. In a few minutes the clouds would disappear as fast as they had come. During the periods of sun in between rain we would try to dry out some of the equipment.

One of the biggest problems that faced us every day was the crossing of streams and small rivers. During the part of the trip in the southern section of Costa Rica, we crossed twenty some of these streams. Each one presented just a little different problem. After several tries at these crossings we got it down to somewhat of a system. When we would arrive at a new stream to be crossed, we would first wade across to look for any holes or big rocks under the water. If there were too many obstacles at that point we would go up or down river a little to try and find a better place. After deciding on our route we cleared the bottom of the stream of any movable rocks and filled in the holes with smaller stones. First the BMW would go across as it hardly ever got stuck. As long as the water did not come over our knees we could make it without much trouble. The water could come over the horizontal cylinders, rear drive and every-

thing else except the air intake as long as the motor kept going forward. Once we were stopped in mid-stream, we were in for some real work. The Lambrettas, however, were not so easy. If the water was of any depth at all, it would drown out the motor and the whole thing would stop. It worked out better to walk alongside the bike without using the motor while one person pushed from behind and the other pulled on a rope from up ahead. Even if the wheels got stuck in a hole or wedged in between rocks, we could pick the whole machine up and out of its trouble. Usually after each crossing we would have to spend at least half an hour to an hour and a half drying out the water from the brakes, spark plugs and other places.

At most of the crossing places there would be a little house and a family living beside the river. This is not uninhabited country. These people would always come out to see our strange machines and talk with us. They of course thought we were completely crazy in our funny clothes. Also they were not much help to us as we could not get them all to pull in the same direction crossing the stream. At first we would ask these people about the road or trail ahead and the condition of the rivers and streams. It seemed they gave us the same answer all the time. The road was worse and the rivers bigger. They would always say, "Yes, Senor, this river here is very easy to cross but the next one is impossible. It is the biggest river in the world. I never go there as it is too large for me to cross."

When we would arrive at the next stream it would sometimes be larger and sometimes not. We came to the conclusion that none of these people ever traveled farther than the land in between the river to the north of them and the river to the south of them.

At last we did come to a river too wide and deep for us to cross, walking. This was the granddaddy of all that we had seen so far. We tried wading across but only got a quarter of the way before we were up to our armpits and the current was sweeping us down stream. It was all of sixty yards across and ten feet deep. Our spirits dropped to a new low for it looked as if we would have to turn around and make the long trip

back. Going back would be mostly uphill and it had been difficult enough going downhill. We had to go on by crossing the river some way. It was late in the day so we set up camp, had a good hot meal of beans, rice, fruit and catsup and gave our weighty problem some thought. There was the usual house alongside the river but the owner had only a small dugout to carry people across. By the light of our camp fire we decided the only thing to do was to build rafts and perhaps float all the way out of this jungle to the ocean.

After sunup the following morning, Juan, our new-found friend from the little house, came down to our camp with a steaming pot of coffee and some fresh bread. We told him our plan to build rafts and he immediately said he would give us a hand. He insisted on helping but could not come until late in the afternoon to start work. Rather than wait all day for him we scouted around and found a huge fallen log that had not started to rot. We got to work with our little hatchet. By the time Juan came back we had just about cut the log through once. We proudly showed him our labors. He let loose a loud unrestrained laugh that could have been heard for miles. These people show their true emotions and do not hold a thing back. When finally he got hold of himself again, he told us we had picked out a tree heavier than the rocks. That was why it had not started to rot. Juan thought we were not too wise in the ways of his jungle so he led us to a grove of straight-looking trees about a mile down river. He whipped out his long knife called a machete and start-

In a small village between Buenos Aires and Paso Real. It was the second time the people had seen a motorcycle. There had been one through here four years ago.

Our camp on the River Terraba, where we made the rafts. We felt as if it would be impossible to find any truer and more open-hearted people than the local natives.

The first raft was launched and checked-out for sturdiness. Logs on the right were used to build a second raft, which was to carry my BMW and me.

Finally setting sail on a short river journey. The river ahead picked up speed and only by chance did we stop short of a stretch of rapids that would have claimed our machines.

ed hacking away. Within minutes one tree came crashing to the ground. The insides of these trees were light and soft. They were pure balsawood. We trimmed all the branches off and removed the outside bark. What was left was about 15 inches in diameter and ten feet long. The trees were light enough for one person to pick up and carry. By the time the three of us had peeled the first tree, our friend Juan had five more on the ground. Whoever said the Latins don't like work should have seen this man with his big knife. We decided on ten logs in order to build two rafts. It took us the rest of the next day to finish cutting, trimming and floating the logs to the site where our bikes were located.

The next morning the rafts started to take shape. Under the guiding hand of Juan and with the help of his son we cut the logs to the desired length, put a point on one end and cut cross members. How we were going to hold the logs together we did not quite know. There were no nails, wire or enough rope. Juan showed us how to cut pegs out of hard wood that we could drive into the soft balsawood. Later he took vines from the trees and wound them around the logs and over the cross members until the raft was as solid as a dance floor. We built two of these rafts, one for the BMW and the other for the two Lambrettas. To us they looked like a piece of art floating high in the water in the little cove where we had built them. At the end of the second day we had a christening party for our two ships. Juan was right in the spirit of things and went out and cut down three dozen oranges. His son brought along a bottle of aguardiente that had been lying around the house and his wife cooked us a big fat chicken. The party, which could not have been more enjoyable in a Hollywood night spot, lasted way into the night as more people showed up from the surrounding countryside with more things to eat and drink.

Loading our bikes on the rafts and setting sail the next morning, began a memorable day for all. The population of the surrounding countryside had all heard about our plans so were all there to send us off down the river. Juan gave us each a big "abrazo," his wife cried, and we were shoved out into the current. We had given our friend and his family a few little odds and ends that we did not need, such as an old screw driver, a shirt, pair of pants, and a cooking pot. You would have thought that we had given them the moon and all the stars. Juan had only helped us with three steady days of work and had made it possible for us to continue our trip by showing us how to build the rafts. To him it was only natural

to help someone who had come along and did not understand the ways of his jungle. We felt as if it would be impossible to find a truer and more open-hearted people inhabiting this atom-aged world in which we live.

Our river cruising was short lived. A few miles below where we had left shore, the river started picking up speed. The raft kept wanting to turn broadside. There were rocks jutting out of the water but the raft glided past. As the water kept picking up speed, we started scraping bottom and tearing off the vines holding the logs together. We poled ourselves to shore to see the damage done and scouted ahead, as we could hear an ominous roar. Our river riding was over. There were small falls and racing rapids that the rafts would never make. If we were going to lose our bikes we did not want them to have a watery grave. It was really impossible to go back now so we had no choice except to unload on the little spit of land where we were. There was a trail of sorts leading away from the river and up a three hundred foot cliff. We had no choice; that was to be our route.

The entire next day was spent taking the machines up this hill. The rains had softened the trail so much that the water oozed from the ground when we walked over it. The wheels would spin, our feet would slip and down into the muck we would go. After the first hour it did not make much difference to us as we were covered from head to toe with mud and grime. We did the job piecemeal. First we would work with the BMW for an hour or so until the engine got so hot I was afraid the oil would boil. Then back down to take the Lambrettas apart as much as possible and carry them up in sections. The path we were following was built with switchbacks for people to walk on and not for motorcycling. The turns were the difficult places. These turns went right back on themselves and the bikes were too long to get around the corners. The back wheel would hang over the side of the cliff until someone pulled from the front. If we slipped at this point, there would have been one less bike to worry about. That night at the top of the cliff we went to sleep alongside our bikes without even bothering to set up camp. I was sure my clutch was burned out from slipping it so much. The boys had doubts that their bikes would ever run again after all the mud we had dragged them through. Our few pieces of bread, oranges, pot of half cooked beans, and last of the catsup did not revive our spirits much. It had taken us almost 12 hours to make the last 100 yards.

Before us lay higher, drier ground. Out of the river canyon at last, the land was

firmer. There were more trees but less undergrowth. In places the path lead across smooth meadows where we could get speeds up to 3 or 4 miles per hour. We were moving again. A group of men and boys who had passed us the evening before at the top of the cliff, came back to see how far we had come along the trail. We had their company for most of the day. We soon found out that we were not going to make as much progress as we had first thought. Cutting this high ground were deep gullies carved out by the rains. The gullies were only about fifty feet across but each one took about two and a half hours. Our friends watched all day and followed us along. After a particularly difficult gully, our friends disappeared up the trail. When the sun came up the next morning so did our friends. This time they brought their wives, daughters, dogs and, best of all, some food. It was not every day that they could see such a sight as we presented. We were glad to have a cheering section as the team spirit was getting pretty low.

Late in the afternoon we arrived at the village where the people lived. They lead us to the center of the village in front of the school house. It was more like a triumphal march. The ones who had gone out to meet us were lording it over the ones who had stayed behind. They all crowded around to see the treasures and strange things that we had with us. The head man came out to greet us with his two words of English, "man," "friend." Two words could not have been better expressed. The conversation that followed and the inspection of our gear was one of the most interesting and enlightening times we had on our whole trip. We talked mostly with the head man as he would ask questions the whole village wanted answered. Afterwards he would explain our answers to his people and fill in our explanations with details. When I told him I was from the United States, he told his people that it was a place near San Jose, the capitol of Costa Rica. When the boys told him they were from Australia, much to our amazement and the boys' delight, he explained that Australia was a colony of the English in the South Pacific. He added on that it was an island near the coast of Costa Rica but the boys did not mind as this was the first time during our trip a person had even placed Australia in the Pacific Ocean.

The path we had been following seemed to go only as far as the village. All our new friends thought we would do better to go higher up the mountain as the gullies around the base were quite deep. Higher up, the land was much better for traveling but much

(Continued on page 46)

45

Two Wheels Across Costa Rica

(Continued from page 45)

hotter and with little water. The sweat rolled off, us in oceans. There was less shade and the sun seemed to burn twice as much. We started to welcome our daily showers and rains. It was the only time we were cooled off. The little bit of rice and beans that we had left and the food that the villagers had given us was now just about gone. We had to find wild fruit where we could. Along the river there had been a lot of fruit but higher up on the mountain there was very little. We were seriously beginning to think we would never get out of this section of jungle land if we stuck with our bikes. Sooner or later we were bound to find the road coming north from Panama. The question was when. We were not even too sure at this point exactly where we were. Our progress with the bikes was only a couple of miles a day. We could walk much faster and cover three times the distance on foot. Our gas tanks were almost empty, food gone, we were filthy dirty, completely fatigued from the long hours of hard work in the steaming sun, and worst of all a bit shaken about our idea to make it to the Panamanian border by land. No wonder our big plan of riding to the border had seemed funny to some of the people we had talked to in San Jose. We also wondered how the daily bus had made it through!

There was nothing else to do except to try and walk out. We had had it! I picked up my knapsack with my passport, camera, a few other important items and started down the trail. The boys decided to try and push on until the last of their gas was gone. Before leaving, I said good-by to my trusty steed not knowing when or if I would ever see her again. Looking back over my shoulder as I went down the trail, the old BMW seemed to be a bit out of place sitting there in the middle of the jungle without a soul around. Hiking across the mountain, through the gullies and over the rocks was much easier than trying to ride my bike. All the rest of the day I went on alone through the jungle until, late in the afternoon, I came across a well traveled path. This path lead to a road a couple of miles ahead. I had found it—the new road that was being constructed north from Panama! Where there is road construction there has to be a camp for the workers, so I followed the road until I could see the lights of the camp in the distance. Never in my life had I ever been so happy to see a small thing like an electric light. The chief engineer was an American who could not figure out where I had come from, as he said his surveyors had all kinds of trouble getting their little bit of equipment through on foot. Lucky I had hit the very northern tip of the construction. A mile to either side and I would have completely missed the road.

Never did a meal taste so good as I dived into three steaks, piles of mashed potatoes and enough ice water to float a battleship. After a hot shower with soap, and a good night's sleep in a bed with sheets, I filled my knapsack with food. The engineer drove me back up the road to the path which lead to my Australian friends and my bike. Hiking back up the trail, everything looked much easier now. We had proved the skeptics in San Jose wrong; you *can* ride to the Panamanian border. If you do not mind missing a few meals, pouring rain, mud filled trails, and disheartening set backs, there is a route across this land of wonders. However, we would not, and could not, recommend this trip for anyone except the very strongest of heart, and those filled with a thirst for adventure and a spirit to see and experience the ways of life in other parts of the world. Not one of the three of us will ever forget motorcycling through southern Costa Rica.

California riders Skeeter Hollenbeck from San Diego and John Hopkins from Long Beach take a break between races at the El Cajon Track in Southern California, just 15 miles from the Mexican border at Tijuana. The semi-monthly races attract many riders from south of the border and hence the growing popularity of the Mexican made Chaleco jackets shown being worn here.

Continued from page 40

Detroit on a 45 Harley-Davidson. Earl's time was 77 hours, 53 minutes, quite remarkable when there were no turnpikes or four lane highways. Rody Rodenburg is credited with a Coast-to-Coast run on an Indian in 1936 but there was some controversy over his run. Some claim he fell asleep and was given help by a truck driver for a few miles. Nothing was ever proved or disproved.

Not since the days of the veteran of all Coast-to-Coast pilots, "Cannonball" Baker, have I known any one with the stamina, ability and general knowledge about tough long-distance riding as likable John Penton. He will go down in competition history along with a few other "iron men" such as Baker, Wells Bennett, Roy Artley, Earl Robinson, and a very few others of long distance fame.

All motorcyclists will hail John for a fine job well done.

John Penton is shown here, the day after the finish, giving editorial highlights to CYCLE publisher, Floyd Clymer. Clymer was curious as to how Penton's BMW R-69 handled after the grueling record run, so he took a spin and his impressions are given in this issue.

Rodger Ward congratulates Penton. Ward, the 1959 Indianapolis champion, was a guest at Ascot Speedway in Los Angeles the evening of the day following the end of Penton's record breaking Coast-to-Coast run. Ward is shown here congratulating Johnny as Ascot promoter, J. C. Agajanian, looks on. At right is attractive Mrs. Rodger (Jo) Ward. Rodger commented "That must have been a lot tougher ride than my 500 miles."

595 c.c. B.M.W. R69S Twin

LUXURY ROADSTER, WITH SUPERB HIGH-SPEED PERFORMANCE, YET DOCILE TRAFFIC MANNERS; MAGNIFICENT STEERING, ROADHOLDING AND BRAKES

IN announcing their 1961 plans last autumn, B.M.W.s virtually claimed to have achieved the impossible—that is, to have improved both the pep and refinement of a range of machines long outstanding for advanced design and superb engineering. To have improved either performance or manners without sacrifice of the other—well, difficult though that seemed, maybe the B.M.W. engineers had succeeded. But to better both qualities—that would be believed when it was proved, so far above average was the blend already.

Proof beyond question comes from an extended test of an R69S, the latest version of the sporting six-hundred flat-twin. With a performance to match that of any roadster in production—and, because of the engine's uncanny smoothness, certainly the most usable—the R69S could perhaps be excused some slight sacrifice of the ultimate polish in traditional B.M.W. manners. But no excuse is required.

Wind open the twistgrip and you are whisked along at 100 m.p.h. while remaining normally seated. Roll back the grip and the machine will tick-tock sweetly along at 11 m.p.h. in top gear without a murmur. Select bottom gear and you can get off and

walk alongside with never a thought of reaching for the clutch lever.

No matter how zestfully the R69S is ridden, the exhaust remains incredibly quiet—inaudible to the rider, in fact, and but a whisper to bystanders. Mechanical sound is confined to a faint chatter from the transmission during cold idling. Indeed, so slight a concession does the R69S make to its voracious appetite for road burning that one has to split hairs to record it: whereas on the 494 c.c. R50 tested by *The Motor Cycle* in 1955 the rider could hear the faint hum of the front tyre above any other noise at 40 m.p.h. in top gear, it proved necessary on the R69S to rise off the seat and lean forward to hear the tyre! In other words, for unobtrusiveness and tractability the R69S is bettered—and that infinitesimally—only by lower-compression B.M.W. twins.

The term "cruising speed" loses its significance. All speeds from a dawdle to maximum proved supremely pleasant and comfortable. Times without number 100 m.p.h. was held with the rider sitting upright, while 110 m.p.h. was occasionally reached downhill. In the face of a strong headwind long upgrades were surmounted

at 85 to 90 m.p.h. Whatever the conditions the transverse cylinder layout kept the engine abnormally cool. Calibrated in k.p.h. (the test model was equipped for use in Germany), the speedometer was as near accurate as makes no difference.

In adverse conditions, the secret of getting the best out of the B.M.W. is to hold third gear up to a speed of 90 m.p.h., which is reached remarkably quickly. And so smooth and quiet is the engine even at peak revs that once or twice 100 m.p.h. was inadvertently touched in third—well into the valve-float range but without adverse effect.

Quite literally there is no more strain in sustaining 100 m.p.h. than 50 m.p.h. The slight forward set of the handlebar and rearward set of the footrests provides just enough forward lean to make it unnecessary to pull hard on the bar in resisting wind pressure. No noise but the rush of wind assails the rider's ears and there is not the faintest trace of vibration—thanks to the opposed arrangement of the cylinders.

Perfect balance prevents any wheel or fork flutter while the springing, a trifle firm at low speeds, is extraordinarily well damped and gives superb roadholding.

(Incidentally no spanner is required to adjust the preload on the rear springs for pillion riding.)

Rock-steady at all times, the steering, too, contributes enormously to the rider's peace of mind. On wet roads raked by fierce gusty cross-winds that had some machines and cars behaving skittishly the R69S felt as stable as if it were on rails; when the going was icy it responded perfectly to the appropriate delicate riding technique.

Maybe in clubman racing on a vicious circuit conditions might be met to warrant use of the ingenious hydraulic steering damper; but certainly 2,000-odd miles of hard riding on main and secondary roads failed to make it seem remotely desirable to bring it into action. On bends of all sorts the B.M.W. could be heeled hard over with every confidence; measuring only 21in across, the footrests never grounded.

In spite of its suitability for ultra-fast cruising the riding position could not be faulted for town threading. In any case the range of adjustment is above average. For instance, besides providing for swivelling, the handlebar clamps have alternative mounting holes in the fork yoke. And the

pillion footrests, as well as those for the rider, are adjustable for position. Excellently shaped, the twin-seat is not merely comfortable—it is luxurious; and with a length of 28in it provides ample room for two.

None of the controls could be better placed and all of them worked sweetly. At the cost of a full movement of three-eighths of a turn (instead of the average quarter) the twistgrip gives a variable throttle-opening rate—slow initially and becoming progressively faster. In traffic crawls the slow action is a boon since it makes ultra-delicate grip twisting unnecessary. Moreover, in effect it combines with the sweet low-speed running and heavy flywheel to conceal the super-sporting potential.

Notwithstanding the high compression ratio (9.5 to 1) little effort was required to

The rear mudguard end can be swivelled up for wheel removal. Below are shown the direction indicators and electric control clusters inboard of the handlebar grips

spin the engine by means of the transverse kick-starter; for this purpose it was most convenient to stand on the left side of the machine. Short riders found the footpiece a trifle high; but the centre stand gave amply firm support for kick-starting.

Since no strangler or air control is fitted the engine proved fairly sensitive to throttle setting and carburettor flooding for cold starting when the weather was really wintry. However, once the best drill was determined—moderately generous flooding and twistgrip set as for a fast tickover—a first-kick response was the rule rather than the exception. In milder weather the drill was not so critical provided the pilot air screws were left a shade on the rich side, as set at the factory. With that proviso again, the engine warmed up fairly rapidly to the stage where throttle response

SPECIFICATION

ENGINE: B.M.W. 595 c.c. (72 x 73mm) overhead-valve, horizontally opposed twin with needle-roller rocker bearings. Crankshaft supported in ball and roller bearings; roller big-end bearings. Aluminium-alloy cylinder heads. Compression ratio, 9.5 to 1. Wet-sump lubrication; sump capacity, 4 pints.

CARBURETTORS: Bing with progressive-rate twin-pull twistgrip. Air filter.

IGNITION and LIGHTING: Noris rotating-magnet magneto with auto-advance, and separate Noris 60/90-watt dynamo both enclosed by crankcase front cover. Varta 6-volt, 8-ampere-hour battery. Bosch 6¾in-diameter headlamp with pre-focus light unit and 35/35-watt main bulb. Detachable ignition and lighting switch.

TRANSMISSION: B.M.W. four-speed gear box in unit with engine; positive-stop foot control. Gear ratios: bottom, 13.03 to 1; second, 8.53 to 1; third, 6.07 to 1; top, 4.82 to 1. Single-plate dry clutch in engine flywheel. Final drive by enclosed shaft and helical bevel gears. Engine r.p.m. at 30 m.p.h. in top gear, 1,915.

FUEL CAPACITY: 3¾ gallons.

TYRES: Continental 3.50 x 18in front and rear.

BRAKES: Both approximately 8in diameter x 1¼in wide; twin-leading shoe front; finger adjusters.

SUSPENSION: B.M.W. pivoted front and rear forks controlled by multi-rate spring-and-hydraulic units. Manual two-position adjustment for load on rear units. Two-position fork-trail and load adjustments at front.

WHEELBASE: 55⅜in unladen. Ground clearance, 6¼in unladen.

SEAT: B.M.W. twin-seat; unladen height, 31in.

WEIGHT: 450 lb fully equipped and with full oil sump and approximately one gallon of petrol.

PRICE: £440; with purchase tax (in Great Britain only), £530 15s.

ROAD TAX: £3 15s a year; £1 7s for four months.

MAKERS: Bayerische Motoren Werke, AG., München, Germany.

BRITISH CONCESSIONAIRES: A.F.N., Ltd., Falcon Works, London Road, Isleworth, Middlesex.

PERFORMANCE DATA

(Obtained at the Motor Industry Research Association's proving ground, Lindley.)

MEAN MAXIMUM SPEED: Bottom: *45 m.p.h.
Second: *68 m.p.h.
Third: *95 m.p.h.
Top: 104 m.p.h.
*Valve float occurring.

HIGHEST ONE-WAY SPEED: 108 m.p.h. (conditions: very strong side wind; rider wearing two-piece plastic suit and overboots).

MEAN ACCELERATION:	10-30 m.p.h.	20-40 m.p.h.	30-50 m.p.h.
Bottom	2.5 sec	2.5 sec	—
Second	3.6 sec	3.4 sec	3.0 sec
Third	5.2 sec	4.1 sec	3.8 sec
Top	—	6.6 sec	5.2 sec

Mean speed at end of quarter-mile from rest: 88 m.p.h. Mean time to cover standing quarter-mile: 15 sec.

PETROL CONSUMPTION: At 30 m.p.h., 100 m.p.g.; at 40 m.p.h., 90 m.p.g.; at 50 m.p.h., 75 m.p.g.; at 60 m.p.h., 66 m.p.g.

BRAKING: From 30 m.p.h. to rest, 28 feet (surface, dry tarmac).

TURNING CIRCLE: 16ft.

MINIMUM NON-SNATCH SPEED: 11 m.p.h. in top gear.

WEIGHT PER C.C.: 0.76 lb.

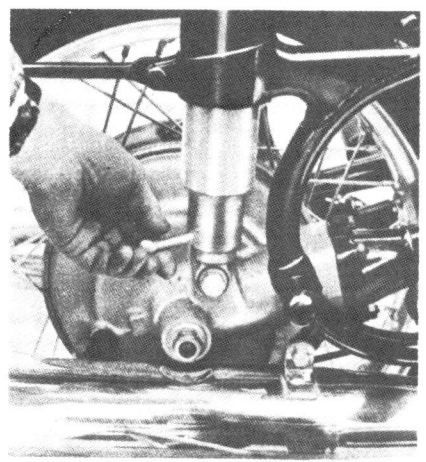

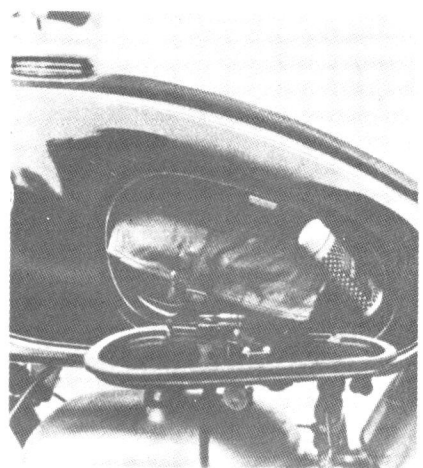

Above: Resetting the rear suspension units for pillion work is done by hand. Top right: A high-quality tool kit, spare ignition key and puncture repair kit are housed in a lockable compartment behind the left kneegrip

fashion, bottom gear usually went into engagement without a sound. Marked by a green light glowing in the headlamp shell, neutral was easy to locate.

Equal to any emergency and thoroughly waterproof, the brakes could bring squeals from both tyres at top speed, yet were smooth and progressive enough to give every confidence on slippery surfaces.

Rubber mounted, the headlamp threw a wide, far-reaching driving beam quite adequate for speeds of 80 m.p.h. and more. The horn, too, did what it should, i.e. gave clear and unmistakable warning of approach, though for really fast riding the thumb-operated main-beam flasher was a most effective substitute.

To comply with a new German law, the B.M.W. has winking direction indicators at the handlebar ends; they proved a great convenience and the firm neutral location of the operating switch prevents overshooting that position when cancelling. The horn button and dip switch on the left and the headlamp flasher and winker switch on the right can all be operated merely by swivelling the thumbs.

As to maintenance, that calls for considerable revision of accepted ideas. No oil is required between changes; and though valve clearances and contact-breaker gap are so accessible as to invite inspection, once the engine is run-in checking between decokes is likely to be a waste of time. Transmission maintenance amounts to no more than changing 150 c.c. of oil in both bevel housing and shaft tube, and just under 1½ pints in the gear box, every 7,500 miles —a fair period for chain renewal on an orthodox model driven the way the R69S can be. Even the tyres on the test model lost no pressure in two months.

As a roadster the R69S is incomparable —the most aristocratic of thoroughbreds. Equally at home gliding through packed city streets with the grace of a Rolls Royce or whispering majestically along at 100 m.p.h. it conceals its iron fist in a velvet glove. To ride it is to appreciate new levels of satisfaction and pride, to understand why connoisseurs who can afford it are prepared to pay a very high price, and to envy the West German enthusiast who can buy it for the equivalent of about £340.

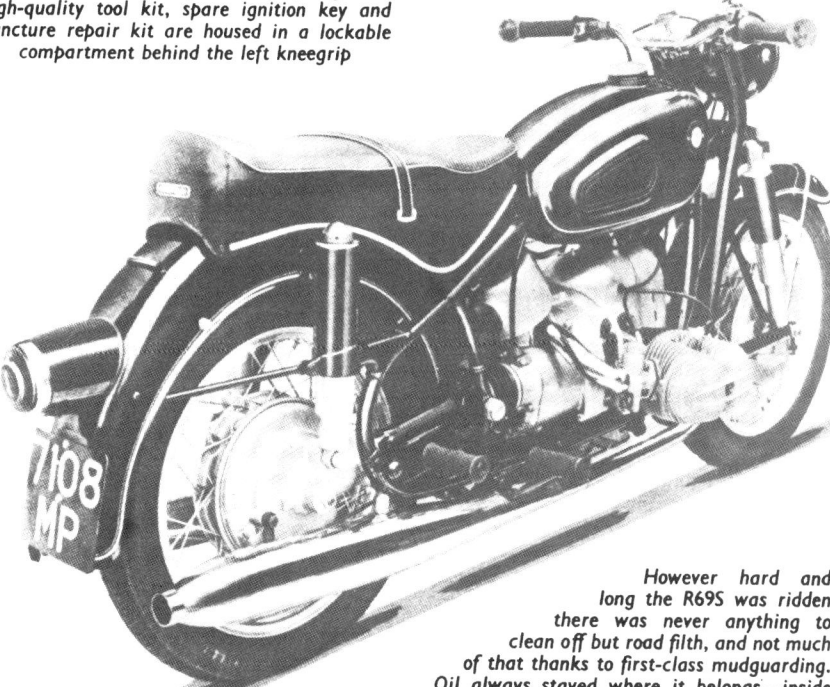

However hard and long the R69S was ridden there was never anything to clean off but road filth, and not much of that thanks to first-class mudguarding. Oil always stayed where it belongs—inside

was unhesitant. The auto-advance worked perfectly so that pinking could not be induced; in deference to the high compression ratio, super-premium petrol was used.

Engagement of the single-plate clutch seemed sweeter than on earlier models and quite as smooth as that of any multi-plate layout. With an engine-speed clutch and heavy flywheel, B.M.W.s have never boasted the slickest of gear changes. Because of the closer spacing of the ratios, that on the R69S is the best of the bunch; and though there may be sweeter changes it is well up to average.

When changing up the best results were obtained by first applying a moderate upward pressure to the pedal so that the dog clutches slipped home as soon as the clutch lever and twistgrip were eased. An appreciable blip of the throttle paid off when changing down. With the engine idling in its customary slow and dependable

Sparking plugs, valve covers and carburettors are extremely accessible. Both cylinders breathe through a large air filter. For the transverse kick-starter there is a rubber limit stop on the lower frame tube

This machine is the 'Rolls' of motorcycles and 'Kit' Kite gives his maintenance tips

SERVICING A BMW

WHEN enthusiasts gather together, it is not long before the conversation gets round to one of the best motorcycles in the world—the B.M.W. And the majority of riders will agree that one has to go a long way to beat this machine. Even so, a B.M.W. does require a certain amount of maintenance if it is to continue to give of its best.

Of course, when you pay £500 for a motorcycle you also expect a very comprehensive tool kit, and the B.M.W. kit is sufficient to do all routine jobs and the spanners are of very high quality.

The horizontal position of the cylinders greatly facilitates the work since the tank and dual seat may be left in situ. When carrying out a routine decoke first remove the silencers. Then loosen the cooling ring at the cylinder heads. It is important to loosen both exhaust systems since there is a balance pipe connecting them together. When the pipes are removed note the position of two washers for each pipe. Remove rocker box. Two small nuts and one centre sleeved nut. The gasket can be used repeatedly providing it is undamaged.

Remove sparking plug and disconnect air intake tube. This is metal, but the Neoprene washer at the filter end is very flexible and the tube can simply be pulled off at the carburetter end. The carburetter is attached to the head with two nuts and these present no difficulties.

Remove cylinder head. There are four long bolts which serve a dual purpose and retain the rocker gear as well as helping hold on the head. Two further bolts at the base of the head and the head can be removed. Light tapping with a hide mallet may be required.

With the head removed decoking can proceed in the usual manner. The valves are taken out by using a standard valve spring compressor and should be lightly ground in.

If it is necessary to check the rings, the barrel will come away by taking off the four nuts at the base. Be careful to prevent the piston dropping as the barrel comes off.

The R.69 tappet clearances are inlet .006 and exhaust .008. When resetting the gaps it is not necessary to find T.D.C. by poking wire down the plug hole. There is a rubber grommet on the nearside of the flywheel housing. Remove this and turn the engine until a small timing mark "OT" appears and lines up with an arrow on the housing. The piston is now T.D.C. and the tappets can be set.

To get at the massive 9 inch, twin leading shoe front brake, the front wheel is removed. Disconnect the front brake cable, undo the spindle nut on the near side, loosen the pinch bolt on the off side, and pull out the spindle. The wheel is then free and the brake plate complete can then be taken out.

To facilitate rear wheel removal, the rear mudguard is hinged. First loosen mudguard stay bolts on the rear springing units, and securing nuts on the mudguard. Spindle nut, pinch bolt and spindle are exactly the same as for the front wheel.

The rear springing units have two positions. When the lever is forward springing is in hard position. Push to alternative point.

50

To remove front wheel first disconnect the front brake cable. Undo the spindle nut and slacken pinch-bolt. Withdraw spindle

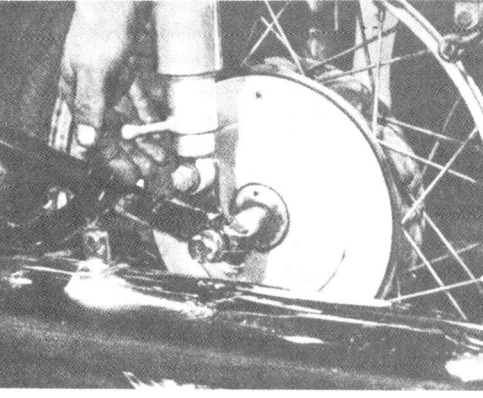

The rear suspension units of the machine can easily be adjusted by hand. A large peg on the unit allows instant tensioning

To take out rear wheel first lift mudguard on hinges. The procedure then is exactly the same as for removing the front wheel

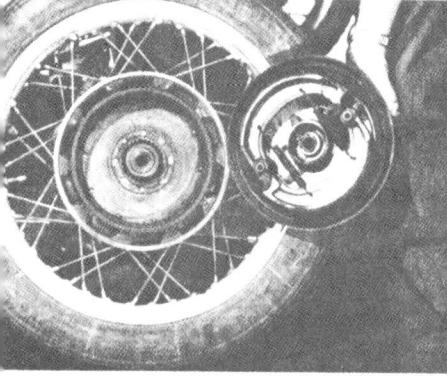

The front brake has a twin leading shoe which gives particularly good braking under all conditions—clean away all dust

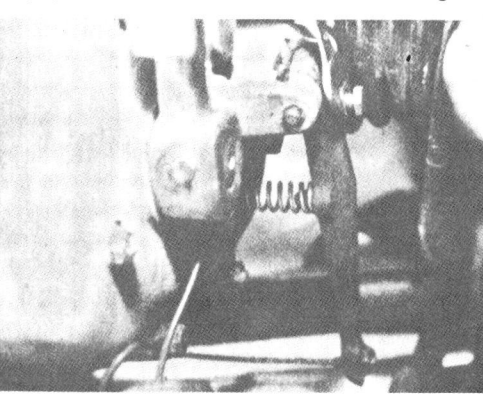

Clutch adjustment is simple. Slacken off locking nut and then adjust with the small bolt on the clutch lever arm on gearbox

Timing is made easy and positive with an "OT" mark on the flywheel. This can be seen through the small hole on the nearside

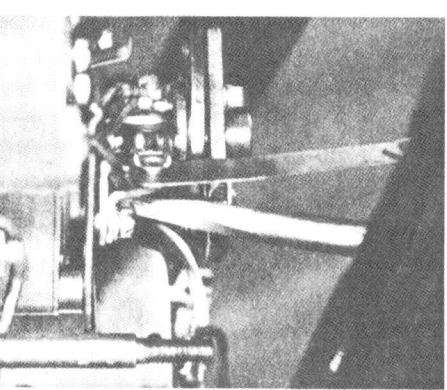

The contact breaker gap is adjusted by loosening the stationary plate with the screwdriver—move until gap is accurate

Air intake tube is pulled free at carb mouth—it is held in place by a Neoprene washer. The carb is held by only two nuts

Tappet clearances are as follows : Inlet is .006 and exhaust is .008. Always see that these settings are accurately made

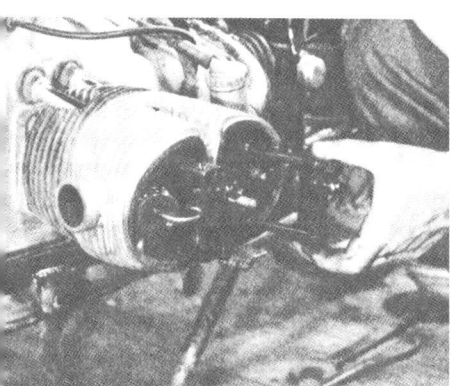

The rocker gear is held to the head by long bolts—make sure that these are not confused if removed for any maintenance

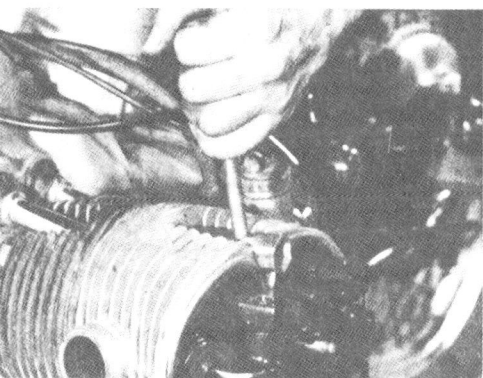

The head is secured by two long bolts and these are placed above and below. Use a box spanner when removing these from head

Removal of the barrel presents no trouble but ensure that great care is used when replacing—it is easier with two people

14 KARAT MOTORCYCLING

by Ted Jacques

Diamond merchant, Morey Lehrman, with his BMW R-60

IF YOU were to do business with a certain merchant in New York City's fabulous diamond center, on 47th St. between Fifth and Sixth Avenues, you would only be too aware of the truth of this statement. Soft spoken, mild mannered Morey Lehrman is somewhat of an anomaly to the guys and gals who deal in the valuable hard carbon, watches and other costly trinkets along this street of gems. They regard him with awe and concern that maybe some of the gears in his mental mechanism need cleaning and adjusting.

You would hardly expect a man who overhauls the finest watches, as well as being versed in the mysteries of diamonds, to ride a snarling scrambler over dirt and through the woods, or to take cross country jaunts on a BMW R-60. His colleagues along the street do not expect such goings on from one of their kind either: hence their concern.

Morey, who saw plenty of Front Line action in World War Two, has a zest for living and stamina that would be the envy of many people twenty years younger than he. A graduate of motor scooters, having owned a Lambretta and a Five Star Prima, the power and acceleration of the Big Wheels has now gotten under his skin. At present he owns the aforementioned BMW and a Triumph Tiger Cub. The BMW is an all-white job, with good taste in chrome and accessories, that never fails to catch the eye of motorcyclists and other citizens who get about on four wheels.

Recently he decided to get a bike rider's view of the country he had flown over so often on business trips. After outfitting his BMW with panniers and a rucksack and packing five more pairs of shoes than he needed, the greatly anticipated day of departure arrived. Rolling along over the Jersey Turnpike the bike swayed most un-BMW-like when it went past the 60 mark. After tightening all the nuts and bolts Morey hit the pike again, but mysterious forces continued to cause the bike to sway like an inebriated sailor. A careful check of the rig revealed a poor job of lashing down his suitcase. Thankful he hadn't gone back to Butler and Smith to have the problem solved, he headed west once more.

The white BMW and its rider rolled happily along down to the Will Rogers Turnpike. After about ten miles on this speedway, Morey glanced at the speedometer and was amazed to find he was roaring along wide open. Not exactly a Sunday driver, he decided to hold it there and clipped off the 98 miles of the Turnpike in slightly over an hour. It must have been lunch time as no law enforcement official interfered with the fast moving diamond merchant.

Barreling along wide open for an hour is not exactly recommended for the proper functioning of a relatively new motor. Morey found this out 30 miles on the other side of the Turnpike when top speed fell off to 45 mph and the usually smooth-purring motor began to sound like a small pile driver. Nightfall found him with a conked out motor and far from a motel, so he bedded down for the night on desert sands with a ruck for a pillow. A good night's rest was out of the question, as what New Yorker doesn't know that coyotes, rattlesnakes and other crawling things are all over the desert.

By morning the overheated motor had cooled off and he was able to fire it up after much prodding. The rucksack back in its accustomed place, he started out in the direction of the blue Pacific again, hoping the machine would hold up until he got to Phoenix. 150 miles further

on he needed some more folding money and dipped into his rucksack where he kept the heavy cash, but none was to be found. Frantic, he remembered he had taken gear out of the bag to make a more comfortable pillow out of it. It was impossible to get up any speed as he crawled back to the spot, or what he thought was the spot, where he had spent the night. The desert is a rather large monotonous piece of real estate and with no landmark to guide him, Morey's quest for the bundle of bills was futile. The only thing left to do was send an S.O.S. to New York from the nearest telegraph office.

Moving westward again, an unfamiliar sound began to plague his ears. The air became a violent blue around him when he discovered he had lost an irreplaceable top to one of his pannier bags, so back in the direction of New York again. After crossing the median line a half dozen times he found the top unscathed by passing cars. In spite of his own problems, he had also spent hours trying to help a fellow cyclist who was stalled in the desert by a dead battery.

As he was approaching Phoenix a black cat crossed his path which, naturally, was not to his liking after what he had been through. The cat had either lost its powers to bring on bad luck or was not as black as Morey thought, because from then on it was smooth sailing. In Phoenix the boys at P. & D. Motorcycle Sales found the valve stems carbonized to such an extent that the valves remained open when the bike was stopped. After the machine was restored to normal, a pleasant night's ride brought him into Hollywood.

The usual tourist's haunts of Los Angeles were of no interest to the motorcycling diamond merchant, and his week in the smog was spent meeting dealers, buying goodies for the BMW and Triumph and taking in whatever activity could be found.

The trip back to 47th St. was a breeze. For some strange reason Morey reports that, "When I look into a diamond it acts like a crystal ball and I keep seeing motorcycles."

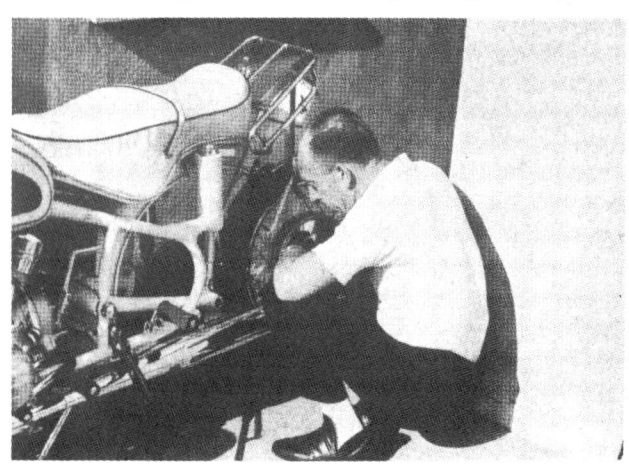

When I look into diamonds, I keep seeing motorcycles

The World-record-breaking 597 c.c. B.M.W. R69S

'Motor Cycling's' 24-hour

record rider tries

the machine which

set new absolute figures

By BRUCE MAIN-SMITH

WITH a near-standard 600 c.c. o.h.v. horizontally-opposed twin-cylinder B.M.W. R69S, the London concern of M.L.G. Motorcycles, Ltd., have just set new world's records at 12- and 24-hour levels in the 750 and 1,000 c.c. classes. The respective speeds (inclusive of all pit stops) now awaiting official confirmation by the F.I.M., are 109.34 and 109.24 m.p.h.

Motor Cycling is privileged to present an extended road test report on this successful machine. With certain obvious exceptions (detailed in their proper places), the test follows our standard routine and—as usual—has been conducted at the Motor Industry Research Association's station at Lindley, near Nuneaton, where we have the use of a three-mile banked circuit and electronic timing apparatus.

The big "Bee-Em" was immediately at home on the high-speed banking, so akin to its recent habitat at Montlhéry, France. With the tester making full use of the dolphin, the rearward rests, the racing seat and with his body draped over the massive tummy-cum-chest pad, a succession of flying laps repeatedly flung the record-breaker through the "magic eyes" at 118 m.p.h.

At this speed the mount was as steady as a modern liner with stabilizing fins. No

World-record-breaking B.M.W. R69S
Road Test

Specification

ENGINE

Type .. Horizontally opposed twin-cylinder four-stroke
Bore .. .. 72 mm.
Stroke .. .. 73 mm.
Cubic capacity .. .. 595 c.c.
Valves .. .. Overhead (push-rod)
Compression ratio .. .. 9.5 : 1
Carburetter .. Bing, type 26/1/9 and 10
Ignition .. Noris magneto, automatic advance
Generator .. .. Bosch, 6-v., 60/90 w.
Makers' claimed output Not disclosed. (Engine "safe" to 7,400 r.p.m; normal maximum, 7,000)
Lubrication .. By gear pump, gravity return to sump
Starting .. .. .. Kickstarter

TRANSMISSION

Ratios .. .. .. 4.6, 5.8, 8.1, 12.7 : 1
Speed at 1,000 r.p.m. in top gear .. 17 m.p.h.
Speed equivalent to revs at maximum "continuous" r.p.m. (7,000): top, 118; third, 93.5; second, 67.0; bottom, 43.0 m.p.h.
Primary drive .. .. .. Direct
Final drive .. By enclosed shaft to spiral bevel gears
Clutch .. .. Single plate in engine flywheel
Shock-absorber Spring-loaded cam in gearbox

CYCLE PARTS

Frame .. Welded tubular construction; duplex main frame, with extended loop-type rear bearers

Front suspension B.M.W. front forks, built under Earles licence, with Girling hydraulically damped suspension units
Rear suspension Swinging-fork, with Girling hydraulically damped suspension units
Tyres .. Avon 3.50×19-in. front and rear
Brakes .. 7.9-in. two-leading-shoe front brake, 7.9-in. rear brake; total lining area, 39 sq. in.
Fuel tank . Welded steel, 5-gal. capacity
Oil tank Reservoir in crankcase, 5½ pints capacity
Lamps .. Marchal 35-w. "Fantastique" head; Marchal spot
Battery · .. .. .. Bosch type 6/12/2
Rev-counter .. Smiths magnetic 8,000 r.p.m.
Seating .. .. Norton racing seat
Stands .. .. None
Toolkit .. .. None
Toolbox Located under fuel tank left knee-grip
Standard finish Black enamel with white lining

OTHER EQUIPMENT

Peel "dolphin" fairing.

PRICES

Not applicable. Standard R69S, £530 15s. inc. P.T.
Tax .. £3 15s. p.a. (£1 7s. for 4 months)
Makers.. Bayeren Motoren Werke A.G., Lerchenauerstrasse 76, Munich, Germany: modified by M.L.G. Motorcycles, Ltd., 105 Goldhawk Road, London, W.12.

Test Data

Conditions. *Weather: Mild, blustery, showery* (Barometer 29.40 in. Hg. Temperature 52°F.). *Wind: West-south-west 11.5 m.p.h. Surface (acceleration): Damp asphalt. Rider: 11½ stone, 5 ft. 10½ in., wearing two-piece suit, boots and safety helmet, adopting racing crouch behind screen throughout.*
Venue: *Motor Industry Research Association Station, Lindley.*
Speed at end of standing 1,000 yd.:
East .. .. 109.2 m.p.h.
West .. .. 91.6 m.p.h.
Best certified M.I.R.A. maximum (rider crouching behind screen) 118.3 m.p.h.
(Absence of speedometer precluded braking and consumption tests)

Engine/gearbox of the record-breaker is similar in all essentials to the standard B.M.W. unit, illustrated below.

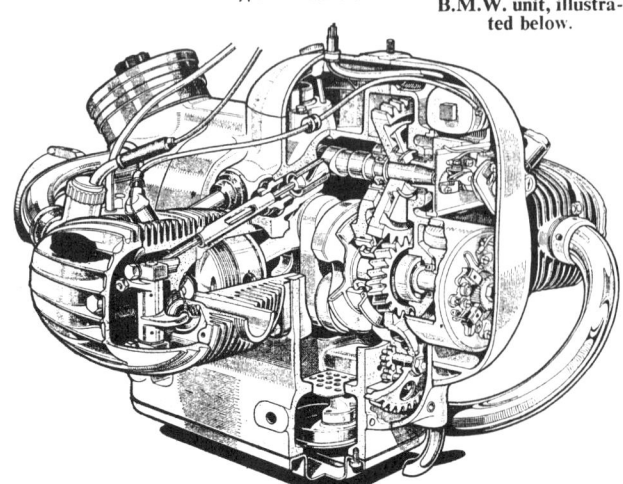

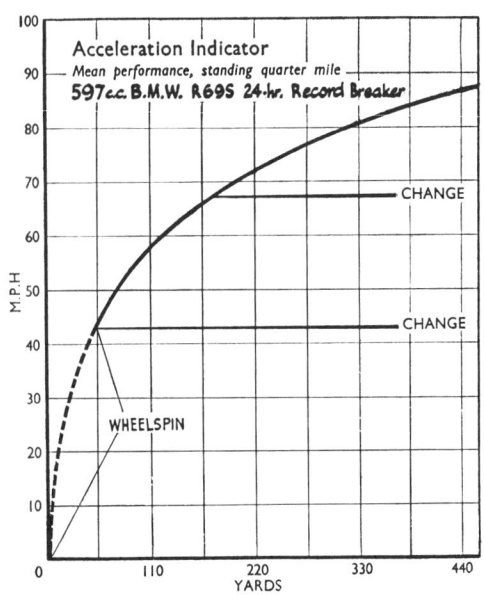

Acceleration Indicator
Mean performance, standing quarter mile
597 c.c. B.M.W. R69S 24-hr. Record Breaker

CHANGE

CHANGE

WHEELSPIN

M.P.H.

YARDS

lurching, wavering from line, tail-wagging, nor anything other than complete tautness and absolute accuracy of line holding was detectable. At this speed, and indeed at all others, the steering damper was set to bite appreciably.

Failure to nip the damper would produce a gentle, almost lazy, oscillation of the front end at the 25- to 30-m.p.h. mark, so it is meant to be used. Respecting this dictate from the steering, the tester found the handling to be excellent—and not only at three-figure speeds on banking or straight. The B.M.W. gave complete confidence to the rider when it was being whisked through fast bends or wheedled 'twixt traffic islands at road junctions. In its Montlhéry trim, the R69S, not unexpectedly, had its lock restricted to a degree that made sharp turns difficult.

Suspension characteristics were good. With the rear damper units in their "hard" position, the rider found the springing aft ideal for the job in hand, namely speed work over mediocre surfaces, such as are encountered at the Montlhéry circuit. But some idea of the efficiency with which bumps were ironed out was gained by hurtling the B.M.W. over some subsided sections of M1, which are becoming notorious for producing full deflection of suspension on cars and motorcycles when taken at speed. The front end was slightly softer than the rear; yet both worked in perfect harmony.

Cruising on M1

The M1 journey to M.I.R.A. was sheer bliss. Knowing the motor to be run-in to a degree that few can ever hope to be (!), the pilot took liberal handfuls of throttle. The dolphin, and the racing crouch behind its protection, were also used 100%. Miles were gobbled up to the melodious accompaniment of a well-muted exhaust and the roar of the wind sneaking past the small double-curvature screen and shrieking around the safety helmet's straps and flaps.

For test purposes, the megaphone exhausts used at Montlhéry were replaced by standard B.M.W. silencers—a necessary action and one, we are told, that brought a mere 2 b.h.p. penalty in the upper register.

Secure in the knowledge of a 110 m.p.h. for 24 hours cruising speed, the tester took the B.M.W. safely and unobtrusively along M1 at an exhilarating "ton"—and sometimes more. The mile-interval telephone posts flicked by at close on steady half minute intervals!

Smooth Speed

With a rev counter as a guide to speed (and to comply with the Road Traffic Act), one had to keep one's wits sharpened. Only the tachometer, the wind, the barely audible exhaust and the relative rapidity at which closing distances on vehicles ahead were shortened, gave a clue to speed. Certainly, it was not possible to use vibration periods for that purpose. The R69S, even after all its arduous mileage, was as smooth as oiled silk and well supported this Munich-made marque's reputation for vibration-free running.

For the record it is observed that, at tickover, the h.c. pistons produced a little "lumpiness" and that, between some 3,500 and 4,000 r.p.m. there was a short spate of tremoring—but *not* vibration. At maximum "continuous cruising" revs (7,000) in the

intermediates, or in top, the unit was as smooth as though it were rubber mounted.

It was possible to feel the machine cant slightly to the right if the taps were opened briskly, for example, at 2,500 r.p.m. in second. But that was the total of detectable torque reaction. Even brisker acceleration at higher r.p.m. gave no indication of this contentious factor. The power came in markedly at about 5,600 and then surged straight through to 7,000.

Gearchange and Clutch

The gearchange was typically B.M.W., for the ratios were the standard wide ones and the clutch runs at engine speed. Consequently, the upward changes had to be made somewhat leisurely if silence was demanded. But the upward flick from third at 7,000 to top at about 5,800 was remarkably rapid in view of these clutch/gear characteristics.

Record-breaking motor. The empty "turret" on top of the gearbox casting is normally occupied by the air-cleaner; also non-standard is the reversed gear lever.

Downward changes were simplicity itself. The gear pedal, on the left, worked one-up-and-three-down.

Clutch action was really perfect. It was light, smooth, easy to slip when required, and possessed an abundance of grip.

Elsewhere in the friction department, namely the brakes, equally pleasing results were forthcoming. If the 8-in. 2LS front stopper and the first-class rear anchor had not been superlatively good, it would not have been possible to gallop up M1 at "the ton" in safety.

In fact, the brakes were perhaps the equal of those on any mount we have road-tested. Their only weakness was a very distinct lifting of the steering head caused by extension of the front suspension as the front unit was used alone. But to be strictly fair it is also necessary to record that the front was inclined to grab when being used during low-speed turns; so, under these conditions only,

resort was made to the back-brake-alone technique. Braking to an emergency stop, straight ahead from any speed between 10 and 100 m.p.h. was fitting work for the front stopper. These anchors are standard B.M.W. roadster equipment.

It was not possible to evaluate several items on the normal road test check list. The riding position, for instance, was decidedly special—and decidedly uncomfortable as soon as one sat up; in other words, definitely not to be recommended for serious road work.

The removal of the speedometer precluded calibration of that instrument and also the taking of a fuel-consumption figure; the horn fitted was of bulb-type; lights were record-breaking "specials"; no stands were fitted; the mudguards had been modified.

For a cold start it was needful to drain the sump and pour in hot oil. It is well worthy of note that the record was set on "green" oil—actually Esso Extra Motor Oil 40/50 and precisely the same lubricant as the ordinary motorcyclist can buy on the garage forecourt. It is to the credit of both Esso and the B.M.W. engineers that such an orthodox mineral oil can today do what yesterday was thought to be exclusively the province of "the vegetables."

By and large, this was virtually a standard R69S with a "works" engine. And it was a remarkably rapid and pleasing hunk of motorcycle. It did credit not only to its German makers but to its British preparers at M.L.G.s not only by taking the 750 c.c. and 1,000 c.c. class records, but by finishing in utterly perfect trim. So sound, in fact, was it when it arrived back from France, that we were able to take it over for road test straight away and do many hundreds of miles without seeing an oil-leak or the level on the dipstick budge one iota!

56

R50 BMW 494 cc Twin

road tests of new models

YOU waft across the sunny countryside with just a rustle of cleft air and, maybe, a faint whine from the tyres. Footrests, handlebar, kneegrips and luxurious seat fit you as unobtrusively as a Savile Row suit. Smooth controls lie close to your fingers and toes. Every muscle is relaxed as you lean imperceptibly on the wind.

As the road veers this way and that your bike curves round on invisible rails. You twist the grip. Silkily, almost apologetically, your bus flows up the speed scale. Caress the brakes and a giant magnet holds you back.

When you want to overtake you choose between a horn that can really be heard and a button that flashes the 35-watt main beam. And there are grip-tip winkers.

Night falls and your lights flood the road with brilliant illumination. Halt and you have to lower your head to hear the slow chuff-chuff of the tickover.

What's this—a *pedal* for starting? Well, yes; but so gentle a prod is called for that a schoolgirl could give it. And the response is certain.

This is a bike for riding, not

The R50 corners as if on rails. The slight forward lean of the riding position takes strain off the arms at high speed without over-loading the wrists in town riding

Finished in black and silver, the R50 has the dignified bearing appropriate to a clean, smooth, whispering roadster. Levers at the base of the rear suspension struts are easily swivelled for passenger carrying

SPECIFICATION
and Performance Data

ENGINE: BMW 494 cc (68 x 68mm) overhead-valve, horizontally opposed twin. Crankshaft supported in ball bearings; roller big-end bearings. Aluminium-alloy cylinder heads; compression ratio, 6.8 to 1. Wet-sump lubrication; capacity 4 pints.

CARBURETTORS: Two Bings with fuel balance chambers. Progressive-rate, twin-pull twistgrip. Air filter and cold-start choke.

ELECTRICAL EQUIPMENT: Bosch rotating-magnet magneto with auto-advance. Separate Bosch 60/90-watt dynamo with automatic voltage control. Varta 6-volt, 8-amp-hour battery. Bosch 6½in-diameter headlamp with pre-focus light unit and 35/35-watt main bulb. Direction indicators, main-beam flasher and stop-light standard.

TRANSMISSION: BMW four-speed, foot-change gear box in unit with engine. Ratios: Bottom, 13.03 to 1; second, 8.52 to 1; third, 6.06 to 1; top, 4.81 to 1. Single-plate dry clutch in engine flywheel. Final drive by enclosed shaft and helical bevel gears. Engine rpm at 30 mph in top gear, 1,900.

FUEL CAPACITY: 3½ gallons.

TYRES: Continental 3.50 x 18in front and rear on light-alloy rims.

BRAKES: Both approximately 8in diameter x 1⅜in wide; twin-leading-shoe front; finger adjusters.

SUSPENSION: BMW pivoted front and rear forks controlled by multi-rate spring-and-hydraulic units. Manual two-position adjustment for load at rear. Two-position fork-trail and load adjustments at front.

WHEELBASE: 56in. Ground clearance, 6½in. Seat height, 31½in. All unladen.

WEIGHT: 415 lb fully equipped and with full sump and approximately one gallon of petrol.

PRICE: £455 3s 3d including British purchase tax.

ROAD TAX: £4 10s a year; £1 13s for four months.

MAKERS: Bayerische Motoren Werke, AG, Munchen, West Germany.

BRITISH CONCESSIONAIRES: BMW Concessionaires, England, Ltd., Victoria Road, Portslade, Brighton, Sussex.

PERFORMANCE DATA

(Obtained at the Motor Industry Research Association's proving ground, Lindley, Leicestershire.)

MEAN MAXIMUM SPEEDS: Bottom, 38 mph*; second, 58 mph*; third, 82 mph*; top, 90 mph. (*Valve float occurring.)

HIGHEST ONE-WAY SPEED: 92 mph (conditions: moderate three-quarter wind; rider wearing one-piece oversuit.)

MEAN ACCELERATION:

		10-30 mph	20-40 mph	30-50 mph
Bottom	...	3.2 sec	—	—
Second	...	4.4 sec	3.8 sec	4.4 sec
Third	...	6.4 sec	5.2 sec	5.7 sec
Top	...	—	8.2 sec	8.2 sec

Mean speed at end of quarter-mile from rest: 75 mph. Mean time to cover standing quarter-mile: 17 sec.

PETROL CONSUMPTION: At 30 mph, 110 mpg; at 40 mph, 84 mpg; at 50 mph, 68 mpg; at 60 mph, 64 mpg.

BRAKING: From 30 mph to rest, 28ft (surface, dry concrete).

TURNING CIRCLE: 15ft 6in.

MINIMUM NON-SNATCH SPEED: 12 mph in top gear.

WEIGHT PER CC: 0.84 lb.

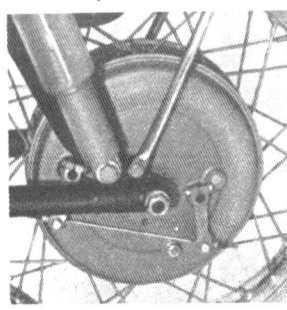

Both cams of the twin-leading-shoe front brake are operated by a single-control cable. The brake has enormous power

tinkering with. Just about all you do is tank-up every 200 miles. Cleaning is feather-duster stuff.

Ah, sweet dream. What a pity to wake to reality. But there is no need if you ride a BMW twin. All these joys are yours on an R50 five-hundred. And, since the compression ratio is low, they are yours on regular-grade petrol.

The R50 is the woolliest of the BMW twins. (Riders who want an out-and-out sports performance may prefer the R50S or R69S.) For all that the

top speed of 90 mph was timed when the test machine was barely run-in.

On first acquaintance, acceleration seems gentle—a deception due partly to the machine's uncanny smoothness and quietness and partly to the progressive-rate twistgrip. This has a slow action at small openings, blending into a quick action at large openings.

In dense traffic the slow action is a boon. And when it's vivid acceleration you want, you have only to take a big-enough handful of grip and let the revs

mount freely through the gears.

Speedwise, the best results are obtained by holding each gear until the speedometer needle reaches the blue mark on the dial that corresponds to peak-power revs of 5,800 rpm. With this technique, third proved to be a very useful gear, especially when a passenger was carried.

Initially, if the engine was allowed to slog very hard in top, there was slight harshness (by BMW standards!) around 56 mph. This was completely eliminated by slightly tightening

Above: Transverse cylinder mounting makes for cool running. Valve clearance adjustment is extremely accessible, as also are the contact breaker and dynamo under the front engine cover.
Below: Both carburettors breathe through a large air filter. The mixing chambers have cast-in fuel-balance reservoirs opposite the float chambers. On the lower frame tube is the rubber stop for the transverse kick-starter

quite easy to operate, either with the right foot before mounting or the left foot once astride.

For cold starting the choke on the air filter has to be closed. It can be part-opened as soon as the engine fires and is easily reached from the saddle for full opening.

When the throttle cables had settled down, it proved worth while to match their adjustments precisely. This eliminated a slight rock on idling.

The clutch is smooth in take-up, though quick because it runs at engine speed and the flywheel is heavy. This layout has never given the slick, knife-into-butter gear changes of the best conventional layouts but, provided the control movements are properly synchronized, it is not difficult to make reasonably fast and quiet changes—especially now the ratios are medium-close rather than uncommonly wide as they were some years ago.

RELENTLESS

In spite of the raising of the lower ratios, the R50 took a 1 in 3 restart in its stride.

Except that the first application of the front brake on a humid day called for a delicate touch if the result was not to be fierce, the brakes proved superb. Smooth and immensely powerful, they pinned the R50 down relentlessly regardless of load or speed.

The progressive-rate springing has the low-speed firmness associated with high-speed stability. Yet there was a remote feel about shocks that got through —as if they were being funneled off to nearby vehicles. Pre-

"Cyril, for goodness sake . . . it's your wedding in 20 minutes"

loading the rear springs for pillion work is a matter of seconds and calls for no tools. You just tweak two levers.

At first the steering had a disconcerting low-speed roll. But that disappeared immediately initial over-tightening of the head bearings was eased. From then on, straight-ahead stability was above average, yet the machine responded precisely to banking.

Nor was there any practical limit to the degree of banking that could be used. For, at 21in, the R50 is unusually slim across the footrests.

CHILD'S PLAY

In dream-bus reveries, of course, the sun always shines. But rain bothers the BMW rider less than most. Waterproofing is extremely thorough, mud-guarding efficient and the cylinders shield the feet.

Maintenance is child's play, for the few routine adjustments are very accessible, as are the oil-level plugs.

What of the debit side? Well, let's be finicky. The R50 is no lightweight and a determined effort is needed to put it on the centre stand. Maybe the twist-grip and front-brake lever are a shade heavier to operate than some. But you can't tell the difference at the end of a day in the saddle.

No, the R50 stands out from the ruck as a superb tourer for the connoisseur— a pride and joy to own. Its impeccable manners inevitably keep the rider always on his best and most courteous behaviour.

the rubber mounting at the top of the engine.

Once top gear was notched the R50 would cruise at any speed between 70 mph, against a stiff head wind, and 80 mph in fair conditions.

Of course, on a machine of the R50's calibre the speedometer was true. It was also very smooth in action.

The BMW kick-starter is on the left side of the machine and moves transversely. Yet it is

At the rider's left thumb are the horn button and dipper switch, on the right the flasher and winker

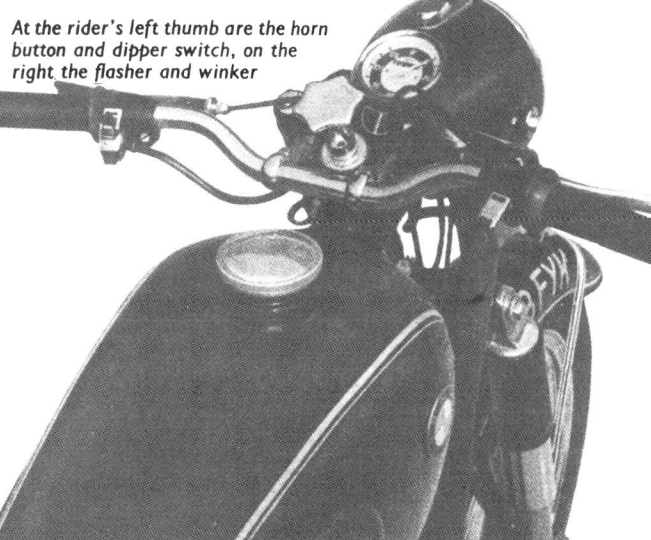

BMW R-27

M OST MOTORCYCLISTS' interests are centered on the sporting aspects of the game, and if they do not race themselves, they at least follow racing closely, and indulge themselves in a bit of brisk riding, on pavement or back-country trails, whenever the opportunity presents itself. However, there is a second group that does not give a hoot for racing; they ask nothing more than to be allowed to ride gently along and enjoy the fresh air and scenery. The first, larger group may be found riding almost anything; the second will, more often than not, be riding a BMW.

The reasons behind this are manifold, but the main factor appears to be that the BMW offers probably the best reliability of any motorcycle in the world, it is also one of the most comfortable. These are things that matter a great deal to the back-and-forth-to-work, touring-on-weekends type of rider.

We have already tested the "top" model in the BMW line: the R-69S; now it is the "economy" R-27's turn. This is the model purchased by those who want what a BMW has to offer, but cannot afford the rather expensive (about $1600) R-69S. Actually, the R-27 is not all that much less expensive than the R-69S flat-twin, and for a very good reason: virtually everything on the bike, excepting the engine, is the same.

The R-27's engine is a vertical single, with pushrod operated valves in a hemispherical combustion chamber.

There is nothing very exciting about this engine, but it does have some rather different features. For example: unlike most single-cylinder motorcycle engines, the crankshaft webs that hold the crankpin are not also flywheels; the flywheel bolts to one end of the crankshaft, just as in an automobile. There is, however, room for flywheels inside the crankcase, which is absolutely cavernous. Of course, part of the great bulk of the crankcase is due to the fact that the engine has wet-sump lubrication.

Another unusual feature is the engine mounting. BMW evidently feels that the vibrations from a single are incompatible with the rest of the machine, and while there is not much they can do to prevent the engine from vibrating, they have stopped these vibrations at the source by mounting the entire engine/transmission package on rubber blocks. This is not effective at all speeds (there is a lot of shaking at and immediately above idle) but when you get the engine cranked up to touring speed, very little vibration can be felt. The R-27 is, when the revs are up, the smoothest of all the 250s we have tried.

As in all BMWs, the R-27 is shaft driven, and so the engine and transmission are "sideways" as compared to the normal motorcycle layout. The clutch is a single dry-plate unit with a diaphragm-type spring under the pressure plate, and as it is bolted to the engine's external flywheel, it turns at engine speed. The diaphragm spring, incidentally, "over-centers" as the clutch is disengaged, so that pressure required at the lever is low.

From the clutch, the drive goes to a shaft that carries a gear for transmitting drive to the transmission, and another gear for the kick-starter drive. Also mounted on this shaft is a torsional vibration damper. Next to this "idler" shaft is the transmission countershaft, and next to that is the mainshaft, which is hooked, at the back end, to the U-joint on the driveshaft. The driveshaft, of course, leads back to the spiral-bevel gears that turn the drive 90-degrees and feed it to the rear wheel. Thus, even in 4th gear, the drive passes through four shafts, and across three points of gear mesh.

All of this whirling machinery can be felt very distinctly when making shifts. Every time you change gears, there is a pronounced clank as one set of fast-turning gears and shafts snatches another set up to speed. The same occurs during down-shifts, obviously, and this is made even more apparent by the engine's unwillingness to rev quickly. The engine carries a lot of flywheel, to smooth out power impulses, and this flywheel makes it quite impossible to blip the engine up to the higher revs needed for a smooth down-shift. On the other hand, we must admit that the shifting requires little pressure on the lever, and it is all but impossible to miss a shift, either up or down. Neutral, so elusive on most motorcycles, was easily found and for those riders who wear very heavy boots or simply have no sense of "feel," a light (green) next to the speedometer winks on when neutral has been selected.

The flywheel we have been talking about makes the bike pleasant to ride in that it does smooth out the widely-spaced thumps from the R-27's single-cylinder engine, but it, in combination with a very "positive" clutch, made it somewhat difficult to make smooth shifts. The gears engage without any trouble (albeit with an audible clunk), but unless the rider waits, holding the clutch disengaged, until the engine speed drops a bit, the engagement of the clutch will snatch the whole bike forward. Naturally, most BMW riders do not make a habit of slam-bang shifting, so this peculiarity will not bother them much, if at all.

Because all of the motion is "sideways" in the BMW's innards, the kick-starter pedal swings outward from the side of the machine. This adds a lot of convenience when you want to start the bike while standing beside it, but if

the engine should stall while waiting for a traffic light, it becomes a distinct disadvantage. We suppose, with practice, one could learn to manipulate that sideways pedal while astride the bike; none of us ever became proficient at it.

Like most of the rest of the world's motorcycles, the R-27 has a swing-arm type rear suspension (the driveshaft housing is one of the "arms"), but it is virtually alone in employing an "Earles" type front suspension. This is, strictly speaking, another form of leading link suspension, but in the Earles fork, the links are very long arms, pivoted at a point just behind the front tire. This layout gives a nearly constant wheelbase, at the expense of small variations in trail, and as braking torque is fed into the suspension arms, the front end of the bike will not dip when the brake is applied. On the BMW, the arms have alternate pivot holes so that the trail can be reduced for sidecar work, and we suspect that this is why the Earles fork has been retained by BMW even though telescopic forks are proving to give superior road holding and handling.

The BMW's handling is exactly in keeping with the sort of motorcycle it is. You will notice that if hard cornering is attempted, the bike will surge softly up and down, which does little to help the rider maintain his "line." Stiffer suspension units would help this, obviously, and it is our opinion that a "cart-sprung" BMW would handle very well indeed. However, stiffening the suspension would also destroy what is a really marvelous ride, and the ride will appeal to the average BMW buyer a lot more than racing-type cornering. And, the BMW handles very well at normal touring speeds, which is really all that matters.

The bike's brakes are good by any standard. The brake drums are quite large, and of aluminum, and a minimum amount of pressure is required at the controls to get a maximum of braking effort. This is not to say that the same brakes would be perfect on a racing machine, but at the speeds of which the R-27 is capable, its brakes give most impressive results.

Hot or cold, the engine is easy to start. We had some difficulty in cold-starting until we learned the combination, which was a little "tickler" and very little throttle, but after the learning phase was past the bike proved to be quite willing to come to life.

With relatively high bars, and a low seat, the riding position was bolt-upright, which is just the thing for long-distance touring. All controls are well positioned, and the saddle is soft enough to allow a rider to spend a lot of time aboard the BMW without becoming unduly fatigued. This is fortunate, because the BMW, with its high tank capacity and low fuel consumption, will go a very long distance before it is necessary to stop. It is, in short, an ideal moderate-speed touring bike.

We have mentioned the impressive reliability of the BMW; that is something that cannot be seen, but is known as a result of long experience on the part of the fanatically-devoted group of BMW riders. What can be seen, by even those who do not know motorcycles, is that the BMW's finish is of the highest standard. Where there is paint, it is of uniformly high quality. The very little bit of brightwork on the bike is really bright, and experience indicates that it will remain bright through a lot of weathering. All of the bike's mechanical elements, and the suspension and frame, are extremely "substantial," and that accounts for the rather high curb weight — and a lot of its reliability.

We can go on to say that the R-27 will take a beating without complaint, although it is not really inended for that, and that the rider's enjoyment of breeze and scenery will not be disturbed by excessive vibration or exhaust noise (things that the sporting rider seems to enjoy more than air or scenery). There are a lot more points to cover, but it is really not necessary for us to do this: people who are not natural-born BMW riders will not care; and those who belong to the BMW cult already know. •

BMW R-27

SPECIFICATIONS

List Price .... $850 (FOB Los Angeles)
Frame Type .... tubular, two-loop
Suspension, front .... leading link
Suspension, rear .... swing arm
Tire size, front 3.25-18
Tire size, rear 3.25-18
Brake lining area, sq. in. 30.1
Engine type .... single cyl, ohv
Bore & stroke .... 2.68 x 2.68
Displacement, cu. in. 14.95
Displacement, cu. cent. 245
Compression ratio 8.2:1
Bhp @ rpm .... 18 @ 7400
Carburetion .... 26mm (1.02") Bing
Ignition .... battery and coil
Fuel capacity, gal. 4.0
Oil capacity, pts. 2.6
Oil System .... wet sump
Starting system .... kick

POWER TRANSMISSION

Clutch Type .... single-disc, dry plate
Primary drive .... gear
Final drive .... shaft and bevel gears
Gear ratio, overall:1
    4th 6.40
    3rd 8.49
    2nd 12.56
    1st 22.17

DIMENSIONS, IN.

Wheelbase 54.3
Saddle height 30.2
Saddle width 14.0
Foot-peg height 10.5
Ground clearance 4.5
Curb weight, lbs. 360

PERFORMANCE

Practical maximum speed
  (after 1/2-mile run)
Max. speed in gears @ 7400 rpm
    4th 84
    3rd 63
    2nd 42
    1st 24
Mph per 1000 rpm, top gear 11.3

SPEEDOMETER ERROR

30 mph, actual 28.6
50 .... 48.2
70 .... 66.7

ACCELERATION

0-30 mph, sec. 6.1
0-40 .... 9.3
0-50 .... 15.1
0-60 .... 21.5
0-70 .... 38.0
0-80
0-90
0-100
Standing 1/4 mile 21.5
  speed reached 60

ENGINE / ROAD SPEED

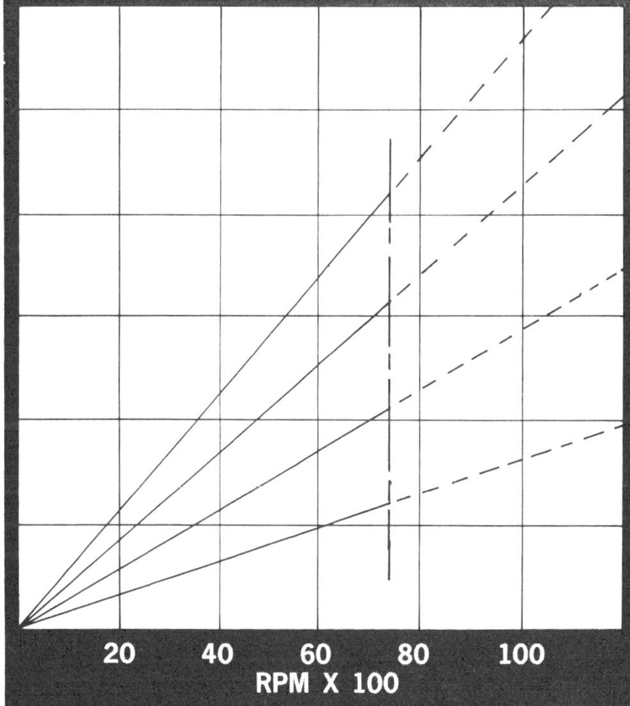

RPM X 100

ACCELERATION

SS 1/4

TIME IN SECONDS

63

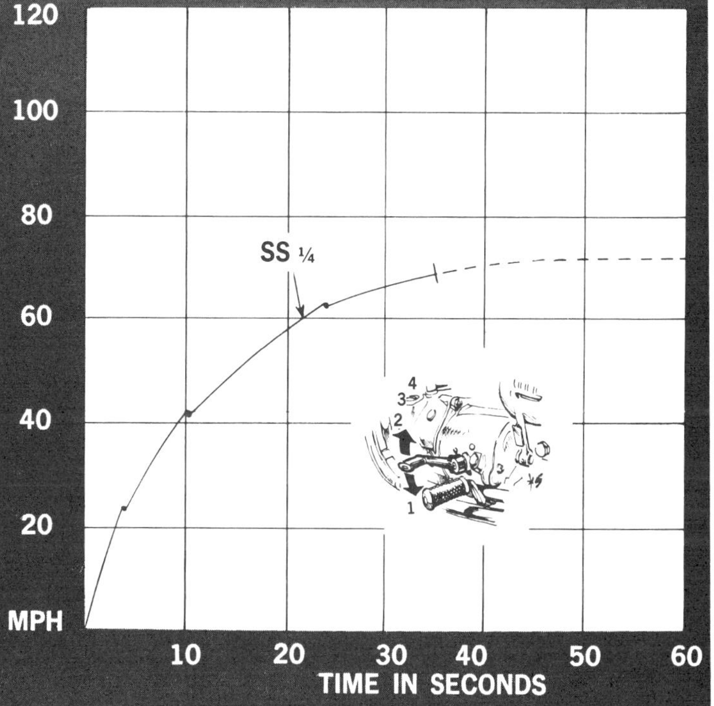

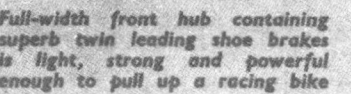

Full-width front hub containing superb twin leading shoe brakes is light, strong and powerful enough to pull up a racing bike

Power pack. Near-side view horizontally opposed motor sh the adequate ground cleara Note kick start at rear of m

UNFORTUNATELY, Rolls Royce advertising men have cornered the " ghost, wraith phantom " market so all that was left to B.M.W. to do was to give letters and nuumbers to their highly-desirable range of machines. Not that it matters really—the fact remains that the Bavarian Motor Works turns out the quietest, smoothest, best-engineered, *nicest* motor-bikes in the world. The fact that they are also the most expensive merely adds to their desirability.

Talk about the iron hand in a velvet glove ! The B.M.W. is so smooth it borders on the sinister, so quietly rapid it approaches the uncanny, so well-engineered one expects it to have a 30-jewel movement instead of the usual engine internals. It's a unique machine.

The first thing you realise when you ride a B.M.W. is that you have just joined the ranks of the motorcycling elite and you must ride accordingly. That miraculously smooth machine insists that you use it in a suitable manner. Gone forever are the roaring nineties—they've suddenly become the purring nineties.

Because make no mistake about it, although the exhaust note is no more obtrusive than an L.E. Velocette, the 600 c.c. R60 touring-sport B.M.W. is a FAST bike. And I received a quick baptism of its handling qualities when I was caught in a cloudburst twenty minutes after collecting it from former T.T. ace " Jock " West at the B.M.W. Concessionaires at Portslade, Brighton. Through all that dreadful weather the big B.M. steered like a train and speed was governed by visibility, not the wet, slippery surface.

SMOOTH, SWIFT, SILENT—THAT'S BILL

LAWLESS' VERDICT ON THE FAMOUS

R.60 B.M.W.

suspension layout is unique ultra-efficient. Look how shock absorber is integral the top loop of the frame

Note the classic angle of brake actuating arm in this shot of off-side of front wheel. Brake lining area is over 28 sq. ins.

Fully enclosed shaft drive is smooth as silk and needs a minimum of maintenance. Large air cleaner is under rear of tank

Another view of shaft drive. Car-type crown wheel and pinion with a needle-bearing universal joint adjusts with wheel movement

Technically, the R60 is a horizontally-opposed twin which turns out a modest 30 b.h.p. at an equally economical 5,800 r.p.m. (The basically similar R69S knocks out 42 brake at 7,000 r.p.m.) This startling difference in output is easily explained—one is a touring bike; the other a sports machine.

The engine housing consists of a one-piece internally stiffened crankshaft bearing cover, gearing cover, magneto and dynamo cowling and a protective cover for the cooling duct connecting the air filter chamber with the generator housing. These are all made from heat-treated lightmetal alloy.

A sectional forged steel crankshaft is fitted with two pressed-in crank pins displaced 180 degrees from each other. The whole assembly has been dynamically balanced with a care that ensures vibrationless running. Oval-section drop forged con rods are mounted on the crank-pins with large roller bearings.

The lubrication system is particularly interesting. A geared oil-pump, driven from the crankshaft by two spur gears, draws oil through a fine mesh filter out of the sump and forces it through channels in the crankshaft housing to the two splash rings on the crankshaft.

Any metal particles in suspension are centrifugally separated and left on the inner circumference of the splash ring, while the cleaned oil enters the con-rod bearings through the hollow crank pins and is then sprayed into the cylinder, pistons, small ends and the camshaft. The splash oil penetrates further through a passage behind the tappets into the push rod guides and flows on to lubricate the rocker arm bearings. It then drains back through borings in the cylinder heads and through an oil-passage press-fitted into each cylinder back into the sump and crankcase.

Oil from the lubrication pump is forced from the oil distribution passage to a spray jet for the spur gears driving the camshaft and to an annular channel around the lower part of each cylinder. Two small holes in each channel provide additional lubrication to the cylinder walls—particularly valuable for cold starting and maximum performance.

If the R60's specification are impressive, the bike's road performance is equally so. While not blindingly fast through the gears—top speeds in the intermediate ratios are 24, 48 and 68—it would cruise all day in the seventies with another 10 m.p.h. on tap if needed. On one slightly downhill gradient I tanked it up to 100 and it was as smooth and vibrationless as ever. It started first kick every time,

Continued on page 93

MOTORCYCLE MECHANICS ROAD TEST No. 85

Vehicle	B.M.W. R60
Engine	600 cc Horizontal twin
Gearbox	4 Speed Unit Construction
Final drive	Fully-enclosed shaft drive

Price new £451 · 13 · 10

GENERAL INFORMATION

Weight	436 lbs
Saddle height	28½ ins
Turning circle	15 ft
Is toolbox lockable	—
Is steering lockable	No
Fuel tank capacity	3¾ galls
Reserve capacity	½ galls
Oil tank capacity	3¾ pints
Gearbox capacity	—
Fuel specified	Regular
Overall consumption	60 mpg
Braking from 30 mph	24 ft
Acceleration 0-60 mph	16 secs

SPEEDS IN GEARS

(tanking)

mph: 110, 100, 90, 80, 70, 60, 50, 40, 30, 20, 10

GEAR: 1 2 3 4 5 6

EQUIPMENT SUPPLIED

STANDARD FITTINGS

Pillion footrests

OPTIONAL EXTRAS

Crash Bars

SPARES PRICES

Engine gasket set	19s 10d
Set valves & guides	63s 8d
Piston with rings	113s 10d
Set of clutch plates	84s 10d
Silencer	210s 1d
Pr Exchange brake shoes	—

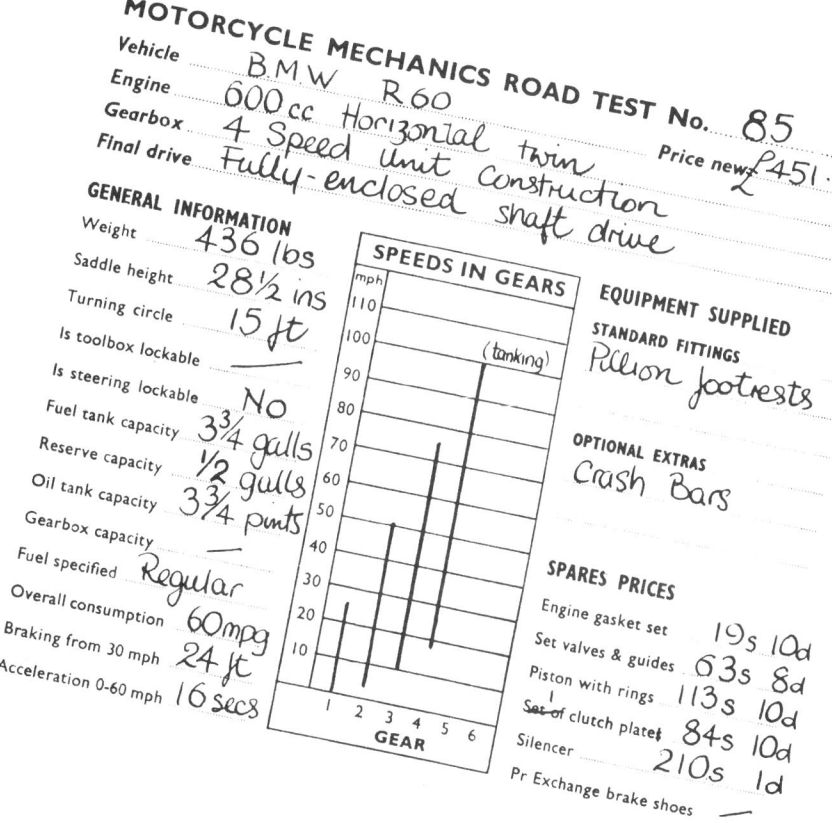

1, Air filter
2, Air intake pipe
3, Bing carburetter
4, Push rod tube
5, Rocker arm
6, Valve spring
7, Piston
8, Con rod
9, Cam follower
10, Camshaft
11, Contact breaker
12, Timing pinion
13, Dynamo
14, Oil filter
15, Oil pump
16, Flywheel

ACROSS THE

BOSWELL and BMW survey the scene at Monitor Pass. Aspen trees, streams, and open meadows remind author of Alpine geography. As usual, the motorcycle performed like a new model, always delivering first-kick starts.

BRING WATER! The Mojave Desert between Barstow and Baker can be threatening to a traveler in mid-summer. Water should be carried and light colored clothes and helmet worn.

MOTORCYCLIST VENTURES INTO
TREACHEROUS TERRITORY

Crossing the great American desert in California, which extends roughly from Mexico to Death Valley, can be a threatening even frightening experience during the summer months of July and August. For a hundred miles at a stretch there is no shade — and no water — no nothing. The unobstructed sun beats down from a clear sky, and heat, reflected from desert sand and roadside boulders bounces off the traveler fit to knock him from his motorcycle.

Better have a canteen full of water and a white helmet to survive such a climate! White shirt and light colored pants help, too.

Yet, how can one enter or leave California headed east or northeast without sampling a portion of its barren hot wastelands? A rider need not worry if his motorcycle is in good shape, if a reasonable speed is maintained, if he is dressed properly, and if a minimum of a quart of water is carried. In case of motor malfunction the light clothing and white helmet ,and canteen of water will assure him of adequate protection until a Highway Patrolman or motorist comes along to lend assistance.

I was out in the middle of this furnace-like country near Barstow (Beechers Corners, to be exact) in August headed for Utah. Temperature was above 100, the wastelands threatened, my motor appeared to be running erratically and too hot, and I began looking for excuses to veer westward to the mountains and call off the trip. Then, into the service station, whose shelter and hospitality I was accepting, came a whole carload of tourists in their air-conditioned car with water boiling from their radiator and their automatic transmission overheating. They looked at me like I was crazy, but I thought, "At least I have Natural air conditioning, and my engine is not boiling, and I have had some experience in desert travel, and I don't think I'm crazier than they;" so I swigged some water from a handy fountain (scrupulously saving my canteen, mind you), started the old BMW with one kick, clanked it into gear and set off down the highway.

About every 50 miles thereafter I stopped where I could find shade, relaxed for a few minutes, drank some water or a cup of coffee. This technique worked satisfactorily, and soon I pulled into Baker, hottest spot this side of Death Valley and just about as remote, except that Highway 15 (Interstate), runs through it. One does not lack for competitive highway companionship.

At this point I knew that the battle with the heat was won; for the highway immediately begins to climb as it leaves this desert crossroads, and finally reaches a respectable 4700 feet. The air is correspondingly cooler at the higher elevations.

However, no sooner did I begin the ascent than the sky clouded over, and a huge black thunder storm moved directly in front of me. I spotted an overpass just in time to pull underneath before the deluge with its ragged gusts of wind struck. In a half hour it had moved westward, and I drove onto the highway with my compass set for Las Vegas.

DESERT TO UTAH

(Above) From near the summit of Monitor Pass the highlands between Gardnerville and Coleville on 395 lie 3,000 feet below. Highway 395 is not visible from this point as it is located close to the foot of this mountain range.

(Right) The eastern shore of beautiful Lake Tahoe near Crystal Bay.

The grade's crest was reached, and I descended into a large lake bed. Gulleys were running full of muddy water from the recent storm, and the road was covered with gravel and mud. Numerous automobiles were stalled with wet engines, or stuck in the silt beside the highway.

Such is the capriciousness of the desert.

I spent the first night at the crest of a long grade in the southwest corner of Utah after polling 525 miles on the speedometer. An old fellow, there, picked a spot for me to sleep underneath some Juniper trees; then took his shovel and smoothed a place for my air mattress and sleeping bag. He was a strange individual who had been savagely burned during the war, and was eking out a bare existence at this remote spot raising bear-hunting dogs for sportsmen. He said that the Indians from a nearby reservation stole his dogs and some of his equipment. He had no electricity, but managed to get along with an old Coleman lantern with delapidated mantles. He was fascinated with my flashlight which I loaned to him until he lit his gas lantern.

I was up before the sun the next morning and getting ready to move when my host arrived to help me pack. After I started my motor I gave him my flashlight, and he said, "God bless you, my friend." Reminded me of the time an old lady in Mexico said to me and Ed Edwards, "Vaya con dios, amigos," which means about the same.

The north side of the grade ushered in a completely new world of scenery. Grey desert reaches were no more. Their places were taken by red clay cliffs eroded into fantastic shapes, and by fertile valleys of irrigated pasture. I was suddenly ejected into the land of the frugal Morman with his neat well-tailored villages, and the strange nether-world of spires, cones and columns of Bryce Canyon and Zion.

Aside from the scenery, the one thing that impressed me most was the huge amount of truck traffic occupying this highway. I would estimate that at least one cross-country truck per 30 seconds roars its way along Highway 15 in Utah. Eventually, something will have to give — will there be special roads for trucks, or will present highways be turned over to them with us ordinary citizens shifting for ourselves as best we can?

Continued on Page **93**

9,000 MILES ... by

Canadian family tours the continent, with exciting stops at Pikes Peak and Loveland Pass, Colorado.

FAIRING was a blessing at high altitudes. Author's BMW was equipped with a Cutlass fairing.

WHITE STEED high in the Grand Tetons. Right cylinder saved author from freezing one night.

CAVALCADE. The author's family; Jim, Ernie, Mary and Barry. This photo was shot at 13,000 feet at Loveland Pass, Colorado. The group skied on that snow in the background.

. . . and every mile of it fun, freedom and thrills . . . from 105 degrees on the Kansas blacktop to 15 degrees over Loveland Pass at midnight . . . and she just kept purring along, my BMWR69S. I had already been to Mexico's west coast from Montreal and back, a couple of years ago on my Harley-Davidson but May 17, 1964 was my son Ernie's birthday and I got him a second-hand BSA 650cc. to go with my BMW. He'd never ridden before, so my wife Mary, I and the two younger boys Jim and Barry, initiated him on our flying field which had a gentle slope. There I started him coasting downhill, motor off, to get balance and feel of brakes; soon he tried it with engine on, then after a couple of trial runs, slipped her into first gear. In a short time, he was running that BSA all over the field like a veteran. One month later, we all took off, BMW, BSA, Mary, Jim, Barry and Audie Jacobs, a silver-haired young grandmother of 52-plus and allround cycle rider, fisherwoman, camper, wood chopper, raconteur and good sport, plus Mary's Olds Starfire, and camping trailer. Montreal to Detroit was an easy first-run for Ernie, although once he did get his front wheel in a soft shoulder and almost flipped . . . but a harder test for a new cycle rider is that snarling hectic swirling traffic on the Edsel Ford thruway coming out of Detroit; however Erine stuck close behind the Olds and got thru o.k. That kind of fast traffic jam is a real challenge to a good bike rider; you've got to be really alert, and with a throttle-twist to a steel steed like ours, you just leave 'em miles behind.

Those U.S. Immigration guys at Detroit like to throw their weight around; Ernie and I would still be waiting there begging to be allowed to tour the United States, if Mary had not come along in the car half-an-hour later and explained to the authorities that these two cyclists, — apparently going for a 6-week trip with hardly any extra clothing, baggage or money — would not really end up being a charge on Uncle Sam, because she had all our extra clothes etc., in the auto.

TROUBLE IN MISSOURI

We sped along No. 94; stopped at Battle Creek and toured the Kellogg Factory, which is a fascinating experience of marvelous efficiency plus free ice-cream! Then south from Kalamazoo and on over to Highway 36 West. Follow the sun, mile after mile. One time in Kansas that sun was obscured with a violent sand-storm of such intensity that our cycles had to lean 20 degrees to port. and once we had to stop in the lee of a house-trailer that had also pulled over for fear of being toppled. We would alternate positions, with no set plan. Sometimes Mary would lead and other times Ernie would be 'way ahead, with the BMW bringing up the rear. Just west of Springfield, Ill., Mary must have been a couple of miles ahead out of sight, and to relieve the monotony, I sped up ahead of the BSA, but after rounding a bend, I did not see him appear; I slowed down and finally BMW and I did a 180. Ten miles back, there was old Ernie sitting dejectedly beside his cycle. His throttle cable had broken at the twist-grip. The only way to get him going was to unsheath the rest of the cable and have him pull it like a conductor on a train, and that was the way we continued to Hannibal, Mo. Just after crossing the Mississippi into town, I

BIKE!

by John Pitt

DEVIL'S PLAYGROUND, Pikes Peak. Auto racer, dust, 10,000 spectators and summer snow combined to make this a highlight of the trip.

FOUR WHEELERS can move too! Huge Crowds watch the action on Pikes Peak.

spied a trooper glancing at the BSA straggling behind with its rider bent over like the hunchback of Notre Dame; being a rider himself, the trooper just said "follow me", and so with police escort, we wended our way to a really fine and cooperative cycle shop. They were closed as it was 6 p.m. but the cop 'phoned the owner, who came flying along in five minutes on his cycle and with two other riders. I left Ernie there in a cycle-jam-session while I retraced my tracks to the Mississippi River to find Mum who, by this time must surely have been 100 miles ahead, or else fractically searching for us. Sure enough, cruising up and down No. 36 from one limit to the other of Hannibal, I saw the Olds and its crew doing the same; we all converged back to cycle shop, where the BSA was repaired. On its way once again the Pitt caravan started out into the setting sun.

At nights we mostly slept in the tent trailer, although once in awhile in motels. Occasionally Mary rode the BSA while Ernie drove the Olds, and of course Mrs. Jacobs cycled at the least excuse. One time Ernie fell asleep riding the BSA, but when his front wheel hit the rough stones on a shoulder he awakened with an awful start and was 'all shook up'

Several hundred miles east of Denver, the highways gradually begin to rise and before you know it, you have gained an altitude of 5000 feet. We got our cycles tuned up at the Fay Myers shop there. I noticed a couple of elderly gents (I hope they don't read this description of themselves) examining my BMW outside. We got to talking and I discovered that they were two attorneys from Indiana, both real old geezers like me (52 years

young) and had ridden their cycles all the way out, with their wives. I'm always especially happy and thrilled to meet the older riders who refuse to be one of the motorist-sheep; there are hundreds of men of my age who yearn to ride a motorcycle but are afraid of criticism and scorn — but let me say to you my friends, — the hell with the critics, and anyway they are either hypocrites who would love to have the courage to ride, or are too darn decrepit to even ride a golf wagon. If you want to enjoy the tremendous exhilaration of riding then just go out and buy yourself a good machine and GO. BEFORE IT IS TOO LATE!!!

FINNED ALUMINUM HAND WARMER

It was here that I gave Ernie my windshield, as I momentarily expected my new Cutlass fairing from California. Actually it did not arrive until ten days later, thus it was that I mighty near froze. Our three vehicles set out from Denver one afternoon to cross Loveland Pass to Dillon. We all rode together until Idaho Springs, then I kept going slower and slower to keep warm, because (A.) I had no windshield, (B.) the sun had set and (C.) the altitude was over 8000'. Pretty soon, they were 50 miles ahead and I was really chilled. Darkness had set in; a restaurant had given me a bundle of newspapers to wrap around my chest under my jacket, but I soon got so numb and my hands were so stiff I couldn't even work the throttle. I pulled over to the side of the road, tottered off BMW and found out that those horizontal cylinders are not just good for vibrationless power — they make

9000 FEET UP! Author and son look down at fine cycling roads and trails in the Colorado mountains near Central City.

9000 MILES (continued)

the most wonderful little stove, whose hot fins I huddled over and caressed until my hands came back to life. Ten minutes of this type of radiant heating thawed me out enough to get almost to the top of the Pass; there once more, amidst howling winds and snow, I took refuge over my cylinder-cum-portable-stove and thus was enabled to proceed to Dillon before rigor mortis set in.

We spent a week around Dillon, Aspen, Leadville (where that fine movie 'The Unsinkable Molly Brown' was filmed) Breckenridge, Frisco, and back over the Pass several times to Denver. One time, taking a hairpin turn near Arapahoe Basin, Ernie saw what he thought were a bunch of tourists waving from the next cliff up, but upon arriving there, he found 18 other cyclists admiring the view; they formed quite a cavalcade from there into Denver. It is not unusual to run into blinding snow-storms in July atop Loveland Pass — the more challenge and fun — just slow down, keep her in 2nd. gear all the time and don't use the front brake. That whole mountainous area is a dream for motorcycling, as the photos show; there is a terrific picturesque road from Idaho Springs to Central City through Virginia Canyon; there, you pass hundreds of abandoned mines and open shafts, with tight turns aplenty; always an adventure to pull over to the roadside (easy with a bike but difficult with an auto) and go exploring. We came across scores of dark mine shafts and entrances plus lots of rusted equipment and once, a whole box of dynamite, but no gold. — yet. The towering cliffs and steep precipices are always better appreciated from a cycle seat, than from an auto. I had the same experience in the mountains of Mexico where cycling is a dream. Here is where a motorcycle shines; you are in much more personal contact, as it were, with the ground and surroundings and with obstacles to battle, like small boulders, side trips across a field, exploring a single trail

in the woods that no car could navigate, etc. Central City itself is another fabulous tourist attraction with old-time honkey-tonk joints, movies of 1920 etc., and thousands of souvenirs. The sidewalks were thick with people jostling and gaping but I imagine that in winter, it is almost abandoned.

PIKES PEAK

The annual road race up Pikes Peak was our goal one week-end. We camped overnight at Castle Rock, an extremely picturesque spot about half-way between Denver and Colorado Springs. Up early next morning, by 9:30 a.m. we had started to climb the long road, with switchbacks, hairpin turns, gravel and dust plus fifteen thousand other vehicles. Of course, as always, the motorcycles are never any problem on a long grade like this, the thicker the traffic and the tighter the turns, — the more the BMW and BSA ate it up, leaving the 4-wheel steaming monsters choking far behind. We all stopped at Devil's Playground, where by 10:30 a.m. there were 10,000 tourists sprawled all over the grass and rocks, waiting to see the big race from this vantage point. (which is the best) This event is really a must, especially for cyclists. We met hundreds of other bike riders up there, from little scooters to the biggest Harleys, and many BMW's. (one was ridden by a U.S. soldier all the way from Munchen, Germany.)

After the race, going down the mountain was a very, very dusty and grimy experience but here again, the cycles could advantageously use the left prohibited lane — until some trooper would frenziedly shout at us to get back into line and what-the-hell did we think-we-were doing anyway; of course once out of sight around the next bend, we'd pop into that fast lane again. Actually it was ridiculous to force all vehicles to use the right lane only, because there was not one single auto that came up the mountain in that left side. It took our two cycles about ½ hour to get down to Colorado Springs, in contrast to the autos, that got into a most formidable traffic hassle due to this right-lane-only enforcement. It took Mary five hours to meet us in the town below!

To Be Continued

9,000 MILES

... by BIKE!

Early morning .... scene in Wyoming, as Mary Pitt with sons Barry (middle) and Jim face breakfast ...e camera.

From Denver we headed north up through Cheyenne and Laramie, Wyoming. Peeling along the highway one day, we came across not one, not two, but dozens of small packages strewn across the road. Close investigation proved them to be little tins of roofing cement, with hundreds of flat-head nails scattered all over. A passing truck had lost part of his load. Motorists went whizzing by as we picked the nails up, but no one seemed to get a flat.

FRONT WHEELS AND STUFFED SHARK

We stopped at a cycle shop at Casper, Wyo. for minor repairs; as usual, the owner himself was a rider, but he was also a master *taxidermist* and we'd find ourselves wandering around the shop between handlebars and owl heads, front wheels and stuffed shark, moose antlers and alligators hanging precariously over Hondas and Harleys! Think it was there that we got a few quarts of good Castrol oil.

CLOVER THE KILLER ESCAPES

Our first goal was Jackson Hole, Wyo., which is the "westernest" town I've ever seen; it is really wonderful. Rimmed by the Grand Tetons, it oozes western hospitality, and every evening at 7, right on the village square, all traffic is stopped, while the local posse on cow-ponies, chase a notorious bad-man named Clover the Killer until

they finally capture him, with guns ablazin' from all sides, roof-tops and other vantage points. After a two-minute trial (over the P.A. system), they finally string him up, but he and his desparado gang shoot their way out to freedom and gallop off up the highway—with tourists mouths agape—until tomorrow evening!

Our first night there, we camped at the Gros Ventre camp ground about ten miles out of town, but them there mosquitoes and black flies outnumbered us, so next morning we moved cycles, car and trailer back to town where a wonderful guy named Burns Ferrin, who owns the Cache Creek Ranch let us camp behind his corrals, next to a cold clear stream. We exchanged our steel steeds for real live ones for a couple of days and had a ball, ridin' into town, mixin' with the real cowpokes and enjoying the whole atmosphere. After exploring the new Jackson Hole Ski Development which is going to be the biggest ski area in the U.S.A., we leaned our cycles in the direction of Yellowstone Park.

FRUSTRATED FISHERMEN

Those bears are fun to watch from the safety of an auto window, but on a cycle they kinda get a bit scary. Bears and bikes tried to outstare each other, but we kept our cycles in first gear and ready to pop if mister bear

by John Pitt

Concluding last month's exciting tour story, the author and his family complete the big circle back to Montreal, Canada...

tried to investigate this new beast. One lake had big signs "Fish for Fun". Yeh. Only allowed to use barbless hooks and, if any fish was chump enough to get hooked onto your line, you had to throw him back. Some fun! However at another spot, we got 22 trout and had us a real fry that night.

Once, out of nowhere, we suddenly came across a fantastic miniature Grand Canyon called "Hell's Half Acre" which aptly described the hugh craters, eroded gullies and formidable rock formations. Very nice souvenir store and restaurant there too. The next town we ran through had a population of ten. Once, separated by a couple of miles, Ernie pulled over at a road-repairing block to allow the oncoming traffic to pass; the flag-man, seeing his Quebec license, opined as how it sure was a funny coincidence 'cos another motorcyclist had passed

that-a-way about half-an-hour before with the same kind of license. Ernie told him that it was his Dad!

COOL, CLEAR WATER

Sometimes we hit torrential rain-storms; when you see them coming far off, the best place to race to is for cover under an overpass; here you could either sit it out, or at least change into a rain suit without getting drenched. Most of the time though, it was hot, and spinning along some of those mid-west baking black-tops, we used to soak our shirts under service-station hoses and then shiver with the rapid evaporation. Jim and Barry, when they weren't riding tandem on the cycles, would fill up empty pop bottles with water and, riding in the Olds they'd sprinkle this water into the air just in front of our cycles; this made a good coolant too. One small roadside parking area in Wyoming was so awfully hot, there just didn't

LEFT — At another Wyoming campsite, the Pitt's swapped cycles for horses. Barry gives last-minute instructions here, while dad's BMW stands protected from the intermittent rain by plastic cover. BELOW — Author and son Ernie near the top of Berthoud Pass, Colorado.

COLORADO COUNTRY — Mary Pitt and Audie Jacobs (facetiously called The Cycling Grandmothers by author Pitt!) relax against a backdrop of breath-taking scenery and challenging roads typical of this region.

seem to be any relief until, wandering down a small path, we came across the most beautiful and tempting stream of cold drinking water, pulsating through a pipe drilled into a rock ledge.

FEW PROBLEMS

In all of our 9,000 miles, we had no accidents (except once when I turned over on a hairpin turn in the snow at Loveland Pass). The BSA, being second-hand, did develop problems, like the night the generator went out and Mary had to guide Ernie with her headlights for 20 miles, and a few other incidents.

Once, when I was alone, and had just pulled into the shade of a big, big tree to eat some fruit, I suddenly could not believe my eyes. There it was right in front of me! My rear tire was slowly going flatter and flatter by the second! On this grassy spot it had picked up the only bent nail around. It would have been a back-breaking job to take this wheel off and get a passing auto to take it and me to the nearest town; not only was the heat intense, but I had worked for hours fitting my carrier and saddle bags over the mudguard and it would have been a long hard job to remove them here. So, the only alternative was to wheel my BMW onto highway, point same toward the next town, pump tire furiously, jump on quickly, ride fast for five miles before it went soft, repeat procedure, on and off, on and off, until, after 21 miles I saw a big "Texaco" sign; I'll never forget the welcome shade in that cool garage, the clean concrete floor, locating the nail and puncture and the ease of patching the leak without removing the wheel. It was worth the pumping and the jumping!

NOTHING BEATS MOTORCYCLING

In conclusion, I cannot recommend too strongly a long, long motorcycle ride to cure you of all ills. You get used to the first fatigue; you wiggle around, you change positions of your feet—sometimes 'way up front on the crash-guards, and sometimes flat out behind, you learn to duck when a 60-m.p.h. semi-trailer juggernaut passes you, and you thank Uncle Sam and American ingenuity for those superhighways, those super service-stations and their clean restrooms, the fine roadside restaurants. Soon, you begin to appreciate the soaring power at your fingertips, unbeatable maneuverability, freedom of movement and the low gas consumption of your flying steed. Any fat-head can drive an auto, but it is that extra challenge, that exhilaration, that zest for living which makes motorcycle touring the pleasure it is. And remember, it's later than you think!

ANYONE FOR CHILE?

My next goal on the BMW is Santiago, Chile, where the best snow-skiing in the world is to be found in July. Anyone wanting to come along (on a cycle of course) will be most welcome. Just drop me a note. END

BMW Twins

Riders'
Report
NUMBER
THIRTEEN

Collated by
MIKE EVANS

THE best motor cycle in the world. Fact or exaggeration? It is all a question of what you mean by best. The BMW may not be perfect—but then, is any motor cycle come to that? The fact which emerges from this 1½-million mile test is that the BMW is only a couple of steps behind its reputation. It may not be as good as it is often made out to be—but it is probably better than most other machines.

Bee-Emming, more so than riding any other machine, is largely a matter of taste. Either you like 'em or you don't. Good as it undoubtedly is, the BMW is not everyone's idea of the ideal motor cycle—and not everyone's idea of the ideal price!

While many reporters point out that the BMW does not fully deserve its acquired reputation—enhanced, no doubt, by the duty-inflated price in this country—the majority learn to live with the few disadvantages and wouldn't change their flat twin for anything else. Take Mr Average BMW owner. He is aged 33 and has 14 years' experience behind him. In fact, if riding careers of reporters were to be placed end to end they would stretch back to AD466! A total of 1,500 years of experience—they should know what they are on about!

Very surprising is the extreme international flavour of the test. Letters have been received from Australia, the United States, Bermuda, Holland, Denmark, Sweden and, of course, Germany.

Machines covered in this report are mainly the R69S sports six-hundred and the touring R60 version. Five-hundred R50s and, to an even lesser extent, R50S sportsters, are poorly represented. All machines manufactured since 1960 were eligible—but the average year of manufacture of contributors' bikes is 1964.

Performance

MAXIMUM speeds are not outstanding. But when the weight of the machines is considered, their performance is surprisingly good.

A very important point for anyone weighing up relative performance is how close cruising speed is to maximum.

With the BMW it is very close indeed. These twins will cruise effortlessly at near maximum and often put up far better averages over long distances than potentially faster machines.

Our figures show the R69S to be capable of a genuine 105 mph; this should be obtainable from any R69S—and some owners have managed 108 or 110 mph. A couple of claims —116 and 125 mph—are so far out that they are discounted.

The touring version, the R60, is 10 mph slower at 95 mph, while another gap of 10 mph separates this model from the smaller, 500 cc R50. Sidecar outfits reported on are all R60s, and top whack here is 76 mph.

Says 40-year-old Denis Saunders of Chessington, Surrey: "The performance of my 1963 R60 is exceptional and deceptive. Exceptional for such a soft tourer to have so good a performance, and deceptive in the ease, smoothness and silence with which it accomplishes this.

"Cruising speed is anything up to maximum and can be maintained all day—the motor is virtually unburstable."

Another R60 owner, Ivor Lawrence of Beeston, is of like mind: "No matter how long or hard my outfit is driven the motor at the end of the trip has the same quiet tickover as when I started. It never seems to get out of breath at all."

Part of the reason for this unburstability and high cruising speed is the turbine smoothness expected from a well-balanced and well-cooled layout such as that of the horizontally opposed BMW engine. It can be buzzed in all gears —and, indeed, the machine thrives on such treatment.

As would be expected, the R69S is not so super-tractable as the R60. Yet it is probably very good in this respect when compared with more mundane machinery.

Starting

Exceptionally good, report the majority. One or two prods after tickling the twin Bing carburettors is sufficient in all weathers.

"Starting is first class. It always fires first kick whatever the conditions. I never have to use the air control, not even below 32 deg Fahrenheit, and she idles immediately with never a falter." Denis Saunders speaking.

Fuel Consumption

AS WITH any twin-carburettor machine, fuel consumption is not a star point. R60 owners can expect an overall consumption of 60 mpg solo or 48 mpg sidecar. The R69S is good for 55 mpg in solo trim.

However, as many point out, when using the machine's potential to the full—and BMWs tempt riders to this—the consumption rises steeply. J. M. Walker of South Africa writes with a strong Afrikaans accent: "My 1965 R69S is a real gas guzzler. Mit der fat vrou on der buddy seat giffs aboudt 30 mpg at 100 plus, against der cape howlers (vind). Und den comes der brainwave, der *fairing*. Now mit fat vrou und suitcase against same vind giffs 40 mpg at 100 plus on two-thirds throttle."

Handling

FOR SOME odd reason BMWs have a bad reputation for handling. Yet only one or two reporters, like John Neave, are dissatisfied. Most think the BMW, in spite of its weight, is well up to scratch.

The low centre of gravity of the flat engine provides a great degree of stability. The much-talked-about torque reaction is a story straight out of Grimm or Aesop.

The influence on corners is something that is noticeable only on first acquaintance with a BMW. A new rider can adjust himself to the BM within ten or twenty miles and from then on he has no bother whatsoever.

Nevertheless, although riding comfort and braking are excellent, handling *could* be bettered.

Says Björn Agnarson of Karlstadt, Sweden: "Being a real heavyweight fitted with an Earles-type front fork, it behaves accordingly. It does not like rippled curves and you have to allow a good safety margin when cornering."

Several mention that the front end becomes light when a passenger and laden panniers are carried.

Left: Most reporters rate handling as good—but not perfect. Here Mike Evans tries his R60 for cornering style

Below: The sporty R69S can be detected mainly by its two-rib rocker-box covers and the massive air cleaner on top of the gear box. Right: The R50 and R60 engines have six rocker-box ribs and an air cleaner incorporating a choke lever. Also, they are slightly narrower than the sports version

Braking

"BEAUTIFUL, both front and rear. I particularly appreciate the Earles fork which does not dive on hard front-wheel braking. No complaints, only praise." That's from Joseph L. Katz, a space programmer, of De Land, Florida.

Confirmation comes from Bob Pilkington, 32, of Royston, Herts: "Without doubt the most powerful and yet the most controllable of any motor cycle I have ridden. The twin-leading-shoe front brake is immensely powerful."

Transmission

"WHAT is there to say?" asks David Dumble of Victoria, Australia. "All you ever do is change the gear-box, shaft and crown-wheel-housing oils every 8,000 miles and check them occasionally. Dead smooth at all times—and there is nothing to adjust."

While the transmission is utterly reliable and sturdy, the gear box annoys most riders. Clonky changes are the rule.

This is caused, to a large extent, by the engine-speed clutch and gear box input shaft. In addition, the progressive-action twistgrip makes synchronization of revs difficult.

Nevertheless, the BMW gear box is something you learn to live with. Upward changes are best made slowly —allowing plenty of time for the revs to sort themselves out.

When changing down a hefty handful of twistgrip is necessary to obtain the sort of blip normal with any conventional machine. Even then, there is a clonk as the cogs are engaged. A way round the problem is to double declutch —cumbersome but effective.

In spite of the rough action, however, the box is sturdy and there is nothing to indicate that it suffers from mechanical troubles.

Electrics

"LIGHTING, with a good dip which does not dazzle others, is good enough for 70 mph cruising. The horn is a real instrument and not a pip-squeak affair as on many machines." Chris Haddon's view is indicative of the general feeling.

The Bosch electrical equipment is thoroughly reliable and of excellent quality.

One snag mentioned by several reporters is that the Bosch sparking-plug covers allow bad shorting in rain. Many, like David Dumble, have replaced the standard metal-shrouded caps by Lodge rubber ones.

Detail Finish

FROM twin-leading-shoe front brake to the distinctive circular tail lamp, the BMW is a quality built machine.

Our Test View		R50 (September 1963)	R69S (March 1961)
Highest One-way Speed		92 mph	108 mph
Mean Maximum Speed		90 mph	104 mph
Standing Quarter-mile	(speed)	75 mph	88 mph
	(time)	17s	15s
Fuel Consumption	(30 mph)	110 mpg	100 mpg
	(40 mph)	84 mpg	90 mpg
	(50 mph)	68 mpg	75 mpg
	(60 mph)	64 mpg	66 mpg
Braking (from 30 mph to rest)		28ft	28ft

Bob Coley of Small Heath gets 70 mph out of his 1960 R60 and BSA sidecar. Fuel consumption is only 50 mpg—but that extra-large German tank helps cut down stops on long journeys

The enamel is universally acclaimed, although some are dissatisfied with a poor standard of chrome work.

Typifying the attention to detail is the toolkit. Listen to David Dumble: "You get a set of first-quality chrome vanadium spanners to fit nearly everything, a set of feelers, good pliers and even a puncture repair outfit with two tyre valves, all in a neat tool roll. There is even a BMW-monogrammed dust-cloth and a lapel badge. British manufacturers, please copy."

Riding Comfort

OF above-average standard, as will be seen from the table of percentages.

Brian Smith, 24, of Appleton, Cheshire, says that with

Here's a smart R69S in Albuquerque, New Mexico. Owner Peter Betz has fitted a large-capacity fuel tank, Avon fairing and Craven panniers

the fully adjustable footrests and alternative handlebar mounting positions, the riding position can be adapted to suit anyone.

However, the BMW usually demands a slightly forward lean of its rider—and Eric Springall, for one, objects. The riding position, he says, is the one fault with the BMW. The too-bent-knees and weight-on-wrists attitude of the BMW rider has to be got used to.

The dualseat is extremely

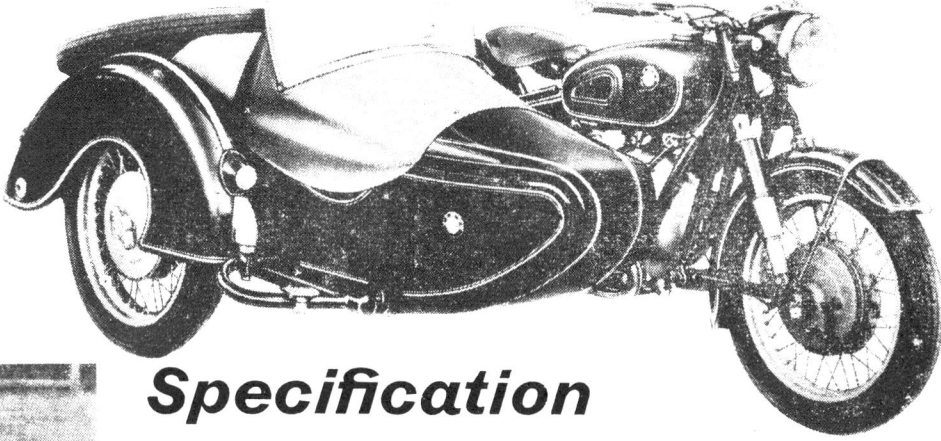

Classic lines of a BMW and Steib—the perfect outfit, according to many. Sidecar outfits like this are used extensively by the German ADAC, equivalent to our AA or RAC

Specification

comfortable, and the suspension irons out the bumps in true Rolls-Royce fashion.

Reliability

"**THE** machine can be caned unmercifully with no protest whatsoever." Brian Smith.

"My 1960 R60, which I have owned since new, has done 60,000 miles and has proved thoroughly reliable." Norman Sharp of Sowerby Bridge, Yorks.

"The only mechanical trouble I have had with any of them at any time is that the rear main bearing of the last one died after 23,000 miles. It gave due warning.

"I also had a little bother with plugs on the R60 when riding to Australia and back!" Eric Springall is a top-line

BMW enthusiast and, as you have seen, thinks nothing of visiting the antipodes on his bike!

It is the nonchalant way in which Eric takes BMW reliability for granted that is the outstanding feature of the above three quotations.

The average BMW twin is reliable—and comment could be left at that.

But since no machine is perfect, it is only to be expected that one or two reporters have suffered uncharacteristic troubles. Some have had repeated (and with the Bee-Emm, expensive) troubles right from new.

Buying a BMW is no guarantee of trouble-free motor cycling. But it is probably the best form of insurance you can take out at the present time. Major engine breakdowns are very rare, and

usually occur only after the sort of mileage that would have reduced lesser breeds to the scrap heap.

Even minor repairs can cost a great deal of money—as any BMW owner will confirm. Parts are expensive and advanced maintenance requires special tools.

One common moan is that the silencers—costing over £10 each—corrode from inside and are ready for discarding within 12 to 24 months.

Reports Denis Saunders: BMs aren't suitable for town transport. Because of the low operating temperature of the engine the corrosive acid products of combustion condense inside the silencers and rot everything. We get through a pair of silencers every six to nine months.

However, the factory acknowledge that their

machines won't reach proper working temperature if ridden at 30 mph in top gear. First and second are the only gears to use in town—and the absolute smoothness of the bikes makes this possible.

If the machine is ridden as it is intended—and as most Germans ride it—the silencer trouble is much minimized.

Many people are put off by the initial cost of a BMW. But the machine lasts so long that even a five-year-old (at about £200) is still a good buy.

Service

"**THOUGH** the cost of spares may be higher than for British equivalents, bits are readily available," says Robert Freeman of Hatfield.

As he says, the price of spares is in proportion to the

original cost of the machine. Good BMW service is not available all over the country.

Most owners seem to have patronized MLG Motor Cycles in London—and they have been well satisfied. Several mention favourably another Shepherds Bush specialist, Ron Perkins.

Accessibility

FOR routine maintenance, marvellous. But for major overhauls, difficult. That is the sum of opinion. Since the BM is so reliable, however, accessibility for big jobs is not over-important.

Everything that needs to be got at regularly is easily reached. Tappets, contact breaker, sump drain plug, gear box and final drive level plugs —all are readily accessible.

Sidecar

"THE R60 must be the best sidecar machine available. Its lusty, smooth pulling makes driving a joy." Bob Pilkington speaking.

No one objects to this view. The R60 is admirably suited to sidecar work. The steering is light and positive—by virtue of the readily adjustable front fork trail.

One snag to fitting a chair is the fact that to lower the gearing it is necessary to change the crown wheel and pinion in the final-drive housing. The cogs alone cost nearly £19 and when various oil seals, a new speedo head and new springs are taken into account, a conversion costs about £30.

Naturally, however, sidecar gearing can be specified as original equipment on a new machine.

Overall View

"IT IS so easy to gild the lily," reports Denis Saunders, "but this is a beautiful motor cycle. Your readers should be warned that once they possess a Bee-Emm they will never be happy or contented with any other make.

"They will want to sell the furniture, dress the wife in rags and starve the kids in order to buy spares and replacements rather than return to an old banger."

As you are aware, this Munich-built twin inspires enthusiasm of the most noble order. It *is* good. And critics should bear in mind the fact that in Germany, without crippling import duties, it costs no more than one of our six-fifties does over here. A sobering thought, surely.

The machine is probably not worth the money asked for it in England. After all, £600 to £700 is a lot of lolly.

But since value, like beauty, is in the eye of the beholder, enthusiasts are prepared to pay for what they consider to be the ultimate available today.

"Extremely smooth, turbine-like performance"—that's the quality admired most by Mike Norman of Chippenham. "I know I can go from A to B and back again week in, week out, as long as I fill it with petrol.

"I don't have to stop to adjust anything. I'm not knocking the British machines, but I have ridden both and if I ever do buy another bike it will be a BMW."

Eric Springall sums up: "I think that riding a BMW makes one behave oneself like a little gent. Even the most extrovert of us seems to realize that by precise, courteous and above all, silent

riding—which the BMW almost insists on—he's putting himself on a plane infinitely above the proletarian masses!"

Contributor Harvey Hoar, who is a bit of a German scholar besides being a BMW enthusiast, adds the final touch, appropriately, in the mother tongue:

"Begeistert durch die Landschaft flitzt,

"Der, der auf einer BMW sitzt!"

which, roughly translated, means that he who sits on a BMW "flits" enthusiastically through the countryside. Seconded by all!

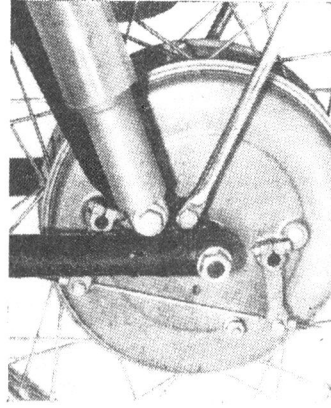

Praise from all quarters for the powerful twin-leading-shoe front brake—one of the star features of the BMW twins

---

PERCENTAGE VOTE

■ After sending in their reports, readers were asked to complete a questionnaire in which they answered specific questions according to the formula good, middling or poor.

In calculating these figures we have allowed two points for good and one point for middling. Poor got nothing.

The marks below are given as percentages of the total possible marks.

	R69S	R50/ R60	R60 Sidecar		R69S	R50/ R60	R60 Sidecar
ACCELERATION	75	68	77	QUALITY OF FINISH	84	90	90
FLEXIBILITY	83	96	98	LIGHTING	88	90	86
SMOOTHNESS	98	99	93	HORN	76	83	83
STARTING	89	92	92	OTHER ELECTRICS	92	96	96
OIL TIGHTNESS	97	97	97	TOOL KIT	92	90	90
RELIABILITY	97	99	88	SPARES FROM CONCESSIONAIRES	58	72	72
CLUTCH	75	75	86	SPARES FROM DEALER	80	82	82
GEAR BOX	48	56	43				
DELIVERY TUNE	56	88	88				
ACCESSIBILITY	86	93	98	OVERALL MARK	84	88	89
HANDLING	78	85	92				
FRONT SUSPENSION	92	93	95	GOOD BUY? (PER CENT YES)	97	94	96
REAR SUSPENSION	98	95	98				
SMOOTHNESS OF CONTROLS	90	93	98				
RIDING POSITION	84	90	91	WOULD YOU BUY ANOTHER? (PER CENT YES)	95	90	91
BRAKES	94	94	93				
MUDGUARDING	97	95	95				
WORKMANSHIP	100	97	97				

■ FAIR SECONDHAND PRICES (for machines in average condition)—1960 R60, £190 (R50, £182; R69S not in production). 1961 R60, £230 (R50, £220; R69S, £260). 1962 R60, £276 (£266, £314). 1963 R60, £328 (£316, £372). 1964 R60, £386 (£372, £440).
NEW PRICES: R50 not fixed; R60, £597 10s 5d; R69S, £694 9s 9d. (These new, higher prices came into effect on January 1 and will affect secondhand values).

The stately handlebar layout of all Bee-Emms. On the left-hand side are the horn button and dip switch while opposite numbers on the twistgrip side are for headlight flasher and indicators. The sturdy Hella indicators are clearly visible from front and rear

BMW R60

Tool kit compartment is located in fuel tank unit.
Note excellent sparkplug cover.

Deep, comfortable dual seat is
optional. Note protected driveline.

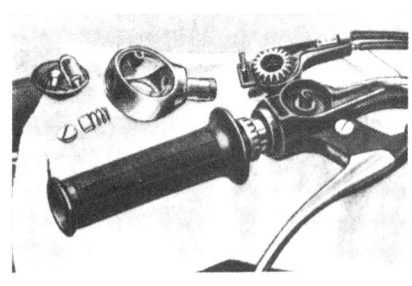

Precision throttle
assembly utilizes gears
as well as cable.

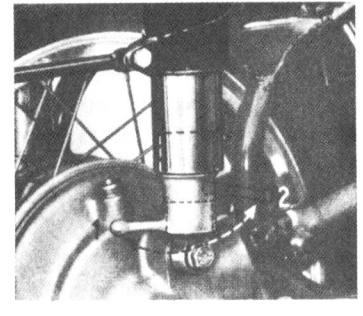

Rear suspension units are 2-way
adjustable by hand; no tools needed.

There is only one way to fully understand the meaning of the many tales about the luxuriousness of the BMW; ride one! Its reputation as the two-wheeled counterpart of the world's most expensive automobiles may only be appreciated by those who have had the opportunity to twist the throttle and sail smoothly down the road.

Smooth is the key word in describing the R60. While many large capacity motorcycles are noted for their acceleration and top speed, the BMW is built for the rider desiring comfort and reliability above all. That is not to say that the BMW is slow. It will cruise at any practical highway speed and will accelerate as fast or faster than most vehicles, although it is no match for the wilder American or European models. (Another BMW, however, the R69S, is considerably faster than our test bike.)

The primary factor contributing to the BMW smoothness of ride is the horizontally opposed twin engine. This design inherently fights vibration, as each motion is opposed by an opposite equalizing motion from the other cylinder. Also, many of the centrifugal forces at work within the engine are directed horizontally making for a smoother operation than occurs with a vertical engine. In addition to the inherent advantages of an opposed twin, the BMW is manufactured with great precision and balancing is given great attention. It goes without saying that a well balanced engine runs smoothly, regardless of design.

Besides the unique engine design, the other major different feature is the driveshaft. Although far more complex than the conventional chain drive, this BMW "trademark" provides an efficient, silent power transmission and adds to the sophistication and prestige of the bike. Chains are a major maintenance problem on motorcycles. The driveshaft eliminates these problems and is generally troublefree. In the event that repair is necessary,

however, much expense would be incurred with this setup. The construction is quite similar to an automobile differential.

With the design differences come a few changes in operation and appearance. Most notable, of course, are the protruding cylinders which never fail to create conversation among motorcyclists. Those who have had little experience with this type of engine layout consider it a handicap and a nuisance. Our experience proved otherwise. The protruding cylinders in no way hamper the machine's handling. Scraping the cylinders on the ground while cornering is so unlikely that it is unworthy of consideration. Perhaps an exception to this would be in road racing, but we doubt if even then there would be such a problem. On the other side of the coin, the cooling capabilities of such an arrangement are superior to any other design. A cooling stream of air is constantly directed to the exhaust system. An unexpected feature is the fact that the rider's feet receive a warm flow of air from the cylinder, most welcome on a cold night, but a hindrance in hot weather.

The kick-starter arrangement is unlike that of a vertical engine. The lever moves vertically, perpendicular to the engine. This is somewhat difficult to become accustomed to. It is necessary to raise the leg quite high to place the foot on the lever. Starting can be accomplished from on or off the bike. The legend about BMW's first kick starts was fully borne out on our test bike. It was necessary, however, to be sure the fuel tap was shut off when parking on the side stand to prevent flooding and fuel leakage.

In spite of the R60's easy starting, we would consider an electric starter a welcome addition that would be in keeping with the luxurious aspects of the vehicle.

The projecting cylinders pose a minor parking problem in that

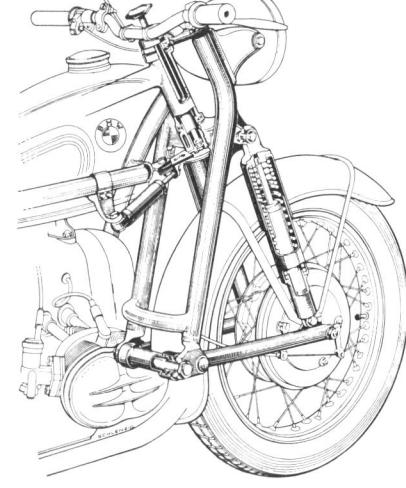

Front Suspension, Fork and
Hydraulic Steering Damper

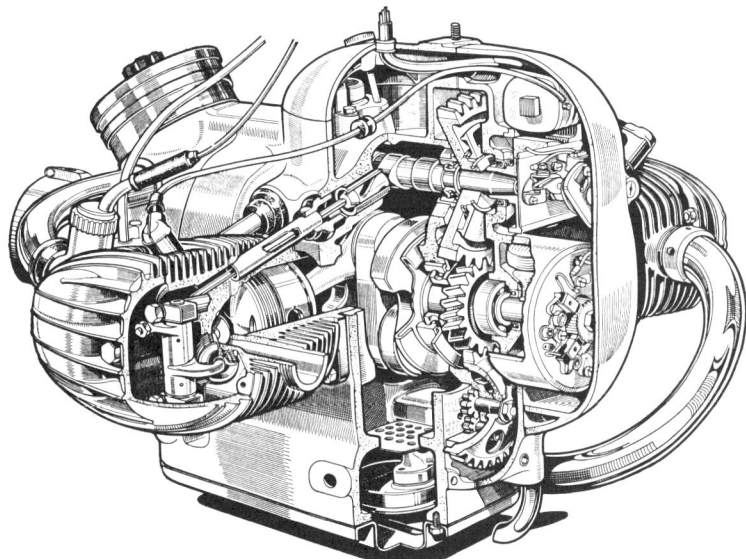

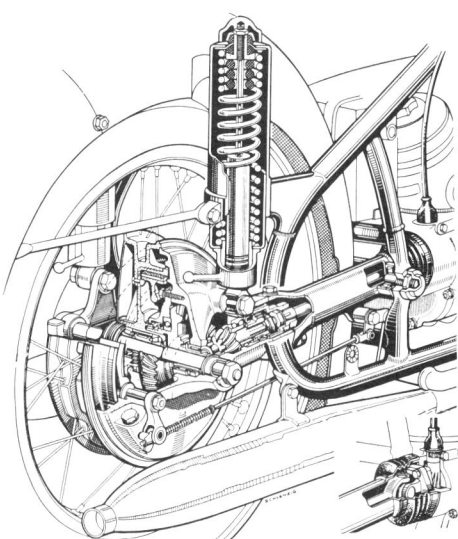

Rear-axle Drive and Suspension

the sidestand may be used only while the rider is off the bike since it is tucked under the frame beneath the lefthand cylinder. Several times we mounted the machine only to remember that the sidestand was down. This necessitated dismounting to fold the stand.

Once underway the immediate strong impression is of quiet, smooth power. The bike is so quiet, in fact, that most auto drivers will not hear you approaching. Cornering is a real pleasure on this bike. Even sharp, tight turns are effortlessly negotiated. The rider is readily aware of the feeling of security that this machine provides. There is little chance of the rear wheel sliding even in the sharpest turns at high rpm.

Freeway cruising is the type of riding where the R60 really shines. Comfortable cruising at 70 mph and faster is routine, with full control and no handling problems. Nighttime riding is aided by an excellent lighting system.

Seating is soft for both rider and passenger, although we felt that rider position could be improved with a lower seat.

Braking is excellent as might be expected. We found the throttle control to be too stiff on our test machine, but quite probably this can be adjusted. An excellent steering damper provides ample flexibility in that department.

Our total impression of the R60 was that this is truly a precision-built motorcycle intended for the serious, experienced rider. It's built to last, and for that reason parts and labor costs for repairs would be high. The important thing to consider here is, however, that this machine will hold up for a very long time without major repairs, and with only a minimum of routine maintenance. With this in mind the BMW rider can enjoy many seasons of carefree, comfortable riding, whether it be to and from work or across the continent. ◀

SPECIFICATIONS
BMW R60

Engine type	Opposed twin, 4-stroke, OHV
Displacement	590cc
Bore	72cc
Stroke	73cc
Compression ratio	7.5:1
Horsepower	30 @ 5800 rpm
Carburetion	2 Bing 24mm
Lubrication	forced feed-centrifugal
Ignition	Bosch mag, battery
Gearbox	4-speed, integral with engine
Gear ratios	4.171:1, 2.725:1, 1.938:1, 1.54:1
Clutch	Sliding dog
Driveline	Universal driveshaft in oil bath
Tires	3.50" x 18" front & rear
Fuel tank	4.5 gal., including ½ gal. reserve
Suspension, front	Leading link
Suspension, rear	Swing arm
Brakes	Alloy full width drums; 28 .2 sq. in. lining area
Frame	Welded duplex-tube steel
Wheelbase	55.7"
Ground clearance	5.3"
Instrumentation	120 mph speedometer, neutral indicator light, batt. chg. light. No tach.
Weight	436 lbs.
Overall length	83.6"
Overall width	26"
Overall height	38.6"
Top speed (claimed)	90 mph
List price	$1260 f.o.b. New York

(Higher in west. Dual seat optional, add $25)

IF A CARTOONIST were to draw a caricature of the BMW opposed-twin he would probably conceive of it as a low-flying one-man cargo plane, skimming along just above the road surface, using its horizontal cylinders as stubby wings. The Bee-Em is a traveling man's machine and this month we renew our acquaintance with the "travelingest" one of the series — the 593cc R69S.

Bayerisch Moteren Werke (Bavarian Motor Works) makes two motorcycles in the 600cc range — the R60 and the R69S. The R69S is the punchier of the two, with 9.5:1 compression (instead of the R60's 7.5:1), bigger carburetors and slightly more radical cam timing, giving a peak horsepower figure of 42 DIN at 7,000 rpm, rather than 30 at 5,800, as is the case with the R60. Just because the R69 has an "S" in its name doesn't mean that one is buying into a fireball solo machine. It must be remembered that BMW does yeoman service pulling a sidecar, particularly in Europe; hence the popularity of the low-rev, low-compression, regular gas R60. The R69S must be regarded as an attempt, pure and simple, to add a few more beans to an essentially conservative machine which filled a great need in the 80-cent-a-gallon economy of Europe long before it ever captured the fancy of the two-wheeled vagabonds in America.

One would wonder how this massive-looking, non-sporting Sport built such a fantastic legend for itself among the far-flung touring clan. Perhaps one must ask the seasoned traveler what he wants in a motorcycle for touring. First, he wants reliability, for he is laying his health and peace of mind on the line by daring to venture far afield without a roof over his head. It is obvious that BMW has that attribute; it just begins to get broken in when many of its like-sized brethren start to fold up. Secondly, he wants a big machine with plenty of reserve power, one that will cruise all day at the legal limit (or higher if nobody's looking). Bee-Em has that attribute in all its big-bore models; the R69S has it in spades and boils along happily at just over 100 mph.

To say that the BMW is big is to put things too simply, and somewhat grossly. Those 480 pounds are gracefully assembled and it looks like nothing could break them or keep them from their destiny. Few motorcycles can boast the attention to detail found on the BMW, from the mirror-like black finish of painted components to the fine contrasting white striping on fenders and tank. All aluminum castings throughout the machine, even the larger ones, are of very high quality and fit with precision. An indication of how well they fit can be determined from the fact that no oil leaks whatsoever could be found during any of our tests. This would help explain why one rarely sees a dirty BMW.

The makers obviously put more importance on longevity and durability than on lightness, as heavy gauge steel is used on all sheet metal parts and the various sizes of tubing that go into making up a complete motorcycle. In the case of the wide double-loop frame, the tubing changes gauge as it passes from a highly stressed area to one that carries lighter loads. Large diameter tubing is found particularly in the main cradle, in the

front Earles-type fork down tubes and around the steering head. At the rear, the cradle continues beyond the normal double-loop rear extremity to a point just ahead of the rear suspension units. Formed sheet metal tabs extend from the side members to support the bottom of the suspension sleeves.

The front forks are of the true Earles type, just as Ernie Earles felt forks should be when he first designed them more than 15 years ago. We see many derivations of the Earles pattern but there is still nothing much wrong with the original layout; it certainly keeps the front end stable under heavy braking. To minimize front end wiggle, BMW has installed a small-diameter hydraulic steering damper between the lower fork crown and a bracket from the frame, just below the gas tank. This miniature shock absorber has heavy damping both ways and tends to keep the front end pointed in the intended direction. Overall appearance of the front fork assembly leaves little doubt as to its robustness. However, it is not clumsy in any way; the Bee-Em floats along very easily.

It is a marvel that the makers can get the R69S engine to turn over so fast, so smoothly. While 7,000 rpm is conservative in these days of the "buzz bomb," it is probably the limit of reliability for an opposed twin of this size (BMW does manage to squeeze 7,650 rpm out of the 500cc R50S). With a single, centrally-mounted camshaft, the R69's pushrods are long and heavy, and the valve gear must do a fair amount of shaking at high engine speed. BMW seems to know where the limit is, though, and the engine runs as smoothly as do the less powerful models in the line. Part of the smoothness is inherent in the engine design. Inside, plain bushings are scarce, roller and ball bearings plentiful. Crankpins,

Born to wander

BMW R69S

CYCLE WORLD

R O A D   T E S T

pressed into place on the three-piece crankshaft, permit the use of one-piece connecting rods. These crankpins are spaced at 180 degrees, so the pistons, moving in opposite directions, cancel each other's out-of-balance forces.

There has been much talk about the torque reaction of engine on frame when the throttle is turned; yes, it does exist and can be felt when the bike is sitting still. But, while this "torque" may have been a problem to riders of the old supercharged works racers of the late 30s, it is hardly relevant to discussion of the handling of the 1966 touring version. This might be a good moment to discuss another BMW bugaboo — the one about hanging up a cylinder by laying it over too far in a turn. It is rather evident that the tires will give way before one of those "pots" ever hangs up. And after all, a tourer is a tourer; one should buy a racer for racing.

BMW's sidecar breeding is most evident in the transmission system, which is quite automobilistic in nature, both in heft and design. A single-plate clutch, mounted on a heavy flywheel, car style, takes the drive to a massive gear train. Shifting is done with sliding dog-clutches, bike style, but the transmission is extraordinarily heavy and strong, as it should be to pull an added quarter-ton of sidecar and passenger. This heft does cause a slight problem for the solo rider accustomed to banging light, fast shifts. The Bee-Em takes its own sweet time, especially between first and second; result of a hurried first shift is a resounding clunk and a bearish lunge as the flywheel chews into that no-give clutch.

The BMW begins to reveal its touring qualities at the back of the engine-transmission unit, from which issues

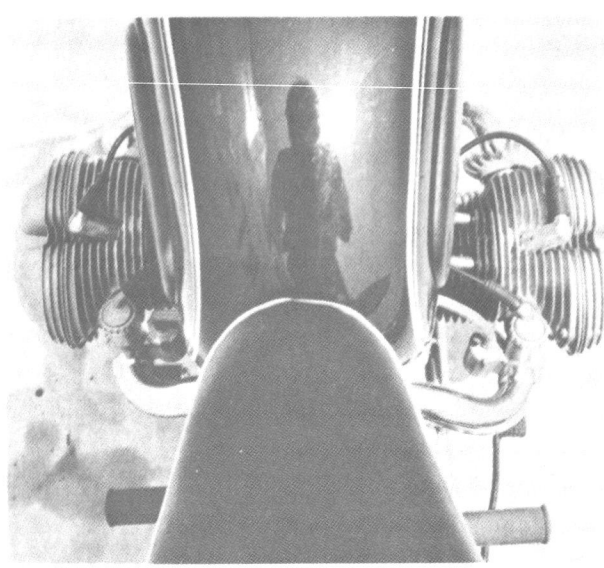

that noiseless, easily maintained and trouble-free drive-shaft. The value of this system to anyone who has rolled off a quick 500 miles on a chain-driven road burner is easily seen.

The Munich twin has other small features which show the great deal of thought put into improving the machine's capabilities for touring. For one thing, the two-way adjustable rear damper units require no separate tools, should one wish to change the setting; handles to change tension are cast in place. Two, the oil level is easily checked with a dipstick built into the cap. Three, the ignition key handle is shaped to fair itself in with the molding of the headlight switch assembly and thus keeps water out when it rains; a sliding cover moves over the keyhole when the machine is stopped. Four, a single air cleaner feeds both carburetors and is placed inboard out of dust's and water's way; it is easily opened for cleaning with one knob. Five, demounting either front or back wheel for tire repair is a cinch, involving removal of but a few bolts and then the withdrawal of the wheel spindle; further, there is no struggling to get the back tire out from under the rear fender, which is hinged just behind the seat and folds up for just that purpose. Six, the muffling system is the most efficient made for any motorcycle in this size category; noise may excite a street racer, but is useless and fatiguing for the man who rides 10 hours at a time. Seven, that big 4.4-gallon gas tank gives the R69S a cruising range of about 250 miles at 60 mph.

And then there is the ride. One would expect such a big motorcycle to be a handful, but this is not the case. Once it is rolling, the machine steers lightly and tracks well. We also discovered that it is a very easy machine to ride at a snail's pace in traffic. Much of this lightness of feel and slow-speed stability is owing to the low center of gravity offered by the opposed twin design. The soft ride is further enhanced by the big dual seat, comfortable both for rider and passenger. At faster speeds, the machine stays firmly attached to the ground and doesn't bounce the rider about the way more "competitive" (whatever that means) roadsters do when surfaces get rough or uneven.

Combine the small features with the ride and the machine's ability to run all day at any speed demanded of it, and one has a near-perfect choice in a machine for serious traveling. ∎

BMW R69S

SPECIFICATIONS

List Price	P.O.R.
Suspension, front	"Earles" Leading-Link
Suspension, rear	swing arm
Tire, front	3.50-18
Tire, rear	3.50-18
Brake, front	7.8 x 1.4
Brake, rear	7.8 x 1.4
Total brake swept area, sq.-in.	68.8
Brake loading (test weight/swept area) lb./sq. in.	8.9
Engine type	opposed twin, ohv
Bore and stroke (inches-millimeters)	2.81 x 2.85, 72 x 73
Displacement (inches^3-centimeters^3)	36, 593
Compression ratio	9.5:1
Carburetion	(2) 26mm (1.02") Bing
Ignition	Bosch magneto
Bhp @ rpm	42 DIN @ 7000
Oil system	wet sump
Oil capacity, pts.	4.1
Fuel capacity, gal.	4.4
Starting system	kick
Lighting system	battery, generator
Air filtration	paper element
Clutch	single-disc, dry-plate
Primary drive	none
Final drive	shaft & bevel gear
Gear ratios, overall:1	
5th	none
4th	4.81
3rd	6.05
2nd	8.51
1st	13.05
Wheelbase	55.7
Seat height	28.5
Seat width	14.0
Foot-peg height	9.0
Ground clearance	5.3
Curb weight (w/half-tank fuel)	452
Test weight (fuel and rider)	612

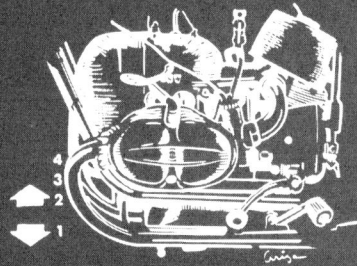

PERFORMANCE

Top speed	101.5
Maximum speed in gears (@ 7500 rpm)	
5th	none
4th	118
3rd	92
2nd	66
1st	42
Mph per 1,000 rpm, top gear	15.6
Speedometer error	
30 mph indicated, actually	29.4
50	47.5
70	66.2
Acceleration, zero to—	
30 mph, sec.	2.4
40	3.8
50	5.8
60	7.6
70	10.7
80	14.5
90	19.8
100	32.7
Standing 1/4-mile, sec.	16.20
Terminal speed	82

ACCELERATION AND ENGINE / ROAD SPEED

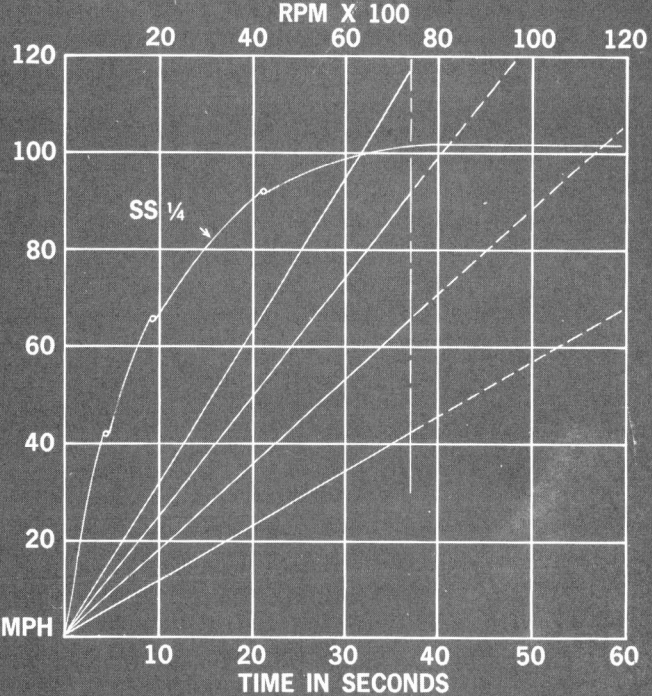

Unusual feature on the big BMW was the kickstart swing, which took some getting used to. The bike was always started easily but it was best to use a little choke

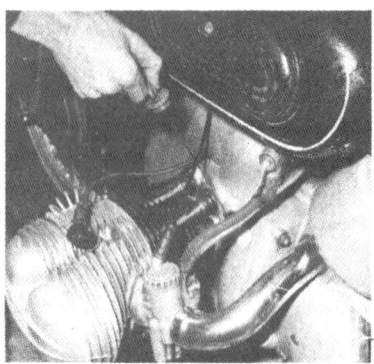

As the bike is wet sump, the filler cap is fitted with a dip-stick. The engine burnt very little oil and there were no oil leaks as picture shows

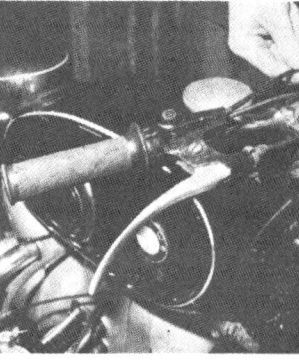

The throttle cable is wou round inside the mould at the twist grip, which is gear to winding drum. Note the fr run on all the control cabl

Eight years old and still running like a clock—only quieter—Fred Secker's . . .

▶ BMW—the machine that every budding long distance enthusiast would like to own. The barrier to these dreams is, of course, price—£485 for a new 600 cc model. Bee-ems, on the other hand, last far longer than ordinary bikes, so secondhand buys are a better proposition.

We wondered what quality of machine could be obtained for about £200, a sum which would buy a three-year-old large-capacity British machine in good condition.

Accordingly, we borrowed a 1959 R69 from BMW enthusiast Fred Secker. The bike had cost him about £200 last year, and was in standard condition.

The only work needed when he bought it was a main bearing replacement, which was carried out by BMW Concessionaires England Ltd, Brighton.

When the bike was delivered, we were amazed at its condition. Paintwork and chrome looked almost new, and there was not a trace of oil on the power unit.

The clock showed only 34,000 miles, and we could not find any parts that were in need of replacement or repair. All the controls and instruments worked perfectly.

Why are BMWs so popular? Firstly, they are extremely reliable, and require a minimum of maintenance.

They are exceptionally comfortable to ride—road shocks are just not felt. On the other hand, there is none of the spongy feeling common to some foreign marques.

They are also very quiet, and practically vibrationless. This means that they can be ridden for long distances with less fatigue.

Finally, they are a reasonably fast motorcycle once the rider has got used to the engine's capacity to rev.

The test bike had all these qualities, and they seemed little dulled by eight years' use.

On the road, the bike was incredibly smooth. Only at tick-over could the engine revs be felt.

The BMW has an engine speed clutch. On the test bike, a considerable dwell was needed between changes. Even then, there was a noticeable clunk as the gear went in.

The brakes were one of the best features on the machine, far better than pratically every British standard brake. Together they would bring the bike to a tyre-squealing halt in 27 ft. from 30 mph. They were equally impressive from high speeds.

The test bike certainly could not be "thrown about like a lightweight". When going into a corner, it felt as though the bike wanted to remain upright, and it had to be forced over to hold a chosen line.

In town, the engine would pull the bike along at very low revs with the minimum of fuss. The unit was so smooth that it was sometimes difficult to tell whether it was in top or third gear at 35 mph.

Once on the open road, the engine would wind on to give impressive acceleration. Second, for instance, could be held comfortably to over 50, and didn't peak until 60 mph showed on the clock. Even then, practically no vibration could be felt.

The only real point of criticism was the lights. After riding modern machines with 12v. electrics, the 6v. BMW headlamp seemed weak and fuzzy by comparison, but not too bad, considering its age.

Apart from this point, the bike was a joy to ride. After eight years' use, it still performed almost as well as a new bike, and its appearance belied its age.

unning these . . . Germans. The olbox hidden in the side of e tank was very nearly over-oked by staffmen. As shown, e box was lockable and safe

The ignition key is turned to the right for driving lights and to the left for pilot cum parking lights. Key can be withdrawn with park lights

The famous shaft drive ending at the gearbox with a car type clutch. Naturally, there is no such thing as snatch and the unit ran smoothly throughout test

The engine breather hangs down in front of the sump plate. Being wet sump, the drain plug for the engine is situated at the back of the plate. Note cleanliness

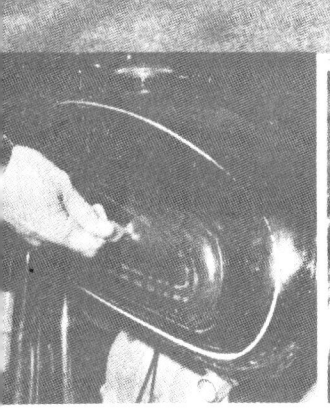

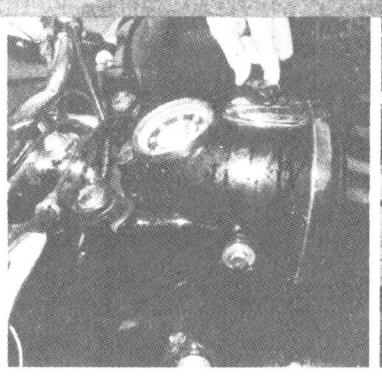

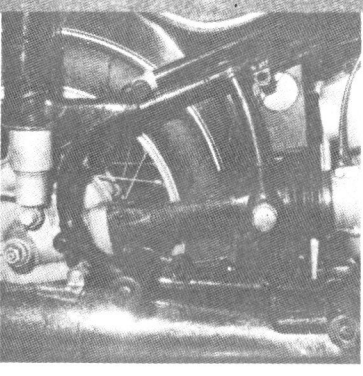

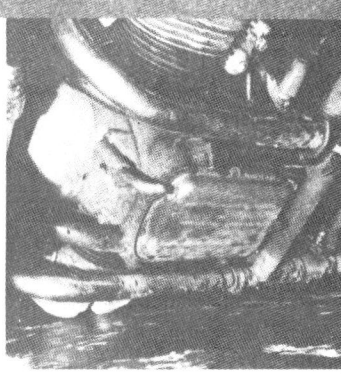

BRILLIANT BMW

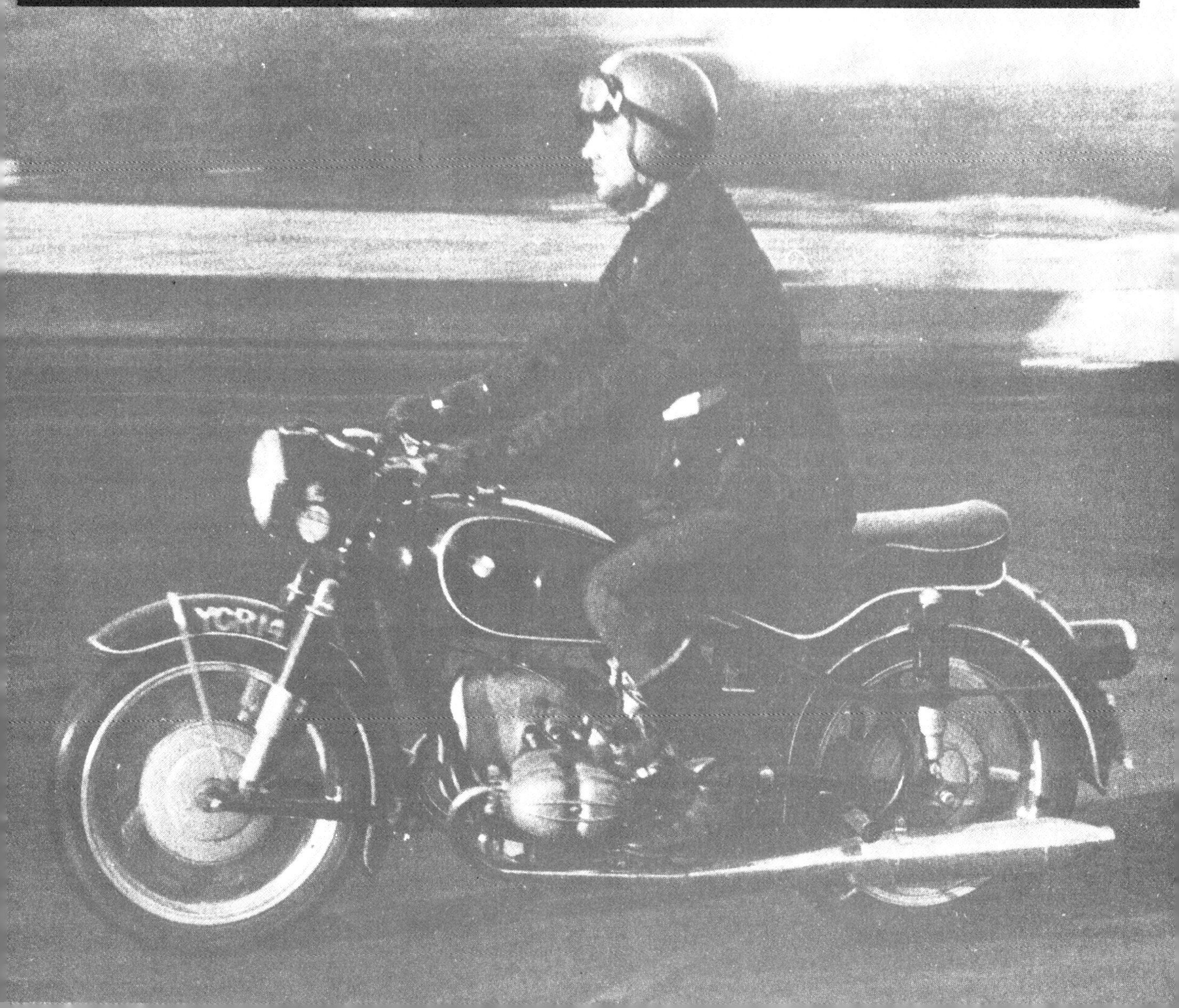

BMW 600cc R60

Once built for sidecars; now a solo line—
BMW owners say the tourer's super-fine—
not just a "triumph of development over design"

Thirteen years ago a sidecar outfit powered by a BMW flat twin won the FIM World Sidecar Championship. It was not the Bayerishce Motoren Werke's first appearance in championship colors, for the factory's supercharged twins had been strong contenders in prewar racing, winning the senior solo championship in 1938. What was to be important about that 1954 victory was its initiation of an uninterrupted series of class championships which continues to this day. For thirteen years BMW has held the sidecar crown, and for twelve years it has been marketing its "sidecar" production motorcycle, the model R60.

In an era of rapid technological change, one might reasonably ask how any motor company could successfully sell the same model for 12 years, especially when the sidecars that model was meant to haul have virtually disappeared from the world's highways. The reasonable answer to that question is complex, for the idiosyncratic mind of the motorcyclist is not about to lend itself to uncomplicated explanations. But we might begin by looking at this month's test R60 for characteristics that prove useful in a solo.

The sidecar outfit was once a sort of poor man's car. A man could buy an inexpensive (by auto standards) motorcycle, ride it solo until he had saved up enough to add a sidecar, then take the wife and kids along with him. Over-all investment would still be less than for an automobile, and running costs considerably less. Well, mass production changed that idea almost before it got off the ground. "Basic transportation" in an automobile has for some time been cheaper than a good sidecar rig with comparable performance.

Other than power, what the sidecar man needs from his engine is high torque and good but not abrupt engine braking. He prefers a reliable, mildly tuned engine over a peaky, temperamental scorcher. Cooling characteristics have to be very good, for a sidecar rig is heavy, has lower gearing, and gets less cooling air at a given rpm than a solo. Owing to the way a chair corners, the engine needs a pronounced flywheel effect to keep power delivery smooth and to prevent wild overreving during wheel breakaway in power slides. Also important is carburetion that does not lean out under horizontal g-loads in cornering. For best stability as well as minimum wind resistance, the sidecarist prefers an engine with a low

height and center of gravity, permitting the outfit to lie close to the ground.

Most of these requirements can be quite useful in a solo bike, depending on one's riding habits. And apparently the R60 suits the riding habits of quite a few for it is the most widely sold BMW in the U.S. A heavy flywheel does contribute to smooth engine output, especially if the firing pulses are even and if the engine's reciprocating masses (pistons, con-rods etc.) are balanced against one another—as they are in the horizontally-opposed R60 powerplant. Low center of gravity helps the handling of any motorcycle. And mild tuning combined with the frame rigidity necessary for a sidecar make for an extraordinary reliable and robust unit.

Most of our readers are already familiar with the basic BMW layout; it has been around in the R60 for 12 years and in other models since 1923, a year after Master engineer Max Friz of Munich conceived it. The horizontally opposed engine, its crank aligned with the fore-and-aft axis of the bike, couples through an engine-speed clutch to an in-unit gearbox at the rear. From the gearbox, a universal joint, shaft, and bevel gears, carry the drive to the rear wheel.

We have known serious motorcyclists in moments of cynicism to remark, "The BMW represents a triumph of development over design." Let us now examine a few developmental details that might inspire such a remark. The BMW is packed with particulars of great ingenuity and high manufacturing skill.

The engine, for example, gets its intake air from two sources. The first is through the centrally mounted air filter, which feeds both carburetors through a common chamber via separate tubes. The second intake is by way of small vents in the nose cover on the engine unit. Under this cover sit the magneto, braker points, capacitor, generator and voltage regulator. Intake air passes over these components, keeps them considerably cooler than crankcase temperature, then passes through a crankcase passage, another air filter, and into the common chamber under the main air filter.

The electrics, made by Bosch of Germany are a bit old-fashioned by present standards, but in the BMW they are far more reliable than the components commonly fitted to other bikes. The 60-watt DC generator puts out an actual 90 watts at any crank-speed over 1700 rpm. The

PHOTOGRAPHY: NOEL WERRETT

The BMW engine's aluminum timing-gear comes in graduated sizes to permit the precise adjustment of "mesh."

At the crankshaft's forward end is a fly-wheel type dynamic vibration damper in the R69S high-speed engine.

magneto is mounted on the end of the camshaft and turns at half engine speed. The braker cam has two lobes, thus opening the points once per crank revolution. This magneto is completely independent of the generator-battery system. Starting is invariably a one-kick job, and the bike can be driven safely, even at night, with a dead battery. The electrics are also completely water proof—mostly undercover and carefully protected.

Behind the enclosure for the magneto and generator is another cover for timing gears. A large gear mounted on the crank drives a gear for the camshaft and a gear to oil pump. A continuous oil stream plays out of a jet into the meshing of the mainshaft-camshaft gears. These have been individually selected and fit at the factory down to the exact size of each crankcase housing, and there is only .0005 inch of backlash. The mainshaft gear also carries a flat plate with cutaways that precisely time crankcase breathing. The cutaways alternately open and cover vents to the crankcase much like the rotary intake valves on modern two-strokes.

The crankshaft itself is a hefty built-up (or pressed together) unit with large roller bearings at the connecting-rod lower ends. The crank turns in two roller-type mainbearings. The lack of a central mainbearing means some crank flexing at higher rpm, but this does not become a serious problem within the R60's rev limit of 6200 rpm. Seen from above, the cylinders are slightly offset, creating a rocking movement about an axis perpendicular to the plane of the cylinders. Not only is this slight, but it is well damped by the R60's frame. In dynamic terms, the horizontally-opposed flat twin is the best balanced of any of the common motorcycle configurations. In the R60, this is felt as extraordinary smoothness and virtually vibration-free operation throughout the power band. With its 7.5:1 compression ratio and conservative valve timing, the R60 is also very tractable with strong pulling power (torque over 26 ft-lb.) anywhere above 2500 rpm.

Although the solo R60 used the same single-dry-plate clutch as the sidecar unit, it has a gearbox and rear drive with taller ratios. At maximum torque in fourth gear (4200 rpm), the R60 is rolling along at 65 mph, a very smooth and comfortable cruising speed that consumes just a shade under 50 miles per gallon of regular gas. The engine will not quite pull maximum power in fourth gear, which at 6000 rpm and 32 bhp would be 92 mph. Instead, it rises to a steady 5800, or 86 mph, and stays there.

Some nice touches in gearbox construction are hard-chromed shifter-fork tips for longer wear, a clutch throw-out bearing running in transmission oil, and gearbox venting to the atmosphere through a small hole in the speedometer drive. The speedometer drive gear has been designed with an extra return spiral that sends any condensed oil vapor back to the gearbox rather than out the breather hole. Result, a clean gearbox that rarely blows its oil seals. The only disadvantage to this gearbox: its input shaft runs at engine speed. A heavy flywheel keeps that engine from changing speed too quickly and often delivers quite hefty jolts to the input shaft on gear changing. Consequently, a spring-and-cam type torque damper is fitted to the input shaft. This protects the gears from the engine side, though the necessity of running two offset shafts for the gear pairs is less efficient mechanically than the more conventional arrangement of two shafts total.

Protection from wheel-delivered shocks is provided partially by the drive shaft itself, which permits a slight amount of both lengthwise and torsional flex. Normal change of length required by movement of the rear suspension is provided by a sliding splined-cup joint at the rear of the shaft. An elaborate linkage to the rear brake arm also keeps an even braking tension on that arm despite vertical movement on the rear wheel.

Counting the rear drive unit, the R60 has four separate oil enclosures, each of which must be sealed off from the others. There is the crankcase and wet sump, the transmissions. The universal joint and shaft drive, plus the rear drive. Virtually every rotating load-carry surface within this series runs on roller or ball bearings and all receive a generous oil bath. Again, a good case for lengevity. The only possible catch is maintaining all those oil seals.

Every enclosure but the shaft drive housing is adequately vented and part of the latter is a *neoprene* expansion boot over the universal joint. This offers enough low-resistance expansion volume to obviate positive venting.

The frame through which this power train passes is basically a sidecar frame. That means it's strong and heavy. BMW uses all kinds of tricks in the basic double-loop cradle, such as varying cross sections at different points according to load. Much of the tubing, oval sectioned and tapered, is very expensive to fabricate. Helmut Kern, service manager at Butler and Smith, the U.S. importers of BMW says, "As far as I know this is the only frame that you can hook a sidecar to, and later ride solo. Any other frame I've tried will eventually distort under the loads imposed by the sidecar, throwing it out of alignment for solo work."

Another vestigial sidecar component that benefits the solo rider are the R60's brakes. The sidecars BMW made (but no longer make) had a brake in the wheel, but many machines were fitted by owners with less expensive, brakeless rigs.

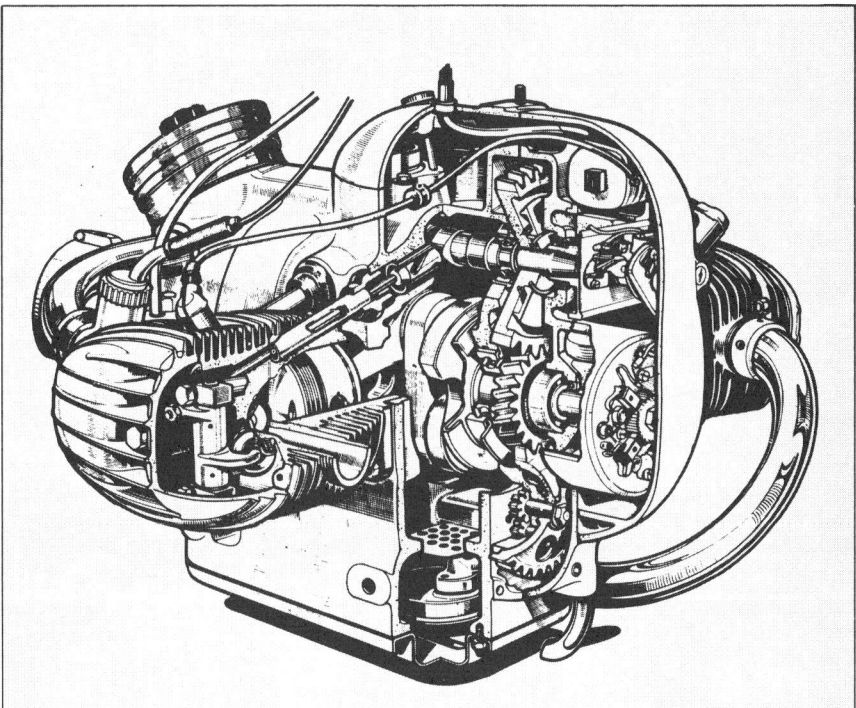

The BMW "Boxer" engine, with its opposed cylinders, has perfect primary balance. Cylinder-cooling is particularly good, as airflow is not obstructed by a wheel.

BMW's shaft-drive feature is cleaner, quieter, less messy and more reliable than the usual roller-chain and sprockets—but expensive and difficult to repair.

BMW R60

This meant that the bike's brakes did all the work, which might be hauling a 1400-lb. package to a standstill from 65 mph. It is not surprising that BMW was the first firm to fit full-width brake hubs on all production motorcycles. They were also among the first to use a double-leading-shoe brake at the front. Twelve years ago these brakes paced the industry and were undoubtedly the best production stoppers available. They are still above average for large-displacement bikes, but technology has caught up with, and in some cases, passed BMW. Our specific brake loading figures show what our riding experience confirms: The R60 has good brakes, but they could be better for such a large machine.

Up front the R60 also features one of the most unique forks in the motorcycle industry. A full Earles-type leading-link fork, it has both advantages and disadvantages compared to the more common telescopic variety. Like so much else on the BMW, the fork is both heavy and strong. It was ball-and-cone bearings at the steering head and taper-rollers at the swingarm pivot. Under heavy braking, the swingarms want to turn forward about the pivot, effectively raising the bike. At the same time momentum transfers most of the weight of the bike and its rider forward, forcing the front end down and swingarms backward. The effects are self-cancelling, and the BMW brakes very evenly without nosedive or lifting.

The rear swingarm of the BMW also pivots on tapered roller bearings. Its suspension units are the conventional coil-spring and shock-absorber combination, but they are secured at the top in housings welded to the rear of the frame loops. The pivot points are located in two vertical members connecting the lower and upper cradle sections. This arrangement does not offer best resistance to side loads at the wheel and we experienced what felt like flexing during hard cornering with two up.

Our test of the R60 was rather more thorough than most road tests, for not only did we run it at the track, we also drove it 1400 miles from New York to Daytona. BMW has produced some 250,000 motorcycles since World War II, and they gave us our test bike to celebrate the fact. It was completely stock, we drove it hard, and we experienced no mechanical difficulties. There was some sweating at the vertical crankcase joints, but no oil leakage and virtually no oil consumption.

The R60 is most at home on the open highway, where it will cruise smoothly at 65 or 70 for day after day almost with-

Continued on page 93

BMW 600 R60

Price, suggested retail	East Coast POE $1420.80
Tire, front	3.50 in. x 18 in. ribbed
rear	3.50 in. x 18 in. ribbed
Brakes, front	Twin leading shoe 7.8 in. x 1.4 in.
rear	Single leading shoe 7.8 in. x 1.4 in.
Brake swept area	56.4 sq. in.
Specific brake loading	10.9 lb/sq. in.
Engine type	Four-stroke OHV twin
Bore and stroke	2.81 in. x 2.85 in., 72mm x 73mm
Piston displacement	36 cu. in., 593cc
Compression ratio	7.5:1
Carburetion	(2) 24mm, Bing
Air filtration	Paper element
Ignition	Magneto
Bhp @ rpm	30 @ 5800
Mph/1000 rpm, top gear	15.6
Fuel capacity	6.4 gal.
Lighting	6 v generator, 60 watts
Battery	6 v, 16 ah
Gear ratios, overall	(1) 13.05 (2) 8.52
	(3) 6.06 (4) 4.82
Wheelbase	55.7 in.
Seat height	28.5 in.
Ground clearance	5.3 in.
Curb weight	440 lbs.
Test weight	615 lbs.
Instruments	Speedometer, odometer
0-60 mph	7.8 seconds
Standing start 1/4 mile	16.2 seconds—79 mph
Top speed	88 mph

B.M.W. TEST

————from page 65————

remained absolutely oil-tight after 1,500 fast miles and returned 60 miles to the gallon.

In the suspension and handling department, the R60 scores another ten out of ten. Front suspension is by two swinging arms with rubber mounted shock absorbers and the front wheel swinging arm pivot can be transferred from the rear to the front of the forks for sidecar work. This gives a smaller trail angle and easier steering. The steering damper is positive to operate and ultra-efficient.

The rear wheel is fixed in a swinging arm which pivots in adjustable taper roller bearings on the frame. Road shocks are absorbed by two quickly-adjustable dampers.

All of which means that the big B.M.W. handles like a dream. It steers as accurately as a sniper's rifle and can be cranked over to improbable angles without anything nasty happening. The double-leading-shoe full width front brake is enormously powerful and coupled with the rear brake returned the most impressive figures of a full stop from 30 m.p.h. in 24 ft.

I should have thought that for the money an owner would be entitled to a set of crash bars as standard. Secondly, because of the method of construction the clutch runs at full engine speed which means the rider has to have a touch like velvet to avoid a slight clunk changing gear.

And finally, one needs a lot of beef and a definite knack to park the bike on its centre stand. The drill is to hold the pillion footrest in your right hand, the rider's footrest in the left and heave!

The electrics are conventional and extremely powerful with a red ignition light and a green light which tells you when you are in neutral. But I did miss some sort of oil warning light—on a bike as good as the R60 this is an inexplicable omission.

The R60 is quite definitely one of the best bikes I have ever ridden—and possibly it is *the* best. It's a pity that a German firm has taken over where Brough, Vincent and Sunbeam (the S7 and S8) left off. Swift, smooth and silent—for the discriminating rider it's worth every penny of the price.

ACROSS THE DESERT
Continued from Page 67

Seriously, truck operators are usually friendly to motorcyclists, and are willing to lend a helping hand when needed. To say that all truck drivers are good ones, though, and are considerate of lesser vehicles would be laying it on too thick. There are poor, even lousy, truck drivers who use their huge vehicles to bully their way along the highways with little regard to the safety or well-being of any one else who happens to be occupying the space considered theirs. With our small two-wheelers we can do nothing but give them room, and if they want to pass, let them. We'll soon catch them, anyway, at the next grade, and will swoop by with no effort at all.

The turning point of my trip ended at a small town on U.S. Highway 40 named Duschene. Located at a 7000 foot elevation, 100 miles east of Salt Lake City it is a gateway to the fabulous fishing and deer-hunting region of central Utah. Hundreds of trout-filled lakes empty into fishing streams along here, and the scenic aspen-covered highlands are loaded with deer. The Strawberry River, near where I stayed overnight, will soon be dammed, furnishing great recreational possibilities.

This is also the land of the Pinon Pine and the Cedar. It is dry with a clear high-elevation atmosphere that is invigorating, healthful, intriguing. Utah is a many-faceted state varying in climate and scenery from the hot salt flats of Salt Lake to towering mountains of the Wasatch and high eastern plains. Certainly, Brigham Young was not in error when he observed that "This is the promised land."

Returning via of Salt Lake City and the great Salt Lake I came across a highway marker, placed many years ago, indicating the passage of the tragic Donner Party across the present highway. In all the annals of the development of our U.S. no single episode demonstrates more clearly the fortitude of our pioneers as that of the passage of the Donner Party across the salt flats and, later, the snowed-in Sierras 100 years ago. The country is hot and dry, each bush has a thorn (typical of desert plants the world over), salty, alkaline dust rises with every footstep, flies and bugs are troublesome, and salty marshes near the lake defy the traveler with impassable mud.

It was a relief to reach Wendover, Nevada, and begin the long trek across the Nevada highlands. Desolate enough, themselves, they are not devoid of beauty when billowy white clouds march across sparkling blue skies trailing their shadows in and out of gullies and over nearby mountain ranges. Such was the weather on this particular day. Needless to say, I knew what to expect later on; for such fleecy white clouds are harbingers of thunder storms.

Near Battle Mountain the storm struck. I watched it build up for 50 miles. The rain does not bother me, but the lightning does. A man on a horse, and, I assume, a motorcycle, is a sitting duck for a bolt of high voltage seeking an easy path from a cloud to the ground. Some of our readers who know more about this subject, can do me and others a favor by sending information via a "letter to the editor" or a personal note to me, % CYCLE Magazine.

BMW R60 *Continued from page* 92

out end. It is a big machine, almost overdesigned and certainly overbuilt for a solo mount. Such a "utility" orientation makes the R60, not surprisingly, the largest selling police motorcycle in the world. But utility demands good manners, strength, and durability. The R60 exhaust note is low and mellow, emerging from an interconnected twin-pipe, twin muffler system. Workmanship, fitting, finishing —all are superb. Buyers have an option of various seats, tanks, handlebars and racks. Ours had the solo seat, which is quite comfortable, but far too low for the high "touring" bars fitted.

The R60 is certainly no road sports machine. It will do zero to 60 in a shade over 16 seconds, and third gear will carry you to about 78 mph for brisk passing. But the combination of 440 lbs., 30 bhp, and a heavy flywheel doesn't make for neck-snapping acceleration, or ear-holing at high speed through a series of left and right hand switchbacks. That heavy front end and over-all weight just can't be thrown back and forth quick enough for hard tight-course riding. This is a machine for long distances, for a comfortable, trouble-free ride, for the rider who wants more to see the country he's passing through than to explore the limits of his cornering and braking skill.

Routine servicing of the BMW is easy. All the oil reservoirs are readily tapped, the electrics can be reached by undoing two bolts, and the valve gear, pistons, cylinders and carburetors hang right out there for ready service and adjustment. Naturally, there is no "greasy chain" to fuss with. In contrast, power-train servicing is a nightmare. Lower end, transmission, drive shaft, and rear drive overhauls require more special pullers, drifts, jigs, wrenches, holders, and fixtures than one can imagine, much less afford. And breaking the power train to service it is a lengthy, exasperating job. Fortunately, for BMW owners, the R60 is built to last, and we know one chap who has 270,000 miles on his bike without ever having so much as removed a cylinder head.

Ironically, as history's clock has caught up with and passed BMW, there has been a recent resurgence of interest in sidecars. The R60 may once again serve for a limited few its original task. Butler and Smith now markets Dutch-made single-passenger sidecars under the BMW marque. Meanwhile, the factory has been blossoming financially under the demand for its automobiles and is completing a new facility for motorcycle manufacture. Although now said to the point of weariness, the near future may bring new models and more modern designs from BMW. Meanwhile, the R60 will continue to do its workhorse chores with the characteristic stamina and unfaltering good manners, that have made it a favorite of long-distance touring riders. ◉

PHOTOGRAPHY: HERMANN BACHMANN

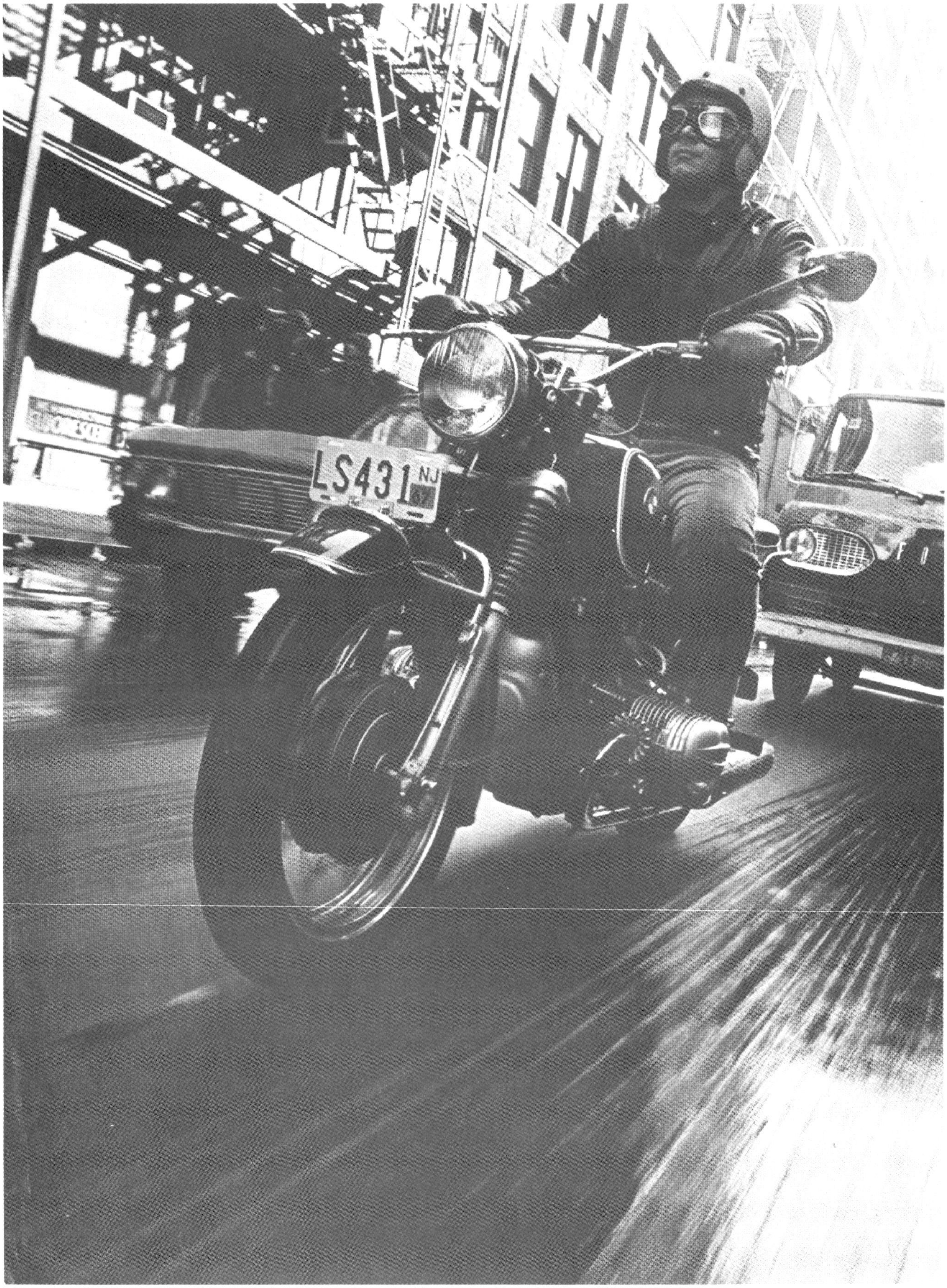

BMW 600 R 69 US

ISDT-bred telescopics trim weight
and add versatility to the fastest
of BMW's sleek, expensive tourers.

Right on the front of a snappy new four-color brochure it says, "BMW is on the move." And there, staring you square in the face, is this pair of enormously long telescopic forks to prove it. BMW, the Bavarian Motor Works, for years the last-surviving champion of Earles-type leading-link forks, has up and moved in the direction of the rest of the world's manufacturers. Now you can get your BMW either way. Reading the brochure will only confuse you as far as making the choice is concerned. Leaping onto two different-but-equal BMW's in quick succession won't help much either, for the two forks have distinctly different "feels"— both quite unlike any other motorcycle you've ever ridden. Whatever else being "on the move" means to BMW, it certainly doesn't mean a loss of identity. The BMW motorcycle remains a wholly unique and distinctive machine that will lose none of its Faithful Followers by this brash new innovation. In fact, it may very well gain some new friends.

Our test machine this month is the R69 US, flagship of a line of six models with three basic engines and now two types of forks. There are two mildly tuned "touring" engines: a 500cc twin that delivers 26 bhp at 5800 rpm; and a 600cc twin that delivers 30 bhp at 5800 rpm. For the R69 US there is a 600cc "sport" engine with a higher compression ratio and hotter cam that develops 42 bhp at 7000 rpm. Our test machine was also fitted with an extra-wide dual seat (we called it the "fat boy") and a 6½ gallon gas tank. Alloy rims, we understand, will be standard on all telescopic-forks ("US") models. Another difference common to the US models is a larger section 4.00 x 18 rear tire and lower rear drive ratio. Net effect is slightly lower over-all gearing with correspondingly slower top end, and better acceleration through the gears. Since as a rule we don't go winging along at 109 mph, we prefer this change. Not that an owner could do anything about it, for altering a geared final drive ratio is very expensive. Naturally, the most noticeable feature of our test bike was the new set of forks, which, when the machine is unloaded, make it look a bit taller than its "S" counterpart.

The new R 69 US showed 40 miles on the odometer when we received it, and we didn't yield it up until the reading was well over 1,200. Since we had driven an R 60 some 1400 miles last year on extended test, we were prepared to compare the handling of a US with a standard model. The first five minutes in the saddle were enough to prove that the US was going to be an entirely different beast. Although the forks feel soft when bounced up and down by the handlebars at rest, they are quite steady on the road, giving no impression of sponginess. At low speeds the forks show a tendency to oversteer, feeling heavy and turning more sharply into the turn than you want to go. This sensation disappears completely at moderate speeds—say, 40 mph and up. At high speeds, 65 mph and up, the forks provide positively superb handling, being both rock-steady and readily responsive to changes in direction. At speed, the forks definitely feel quicker than their Earles-type counterpart. On winding, rough-surfaced roads, they offer a distinct advantage, assuming you're a sprint-and-brake enthusiast.

Now the story behind these forks is a long one in time, and when you understand the effort that went into their development, you will appreciate the effectiveness of their operation. Several years ago, BMW built a surprise fleet of ISDT bikes, equipped with telescopic forks and a double-cradle frame that held those flat-twin engines about three inches higher off the ground than did the production frame. Many people felt that running a flat twin engine on a cross-country enduro-type bike was absurd, even if the weight could be pared to less than three hundred pounds. But the factory line was, "If it won't break in the toughest off-the-road competition, it won't break on our production bikes." Well, the factory BMW's didn't do so well—they were just too heavy and too wide to outmaneuver the 200-lb. two-stroke singles. But they didn't break. This year's production bikes therefore have forks that can take the rigors of ISDT competition. The only change made for the street is slightly stiffer springing.

One great advantage of that cross-country background is an extraordinary 8.4 inches of fork travel (214mm). Under normal load this is distributed as 5.47 inches of compression and 2.95 inches of extension (or rebound). Not only springing, but damping also is progressive, meaning that the further the forks are compressed (or extended), the stiffer they get. In fact, just before these forks reach mechanical bottoming (full spring compression) they reach a hydraulic lock-stop. This is accomplished by having a hydraulic metering rod that tapers in toward the center and out toward each end. This rod passes through an orifice at the bottom of the fixed fork tubes. When the bottom section of the fork moves up or down oil is squeezed through the space between rod and the orifice. As the fork is compressed further in either direction, the taper causes the rod to fill more of the orifice, making the squeezing action more difficult. Eventually the orifice is almost completely filled and the forks, at the very limits of compression, become immovable. Valving in the hydraulic rod makes damping on compression about one third as firm as damping on release. All of which leads to excellent tracking over rough surfaces, and great smoothness on level surfaces.

The heavy feeling and oversteer at low speed from these forks owes partly to the rather large rake angle and partly to the considerable trail that have been designed into them. Actually, steering-head angle was fixed before the design was begun, for BMW wanted the telescopics to be interchangeable with the Earles forks. Factory designers chose to make the downtubes exactly parallel to the steering head. All production-line frames for all models are the same at present (except that US versions don't have sidecar mounting lugs). Present BMW owners can bolt-on the telescopics if they want to, although the present total parts cost of almost $350 makes this a rather prohibitive venture. Commonly, fork rake varies between 25 and 30 degrees for all types of motorcycles, the 25-27 range used mostly for street machines, and the 26-30 range for high-speed dirt bikes. BMW's forks, first tried in the dirt, are raked at 26.5 degrees from the vertical, thus exhibiting some

BMW R69US

of their ISDT heritage. Trail, which provides a self-correcting, self-aligning steering effect, is usually between three and four inches on high speed touring machines. The BMW trail at 3.34 inches is solidly in this range. Knowing this and the rake angle, one could reasonably predict that the BMW forks would handle heavily at lower speeds but firmly (not light) at high speeds. And that is how it works out.

From the steering head back, our BMW was mainly old news, though much of it is good news. The frame, engine, brakes, transmission and rear drive—except for detail improvements—remain the same as they have been for many years. One of the virtues of this continuity is the BMW's much-celebrated reliability. This machine has been debugged with a thoroughness that borders on obsessive. Our test bike had not one single mechanical complaint during those 1200 miles of hard testing, and *that*, friends, for a brand new motorcycle, is very unusual. The same thing, incidentally, occurred with last year's test BMW.

Regretfully, at least part of the BMW's reliability owes to sheer mechanical bulk. The basic frame, a long double-loop tubular affair (except for one single-tube section under the gastank), is sturdily made to resist the rigors of sidecar attachment. It is expensively produced, with tapers, round-sections, oval-sections and other variations introduced to deal with specific loads at specific points. The result weighs nearly fifty pounds, less forks—strong enough for two up, two in a sidecar, plus a mountain of luggage. This frame will also survive most spills without a trace of misalignment. We have a hunch, however, that BMW will eventually produce a stronger, simpler, lighter, and still more rigid frame. Meanwhile, your BMW frame will never have to answer for want of durability.

Cradled comfortably in this frame is the familiar R69 S (and now US) engine, which stands as a remarkable piece of engineering in its own right. Probably the last of the flat or horizontally-opposed twins, it is the smoothest running motorcycle engine we have tested, bar none. The pistons reciprocate in their cylinders simultaneously, exactly cancelling reaction forces and offering perfect primary dynamic balance. You feel this when riding as an eerie, almost motorless, effect. Because the exhaust note is so well muffled, new riders run a fair chance of overreving the unit. Eventually you will hear valve crash, but on an engine in this state of tune, that kind of revving is not recommended. The only imbalanced force in the BMW is that caused by a slight offset of the cylinders when seen from above. This produces a rocking moment in the horizontal plane, but one that is well damped by that long, heavy frame. Another dynamic problem that arises in a flat twin at higher rpm is crank flexing, especially when (as in the BMW) there is no center mainbearing. The two mains consist of a ball bearing in front and a spherical (barrel-shaped) roller at the rear to endure this unavoidable shaft rocking or flexing. Meanwhile, up front at the very tip of the crankshaft, outboard of the crank-mounted generator, sits a flywheel-type vibration damper. This device appears only on the high-revving R 69 S-US engine, and it works by putting a rubber cushion between the crankshaft and a heavy, rotating mass. The cushion firs absorbs the impulse from crank flexing, then transfers it to its own damping mass. The damping mass reacts, sending another impulse back through the cushion. Because the reactions are out of phase (ideally by 180 degrees), they are completely or partially self-cancelling. Vibration from crank flexing is therefore very effectively damped. The only fault with this unit is that the rubber cushion eventually loses its resiliency and may even harden and disintegrate. Naturally, when it is rigid, the damper will promptly *amplify* crank flexing. The solution is a simple, sixty-cent replacement rubber cushion, renewed every 4000 miles.

About the only drawback to this power-plant for all-purpose use is not that its state of tune jeopardizes reliability (most "sport" four-strokes are more radically tuned), but that it *is* cammy enough to lose good low-end torque. For stop-and-go driving, the R 69 US simply *won't* get off the line. And if you wing it up to 7000 rpm and dump the clutch, the clutch slips a bit before it grabs. Our best ET of 15.3 still shows pretty good performance for a machine of this size and weight. A very significant indication of power-torque characteristics is that we could get trap speeds at the end of the quarter well into the nineties, but were turning ET's in the sixteens. Best ET resulted from holding the bike in third gear just at valve float (about 7200 rpm) through the traps, giving a top speed in the upper eighties.

Out on the highway, this off-the-line deficiency is completely obviated by better-than-average acceleration, and excellent top speed. The R 69 US would cruise comfortably at *any* speed we felt comfortable to maintain. Even with a windshield and two saddlebags, it would pull quickly to over the 100 mph mark. The more miles we put on the machine, the more readily it would surge up to the ton and beyond. At about 75 mph there is a mild vibration resonance somewhere in the engine-suspension system, but

Immaculate finish, wide seat, and substantial bulk add to luxury image. Forks are mostly alloy.

Flat-twin engine and shaft drive are clean and quiet. Full tank carries bike 300 miles.

BMW R69US

throughout the rest of the range, our test machine was astonishingly smooth. Fourth gear will haul two-up very comfortably at 65-70, and you can quickly drop into third for passing speeds up to 85. The closeness of third and fourth is a very useful high-range touring combination. For about-town riding, you rarely shift past third.

Power from the R 69 US engine is carried to the transmission by way of crankshaft-mounted flywheel and clutch. The crank passes through an oil seal at the back of the crankcase and into the dry flywheel-clutch housing. This oil seal has, as in many automobiles, been a source of trouble, for it is an expensive and tedious job to remove the transmission and flywheel to get at the seal for replacement. Large crank diameter means high radial speeds at the

seal lip, and this often leads to leakage. Now BMW has redesigned the seal, using a new proprietary material and including swirl-patterned grooves on its inner face. Oil that reaches the seal is first trapped in the grooves and then spun away by centrifugal force. Our test bike showed no leakage whatever at the small lower vent hole in the flywheel chamber.

The dry, automotive-type clutch frees easily and cleanly and will only slip momentarily when used in dragstrip-like starts. It's dry plate is splined to the transmission input shaft, which goes through another oil seal into the three-shaft transmission. Somewhat less efficient than conventional motorcycle transmissions, this version offers the benefit of a heavy spring-and-cam type shock damper on that extra shaft to prolong gear life. A new shifter-cam

mechanism in the transmission guarantees positive shifts. Once the shift pedal has been operated the transmission will, because of internal spring loading, drive a sliding dog into place to insure engagement. If the pedal is not operated through the full positive-stop throw, the transmission will drive the previously engaged shifter-dog back into place. Thus you simply *cannot* get a false neutral in this transmission, no matter how violently or timidly you pump the shifter pedal.

The transmission, the universal joint and drive shaft, and the rear pinion-gear drive units all now run in SAE 90 gear oil. This helps to quiet the great clunking shifts common to BMWs, and the reduced frequency of changes means even less attention to this quiet, indestructable

Continued on page 137

BMW R69 US 600

Price, suggested retail	East Coast, POE $1712.75
Tire, front	3.50 in. x 18 in.
rear	4.00 in. x 18 in.
Brakes, front	7.8 in. x 1.4 in.
rear	7.8 in. x 1.4 in.
Brake swept area	68.6 sq. in.
Specific brake loading	8.95 lb/sq. in.
Engine type	Four-stroke OHV twin
Bore and stroke	2.83 in. x 2.87 in., 72 mm x 73 mm
Piston displacement	36 cu. in., 593cc
Compression ratio	9.5:1
Carburetion	(2) 26mm, Bing
Air filtration	Paper element
Ignition	Magneto
Bhp @ rpm	42 @ 7000
Mph/1000 rpm, top gear	15.1
Fuel capacity	6.5 gal.
Oil capacity	4 pt.
Lighting	6v, 90 watts
Battery	6v, 16 ah
Gear ratios, overall	(1) 14.11 (2) 9.20 (3) 6.55 (4) 5.14
Wheelbase	56.18 in.
Seat height	29.1 in.
Ground clearance	5.9 in.
Curb weight	439 lb.
Test weight	614 lb.
Instruments	Speedometer, odometer
0-60 mph	8.2 seconds
Standing start ¼ mile	15.3 seconds—89 mph
Top speed	103 mph

DON'T READ THIS AD

BMW breaks coast-to-coast record. 45 hours, 41 minutes!

BMW has done it again. On August 28-29, 1968, Tibor Sarossy, 22 year-old Ohio State student, rode a BMW R 69 S from New York to Los Angeles to break the 1959 coast-to-coast record of John Penton, also on BMW, by fully 6½ hours.

2687 grueling miles on all kinds of road. In all kinds of weather. Over cold mountains and through the hottest of deserts. And Sarossy's BMW had already traveled 22,000 miles

before starting this punishing test.

Traveling 100 mph on open highways or 30 mph on rain-flooded roads in Texas and New Mexico, the BMW never stalled or missed a single stroke. And after more than 45 hours of a practically non-stop ride, it ran as quietly and smoothly as ever. Said Sarossy, "The virtually vibration-free ride assured me maximum comfort and reliable performance."

Back home in Cleveland, after a total of 5460 miles, a service check revealed that no repairs were needed. Not even a lightbulb had burned out.

That's a BMW motorcycle for you. Remarkable!

See your nearest authorized BMW dealer, or for information write to: East: Butler & Smith, Inc., 160 W. 83 St., New York, N.Y. 10024. West: The Flanders Co., 200 W. Walnut St., Pasadena, Calif. 91103.

Where the action is: 3 great all-new BMW models!

R 50/5 500cc. Horsepower: 36 at 6600 rpm. Stroke/bore: 70.6/67 mm. Carburetor: Bing float. Weight: 410 lbs. Top speed: 100 mph. Acceleration: 0 to 60 mph in 9.8 seconds. Electric starter optional.

R 60/5 600cc. Horsepower: 46 at 6600 rpm. Stroke/bore: 70.6/73.5 mm. Carburetor: Bing float. Weight: 421 lbs. Top speed: 105 mph. Acceleration: 0 to 60 mph in 7.8 seconds. Complete with electric starter.

R 75/5 750cc. Horsepower: 57 at 6400 rpm. Stroke/bore: 70.6/82 mm. Carburetor: Bing vacuum. Weight: 421 lbs. Top speed: 110 mph. Acceleration: 0 to 60 mph in 6.1 seconds. Complete with electric starter.

One glance at these extraordinary machines tells you they're completely new from the ground up.

To begin with, they have more horses than ever. 36, 46, 57 respectively. Top speed? 110 mph. Acceleration? Terrific. 0 to 60 mph in 6.1 seconds.

Those famed horizontally-opposed cylinders of ours now utilize a casting process unique in motorcycle engines. By this special process, aluminum alloys are cast to the cylinder sleeves, resulting in lower weight and optimum heat dissipation.

Our new crankshaft, forged in one piece, is even stronger to permit the higher power-output.

Completely new Bing constant-velocity vacuum carburetors on the R 75/5 and concentric float carburetors on the R 50/5 and R 60/5 give the new BMW's instant throttle response.

The variable cross-section, oval-tube cradle frame, incorporating a detachable rear section, is very light and capable of taking enormous stress. Its design makes it possible to mount a reshaped tank with a capacity increase of almost two gallons, without a change in outside dimensions.

The new telescopic front fork has hydraulic stops for extension and compression. For all practical purposes, it can't be bottomed. Its more than 8-inch travel is now matched by rear wheel travel of nearly 5 inches, providing maximum riding comfort.

An excellent optional feature is the self-leveling suspension device, the Boge-Nivomat. This device, a first on any motorcycle, keeps the machine level automatically, regardless of whether you are carrying a passenger and/or luggage.

The geometry of the braking system is such that no distortion takes place, and full contact is maintained between drum and bonded shoes. As a result, the brakes simply will not fade.

In the new BMW's, electric power is supplied by a 12-volt, 3-phase alternator with six silicon diodes for full-wave rectification. The specially developed 15-Ah battery takes little space, is light-weight, and has a window for acid-level control. It provides for reliable starting even in cold weather.

The newly-designed Bosch headlight throws an asymmetric beam pattern, minimizing glare and increasing illumination for safe night riding.

Mechanically-driven tachometer, front and rear turn signals, are now standard equipment. So is the electric starter (optional on the R 50/5).

There is more. A lot more. Not to mention factory-approved accessories. We could fill a book. But why not go to your nearest dealer and see the real thing? White, black or Polaris silver, the all-new BMW's have to be ridden to be believed.

See your nearest authorized BMW dealer, or for information write to:
East: Butler & Smith, Inc., Walnut Street and Hudson Avenue, Norwood, N.J. 07648
West: Flanders Company, 340 S. Fair Oaks Avenue, Pasadena, California 91101
Canada: BMW Motorcycle Distributors, 3335 Yonge Street, Toronto 12, Ontario.

Bavarian Motor Works

Why does a BMW cost more than an ordinary motorcycle?

Because a BMW is no ordinary motorcycle. Instead, it's something else: the finest motorcycle built anywhere in the world, bar none.

How does it lay claim to the title? By virtue of craftsmanship you won't believe. By way of quality that has just one standard—the best, or forget it. We've been building them that

way for 45 years. And the result has been more world championships and more world speed records than have been won and set by any other make.

So if you want an ordinary motorcycle, okay. But if you want the greatest machine you can swing a leg over, if you want the riding thrill of your life, it's got to be a BMW. And

when you look at it that way, the few extra dollars make a BMW a bargain.

See your nearest authorized BMW dealer, or for information write to: East: Butler & Smith, Inc., 160 W. 83rd St., New York, N.Y. 10024. West: The Flanders Co., 200 W. Walnut St., Pasadena, Calif. 91103.

Bavarian Motor Works

BMW R 60 U.S.

The Telescopic Tourer

A TEST RIDE on a new BMW reveals a strange and, to some, unwelcome sensation. The front wheel actually dips under braking! For years BMW owners have boasted of the way the Earles type front fork has enabled their bikes to remain level despite the weight transfer that occurs when a motorcycle's brakes are used fiercely. Now the factory has made a departure from tradition by offering three machines with telescopic forks fitted as standard.

The reason is that BMW has recognized the growing tendency for American riders to take their machines off the freeways, throughways, and city streets, and onto dirt roads and rough byways. The new light alloy front fork will cope with this type of riding more adequately than the Earles usually associated with "Bee-Ms."

Yes, the new fork does allow the nose of the machine to dive under braking, but this is a feature of all telescopic units. Otherwise, the fork offers a smooth and luxurious ride that is always associated with the German bikes.

The new machines are the R 50 US, R 60 US and R 69 US. The only difference between these and the established models lies in the front forks—engines and other specifications are identical. CYCLE WORLD's test machine was the 593-cc R 60 US, a 457-lb. tourer that develops peak power of 30 bhp at a leisurely 5800 rpm. It is a close relation to the R 69, which uses a similar engine tuned to develop 42 bhp.

The R 60 US, like all large BMWs, offers a unique form of motorcycling. What other machine could be so silent, so free from vibration, so effortless at cruising speeds? Even its appearance is unusual. It stands high and proud, and offers few

concessions to modern styling. No bright colors distinguish its bodywork—fenders, tank, and frame are painted a gleaming black.

Chief characteristics of the BMW are its opposed Twin engine, and shaft drive, features which also contribute most to its uniqueness. Both have been retained ever since the factory started manufacture of motorcycles 45 years ago. BMW goes to great lengths to insure that its machines offer reliability and smoothness, and the engine layout plays a great part in this. An opposed Twin has excellent inherent balance, with the motion of one piston automatically counteracting the motion of the other.

The crankpins are set at 180 degrees to each other, and another feature which aids smooth running is the dynamically balanced crankshaft. The forged steel crank is carried in two ball bearings, while roller bearings carry the oval section connecting rods. A bushing is used at the piston pins. A massive alloy cover houses the engine and transmission, apart from the cylinders.

Three-ring, alloy pistons run in cast iron barrels, which also house the upper ends of the pushrod guides. These guides are rubber-seated against the engine cover. Gray cast iron is used for the intake valves, and heat resistant steel for the exhaust valves, which have to cope with far higher temperatures.

The single camshaft is mounted above the crankshaft, and turns in ball bearings. It is driven at half engine speed by a pair of helical gears for quietness.

Like several other features on the R 60 US, the lubrication is similar to automobile oiling systems. There is no separate oil tank. Instead, the engine lubricant is contained in a sump under the crankshaft. A gear type pump draws oil from the sump, and feeds it along the crankshaft. After the oil has been fed to the cylinders, connecting rods, and valve gear, it drains through borings in the cylinder heads, through an oil passage press-fitted into the underside of each cylinder, and back into the sump.

The same rather massive, unstinting design appears in the clutch mechanism, which also is very similar to those found in cars. In place of a multi-disc clutch, a single plate, spline-coupled to the gearbox input shaft, is used. When the clutch lever is operated, the pressure plate is forced off the clutch plate, and drive from the crankshaft to the gearbox is then interrupted.

The heavy flywheel is the cause of the slow gear change action for which BMWs are infamous. This large mass of metal keeps the engine turning quickly even when the clutch lever is operated. The result is an evil-sounding crunch if changes are made hastily or awkwardly. There is only one way to make a noiseless change; be patient, and take it slowly. Even then, the gear pedal must be eased very gently and accurately. Gear action on the test machine was probably the noisiest test riders had encountered on BMWs, and became acutely embarrassing in city riding. Uninitiated car drivers tend to think the hideous crunching sounds are the rider's fault!

Even worse are times when vivid acceleration is required in city traffic. Then the BMW rider has a choice; he can rush the change and endure the accompanying graunching sounds, or he can wait for a couple of time devouring seconds before easing the pedal through.

From the gearbox, power is taken by the shaft drive system to the rear axle. The shaft runs in its own oil bath inside the right swinging arm, and is linked to the transmission by means of a universal joint running in needle bearings. The entire assembly at the rear is carried in a series of ball and needle bearings, and the crown gear and drive pinion are both spiral bevel gears which run noiselessly in an oil bath.

The shaft drive causes no problem with rear wheel removal. The folding rear fender is swung upward, two nuts, one on each side of the wheel, are undone, the axle spindle is withdrawn...and out comes the wheel, leaving the bevel housing and brake intact.

The R 60 has one more major disadvantage, in addition to its outdated gearbox. The combination of a meager 30 bhp, and the hefty weight, makes it distinctly underpowered in comparison with more modern machines. Many 250-cc machines are blessed with an equal amount of horsepower, and have the advantage of far less weight. The result is that the R 60 is no champion of the Greenlight Grand Prix. On other machines of similar engine size, full throttle acceleration is an exciting, hustling sensation as the bike rushes to 70 mph in a few seconds. The R 60 takes things in a far more deliberate manner.

Even with this handicap, BMWs have gained a fanatical following. Clearly, its supporters look for something else in a motorcycle than dragster style power. What they admire is the BMW's smoothness and ability to travel long distances with minimum fuss. BMW's careful construction has insured that the engine runs quietly, and this is complemented by an excellent exhaust system.

A vast dual seat contributes much to the comfort of rider and passenger. The seat is a generous 13.8 in. at its widest point, and is so long that two bulky humans have plenty of room. The R 60's capabilities as a touring machine were excellently demonstrated during the test period when it was taken for a 300-mile round trip which involved a climb from sea level to 4255 ft. Total weight of the bike, its two passengers, and their gear was around 840 lb., yet it cruised easily at 75 to 80 mph in a zone with no speed limit. A cruising speed of around 4400 rpm in fourth gear, equivalent to 65 to 70 mph, can be held indefinitely.

A handlebar screen fitted to the test bike was no handicap in windless conditions, but crosswinds of 25 mph treated it like a sail, and made hard work of high speed riding. No screen at all, or a full fairing, would probably have been better. But the way the R 60 hauled a heavy load at high speed over an arduous route was magnificent.

A pair of two-position springs and telescopic hydraulic shock absorbers comprise the BMW rear suspension. Adjustment from one position to another is achieved simply by turning a handle cast onto the suspension units. No tool is required for this task.

The frame is a duplex unit of rolled steel tubing, which actually changes diameter and shape as it passes from a highly loaded area to an area which is more lightly stressed. At the steering head, for example, very sturdy oval tubing is used, but this becomes circular, and of smaller diameter, farther down the front tubes. Top and lower frame members extend much farther to the rear of the machine than on most motorcycles. Another unusual practice is that rear suspension units are not pivoted at their upper ends. Instead, they are attached to the seat mounting, and to the rear of the frame.

Seat height of 33.3 in. means that shorter riders make a long stretch when placing their feet on the road. Hand and foot controls are located so that they are immediately accessible. Handlebar on the test machine was the optional type that BMW calls "Cross-Country." It entails an upright riding position that is comfortable enough for the longest journey.

A twin leading shoe brake is fitted at the front, and a single leading unit is used at the rear, in keeping with modern practice. Both are housed in large alloy hubs, and can slow the machine from high speed, even in the two-up situation, with a minimum of fuss. There is no jarring or shuddering of the front end under fierce braking, merely the aforementioned dipping of the fork. The R 60 equipped with an Earles fork actually costs $12 less than its stablemate with the telescopic unit. An additional, but less important, advantage with the new component is that it considerably cleans up the front end appearance of the bike.

Handling and cornering is safe and predictable. There is the danger that a cylinder could be badly mauled if the rider cornered too fast and the machine slid away, but BMW offers a "cylinder guard." a sort of small crash bar, as an optional extra. These bars are controversial items, because it is easy to dig them into the ground on corners and cause a spill. The BMW rider also must exercise care not to crunch the heads against high curbings. Width from the outside of one head to the outer edge of the opposite one is 27.75 in., approximately the same width as the handlebars.

Two 24-mm Bing carburetors are mounted one each side of the machine, behind the cylinders. They are fed through a single air cleaner which is one of the most efficient ever fitted to a motorcycle. In common with several other BMW features, it is based on automotive practice. The circular paper dry element is accommodated in an alloy housing. Air passes through the filter into an inner plenum chamber, and then along feed pipes to the carburetors. This system also eliminates induction roar.

A magneto supplies the sparks on the R 60, while a battery and generator form a completely separate electrical system which provides power for the lights and horn. All electrical components, apart from the battery, are housed under an alloy cover in front of the crankcase. This location protects them from water, yet allows easy access for maintenance. The headlight is fully adequate for night riding.

The BMW also offers its owner several less obvious pleasures, such as a lockable tool box mounted in the top of the optional 6.5-gal. fuel tank, and an excellent tool kit. This kit contains a variety of equipment ranging from wrenches and screwdrivers to a pair of pliers and a full tube puncture repair kit. Engine oil must be changed every 2000 miles, but transmission, rear wheel drive and right swinging arm oil must be replaced only at 16,000-mile intervals.

The German factory seems able to sell with no difficulty all the machines it can produce. Undoubtedly, the BMW is a great bike, with a charm it shares with no other motorcycle. ∎

BMW R 60 U.S.

SPECIFICATIONS

List price	$1376
Suspension, front	telescopic fork
Suspension, rear	swinging arm
Tire, front	3.50-18
Tire, rear	4.00-18
Brake, front, diameter x width, in.	7.8 x 1.4
Brake, rear, diameter x width, in.	7.8 x 1.4
Total brake swept area, sq. in.	68.5
Brake loading (test weight/swept area) lb./sq. in.	9.16
Engine type	ohv opposed Twin
Bore x stroke, in., mm.	2.81 x 2.85, 72 x 73
Displacement, cu. in., cc	36, 593
Compression ratio	7.5:1
Carburetion	(2) 24-mm Bing
Ignition	Bosch magneto
Claimed bhp @ rpm	30 @ 5800
Oil system	wet sump
Oil capacity, pt.	4.1
Fuel capacity, gal.	6.5
Starting system	kick
Lighting system	battery, generator
Air filtration	paper element
Clutch	single plate, dry
Primary drive	none
Final drive	(3.13:1) shaft and bevel gear
Gear ratios, overall:1	
5th	none
4th	4.81
3rd	6.05
2nd	8.52
1st	13.05
Wheelbase, in.	58.6
Seat height, in.	33.3
Seat width, in.	13.8
Footpeg height, in.	10.0
Ground clearance, in.	7.1
Curb weight (w/half-tank fuel), lb.	457
Test weight (fuel and rider), lb.	627

PERFORMANCE

Top speed (actual), mph	97.5
Calculated top speed in gears (@6400 rpm), mph	
5th	none
4th	100.0
3rd	79.5
2nd	56.4
1st	36.8
Mph per 1000 rpm, top gear	15.6
Speedometer error:	
50 mph indicated, actually	46.10
60 mph indicated, actually	54.81
70 mph indicated, actually	63.78
Acceleration, zero to:	
30 mph, sec.	2.8
40	4.0
50	5.3
60	7.6
70	10.9
80	16.2
90	22.6
100	...
Standing 1/8th mile, sec.	9.83
terminal speed, mph	67.36
Standing 1/4th mile, sec.	16.03
terminal speed, mph	79.85

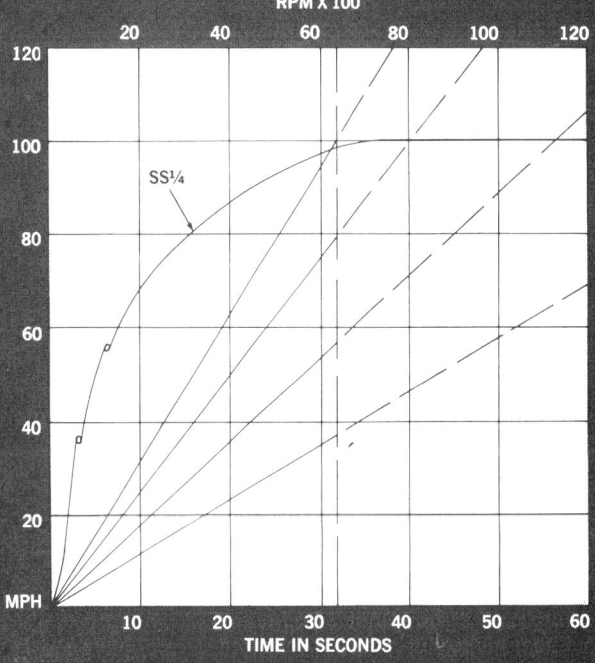

ACCELERATION AND ENGINE / ROAD SPEED
RPM X 100

Big Bore BMW

Walter Gruenberg's special has enlarged bore and stroke, raised compression, and careful valve train work.

Built By the Braniff Boys

WHEN Walter Gruenberg bought his BMW R69S, it was "one big ball of rust and dents, the fork was way out of line, and it was leaking oil badly. The bike had been wrecked in Panama." Six months, $2300, and endless hours of work later, Walter was the owner of a super-fast BMW with the appearance of a showroom model.

BMWs are superb machines in standard trim, and owners are content to leave them unmodified and uncustomized. Not so, Walter, a 33-year-old mechanic from Carrollton, Tex. Displacement of his machine has been increased from 593 to 700 cc, and it now has very un-BMW-like performance.

He says: "The top rpm limit must be over 8000. The bike is about 13 mph faster in every gear than a standard R69S. It was built primarily for high speed touring."

The project is a result of cooperation between engineers, welders, and machinists at Braniff International Airways, where Walter works, several specialist motorcycle companies, and Leon Pratt, the BMW dealer in Denton, Tex.

Cylinder head work, including installation of 42-mm intake valves, and enlargement and polishing of the ports was undertaken by Amol Precision, of Dumont, N.J. "The port surfaces are just like glass," reports Walter. Heavier valve springs, and lighter valve spring retainers and pushrods also were fitted.

Standard dimensions of the opposed Twin R69S engine are 72 mm bore and 73 mm stroke. The engine in the Gruenberg BMW has been enlarged to 75 mm bore and 79.5 mm stroke. This has been achieved by the use of 10.5:1 pistons from Bowman Products of Montrose, Calif., and offset crankpins machined from titanium stock by one of Walter's colleagues at BI. The crankpins were drilled and lightened, and small amounts of metal were ground from the big ends of the connecting rods, to prevent them from hitting the crankcases. Spacers of 0.25 in. had to be placed under the cylinders, and the same amount was cut from the bottom of the pistons. The latter modification was made more for balance than clearance.

A lightweight aluminum flywheel saves two-thirds the weight of the original unit, and converts the previously slow BMW gear change action to a very rapid movement. The clutch diaphragm was heated and bent for

more spring pressure, and then re-heat treated by the same BI machinist who worked on the crankpins.

A special oil pan with 4-in. cooling fins, and rocker covers with cooling fins, also were made by BI employees.

Carburetors are 30-mm Dellortos, from Mustang Motor Products Corporation, Sun Valley, Calif. The standard R69S cams have been retained, and a tuned BMW exhaust system is used. Gearing also is standard BMW, giving ratios of, from first to fourth, 13.05:1, 8.51:1, 6.05:1, and 4.81:1. An 8-gal. racing fuel tank, and Pirelli racing tires are fitted. Tire sizes are 3.00-18 in front, and 4.00-18 in the rear.

Walter gives credit to local motorcycle builder and race rider Don Turner, who planned the majority of the changes on the machine, and accomplished much of the engineering involved. BMW man Leon Pratt also provided much help, particularly by offering the use of all his special BMW tools. After tuning and riding the machine, Leon commented: "It sure doesn't feel or sound like a BMW. It goes like hell!"

Walter claims maximum speeds in the gears of 55, 79, 105, and 124 mph. Now he has a BMW-plus! ∎

FROM THE STABLE OF THE KAISER . .

YOU know the feeling. Winter has been a long, grey, wet, dullness; even the snow gave up and melted away in disgust of the damp, gritty filth beneath and the sodden grime splashed above. Even the vague memory of one bright, sunny January morning remains, almost hidden under a smothering blanket of foggy drabness. You don't just feel it will go on for ever and ever, or even realise you do. By now, the routine is accepted and the pattern set. This is life and there is no other. But one morning you wake a little earlier. The sun is shining, blazing through the by-now permanently drawn curtains. Something is different. Weekend? Holiday? Inherited a fortune? Whatever, it is more than the sunshine. Like the centre spot on a page of doodles it stands out, tiny, but with realisation, suddenly exploding gloriously. Garage! Now! Black and gleaming. Chock full of past reputations, myths, rumours and legend. It is early, but bed is for the world of boredom, and breakfast an obstacle between you and a new freedom. Long, frustrating, impatient minutes later you swing open the garage doors and there it stands leaning rakishly on the prop-stand as arrogant as a dream of knighthood. Contempt for anything outside its own traditions showing plainly in every line but just as obvious the proud acceptance of the rigid conventions im-

Not the Rolls Royce of motorcycles as is so often (mis)quoted, but the Porsche.

posed on all those descended from a long-established nobility.

You ride, in the new morning sun, through the empty streets. The frosty air pricks your nose, and slowly the concrete walls of the city streets shrink, to finally disappear, leaving the horizon as your only boundary. No maps in your pocket, and no route in your mind, so just follow the signposts; to "the North", where the high, rugged hills are more suited to the big German tourer than the lush green fields of the South and West. So went my thoughts, and my riding, during my week's riding.

Compiling a test was not easy, at least not a fair one. It would have been easy enough to deride it for its apparent lack of speed or some other inconsequential observation, but providing the concept of its original purpose was kept in mind, and its value towards only that judged, rather than a direct comparison with any similarly sized motor cycle, then it was difficult. Only two others in my opinion have any relationship anyway: the Moto-Guzzi V7 and the Harley-Davidson Electraglide, and as I have never ridden them, then for me and the purpose of this test then they might as well not exist. We in this country can buy nothing on the home market manufactured to compete; neither Norton Commando, nor BSA/Triumph Three. At the start of the week we (the Editor and I) were lucky enough to find ourselves with a Royal Enfield Interceptor, and after the first few moments with both, I considered conducting a comparison test; but as the week passed, so grew my reluctance to carry it out, for familiarity only accentuated the gap between the two. One is a rough, tough sportster, and the other a luxury tourer; both can do the other's job, but only at the expense of their true function, although it is not quite such a hard-and-fast rule with the Enfield.

After producing aircraft engines for many years, in 1923 the first horizontally-opposed, shaft-driven motor cycle was produced. Although a side-valve, it was the foundation upon which, with very few exceptions, every other machine produced by the company was built. Three years later, the first ohv engine appeared, and immediately pre-war came the first telescopic forks and rear suspension. 14 years ago in 1955 the present range of machines started with the introduction of the R50, a 500 cc tourer, identical in every respect save minor changes, to the present-day models. In consequence it can be safely said that except for improvements, the R60 I used owes its superlative performance to 46 years of production, albeit thorough; so surely after such time, with a sound basic design, any

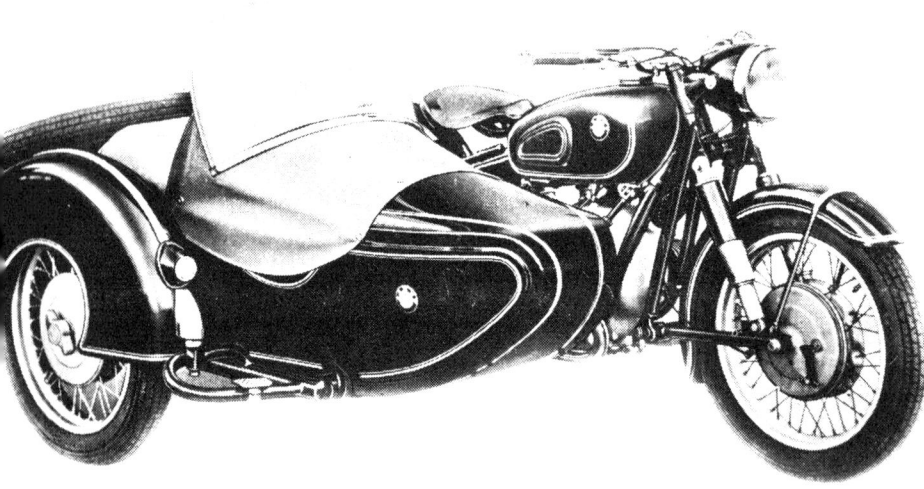

The world's most famous combination: an R60 BMW and a Steib S501. An historic pair setting a standard by which all others follow.

motor cycle company could turn out a similar machine. After my introduction to it, I can all too well understand the supporters of the policy of improvement through refinement, instead of replacement; it has much in its favour.

Until a very short time ago we had nothing even remotely approaching the price, so that could well be claimed as the reason for unpopularity. But years ago, the Vincent twins equalled it, yet it still was unpopular. Two British manufacturers introduced similar machines, both without any great success. The Wooller shaft-driven flat four—killed by an unimaginative public, disinterested in anything but the cheap, samey old stuff they were deluding each other and the manufacturers (to their lasting discredit and misfortune)—was best, and the Sunbeam. These beautiful motor cycles, so far advanced of their contemporaries, not only in performance but engine design, suffered a long, lingering death from the instance of production. It was the motor cycle everybody wanted to admire as a national prestige piece, but nobody wanted to buy. A few people did, although even they generally, probably because of the fat styling, killed its charm by manacling it for life to a sidecar as big as a saloon car. Maybe we know something the Germans don't. Maybe there is something inherently unsound in a frame-line crankshaft. Even Douglas gave up in disgust in favour of scooters.

There is no getting away from the fact that a generous re-assessment of one's previous standards is necessary to enjoy to the full the complete satisfaction obtainable from the machine. Not un-naturally, at first hand they clash, and certainly my initial reaction was to shrug off my own failings to adapt to the new personality, and blame the motor cycle as inadequate. Once the partnership is complete, though, few machines are capable of impressing their owners (and long term borrowers) quite as deeply. I found dozens of ''faults'' within the first day, but as the initial strangeness wore off they disappeared, and in most cases, one in particular concerned with roadholding, showed themselves as functional benefits. So many people, their interest aroused by the sight and sound of the big, flat twin proudly admitted to a ''quick run up the road and back'' at some time or other on one, and just as proudly boasted that it had not come up to the performance standard set by their own machine. These people are a manufacturer's delight, for in every case it boiled down to one thing: speed, or the lack of it; nothing else except for a vague inexpressible discomfort that it was

Observe the width of the machine, no more than any other, and also the clean, uncluttered simplicity of its whole appearance.

not quite right; nothing more or less than an excusable (because of the short ride) misunderstanding.

Speed is the easiest of all qualities to build into a motor cycle providing others are sacrificed, and they generally are. You or I can add enormously to the power of a machine by simply opening out gas tracts, skimming heads, reamering out carbs and rejetting. For manufacturers and tuning component companies it is even easier to fit high-lift cams, bigger valves and what-have-you. Mechanical, inlet and exhaust silencing is lost. Flexibility becomes a memory, reliability forgotten in the tasteless scrabble for speed, and comfort ignored altogether. Until the experience of riding a motor cycle designed to cruise—and the accent is on cruise—at high speeds indefinitely and carry the rider in all possible comfort is enjoyed, then it is almost impossible to realise just how poorly designed most of our machines are. Without doubt the front suspension is unsuitable for ultra-fast sports machines. It can be argued that the gear change cannot be raced through without use of the clutch. That the footrests are too far forward to allow a racing crouch to be adopted in comfort. Gear ratio changing to match the new power output after tuning is an expensive and difficult process, if indeed it is possible. So on and so on. Is it any less of a machine for all this? Certainly not. It brings home with a wallop just how perfectly suited to its purpose it really is, and how so many other machines are

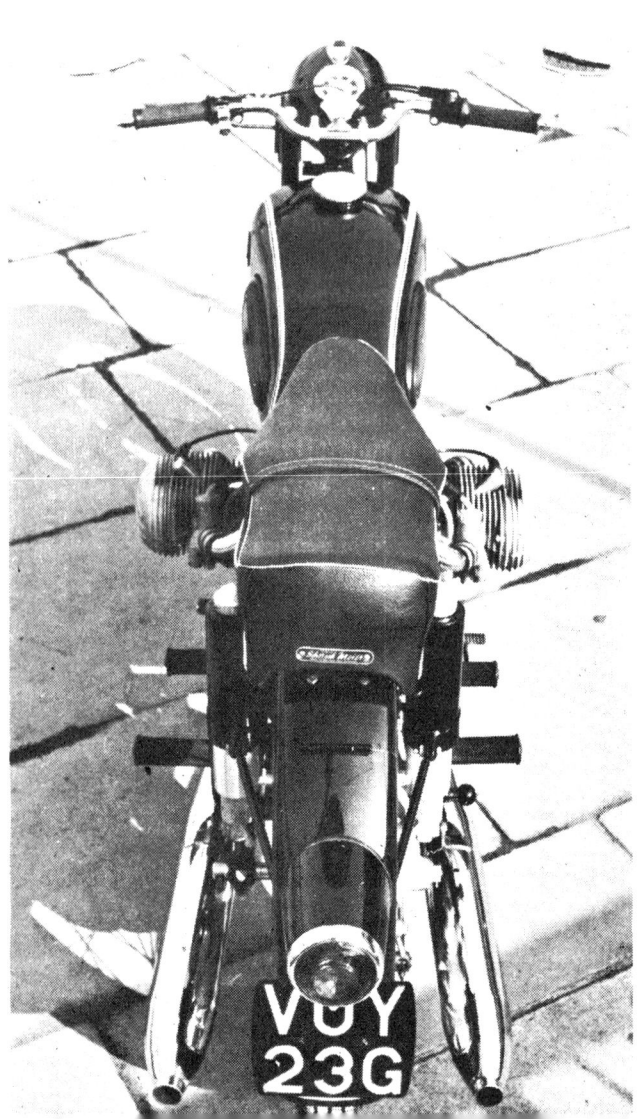

merely the adoption of one single basic design, and the attempt to adapt it for all purposes in much the same manner as those awful old pannier sets advertised as having universal fittings; they fitted everything badly and nothing properly. A few days with "my" R60 convinced me that with precious few exceptions, everything had a reason, and there was a reason for everything.

I was very reluctant indeed to hand it over to its temporary owners, but as it was not planned in the first place merely a happy surprise I could scarcely grumble. I was paying a visit to the Elite Motors of Tooting, just chatting to Ron Welling the manager about their motor cycles, when he grinned and mentioned IT. Would I like to ride it? Would I? WOULD I!? Act cool, I thought; play it down; it's the casual approach that impresses. But I am me, so that all went by the board and once I had hold of the throttle absolutely refused to let go, grinning immensely the whole time. My first reaction, once I had stopped foolishly attempting to start the engine by straddling the bike, simply radiating synthetic confidence, kicking awkwardly at the radially-transposed crank, was one of pleasant surprise at the gently murmuring exhaust. While stationary at traffic halts it was often impossible to hear or even feel the engine and I had to blip the throttle to recognise the fact that it was turning over. Secondly was the apparent light weight, brought about by the very low centre of gravity; to my mind one of the most endearing features of the machine. Thirdly came the impression of the superb riding position. Everything seemed a long way down: tank, handlebars and engine. Overall, it felt to be a comfortably small controllable motor cycle. Fourth was delight at the light, positive, firm controls, and fifth I discovered when I rode away. Satiny, velvety smoothness. After the initial tickover tremors as the clutch was released, nothing, just a whispered suggestion of energy from the silencers. Not the trundling weight of a well-balanced single, or the dynamo thrill of a two-stroke twin. but a featureless, flat "nothing". Images reflected in the twin mirrors remained as steady as the objects they framed. All this and nobody noticed. Even other motor cyclists ignored our passing, and why not? The eyes notice only 50% of the world around, the ears are attracted by the rest, and to most people we remained unheard. Later in the week I grew used to using the powerful Klaxon horn more than is usual on a motor cycle for this reason.

The most recent USA models have thrown away the Earles type front suspension, and reverted to telescopic forks; well, providing the latest models are lightweight sports machines all well and good, but if not it is a retrograde step. To improve on the present layout I would categorise as possible, but improbable. The design engineers must have decided exactly what would be required of a tourer's front end and exploited (not designed, for it was an Englishman's idea) a system that would fill the role practically, instead of attempting to modify an already existing and accepted method to suit the need. Front and rear springs are variable coil type, so small irregularities are completely absorbed by the softer leading coils, and the bigger bumps by the harder ones following. An example of the system's effectiveness came to light as I was pushing the bike to its parking spot beneath the office. A sandwich crust lay on the ground and as the wheels rolled over it, both sets of springs moved. I tried again, and sure enough once again, only lightly, but the sliders lifted and dropped. Try it with your own mount sometime; it's a disappointment. I would imagine, although I can find no reference to it, that a variable damping system must be incorporated as well, for generally this alone is enough

Just to prove that a 'Bee Em' is more than a tourer—Ellis Boyce riding MLG's R69s to victory in the 1961 Thruxton 500.

to cause a certain "stiction" if the action is constant regardless of inertia. At all speeds and over all road surfaces I could not seriously fault the suspension, and found it fascinating to watch the front mudguard's never-ceasing movement as it rippled gently on even the smoothest roads. Unsprung weight is, I suspect, a little high, because on a sudden drop caused by, say, a frost hole or a resurfacing gang's half-way progress, I could feel a definite thud as the wheels hit the hole's floor. It did not show up on a lifting bump any more than any other type, in fact it was better, but on a drop away: shock! No movement took place on the handlebars, and even the mirror images remained still, but I could still sense the wheel's weight. For all that, though, combined with the luxurious dual seat it was the most comfortable ride I have yet to enjoy on any motor cycle and a goodly number of cars. The seat incidentally has no pressed steel pan, but a skeleton frame, supporting a web of springs upon which an inch or so of firm foam rubber sits. How sensible. Unsprung foam collapses the instant you sit upon it into a non-resilient squash; in a long run, and I mean long, first producing an ache and finally numbing. Normally the machine remained parallel to the ground even while braking; only if a crash halt was tried did it lift, and then only slightly. Altogether it gave a feeling of great security, without any yawing forward from weight transference, easier on the arms as well. At the rear end, springload adjustment could be carried out by simply operating an aluminium peg at the base of the spring unit. The driving shaft is carried within the offside rear fork leg, and except for the plastic bellows covering the universal joint at the front, is completely hidden. Obviously that part of the drive is sealed from the oil everything else runs in, but I do not like the idea. A metal sheath would be a better thing, for once the plastic convolutions crack—and all plastic brittles with age—it would have to be replaced, and that would require a tiresome strip-down of the rear end and drive.

As with other components the frame is massively constructed, and must contribute enormously to the overall weight. Whether any motor cycle really needs such a gargantuan skeleton I doubt, and suggest it is a prime example

Road test by DAVE MINTON

Was ever a machine more courageously unsuitable? One of the flat twins prepared for the 1964 ISDT.

of the argument against gradual evolvement rather than fresh planning. Studying it I could not but help the impression that any weak points in the design had been overcome by brutally strengthening the construction. For instance, the pivoted fork support. Two vertical struts run parallel each side of the frame connecting the top and bottom tubes, and that is all the support the rear end has. In what I imagine to be a pretty desperate attempt to stall movement under stress at this point, the struts have been cast in solid iron or maybe steel, but it does not matter which. Why a simple triangle could not have been fabricated with its apex at the pivot bearing is puzzling. Unarguably lighter and stronger, it would possibly cost less as well. Although I found nothing lacking on the R60, I know full well road-holding on the R69S does come in for criticism. Maybe the extra power has something to do with it at this point. This however is scarcely fair, for my concern is with the R60 and to this end I have great respect for its handling characteristics. It took a little time in getting used to, but once familiar it was superb. The only fault became apparent on one favourite local road. A steep hill ends in a swooping valley, curving to the right and climbing hard upward again. Just there the exaggerated "G" effect, coupled with the turn, set the stressed frame and suspension shrugging its protest with an even, regular waver that I could not pin-point to any particular spot. Under any normal conditions though, bend swinging was good enough to relax with and enjoy, and at any speed I was able to remove my hands with never a movement from the handlebars. Until used to the manner of cornering I found a certain vagueness about the procedure but only after a couple of days did I discover what should be a very basic fact. We are used to vertical engines and their partnering high gravity centre, while this one's flat and low engine pulled it down to not much above the wheelspindle, hence the ease with which the top of the machine could move. Take a pencil, hold the base between your fingers and waggle it from side to side. It is an easy enough and quick motion, and instantly controllable. Now push the same pencil's point into an apple or cotton reel and try the same thing. Although more effort is required to start the rocking movement, once it has it is not as controllable as previously, and it also affects the base of the pencil to a greater extent. It is much the same with any motor cycles with a high centre of gravity. It may feel more stable due to the initial effort required to start the high mass rocking, but once you do it can be dangerous. But a flat twin because of its low centre of gravity can be moved relatively easily at the top, but in reality is a far more stable proposition. Quick direction changes and line-swopping were a thrill and could be easily accomplished without the cylinderheads scraping. That it could be done at speed enough to crush the suspension I have no doubt, but what I do doubt is the ability of any man to carry it out on the road whilst in full possession of his senses, and to (a) come out of the corner, (b) do it again on the same machine or (c) be able

to do it again. Probably it could be done on a very slow, tight curve by dropping the bike down and back up again before time enough has passed for anything "funny" to happen, but that is cheating. Another silly rumour has ended for me as well. You would no more wipe off one barrel because "they stick out and might hit something" than you would remove a foot under identical conditions on a vertical twin, for although the machine is wider than most, with the rider aboard width is about the same. Traffic threading was if anything easier than with most big machines because of the superior direction-changing ability, and certainly width was no greater problem.

The touring image follows through everything, even the gear ratios. Bottom considered in this context is just right; a little high, but low enough to pull away from a standstill easily. Second follows suit, high enough to be used at touring speeds, and low enough for traffic; actually I found the bottom two gears the most comfortable to use in town. 25 mph in bottom and 40 mph in second proving happy change-up speeds. Third blends in at 60 mph without any step in the ratios so often found in an attempt to make up for the lacking fifth ratio, and top fits the pattern. All in all a well-chosen set of gears complimenting the engine's power characteristics to a "T". Without the quiet exhaust note the speeds in the lower gears would not have been practical, but as it was I could and did accelerate hard away from a standstill without disturbing a soul.

Most interesting of all is the power unit. Compared to it the rest of the machine though unconventional by our standards becomes merely ancillary. Many, many years of development have resulted in an almost faultless performance, within its own limitations of course, but even this cannot hide the fact that it is a very old design. I remember some time ago, either reading or hearing a quote to the effect that it was in fact a refined vintage engine, and frankly I agree wholeheartedly, but to avoid any misunderstanding I should point out that it is not necessarily a criticism, merely an observation. Other machines have this in common. Big twin Harley Davidsons and Velocettes, even Triumph Bonnevilles have their roots sunk deep in pre-war engines. The R60 is quoted as producing 30 bhp at 5800 rpm, and on this point I have nothing but admiration. So many manufacturers celebrate their machines' anniversaries by quoting an extra horsepower, like parents adding a candle to their children's birthday cakes, yet speed remains remarkably constant. Top speed is also modestly given as 84 mph, so from my experience both power and speed match exactly even to the point of pessimism. Compression is comfortably low at 7.5:1. Very quickly I discovered the enjoyable sensation of surprising pump attendants by ordering a few gallons of "the worst". Even with this, pinking could not be provoked by the most hamfisted jiggery-pokery, so whoever buys VOY 23 G from Elite Motors—who, incidentally, have a couple of Continental mechanics so familiar with what we regard as a rare, precious motor cycle as to suggest they are not quite what they appear to be to us—might well be able to save enough money by buying cheap petrol to pay for his road tax. It is quite possible; I worked it out. Previously I mentiond the vintage performance. From the drop of the clutch it stands out. It is safe to say that despite the smoothness and quiet performance of the motor, the power band is comparatively restricted; one reason for the semi-close gears. The engine is unhappy at anything under about 3000 rpm, not that it will not, but it is hesitant and unusable power, and then at the other end of the scale power falls off at about 6000 rpm (maximum comes at 5800). For a touring machine it is not so good, and anyway, nobody wants to rev up to maximum the whole time; besides it is out of character to do such a thing often. Doubtless, German silencing regulations (the only reason for the whispering exhaust note) absorb a lot of power at the top end of the scale, and were an owner to fit a pair of efficient Dunstall type, he might well notice a big improvement. But if it were mine I think I would forsake the few extra mph for luxury of true silence. Tick-over was so slow it sounded like a good, soft old single. Had I had the time an even slower one could have been achieved by careful tuning. Comparing it to the Interceptor, I estimate it to have been around the 700 rpm mark, and it was reliable. At what felt to be 4000 or so rpm a very satisfying power increase developed; enough to get things really moving, but it was all a little bit out of character to suddenly feel the distinguished tourer beneath suddenly start punching out power with the wicked, gleeful abandon of an otherwise obedient dog chasing a rabbit away from its master. Holding on to this range, very good acceleration indeed for a heavy 600 could be encouraged, and compared favourably to a Gold Flash or Thunderbird. Low down it did not have the power of either; to be honest I expected a little more, especially knowing their popularity with chair enthusiasts.

Like a Volkswagen, because of their robustness and sensibly low-placed power output, top speed is cruising speed. Why not? The same components are used to propel the much faster R69S along at greater speeds, so this model will never snap inside. Sitting bolt upright and using throttle stop acceleration methods, speed increased hard and persistently up to just beyond 80 mph, and then steadily weakened until the needle was only moments away from 90 mph. As only 800 miles had registered on the clock, and not wishing to spoil the next owner's chances of a superb, trouble-free machine I tried once only for top speed and then only momentarily. I have no doubt that with more miles on the clock, and lighter clothing or a slight crouch (very easy with the riding position on the R60) a genuine 90 could be within easy reach. I did not check the speedometer's accuracy but I have no reason to doubt it; should you prefer, then dock a couple of degrees for the sake of tradition. I am not, though.

Throughout the test I have referred to a tourer, simply for the sake of easy classification, but in fact a term so popular with car enthusiasts is much nearer the truth—GT. If any motor cycle deserves to be classified as such then this one does. Oh, I know the R69S is faster, but for the sake of my argument the two are the same. Ignore the shoddy, mass-produced rubbish that the PR and ad-men have deluded the public, and themselves by now, into believing is a GT; it is not. A GT is more than a cheap family saloon with a stripe down the side and another carburetter. It means Gran Turismo and was conceived by the Italians to describe the kind of car which they excel in building. One for the millionaire set, manufactured on a small production scale for a driver seeking the best performance and the greatest comfort without over concern for the cost—a fast luxury cruiser. The Editor and I enjoyed more conversation about this than we do on a good many machines, and concluded that "GT" fits exactly. The fact that other motorcycles may have a higher top speed is irrelevant.

Again the vintage (though not old-fashioned) traditions repeat themselves in the electrical system. Magneto and dynamo supply the power to their respective systems, but neither bear the faintest physical resemblance to their British counterparts. The magneto is a rotating magnet type, which means it should last for ever, and is driven from the camshaft. The dynamo is a 6v 90w output unit driven from the crankshaft. Both are located behind a cast aluminium cover in the front of the engine. I think that the electrics alone could persuade me to buy. When I think of the breakdowns I have suffered because of the incompatability of machine and electrical unit, or simply the shoddy, cheap, penny-pinching attitude of the motor cycle manufacturers (not Lucas), I wish for the good old days back again with simple but effective electrics. Admittedly, though, since the

introduction of the latest 12v systems things seem to be improving.

Braking is like the rest of the machine, as efficient as could be imagined. As well as being immensely powerful, leverages have been carefully arranged to fit the rider's purpose. They are good and smooth at light pressure, but with any hard increase in fist or foot pressure, respond accordingly and grip the wheels as though some cogs had suddenly engaged. That is all I can say about them, simply that for this machine and its purpose they would be hard to better.

The price in this country is around £650, but in Germany the same as ours are here, about £400. Other little points I noticed. The clever, hidden tool box behind the left knee grip on the petrol tank. The stupid lack of an air lever making it impossible to tell why it would not start in the morning. The very peculiar advice in the instruction book to "Remove and dismantle the carburetters every 4000 miles". On a leave-well-alone machine like this? No ammeter either; it is madness. They are as important as a speedometer, more in fact. Winking lights are utterly pointless, and satisfy only the ignorant to whom they appeal and tell nothing. The sheer snobbery I found in myself, riding around Knightsbridge trying to feel at home amongst the Alvises and Bentleys—and succeeding.

It is probably still in Elite Motors right now. A glossy, arrogant thoroughbred among a host of bright-coloured toys. It stands out a mile as a motor cycle incomparably right in every respect. Whatever the means taken to achieve it, the end result is near perfection.

And now dear reader forgive us, for silence under such conditions is impossible. Groan if you must, but the choice is yours alone—To be or not to BMW.

PREVIEW: BMW 750-cc R 75 US

The Opposed Twin Follows Suit

BY IVAN J. WAGAR

AMONG THE hard core motorcycle touring enthusiasts of the world there are about three groups that favor Twins. These Twin devotees can be divided into Vees, Verticals and Horizontals. The latter group, for reasons known only to themselves, have developed into the most rigid, adamant bunch of "individuals" in motorcycling. They are "individuals" because the near $2000 price tag is nothing for the supreme product. Most Horizontal fans think nothing of spending another $200 for a pair of upswept pipes or $350 for a pregnant gasoline tank to make their "pure" Horizontal different from the one down the street.

Not only is the hard core Horizontal addict prepared to go on an enormous dollar binge, he also reads every word published anywhere in the world for and against his brand. To this group, the advent of a 750-cc BMW will be no surprise. They have read for the past couple of years accounts of experimental 750-cc mounts in the International Six Days Trial, and of a down-the-street machinist in Germany making 750-cc conversions for existing BMWs.

So, to the Horizontal Bunch, the all-new R 75 might be old hat. On the other hand, those among us who look on motorcycles as fun, rather than tradition, will find it interesting that Bavarian Motor Works has not been sitting still while manufacturers in England and the Orient have built and shipped their 750-cc muscle machines to this country.

The R 75 truly is a fine looking machine. Engine castings and gasoline tank have been blended to eliminate the ugly air gap of previous models. The massive central engine casting now extends higher for its full length to provide a housing for the previously bastard looking air cleaner. The tank is similar in concept to the conversion BMWs customizers have been paying fortunes for. In reality the tank is extremely humped, but the fact that the frame toptube passes very high through the center shows it is of deep saddle construction. That is, the tank has been designed to fill in an undesirable "hole" with the deep side sections.

Previous BMWs, including the R 69 U.S., featured a frame which was a hand-me-down from the rigid frame era. The main cradle lower loops extended from the front of the engine to just ahead of the rear wheel spindle. Rear suspension units were supported—as an after-thought—in an outrigger housing. The new frame layout obviously is constructed without the restrictions of heritage. The R 75 frame almost is a takeoff on the trend-setting, classic Manx Norton design. About the only visible exception is the fabricated single toptube. Otherwise, the Manx enthusiast would be lost. The new frame begins the two loops at the bottom of the steering head and, instead of continuing to the rear wheel, loops upward immediately behind the engine mass. At the junction of the seat and tank, the loop tubes join the top backbone frame member. Two small tubes, also very similar to the Manx Nortons of 18 years ago, sprout from the swinging arm pivot juncture to the top of the rear suspension units.

The cast iron swinging arm pivot junction has been eliminated on the R 75; note that the rear fork is mounted inboard of the twin downtubes. Structurally the new layout should be much stronger because twisting forces at the pivot point are more easily contained when the swinging arm is inside the frame members. As before, the final drive is by shaft through the hollow right-side swinging arm tube which bolts to the bevel housing in the rear hub. The old style rear suspension legs featured a cast alloy lower section, with integrally cast

knobs which permitted the operator to adjust the stiffness of the springs without the aid of tools. The new units on the R 75 are very similar to Girling legs, but have a sheet steel handle welded to the adjusting cam on the lower spring flange. The complete front fork assembly is identical to that used on last year's U.S. models.

Mounting passenger footpegs and mufflers was an easy task on the old frame with the loops extending to the rear wheel. Now that the frame is similar to current design trends, it has been necessary to build two small sheet metal fabricated mounts to perform the chores. The mounts are welded to the swinging arm juncture of the main cradle, and are quite short, leaving some 20 in. of overhang for the heavy mufflers.

The new BMW's rear fender is quite interesting from an engineering point of view—there is no hinged rear portion to permit easy removal of the wheel—another indication of appearance taking precedence. CYCLE WORLD's last BMW test machine was the R 60 U.S., which featured alloy rims; previous models used steel rims. The R 75 employs the new steel deep side rims, which offer light weight but are very strong, and have a similar appearance to alloy wheels. The front brake is a twin leading shoe unit, while the rear is of single leading shoe design. Both front and rear hubs are cast alloy, with iron liners, and have chrome-plated discs on the side opposite the brakes. Recently at Hockenheim, a four-shoe, dual front brake was tried on a machine based at Munich (factory sponsored), and it is assumed that this unit will be fitted to future larger displacement BMW models.

Heart of the R 75, the engine, is an all new design, not simply a punched out version of an older configuration. The whole engine is slightly tilted in the chassis so that the drive shaft line is nearer to the angle of the engine in the frame. All major engine castings, besides being much more massive, are different from previous engines. The camshaft now is located below the crankshaft, and pushrod tubes are underneath the cylinders. Thus the visible top of the engine is more attractive. Cylinders now are cast aluminum with iron liners, and the finning blends with that on the cylinder heads.

Throughout the engine, extensive use has been made of deeply recessed allen head screws. All flanges have very thick reinforcing bosses for the screw heads to bottom in the aluminum castings for maximum support at the flanges. Mating widths at all joints are sufficiently wide to ensure an extremely oil-tight engine, despite the enormous castings which will grow and shrink rather large amounts during use. The R 75 which was made available to CYCLE WORLD featured sand castings throughout. And, while the factory would like to adopt die cast techniques for production models, no top level decision has been made at this point to eliminate the rough sand castings.

Overall appearance of the machine could have been improved in the region of the battery if some sort of sheet metal or cast aluminum covers had been designed to continue the upper engine castings rearward beyond the air cleaner compartment. As it is, the battery is the only ugly spot on an otherwise pleasant design.

Basic engine layout is the same as on the first BMW motorcycle introduced some 46 years ago—the horizontally opposed Twin. The advantage of an opposed piston engine is that almost all reciprocating forces are canceled, and vibration is quite nonexistent. One of the major disadvantages—and one blissfully ignored by the Horizontal Bunch—is the effect of the machine attempting to rotate about the axis of the crankshaft under acceleration or deceleration. It is, after all, a very basic fundamental of physics when the crankshaft is in-line with the motorcycle. And the greater the flywheel effect, the greater the tendency for the machine to exhibit this unusual characteristic. After a rider has spent some time and miles on a transverse design, he becomes accustomed to rotational effect and allows for it in his riding habits. From that point on, the pluses of smoothness seem to offset the minuses of an in-line crank.

The crankshaft of the R 75 is mounted in four main bearings. It was suspected that BMW would make an attempt to incorporate a center main bearing assembly in the new design to eliminate crankshaft whip at high crankshaft speeds. That would mean, however, that the cylinders would necessarily be considerably out of line, an undesirable trait in an opposed Twin layout. In an attempt to overcome the need for the rigidity of a middle main bearing, the crankshaft has been made huskier than even before.

To emphasize the strength of the crankshaft we should explain that this engine has been built in versions up to the 900-cc, without crankshaft failures. The 900-cc R 90 is due to be released later. Along with the R 75 will be two smaller versions, of 600- and 500-cc displacement. The R 50, R 60 and R 75 all feature the same stroke of 70.6 mm, resulting in an extremely over-engineered bottom end for the 500 in order to have tooling uniformity throughout the line. Where the 500 has an undersquare bore/stroke ratio of 67/70.6, the 750 engine is in much better shape at 82/70.6, considerably oversquare. Thus, the R 75 has a very low piston speed (in the region of 3000 ft./min.) at the rated maximum of 6400 rpm, where the engine is claimed to produce its maximum output of 57 bhp, to give a claimed top speed of 115 mph.

Carburetion for the R 75 will be handled by a pair of Bing units, new in concept. During tests of BMW prototypes in the ISDT in the past few years, various types of Japanese Keihin carburetors were experimented with to discover the satisfactory balance between demand and consumption on quick throttle openings. Bing now has produced a carburetor so close in design concept that it must in some respects infringe on Keihin patent rights. Be that as it may, the new Bing has a vacuum demand operated slide which produces an over-rich mixture during the crucial first instant of rapid throttle opening, much the same way as the acceleration pump on American automobiles. The major difference is that the accelerator pump tosses a gush of raw gasoline into the inlet track, whereas the diaphragm carburetor causes a delay in admitting more air quickly. A greater vacuum is produced in the venturi and the engine sucks in a larger portion of fuel until the slide begins to open. The system is extremely efficient, and more economical than the squirts of raw gasoline from an accelerator pump.

Altogether new for BMW is an electric starter, which will be standard on the 600 and 750 models, and an optional item on the 500. However, the factory has opted to retain the traditional side acting kick starter, probably because of the smallish battery. Most factories going to electric start have done away with the kick starter, reasoning that, with sufficient amperage available, the chances of not starting are the same as with the modern auto—just about nil.

At this time plans are going along very well for the new units. Early in the year it was believed the new machines would be ready for release in June. But production delays moved the date to August. Now Berlin skeptics have predicted a delay until December. The new R 75 will not be built at the old Munich plant, but at a new plant at Spandau in Berlin. This does not, of course, mean the machine's name will be changed from the traditional BMW. It does mean that the present work force of 450 employees is to be increased by 50 to meet the demand schedules imposed by the need to have the new models in production at a rate of 1000 units per month before September. CYCLE WORLD's advertising department has a special all-color layout for the October issue to announce the R 50, R 60 and R 75. From that we can assume that everything is going as planned, and that the machine will, indeed, be available for sale in September.

The R 75 marks a completely new trend for BMW. Gone is the strict adherence to 46-year-old practices and design innovations; in most respects, the new R 75 is in line with what everyone else is doing and, therefore, it will be interesting to see how BMW fares when meeting the competition head on.

R27 250 BMW

Surprise, surprise . . . it's not so gutless!

THE tester, faced with the job of assessing a 250 B.M.W., has to consider whether to report on it as "just another 250" or as a B.M.W. product. Its price encourages one to judge it by the standards of other B.M.W.s. With this in mind, we have drawn comparisons with other B.M.W.s where the situation has demanded it.

Of course, everyone knows that a "proper" B.M.W. has a cylinder poking out either side. When the 250 B.M.W. is discussed in select circles it is, at worst, dismissed as never having been heard of and, at best, as "half a bike" (a label that a malevolent twin owner pinned on the 250, having just been "seen off" by one !).

And, yet, it is still a B.M.W., with the blue and white badge on the tank and most of the features of the bigger B.M.W.s —except that it hasn't got those famous cylinders pointing out at the sides. The suspension is the same, the seat is the same, the lights, controls, cycle parts, are the same. Both have the same shaft drive, engine-speed clutch, fore and aft crankshaft, clunky (if you're careless !) gearbox,

and, of course, the same peerless workmanship.

The heritage of the R27 goes right back to pre-war days, when it was sold as the R23 and was considered one of the best two-fifties on the market. Steady development produced the first post-war version, the R25, with the R26 being introduced in 1955, looking very much like the R27. When the R27 was introduced six or seven years ago, you had to peer very closely at the engine to discern that there was a difference from earlier bikes. There wasn't much to see . . . but what an improvement!

> We are indebted to Herbert Kennard, B.M.W. Club P.R.O., for the loan of his 1967 R27. It was supplied at only a few hours' notice "as it stood" without even a wash—and it had been used for a 200-mile trip a few days previously. Perhaps readers will forgive any road grime showing in the photographs, which were taken soon after delivery.

What had they done ? Why, rubber mounted the engine. And I bet you thought that the Commando was the first ! In the same way that rubber mounting transformed the Norton, so it transformed the R27—but more about that later; first let's tell you something about what makes the bike tick.

The engine is "square" (68×68mm), of 245 c.c., with pushrod-operated valves. As already stated, it is unusual in having the crankshaft running "the wrong way". This means that the single-plate, disc-spring pressured clutch is running across the frame, transmitting power to a four-speed gearbox. From there the power is taken by shaft to the rear bevels. All these parts run in oil. This inevitably means that the slow B.M.W. gearchange is retained. It also means that the clutch is well nigh unburstable. So, for that matter, is the bottom half of the engine. This is hardly surprising when you consider that the bearings and crankpin used are of the same dimensions as those on the 500 twin. The wet sump oil system is, if anything, an improvement on that of

And now: the new BMWs

Which have telescopic front forks (with $8\frac{1}{2}$in travel), oval-tube cradle frame incorporating detachable rear section (9 lb lighter than the old), redesigned cylinder heads, new crankshaft, 12-volt, 180-watt alternator, $5\frac{1}{4}$-gallon tank

R50/5—the five-hundred: 70.6mm stroke, 67mm bore. Power: 36 b.h.p. at 6,600 r.p.m. Bing "float" carburettor. Weight: 410 lb. Top speed claimed: 100 m.p.h. Acceleration: 0-60 in 9.8 seconds. Electric starter optional. Silver-grey finish

R60/5—the six-hundred: 70.6mm stroke, 73.5mm bore. Power: 45 b.h.p. at 6,600 r.p.m. Bing "float" carburettor. Weight: 421 lb. Top speed: 105 m.p.h. Acceleration: 0-60 m.p.h. in 7.8 seconds. Electric starter. Black finish

R75/5—the seven-fifty: 70.6mm stroke, 82mm bore. Power: 57 b.h.p. at 6,400 r.p.m. Bing "vacuum" carburettor. Weight: 421 lb. Top speed: 110 m.p.h. Acceleration: 0-60 m.p.h. in 6.1 seconds. Electric starter. Silver-grey finish

the twins, with the oilways drilled in the crankshaft to allow oil to pass right through. On the twins the oilways in the crankshaft are blind and, inevitably, get bunged up with sludge. Oil is delivered by gear-type pump under pressure. All these are reasons why you will rarely see a 250 B.M.W. owner (when you see one at all!) with bottom-end trouble.

The R27 was, until recently, the only modern B.M.W. to use a chain—to drive the camshaft. The latest B.M.W.s (reported elsewhere) have now reverted to this system. With adjustment by tensioner, it is noiseless and efficient. The engine, with a compression of 8.2 to 1, revs to 7,400 r.p.m. and develops maximum torque at 6,300.

Disasters of my youth have left me unreasonably prejudiced against coil ignition and I have always tended to regard it as a fault that the 250s should use this system. Yet with power supplied by a Bosch 90-watt generator there shouldn't be trouble, and on the model tested the system behaved faultlessly.

The cycle parts on the R27 differ little from those of the twins. The frame is the familiar duplex cradle type, of slightly lighter manufacture, with the swinging-arm rear suspension identical to that of the bigger model. Earles-type front forks are fitted, again of a slightly lighter construction. Eighteen-inch wheels, 3.3-gallon petrol tank and well-valanced steel mudguards complete the picture of a very well-made lightweight. Though the term "lightweight" is more a description of its capacity class than its build, for the B.M.W. turns the scales at 356 lb, laden with petrol and oil.

The whole model gives an air of solidity and longevity. Indeed, they must be more than confident of the sturdiness of the Bee-Emm in Munich, for the instruction book positively encourages the owner to fit a sidecar, with literature on fitting and alignment and special gearing available. I can vouch that this is no idle boast for I have a friend with the earlier R26 attached to a S350 Steib, and it has hauled this sidecar uncomplainingly these last five years or more. Mind you, he's nearly gone mad having to be satisfied with a top speed of 55 m.p.h.

On the road, the rider who expects to get the dynamo-smooth power of the twins is going to be disappointed. The first impression is of lightness, especially at the steering. Maybe the bike does turn the scales at over 3 cwt but, like the buxom beauties of yesteryear, it carries its weight well.

The fat spark supplied by the coil makes starting child's play and the engine immediately settles down to a steady, muffled, plonk, plonk, plonk. You think the twins are quiet? You should hear the R27. Stationary and on the move, noise is just a dirty word. Mechanical "off" noises are just audible if you listen intently, and the large silencers absorb the exhaust noise so well that one almost feels that the phons are being strangled. On

TEST : 250 BMW

the move you notice that the loudest noise comes from the induction.

First impressions of the motor is that it is "gutless". A very slow-action throttle combines with the extremely efficient silencing to make the engine *seem* very sluggish. A more determined grip on the throttle soon dispels this illusion and, provided the rider watches the speedometer rather than listen to the exhaust note, the impression of speed is re-established. Vibration is non-existent all the way up the rev range. Those engine rubbers absorb all the shake. Only when the bike is on tickover does some slight vibration show itself by gentle juddering of the rear number plate. The merest whiff of throttle clears this.

This is not to say, of course, that the engine is as silky smooth as the flat twin. Most riders judge vibration by the effect it has on them, and if none reaches them they are not going to be too bothered by the theories connected with the problem. That the engine itself is far from vibration free is readily apparent to anyone who has ridden the R26. Of course, there is no point in rubber mounting the engine if you leave various bits undamped, and B.M.W.s have avoided this by completely rubber mounting the engine/gearbox unit *and* the exhaust system. Nothing is allowed to pass from the engine to the frame without a generous layer of rubber. It is recommended that the rubbers be inspected for wear every 10,000 miles, and it would be a wise rider who did so, although their active life should be considerably more for OWP 181E has done over 17,000 miles on the original rubbers with no deterioration discernable.

Gearchange on the R27 is typical B.M.W. Silent changes are easy *if you have the knack*. Some riders learn it immediately, others never. Briefly it means that on upward changes a dwell must be allowed between gears, then the lever is "felt" in. Like double-declutching on a car, but without the extra clutch movements. On downward changes a gentle pressure coupled with a slight roll of the throttle does the trick. The clutch plays little part in this operation, for quiet changes can be achieved with or without the clutch.

The old R26 was infamous for its ultra-low bottom gear and, although the gearing on the later model seems to have been raised slightly, it is still too low. Perhaps the prospect of its being used for sidecar work influenced the choice? Once the jump to second has been made the remainder of the gears are ideally spaced, with no great leap to the next gear. To all intents and purposes, top gear can be used by the lazy rider for all speeds above 15 m.p.h., but if anything approaching snappy acceleration is to be achieved the gearbox must play its part.

For town work the R27 was just the job, light to steer, narrow, flexible and economical (between 70 and 80 m.p.g., or

more, can be expected). And on the open road the B.M.W. was a revelation, 120 being easily obtained on the clock. Ha. I thought that would make you sit up! It's a kilometre clock . . . . still, 120 k.p.h. translates to 75 m.p.h.; with 80 or so as the maximum. The engine at full throttle is still vibration free and burbling happily. This engine has shown itself over the years to be as tough as they come and can be, and has been, cruised at 70 m.p.h. all day long. The owner of OWP 181E treats his bike in this way and expects it to do 300+ mile trips whenever the mood takes him.

The motor was completely oil-tight, the only oil that was visible coming from the clutch cable. Although this R27 is two years old and is given no more than average grooming it is still in very good condition, with all chrome work unblemished and paintwork equally so.

The "little" B.M.W. was a most comfortable bike to ride, the suspension effectively ironing out all road surface blemishes. The dual seat was extremely comfortable, although in theory, at 33½in, was a bit high. In practice it didn't present any problems. The impression given by such a robustly built machine is that of riding something much larger than a 250, with the 3.3-gallon petrol tank contributing to this. The 35/35W light is in character with the view, giving a beam that is the envy of machines of twice the capacity. The rear light, large and bright, is superb and the horn was excellent, loud and clear.

Handling of the R27 was a little "soft" with the rear end tending to drift a little at speed on bumpy bends. For everyday use it presented no problems. Controls, by Magura, are well made but suffered a little from the owner's preference for down-turned handlebars. He likes them like that, but they were not to my taste. The brakes were probably considered good when the model was introduced, but the improvement in brakes these last few years has been tremendous and the R27, lacking the twin-leading-shoe front brake of the rest of the range, suffers by comparison.

Now, supposing you have read this test and decide that you would like to own an R27. Could you still get one? Perhaps I'd better tell you what it will cost first . . . .? I am reliably informed that it might just be possible to get hold of a new one at—hold your breath—something over £500. You've lost interest a little? I thought you might.

I liked the little R27. It offers a fuss free, civilized sort of motorcycling that few other lightweights can equal (but at £500 one would expect it to). B.P.

BMW R75/5 Sport

BMW has made a bold risk-bid for the performance buyer. Will a flat twin as big as the R75 really handle? Take a ride, baby—you'll see.

PHOTOGRAPHS BY ROBERT LACKENBACH

• Back in the good old days, Bavaria was ruled by an emperor looked on most fondly by today's Bavarian. He was Emperor Ludwig II—or "Mad Ludwig"— whose particular bag was building castles. Nineteenth-century Ludwig wanted to recreate the glories of the past by building castles all over Bavaria. He built so many that he eventually bankrupted the state, but the Bavarians admire him anyway. After all, he had style and, though "mad", he did in fact do his own thing. In some ways, the spirit of Ludwig II lives on at the Bavarian Motor Works, whose motorcycle division continues relentlessly to do its own thing. That means it

produces motorcycles with horizontally-opposed flat-twin engines and with power transmission to the rear wheel by shaft drive. Now BMW has introduced a new series of these devices, the biggest and fastest of which is our test bike—BMW's 750cc model R75/5.

For BMW the new models, and particularly the R75, signify a great leap forward into the present. That is, the firm senses that today's big-bore motorcycle buyer doesn't buy utility transportation. What he wants is a street sport machine with emphasis on good handling and high performance. BMW wants to please the new breed of rider, but not by sacrificing its hard-earned reputation

for quality and durability—certainly not by abandoning a basic design concept so integral to its identity.

The new BMWs are lighter and faster than their predecessors and they have been brought up to date technically in many ways. They now have alternator-fed 12-volt dc electrics. They now have electric starters, concentric float bowl carburetors, battery-and-coil ignition systems, plain bearing crankshafts and high-volume trochoidal-type oil pumps. The new machines have received such thorough redesign that they genuinely deserve the label "new".

A look at the R75 tells you instantly that this is a motorcycle created by

It's got all that touring stuff: electric start, turn signals. But you can corner it honked way over, stand it on end with a throttle twist, and cruise full-song all day long.

engineers. The hand of a designer or stylist has never been laid on that metal. If you ever wondered what happened to the Honda hump, now you know. A short wheelbase and a high, arching gastank give the BMW a stubby, lumpy appearance that takes getting used to. From the side, the BMW's crankcase castings resemble a giant tadpole just before it sprouts legs. And then there are those turn signals front and rear, sticking out on stalks like monster eyes. In styling, you might call the R75 motorcycling's own Volkswagen, except

Not much has changed in the final drive department: an enclosed, rubber-bushed shaft takes the place of the more prosaic motorcycle's chain.

Long through-studs hold rocker gear, cylinder-head and cylinder—minimize heat distortion. As usual, rocker covers are very strong.

that the power of this machine rules out an image of homely cuteness. Maybe some people will regard its appearance as a kind of blocky muscularity. Certainly it looks big.

Fortunately for BMW, going, not looking, matters most in motorcycling and the R75 will go like no BMW ever before and like few other motorcycles today. That redesigned flat-twin engine delivers 57 bhp at 6200 rpm, which puts it squarely among the new superbikes and ahead of the sport 650s. I tested the new bike in West Germany, shortly after

its official September introduction. There is no better testing area, for not only are there Germany's fabled no-speed-limit *autobahns*, but also the incredibly challenging roads of the Bavarian Alps. Road surfaces vary from seamless cement to gravel and *pavé* (a kind of granite cobblestone). And the Alpine roads offer grades and turns that would never meet U.S. highway codes. Steep and tortuous. They are a motorcyclist's delight. For three weeks I thrashed the R75 along those roads and I can tell you, it has a long suit in going.

But first I got a thorough grounding at the factory on the nitty-gritty of design. This R75 engine is a remarkable piece of work. Perhaps the best way to see what BMW's engineers have done is to start with air intake and follow all the way through combustion and power transmission to final delivery of drive to the rear wheel.

In the manner of an enduro bike, the R75 gets its air high and dry through an intake located well up under the gastank. The air intake grill faces rearward in a pocket of relatively still air. Intake air gets no ram effect from the velocity of the machine, but this would be cancelled by the elaborate filtering system anyway and at least the air is cool and relatively dense. Gross impurities (birds, twigs, etc.) are blocked by the grill before the air swirls in and around the starter motor and then into a gigantic paper-element filter. This filter (disposable) has 60% greater area than the filter used on BMW's R69s. A small amount of air in traditional BMW fashion is taken in through orifices in the electrics housing at the front of the engine to cool these heat sensitive elements before it also enters the main filter.

From a common chamber under the air-filter element, air is drawn individually through ducts into each carburetor. I asked BMW's engineers why they had created such an elaborate intake path. Every time air changes direction on its way to a carburetor and every time it passes through a filter some energy is lost. That is, the engine has to suck a little harder to get the same amount of air. The answer I got was noise. A 750 turning six grand sucks a lot of air, enough to raise an ear-rending howl unless it is muffled by the same filters that extract dust and grit. Part of the reason that the new engine housing is so large is that it must provide sufficient flow for all the air a hungry 750 on full song needs. In any case, the BMW's intake muffling system works splendidly. It filters splendidly. You might get five easy horsepower simply by venting those carburetors directly—but you'd get a lot of noise and you'd reduce engine life by at least two-thirds.

The carburetors on the R75 are wholly new products from Bing, though they look suspiciously like the constant-vacuum carbs on Honda's 450. (Actually, CV carbs have been around for some time in the automotive world: England's SU firm had them before Keihin.) Their operation is simple in principle though complex in execution. Twisting the R75's throttle-grip doesn't lift a slide as in most motorcycle carburetors. It rotates a butterfly valve in the tract leading directly to the cylinder intake valve. For this carburetor, full throttle means minimum interference with all the vacuum (or suction) that the cylinder can draw. A tube from the same valve-side tract leads to chamber above the carb slide so that both have equal pressure (equal vacuum). Mixture rushing under the slide provides a positive pressure, lifting the slide until the pressure over it and under it are the same. In the new Bing, pressure masses above and below the slide are kept separate by a flexible rubber diaphragm. Honda's Keihins count on the slide working as a piston with close fit provided the seal. In any case, the big advantage of a CV carburetor is that it delivers only as much mixture as the cylinder can draw. Whacking open the throttle won't flood or starve the engine: it just allows the carburetor to adjust itself to maximum draw. Result: very progressive power transitions and very efficient carburetion (good mileage).

The R75 is, above all, technically contemporary. It incorporates a one-piece forged crankshaft, an alternator good for 180 watts—and more.

Only the R75 has CV carburetors; the other models (R50/s and R60/5) have new Bing concentric floatbowl models with cable actuated slides. Concentric floatbowls with nylon floats on all three bikes keep the fuel level constant no matter what the cornering angle or how steep the grade. Provision has also been made to prevent carburetion irregularities from fuel surging during hard braking or acceleration. The R75's carburetors have also been isolated from the cylinders by a short rubber sleeve to prevent vibration interference with carburetion. A rich cold-starting mixture is produced by an independent mixing system similar to that on most Japanese carburetors. Rotating a choke lever on the side of the engine housing opens this system by cables to both carburetors. I found this location easy to get at, yet out of the way—unlike the handlebar mounted chokes that clutter up the control layout on so many British bikes.

Mixture rushes into the combustion chamber through an enormous 42mm intake valve. There are 88° of valve overlap (both intake and exhaust open) so that intake mixture is drawn along by departing exhaust gases. Momentum acquired by the mixture stream tends to stuff additional mixture into the cylinder when the exhaust valve closes. Just eyeballing that cylinder head tells you that considerable thought has been given to gas flow. With the valves removed you can look through the inlet part straight out the exhaust port. An oversquare bore-stroke ratio of 82mm x 70.6mm provides plenty of room for valves. BMW's designers chose a very flat combustion chamber with an included angle between valve stems of 65° (versus 80° in the R69s). Compression ratio is a relatively mild 9:1. Perhaps the best indication of the efficiency of this cylinderhead design is the fact that maximum horsepower (57 SAE) is produced at a relatively slow 6400 rpm.

After combustion, the exhaust gasses depart through a 38mm exhaust valve into an exhaust plumbing system of enormous volume. A crossover pipe just below the front of the engine lets each cylinder exhaust into the whole system including both mufflers. The system isn't "tuned" for wave-type gas extraction at the exhaust valve, but it is designed to minimize backpressure at all operating rpm. Sound muffling in traditional BMW fashion (because of strict noise-control laws in Germany) is superb. This big bike whispers along so rapidly and so silently that a good horn is absolutely necessary. Unfortunately, the bike doesn't come with one.

The R75's large, flat pistons require only the slightest valve cutaways. Working through such a short stroke, they should last a long time. Each piston has three rings: a chrome-plated compression ring, an "L"-shaped compression ring (Dykes pattern), and an oil-scraper ring. The top compression ring is very thin, specially designed to avoid flutter and thus loss of compression at high operating rpm. The R75's cylinder consists of a cast iron sleeve molecularly bounded by the "Alfin" process to an aluminum-alloy fin casting. This combination, along with the horizontal positioning of the cylinders directly in the airstream, provides excellent cooling. Operating oil temperature of the R75 engine under full load in the 4th gear is between 175°F and 195°F, which compares with, say, a 270° oil temperature for a Porsche engine under load.

Oil temperature is particularly critical because of BMW's radical conversion to the use of plain bearings in the crankcase. Fifteen years ago, BMW set a kind of milestone by producing a street motorcycle whose running parts turned exclusively in ball and roller bearings. Roller bearings are expensive, but they don't generate much heat. That early, pressed-together (or built-up) crankshaft acquired a much celebrated reputation for longevity—so long as maximum power was kept under 50 bhp. More power tended to flex the crank excessively and roller bearings don't respond at all well to flexing. When BMW chose to stick with the flat twin as a solo engine, they also chose to live with an inherent weakness in its design: no center mainbearing. To include a center mainbearing would mean to offset the cylinders even further (as seen from above) and such an engine would generate a rocking couple large enough to effectively cancel its chief virtue—perfect primary balance. An alternative solution to the demand for more power was to make a stronger, more rigid crank. For BMW that meant a one-piece forging with considerably increased bearing diameters.

The new crank got rigidity with a vengeance. A 5000-lb sideload or the center will deform this crank less than half as much as the pressed-together R69s crank. Where the R69's had mainshaft diameters of 35mm and 36mm, the new crank measures 60mm and 48mm. Rod journals are up to 22mm from 15.2mm. Plainbearing materials have been lifted right out of BMW's cars (trimetal-bronze, tin and indium). The new crank will live

comfortably with 80 bhp and thus is considerably understressed in the 57 bhp model R75. R75's short, forged connecting rods look as if they had been lifted right out of a Porsche, as indeed have many parts on this machine. (eg—the bonded brake and clutch linings).

To solve the cornering interference problem of a flat twin, BMW's engineers decided to get the cylinders higher off the ground. To do this and still keep the center of gravity low, they moved the camshaft from directly above the crank to directly below. Instead of a geared cam drive, the R75 now uses a duplex chain with automatic tensioning—vast as in the BMW overhead-cam auto engines. Mounted on the rear of this camshafted is the rotor of an Eaton (trochoidal) oilpump, very similar to the one used in Honda's 750. The life of a plainbearing engine can be credited directly to this device and BMW's does its job well. At 6000 rpm it will circulate over 800 quarts an hour. That means the entire oil capacity of this engine (2.4 quarts) gets circulated 355 times in an hour of hard riding. Oil is pressure fed to the mainbearings, lower end bearings, camshaft bearings and rocker arm bearings. The pump draws its oil from the sump through a disposable, automotive-type oil filter.

At the extreme forward end of the camshaft, past its driving sprocket and into the dry electrics housing, sits a new Bosch centrifugal ignition advance unit. This is only one element of a completely redesigned electrical system common to all models. The primary power source is an automotive-type 12-volt alternator located on the end of the crankshaft. Rated at 180-200 watts, this new unit was designed at the BMW factory and then given to Bosch to manufacture. In automotive fashion voltage is regulated by varying the current in the rotor—some DC current is always needed for starting. According to BMW engineers, the engine will fire up even if the 12-volt battery has decayed to 7 volts. If it has gone lower than that, you have to spin the rotor at 2000 rpm to get enough primary juice for a spark. That's one helluva bump start for a 435-lb motorcycle. But the generous capacity of the alternator should keep the battery charged even if the bike is only used occasionally. Obviously there is wattage to spare—enough to power flood lights, radios, compressor horns, police transmitters or whatever other accessories amuse you.

Above the crankshaft, situated where BMW's camshaft used to be, sits a

Big 32mm constant-vacuum carburetor is similar to Honda's, but uses neoprene diaphragm to separate pressure masses. Throttle actuation turns butterfly in valve-side throat; mixture velocity adjusts the slide to engine's needs. The float bowl is concentric; the float is made of nylon.

Massive engine housing includes most of the electrics and other hardware usually left flapping in the wind. Camshaft now rides below crank with the starter motor above (making for a lower center of gravity). Massive housing shown at top rear contains a large air filter.

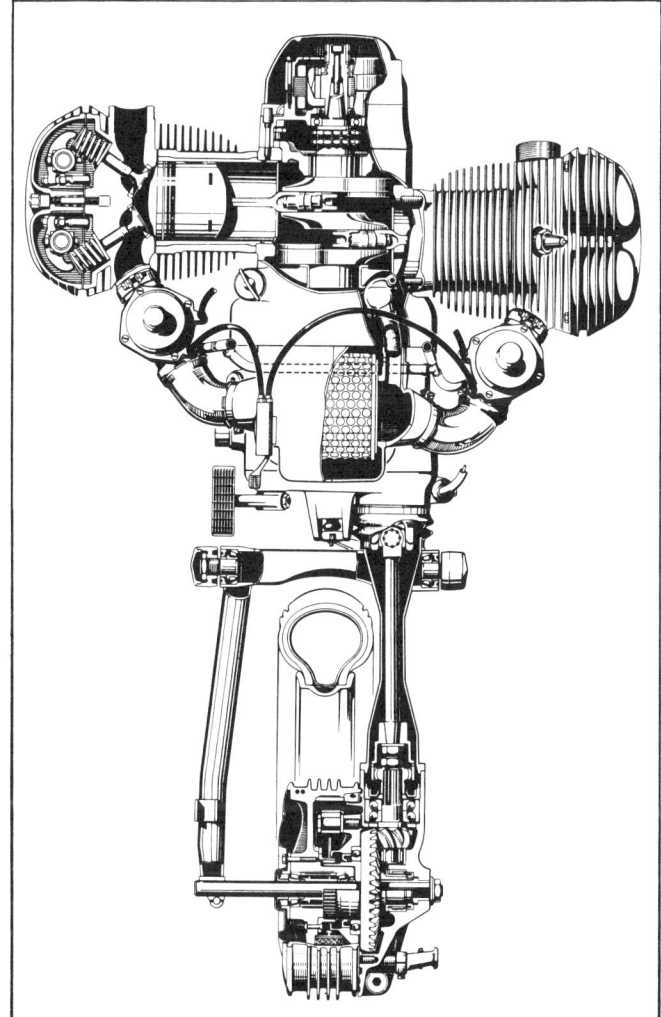

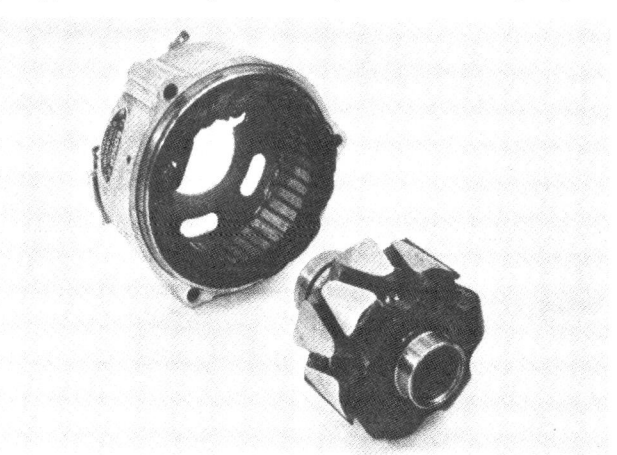

Three-phase 180-watt alternator gets magnetization current for rotor from the battery. Alternator has advantages of compactness, efficiency, and no rubbing connections (brushes) for high currents. The alternator output will fire plugs—even if battery fades to seven volts.

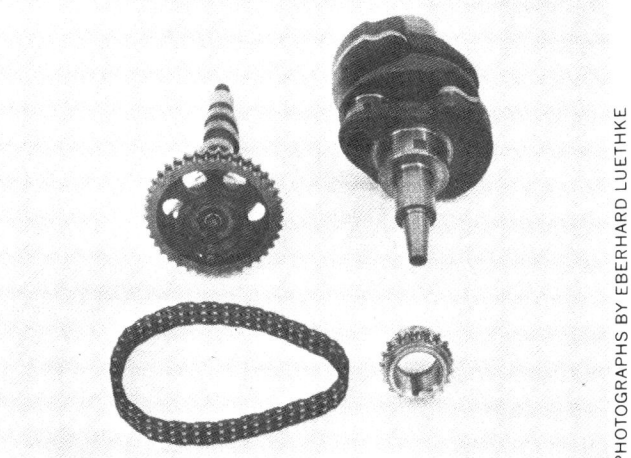

Symmetry of flat twin dramatically emphasizes cooling virtues. With camshaft under crank, the cylinders are raised, providing greater cornering angles. Nose casting covers automatic ignition advance unit, alternator, and rectifier, and permits air entry for cooling of electrics.

Camshaft drive by automatically tensioned duplex chain comes straight out of BMW's rally-winning sports sedans. Valve timing affords a generous 88 degrees of overlap, which makes for good combustion chamber filling, easier starting, higher midrange torque.

It may be disappointing at the top end, but the BMW has splendid midrange acceleration and an operating smoothness that's yet unequalled by any of the multis.

starter motor with capacity of 0.7 hp. With its automotive-type flywheel and dry clutch, the BMW has long been a natural for this addition. A ring gear was simply added to the flywheel, driven by a tiny throw-out gear on the starter shaft. A quick punch at the starter button fired up our test bike every time, even in some very cold, damp weather. The system was designed to work down to 15°F, yet it isn't burdened with the gigantic 32 amp-hour battery common to some electric-start bikes. A new, remotely vented battery of 15 ah capacity handles the job quite satisfactorily.

BMW's drive train remains virtually unchanged in the new machine except for strengthening to accept the additional horsepower. Again, everything seems set up for 80 bhp. A single dry plate clutch, compressed by a diaphragm spring, is mounted to the flywheel. Drive is transmitted to a three-shaft transmission that includes a spring-and-cam type shock damper. Transmission output passes through a universal joint to permit up-and-down motion at the rear swingarm. The driveshaft turns within the righthand swingarm tube, driving a piston gear engaged with the ring gear that turns the

rear wheel. It is a quiet, maintenance-free system, everything running in an oil bath and turning on ball, roller or needle bearings. That rear wheel actually has a splined coupling to the drive unit so that it can be quickly detached for tire or brake work—a useful feature I discovered after spearing a horse shoe nail in Bavarian farm country. Somehow the engineers' ingenuity ran out just short of completion, however. The lefthand muffler is notched so that you don't have to remove it to draw out the axle. But there is no flat wrench in the tool kit for the axle nut, so you have to

BMW R75/5 750 cc Sports

Price, suggested retail	East Coast, POE $1696
Tire, front	3.25 in. x 19 in.
rear	4.00 in. x 18 in.
Brakes, front	1.18 in. x 7.8 in.
rear	1.18 in. x 7.8 in.
Brake swept area	58.6 sq. in.
Specific brake loading	10.8 lb/sq. in.
Engine type	Electric-start boxer twin.
Bore and stroke	3.23 in. x 2.78 in., 82 mm x 70.6 mm
Piston displacement	45.0 cu. in., 745 cc
Compression ratio	9:1
Carburetion	(2) 32 mm, Bing Constant Vacuum
Air filtration	Paper element
Ignition	Battery and coil
Bhp @ rpm	57 @ 6400
Mph/1000 rpm, top gear	17.7
Fuel capacity	6.1 gal.
Oil capacity	4.9 pt.
Lighting	Alternator 12 v, 180 watts
Battery	12 v, 15 ah
Gear ratios, overall	(1) 11.31 (2) 7.49
	(3) 5.48 (4) 4.35
Wheelbase	54.7 in.
Seat height	33.4 in.
Ground clearance	6.5 in.
Curb weight	436 lb.
Test weight	611 lb.
Instruments	Speedometer, tachometer, odometer
0-60 mph	6.1 seconds
Standing start ¼ mile (see text)	14.5 seconds-90 mph
Top speed	103 mph

remove the righthand muffler to use the deep socket wrench. I suggest that owners add a flat 22mm box wrench to the kit—which is otherwise probably the best tool kit in all of motorcycling.

Testimony to the fact that BMW isn't completely hidebound is its outright abandonment of a sidecar tradition older than most of us. Until last year, every BMW made came with sidecar lugs welded on the frame. Now there is a wholly new frame, a lightweight backbone-type double-loop frame exclusively for solo riding. In traditional BMW fashion, the frame is expensively made of variable section tubing that includes both tapers and ovality according to the stress it must deal with. One aspect that I find suspicious is BMW's claim to have designed in a little flex at the steering head along with strong (fore and after) resistance to torsional flex. The only practical way to test this claim is by riding. I was unable to feel significant flex.

Increased performance also required a redesign of BMW's brakes. These units were already marginal by present day standards on the R695. Hard braking pressure alone would flare the drums slightly and heat only compounded the effect. The new brake drums are vastly more rigid with deep stiffening (and cooling) ridges in the alloy housing. The drum itself has a cast iron insert. New (from Porsche) bonded brake linings offer considerably more grab. The brakes have the same diameter (200mm) and slightly narrower width (30mm), but they are far more effective than their predecessors. On the very rapid R75, you can even work these to the limit. I can remember rounding one mountain donwhill at about 90 only to see two gigantic semis in the roadway, headed uphill. I thumbed the handy headlight flasher and hauled on as much brake as I could. The rear wheel did a few hops and judders and then began howling; the front end dove almost to full compression. I could see the expression on the outside drivers face, his mouth wide open and his eyes as big as fried eggs. That big rig was pulling maybe 2-mph on the other one and he had simply nowhere to go. Luckily the anchors worked and I had reached virtually a standstill before cutting across his outside fender onto the soft, foot-and-a-half wide shoulder. I felt then I could have used a little more braking power up front.

When you first get aboard the R75 you know instantly you're in for a very unique riding experience. When you put your weight on the seat, the bike seems to sink about four inches. Actually there are five inches of vertical travel at the rear wheel and *eight* inches in front. You prepare yourself for a very mushy, wallowy ride. Mechanical tach and speedo are combined in one unit up front, along with a bunch of signals and warning lights. I would have preferred separate units, *á la* Triumph and Honda. One glaring omission was a winker indicator light to let you know when the turn signals are on. I asked for the low European-style handlebars and the handgrip units completely obscured the lights mounted at the lower fork yoke. Even the higher, American-style bars would have the same effect. Sometime when you first get aboard your thumb will brush the righthand signal switch and you might ride 50 miles before you catch a reflection that tells you you're about to turn.

Anyway, the control layout is clean and nicely nodularized. High beam, low beam, flash and horn with the left thumb, signals and starter button with the right. It would have helped if BMW's designers had realized, as Honda's designers have done that the human thumb is *below* the grip in normal riding position. Better to be able to flick those switches without compromising basic grip pressure. You push down the spike-type ignition key on the headlight, then jab the starter. The engine lights up instantly with a very satisfying well of smooth sound. While you wait for it to come up to temperature you notice that the control cables have been waterproofed. Neat rubber cuffs surround the end of each and inside, I learned, are complete nylon cable linings.

When the engine settles down to an even tickover, you pull in the clutch and press down on the left foot shift lever. You hear the transmission sort of punch into gear. Last year BMW initiated a spring-loaded shift mechanism and this year I guess they increased the spring's strength. Actuating the shift lever is like switching on a solenoid. Punch, punch, punch—through the gears. At first I found this effect unnerving, but later grew to like it. That gearchange punch is a very solid, reassuring sound. You *never* get a false neutral with this gear box. If you don't move the lever far enough along its arc, the spring load mechanism will drive the previous gears back into engagement.

Out with the clutch and you're off. It takes awhile to learn to feather that big dry-plate clutch. Engagement is just a degree or two of hand lever movement. You hear a very muffled click as the engine pulls all of those drive-train components into tension. You wind on throttle and that's when it happens. That's when you discover what this meticulous, painstaking redesign has been all about.

You move out fast, really fast. Shockingly fast. I have never seen as many white-faced journalists as at that press introduction at the Hockenhein race course. One after the other, they got off the R75, a nervous look of incredulity on their faces. One of the reasons was that on-off clutch. The track was wet and, when you wind the R75 up to six grand and charge up, you dump an awful lot of torque very suddenly on the rear wheel. On dry pavement, you can get a very satisfying chirp. In the wet you get some real slithering. Along a straight, the bike won't get away from you, but beware in the corners. I expected to see eight test bikes in pieces that afternoon, but they crashed only one.

What this means is quarter-mile elapsed time is mid-fourteens at about 90 mph. I couldn't check it exactly because they don't have quarter mile dragstrips in Europe. In any case, for a 430-lb bike that's a respectable, though far from staggering figure. I can't imagine why BMW put so much money into updating this machine without including a five-speed gearbox. A five-speed box and slightly more radical tuning would put this bike in the thirteens with no real compromise to roadability.

Roadability is precisely what BMW has to say with the new R75. I mentioned that with a soft, long-travel suspension you would expect mushy cornering. Not true at all, though I can't say why. The R75 corners superbly—very steady, very firm, very controllable. The whole machine has been set up for hard cornering. Footpegs, control levers, mufflers—all tucked up high and inside—out of the way. If the suspension is not compressed, you can get it over 47° from the vertical before a rocker cover scrapes. Not many of us are brave enough for that kind of cornering. Only twice was I able to just nick the right footpeg (suspension compressed) and never grounded anything on the left. On this bike, even the traditional low-hanging entrails, the side and centerstands, have been tucked away.

Some of those little, winding roads through Bavarian farm country are only about ten feet wide. The road bed itself has never been graded, but the pavement is smooth and (usually) clean. There is little traffic on these roads and no speed limit. Sometimes I would tell myself, "Don't let the speedo fall below 140." That's about 83 mph. I didn't always succeed, but I learned a lot about how this machine corners at high speed. On both smooth and rough surfaces it will hold a line as if it were running on a rail. Not only is the bike delightfully quick and quiet, it has a snug, very compact feel when you get down on the tank. It feels so well integrated that you sometimes forget it is a 435-lb machine doing over 90. A good way to scare yourself. The problem of spinning out the rear wheel with 57 bhp doesn't occur—so long as you use the clutch wisely. You just have to avoid dumping it all on at once.

Continued on page 137

IT WAS WORTH THE WAIT

Can Joe Roadrider find true happiness with the acquisition of a new BMW 750?

You can bet your booties he can! Up to this year, if you were a sports minded enthusiast, and a BMW lover, all rolled into one, the choice was obvious — an R69S. This top of the line model was the only one offered by BMW that offered quality and performance in large enough quantities to keep most riders happy.

Now the Bavarian Motorcycle concern has gone even further with the new

75-5. The first thing they did was to up the displacement to a full 750 (the displacement is actually 745cc) and the difference in power output is quite noticeable. As might be expected, with the added inches the torque that is available at the rear wheel is considerably greater than the old R69S. Also, the engine has none of the caminess that last year's super sport model had. Like all BMW models, it's extremely smooth once over

3000 rpm and will run clean up to 100 miles an hour without the slightest quiver, and it will get to 100 very quickly, at which point the engine flattens out and the rider is obliged to crouch somewhat if he is to get over the magic ton mark.

But our feeling on the matter is, so what? Who wants to go faster than 100 anyway? It will jet past slower moving traffic with just a slight twist of the throttle, whether you're going up hill, or

of fuel sloshing around on the top portion of the motorcycle, and there were no baffles inside the gas tank, this weighty mass of fuel would tend to push the motorcycle around somewhat, especially when trying to find the shortest way around a given corner.

The styling is something that will probably take a little getting used to. It looks heavy and massive, when in reality it is lighter and more agile than the older models, so here again, looks are deceiving.

The handling has got to be the new BMW's long suit. It's out of sight, a real mind bender. We found ourselves doing wild, impetuous things that on a lesser motorcycle would have deposited us in the shrubbery alongside the road. This motorcycle is a paradox, in that it feels heavy and agile, both at the same time, if you can imagine that. When thundering down the freeway at high speed, it imparts to the rider a feeling of solidarity and smoothness. When moving out to overtake a car, or just whistling down the offramp with the motorcycle cranked over at an alarming angle, the agility portion comes to the fore. It would appear that BMW is making a mighty effort to penetrate the sports minded motorcycle buyer market. We would suspect that it takes one quite awhile to get used to the fact that there is a cylinder protruding from each side of the crankcase. On a number of occasions, we would glance down and to our alarm discover that it looked as though there was zero clearance between the cylinder and the ground. This is deceiving. BMW has actually raised the cylinders even higher than they had them last year. This was accomplished by moving the cam shaft to the lower portion of the engine, thereby making more room topside.

While providing more ground clearance, this also raises the center of gravity, and this is probably another reason

The headlight is one of those units that provide a flat wide beam that will not blind oncoming drivers. The turn signals are a handy touch for changing lanes on the freeway.

on the flat. It makes absolutely no difference to the flat Twin power plant.

Speaking of throttles, we did not care for the quick throttle that comes equipped on all of the new BMW's. We prefer the slower older style, since it makes riding the motorcycle considerably easier. The throttle itself was quite stiff and took a great deal of effort to keep the wick turned up, and after half an hour on the highway we discovered our right hand getting tired. This was not merely one rider's impression, but everyone that rode the bike. This, however, is a small thing and quite easily can be changed.

From the time you first lay your eyes on the new BMW you have mixed emotions. We did too. Our impression was we were not quite sure what BMW was

up to. The high, deep chested gas tank, plus the massive crankcase castings give the motorcycle a fore-shortened and stubby appearance. The truth of the matter is, it has a 54" wheelbase which is really not all that short. However, it is the styling that gives it this fore-shortened appearance.

For those individuals who really dig really long trips, that 6 gallon gas tank will be a boon. It will not be necessary to stop nearly as often as it would with any other motorcycle. However, this in itself created a problem for us. Inasmuch as we now had 42 pounds of fuel topside, we discovered the handling deteriorated rapidly. But as the fuel level dropped, the handling improved considerably. The reason for this is really quite simple. Inasmuch as we had over 40 lbs.

It would be difficult indeed to find any motorcycle more flawlessly finished than the new BMW. That dual saddle is as comfortable as it looks.

We found at night the speedo unit is easily read, but the cables cover up the lower portion of the instruments and the tach is all but useless.

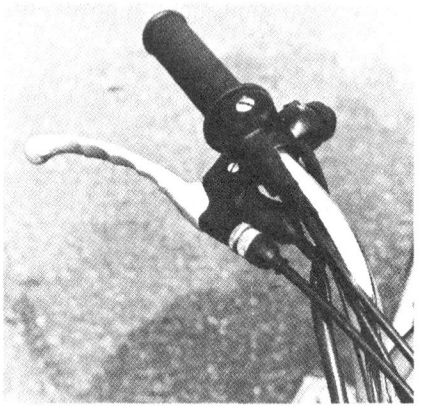

The right handlebar half is busy indeed. One thing we liked was the electric starter, but the throttle was a little too quick to suit us. The older slower throttle was better.

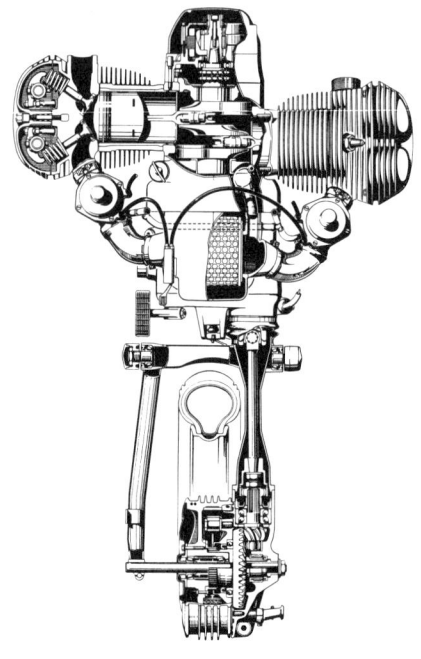

why the motorcycle might be sensitive handling-wise at higher speeds with a tank full of fuel.

That old wive's tale whereby the BMW has been credited with providing the rider with a torque reaction when the throttle is turned on, is nothing but a lot of overrated nonsense. If you're sitting at a stoplight, and you suddenly turn the throttle on, you will notice a definite torque reaction, but once under way, this sort of thing is barely discernible, if at all.

Located just below the speedometer you will find a small tach. This is a nice touch, but it is very difficult to read since the cables intersect directly in front of the tach face. In reality, the tach is not really all that necessary anyway. There is very little danger of the rider ever lugging the engine down to where he is going to harm something. Once the rpm drops down to 3,000, the machine suddenly, and we mean suddenly, starts to run quite rough and the rider will be forced to shift to the next lower gear, unless, of course, he is the type who is

completely insensitive to any vibration whatsoever. We never once had to look at the tach to tell when we were down close to the 3,000 mark because the motorcycle let us know almost instantly when we reached this point.

We discovered that the engine will spin quite happily well over 6,000 rpm, although it is very unnecessary to do so. Because of the huge quantitites of torque available, it was merely necessary to turn the engine up to approximately 5,000 and then shift to the next higher cog. When the next higher gear was engaged and the clutch was engaged, the machine would leap forward with an eagerness that is hard to describe. Also, it almost felt as though the machine reared up slightly when moving away from a stop light as quickly as possible, or speed shifting to the next gear. Not just the front end, mind you, but the back end would also come up. At least it felt as though it did.

All of the attributes previous BMW owners have heaped upon their motorcycles are still evident in this new machine. The same low mechanical noise, riding comfort, and superb quality are quite evident from the first time you lay your baby blues on one. Everything is well thought out, solid, and beautifully executed. There is one thing we are

Pegs and mufflers are tucked up high enough so the rider needn't worry about grounding them when cornering hard. Brakes are excellent and do not fade.

Under the seat we found a plastic tool tray, tool kit and a BMW shop towel. The tire pump (and it works very well too) is also tucked away under the dual saddle.

The vacuum operated 32mm carburetors were not as faultless as they should be. Turning proved to be something of a chore. Starting was instantaneous.

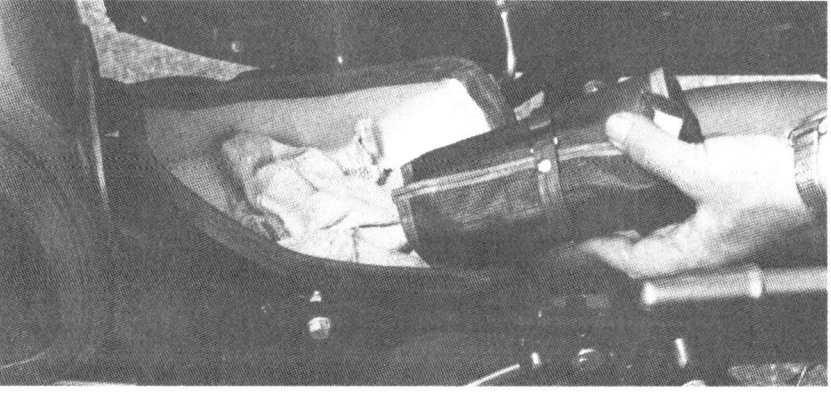

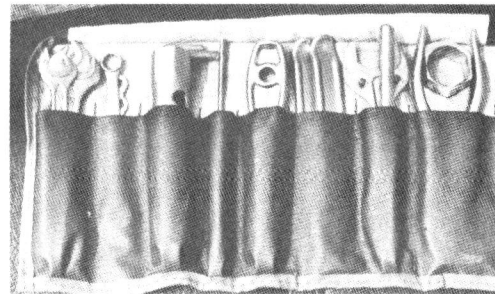

This is probably the nicest looking, and best made tool kit in the industry. All the tools are included for average home maintenance.

rather curious about. Inasmuch as BMW started with a clean piece of paper (this new machine is all new — there are only a handful of parts that can still be interchanged with the older machine) we wonder why they chose to stick to a design so reminiscent of the earlier models. We would have suspected that they would have chosen a more contemporary design. In actuality, the older model had a sleeker design than the new one does. The factory obviously feels, and they may be right, that the opposed twin shaft drive design offers the least number of problems in coming up with a power package that has little vibration and will attain the goal they set out to conquer.

Inside those massive engine cases you will find the clutch and gearbox just to the rear of the power plant itself. Like its predecessors, the new BMW has a single plate dry clutch which is silky smooth in operation and requires very little to depress the clutch handle on the handlebar.

The output portion of the clutch itself is coupled to the transmission and here again it is not unlike the earlier machine. Here is another area we felt should be improved upon. There is still the same "ca-chunk" when the next gear is engaged. We would certainly think that in all the time the BMW has been manufacturing motorcycles, they would have found a way to produce a transmission that didn't clunk when shifting gears.

This gear clunking can be minimized somewhat through judicious and careful shifting. But we don't feel that a motorcycle that has the tremendous inbred quality that this one has should be burdened with a gearbox of this type. You do get used to it somewhat, but it is annoying and unnecessary.

The only source of bother came from the carburetion department. The new 75-5 is equipped with a pair of Bing demand type carburetors. In other words, when you jerk open the throttle, there are no slides to go up and down. The cable operates a butterfly which in

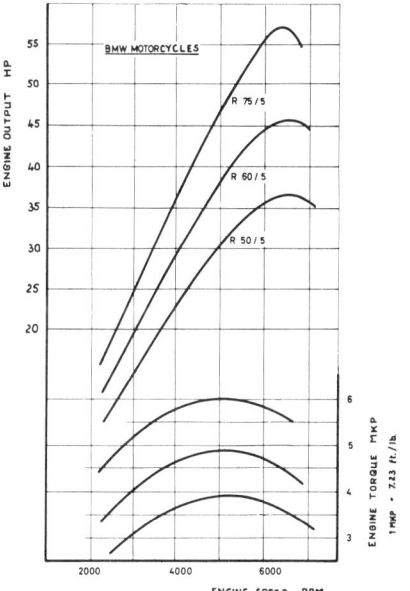

turn lets the engine vacuum perform its function in lifting a piston in the top part of the carburetor. This is the same type of unit, or basically the same type that Honda has been using on their 450 for quite a long time now. The one really nice thing about this whole design is that if the throttle is opened suddenly, at low speed, there is no flooding or starving since the throttle cable does not

operate that portion of the carburetor which allows fuel to be dumped into the engine. A very nice idea indeed.

One reason the crankcase is as large as it is, is because of the air filter. Any engine that displaces 750cc needs a lot of air to run efficiently. The BMW is no different. We might mention also that a good proportion of the reason the BMW runs so quietly is due to the fact that the

intake and filter system is designed in such a manner as to allow the engine to take in all it requires without any unnecessary noise. This noise factor is probably the one major reason BMW has gone to the length it has to produce such an elaborate filter system. By the way, we might also mention that on the very top portion of the crankcase, you

Continued on page 151

BMW R75/5

ENGINE

Type	4 cycle opposed twin
Bore and stroke	82 x 70.6 mm
Displacement	745cc
Compression ratio	9.0:1
Max. horsepower	
Max. torque	43 ft. lb. at 5,000 rpm
Ignition	alternator/battery
Carburetion	twin constant velocity 32mm Bings
Lubrication	wet sump

DIMENSIONS

Length	82.7 in.
Seat height	33.5 in.
Wheelbase	54.5 in.
Ground clearance	6.5 in.
Dry weight	419 lbs.

WHEELS AND BRAKES

Front tire size	3.25 x 19″
Front brake type	internal expanding-double leading shoe
Rear tire size	4.00 x 18″
Rear brake type	internal expanding

TRANSMISSION

Type	4-speed claw type w/enclosed drive shaft to rear wheel
Clutch	dry single plate
Internal gear ratios	1st 3.896:1, 2nd 2.578:1, 3rd 1.875:1, 4th 1.50:1
Final ratio	1:2.91
Countershaft/Rear wheel teeth	11/32

PERFORMANCE

Indicated highest one-way speed	102 mph
Acceleration 0-60	5.9 sec.
Braking distance 30-0	29 feet

GENERAL

Air filtration	dry paper
Battery type	12V 15AH

CAPACITIES

Fuel tank	6.3 gal.
Engine oil	4.75 pts.
Gear box	1.7 qts.

FRAME AND SUSPENSION

Front suspension	telescopic-double damping
Rear suspension	adjustable shocks
Frame type	tubular-cradle
Steering damper type	friction

COLORS — Silver, Black or White

PRICE AS TESTED — $1750.00 FOB West Coast

DISTRIBUTORS

BMW West:
Flanders Co.
340 S. Fair Oaks Ave.
Pasadena, Ca. 91101

BMW East:
Butler & Smith Inc.
Walnut St. and Hudson Ave.
Norwood, N.J. 07648

MOTORCYCLE
SCOOTER & THREE-WHEELER
MECHANICS
THE ILLUSTRATED HOW-TO-DO-IT MAGAZINE

ENGINE ANALYSIS
No. 7

BMW R69S

M M dissects this Bavarian beauty

▶ The BMW flat-twins must now rate as one of the classic motor-cycle engines of all time.

Modern machines from the Munich factory still present a unique layout of engine, transmission and frame, with a nostalgic similarity to the pre-war designs.

Those early BMs, 500s, 600s and 750s, had the same concept of a flat-twin motor, single-plate clutch and shaft drive and were produced as side-valves and ohv units.

Apart from use as touring units, military and police vehicles and the heavy sidecar outfits, the real fame and glory came with the successful model 252 racing machine.

This was a blown 500 which in the hands of such riders as Georg Meier and Jock West, swept the international racing scene in the years just before the last war.

After the war years, the factory managed to continue production, and in 1952 the R68 appeared in this country. This was continued until '54, and the first R69 was delivered in '55. The R69S superseded this in 1961.

Some of the touring type BMW's fame undoubtedly stems from the R69S which broke the 24-hour speed record at Montlhéry in 1961. The machine, which was standard apart from megaphone exhausts and Dell'Orto carburettors, was prepared by MLG motors and averaged almost 110 mph for the 24 hours. Just to prove the point, Sid Mizen then made a flying lap at *135.7 mph*!

Of the current machines, the R69S 600 cc has the sportiest specification and makes quite a fast and comfortable tourer. The new 750, which will be available in this country from November, will of course be more powerful, but retains the basic engine design of all the road-going flat-twins.

Finally, BMW's other flat-twin deserves a brief mention. This is the Rennesport, the 500 cc factory racer used mainly as a powerhouse for racing sidecar outfits. At a glance the engine may look like any other BMW, but in fact it has a complete racing spec, from the overhead cams inwards.

lubrication

wet sump, forced feed from gear pump combined with centrifugal lubrication

engine

horizontally opposed ohv twin

capacity	590 cc
bore × stroke	72 × 73 mm
compression ratio	9.5:1
nominal rated bhp	42 at 7000 rpm

cylinder bore:

1st oversize	72.5 mm
2nd oversize	73.0 mm
piston skirt clearance	.08–.09 mm
(for sidecar work)	.09–.10 mm
maximum permissible	.12 mm

piston rings:

gap	.25–.40 mm

side clearance,

top ring	.07–.10 mm
second ring	.07–.10 mm
oil control ring	.03–.05 mm

valve gear:

inlet port size	38 mm
exhaust port size	34 mm

valve clearance (cold)

inlet	.15 mm
exhaust	.20 mm

valve timing: (measured with valve clearances of 2.0 mm)

inlet opens	4° btdc
inlet closes	44° abdc
exhaust opens	44° bbdc
exhaust closes	4° atdc
valve seat angle	45°
valve seat width	1.5 mm (both)

correction angle:

inner	75°
outer	15°

valve springs:

free length, inner	42 mm
outer	43.25 mm
ignition:	Bosch magneto driven from camshaft at half engine speed with automatic advance/retard unit
contact breaker gap	.4 mm
ignition timing	9° btdc (static)
advance range	30° crankshaft on
max advance	39° ± 2° btdc
spark plugs	Bosch W 260 T1
plug gap	.6 mm

electrics

6 volt dc lighting from battery and crankshaft-mounted dynamo with integral voltage regulator. Ignition by magneto (rotating magnet).

battery	6v, 8 a-h
generator	Bosch LJ/CGE 60/6/1700 R5
magneto	Bosch MZ ad/R
generator output	60 w at 1700 rpm

bearings

mains: built-up crankshaft supported in one ball bearing (front) and a fully floating barrel roller bearing (rear)

crankpin diameter (std)	36 mm
max ovality	.02 mm
maximum permissible out of round on flywheel commutator	.04 mm
big-ends	roller bearings
oversize rollers	4.994 to 5.004 mm, in increments of .002 mm; and 5.01, 5.02 and 5.03 mm
endplay of conrod on crankpin	.07–.10 mm

carburettor

type	two Bing model 1/26/29 (left) and 1/26/70 (right)
venturi	26 mm
main jet	135
needle jet	2108
jet needle	934, no 4
needle position	2
idling jet	35
idling mixture adjusting screw	open 1½–2 turns
throttle slide	22–531
weight of float	7 gms (.25 oz.)

transmission

single plate clutch driven from engine flywheel driving through four-speed cross-over gearbox. Final drive by shaft in oil bath mounted in right-hand swinging arm fork. Rear wheel driven by spiral bevel gears.

clutch	single plate, operated by diaphragm spring
clutch spring load	341–363 lb. installed

flywheel clutch face, max runout .1 mm

gear ratios (gearbox)

1st	4.171
2nd	2.725
3rd	1.938
4th	1.54

rear axle bevel gear ratio

solo	3.13
(no of teeth	8,25)
sidecar	4.33
(no. of teeth	6,26)

torsional torque damper spring,

free length	1.75 in.

dimensions

sump capacity	2 litres (.44 gal)
gearbox capacity	150 cc
rear axle capacity	150 cc

torque wrench settings

cylinder head bolts	25 lb. ft.
flywheel retaining nut	123 lb. ft.
generator armature on crankshaft	14.5 lb. ft.
magneto rotor on camshaft	14.5 lb. ft.

Note:

most measurements are quoted in metric sizes. Useful English equivalents are:

1 mm = .0394 in., 1 in. = 25.4 mm
1 kg = 2.2 lb., 1 lb. = .454 kg

FINAL DRIVE

● *The rear wheel's shaft drive is one of the features which distinguishes the BMW. The cross-over gearbox is arranged so that the output shaft connects with the prop-shaft via a universal joint. This runs in the swinging fork which is also used as an oil bath. The rear end of the propeller shaft is connected to the pinion shaft which runs in ball and needle roller bearings in the axle housing. The pinion drives the crown wheel which is splined to the hub and also runs in ball and needle roller bearings.*

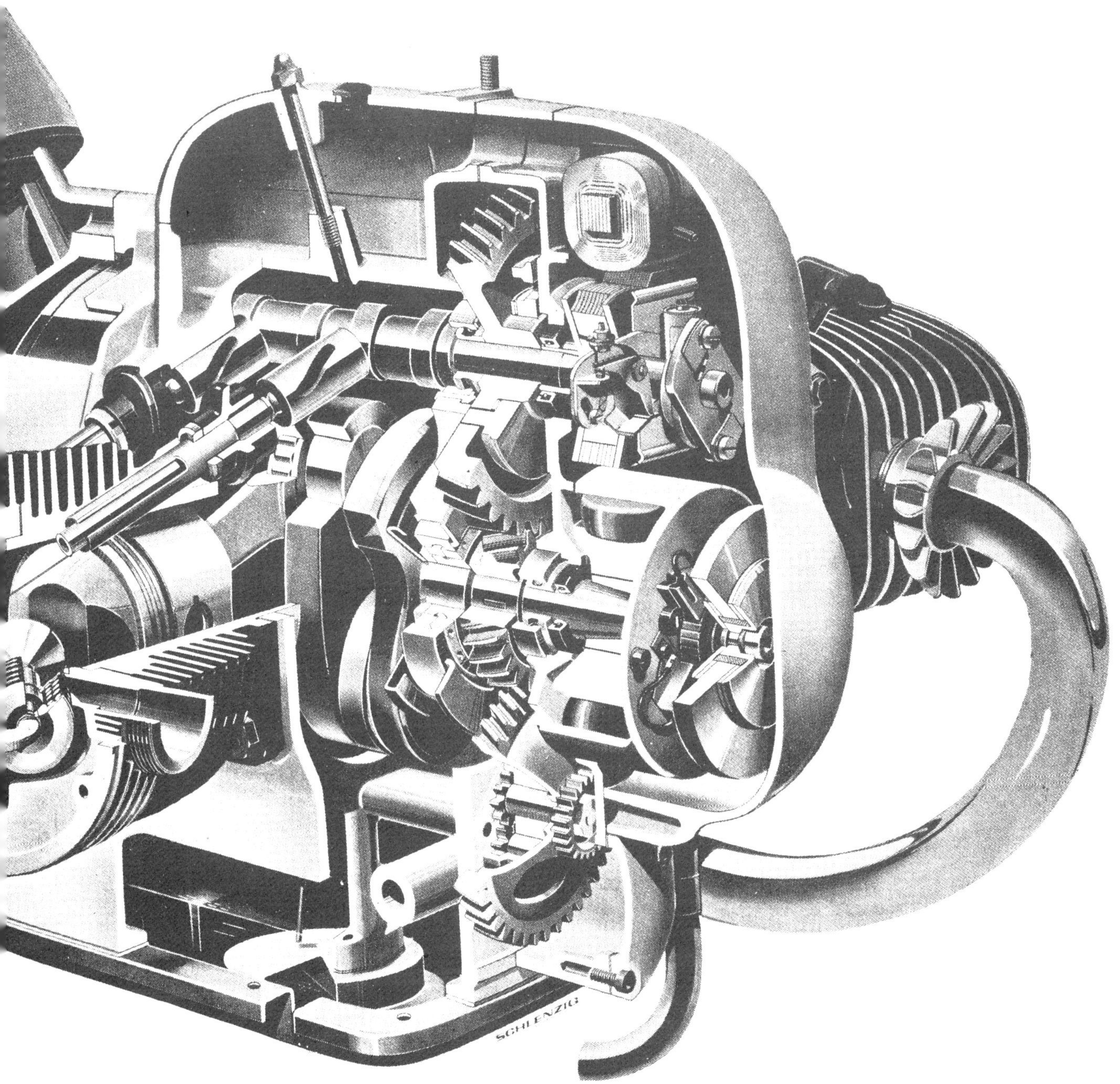

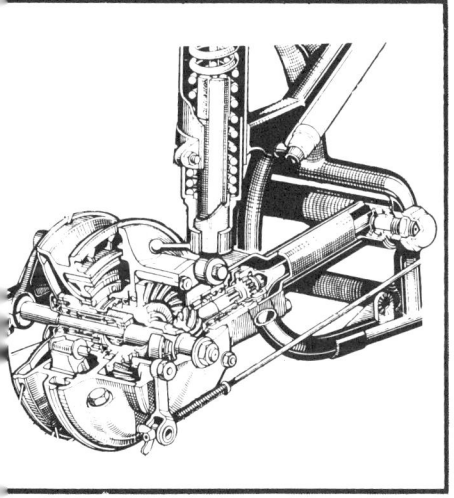

BMW R69S
ENGINE
ANALYSIS

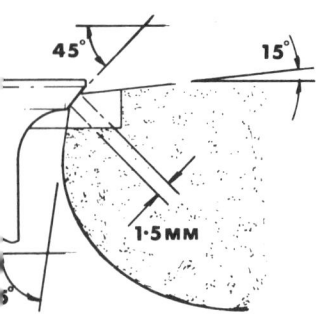

To keep the gas flow at maximum efficiency the valve seat dimensions are critical. Use inner and outer cutters to cut seat width

Leaking pushrod tubes can be cured by tapping the tube down to make the rubber seal at the cylinder base seat properly

The high domed pistons from the R69S give a compression ratio of 9.5:1. Lower cr pistons from the R69 fit giving smoother running

The flywheel drives the clutc and run-out must not excee 0.1 mm. Check pressure face for any signs of cracki

This is the diaphragm spring and driven plate assembly. Clutch release is by rod through spigot shaft bearing on pressure plate

Drive to the camshaft is by this helical gear train. The gears are machined as matching pairs and should be changed together

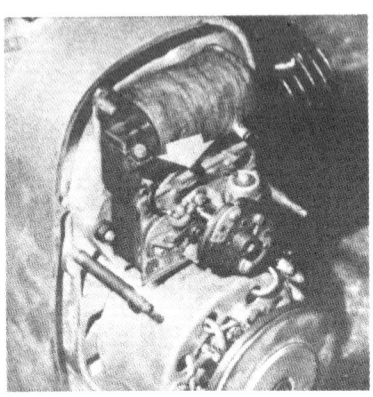

Set up the magneto timing on full advance by rotating rotor with flywheel held still until the marks (arrowed) line up

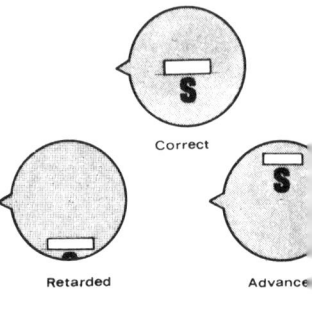

Check timing with motor runnir at tickover (500–750 rpm)- using strobe the S mark shou appear in centre of hole (9° btd

▶ **The massive casting of the flat twin's crankcase assembly may make the motor a shade bulky, but at least the cylinder heads and barrels are easy to get at!**

A fairly common complaint is oil leaking from the pushrod tubes at the base of the cylinder. This can be cured by reseating the tube. When the head has been removed, use a suitable drift through the pushrod tunnel in the head to tap the cover down towards the crankcase and give the rubber seal a better fit. There is a special tool for the job, Matra 530a.

When the valves need reseating, it is important to maintain the correct seat width on the head in order to keep the gas flow as efficient as possible.

After using the 45° cutter to clean up the seat, it will be necessary to use a 15° cutter or 75° cutter (or both) to reduce the seating surface to the specified 1.5 mm (see diagram at top of page).

Another point to watch when replacing the valves is that the springs are fitted with the close coiled ends towards the barrel.

When installing the magneto, the best procedure for retiming the engine is as follows: turn the flywheel until the "S" mark lines up with the mark on the engine housing. (S stands for *spätzündung* meaning retarded ignition.)

Timing

Fit the rotor on to the camshaft with the timing mark upwards, but do not tighten it up yet. Then place the magneto body on the timing cover and secure with the screws approximately in the centre of the oblong holes.

The auto advance unit should then be fitted on the (lightly greased) rotor shaft and the central mounting screw done up finger tight.

Hold the flywheel still and turn the rotor on the auto advance unit until the marks on the rotor and the mag body line up. The timing is now fully advanced, and the central mounting screw can be tightened up to a torque of 14.5 lb. ft.

Check that the advance unit springs are working correctly and that the cb cam has an endfloat of 0.008–0.024 in. and is easy to rotate.

A final check on the timing is made with a stroboscope on the "S" mark— see diagram above.

The generator can be tested *in situ*, but the battery must be fully charged and in good condition. Test by running the motor up to about 2500 rpm with full lighting switched on. Remove the battery negative lead—the light intensity should increase slightly and diminish when the negative lead is touched on the battery terminal.

If the reverse happens, the generator is suspect and should be checked accurately by an appointed Bosch agent.

BMW 600cc R 60/5

The BMW engineers have yanked the R 60 out of its hiding place on the edge of motorcycling and planted it squarely in the middle of the action.

The success of the earlier R 60 model in this country has been one of the wonders of motorcycling because the machine was designed primarily to pull a sidecar, and not for solo riding. For that reason, the bike had a number of characteristics completely different from those of most other brands. But a certain type of rider latched on to the R 60 like glue; rode it without a sidecar; was absolutely enchanted with it; and only parted with it when it had 50,000 miles or so on its odometer and the time had come to get a newer R 60.

wanted a responsive bike. To get these features, he was willing to put up with vibration, and the need for a lot of maintenance. But the R 60 rider wanted—and got—just the opposite.

The old R 60 was the most unobtrusive, conservative motorcycle that you could buy. It wasn't pretty, but its lines were so clean and simple and functional that a lot of people really dug its looks. With its standard funereal-black paint job, the R 60 wasn't *quite* invisible on the highway, but it came mighty close. On any other brand

Dance would have had trouble manipulating the controls on the old R 60 for around-town riding, but everybody else should have been able to manage the job in their sleep. In fact, the bike actually penalized the use of dexterity and skill. It had a specially designed long travel twistgrip that you had to wind up like an alarm clock before it would reluctantly lift the carburetor slide to give you some forward motion. This feature, combined with the wide powerband of the engine (which came on at 2500 rpm and pulled up to 6000

PHOTOGRAPHY: JIM McGUIRE

The R 60 owner was about as dissimilar to the average rider as a man could be and still get transported on two wheels. The average motorcycle rider was not bashful about being noticed: he enjoyed riding a bright, shiny, distinctive-looking machine. He liked the feel of power: when he grabbed some throttle, he wanted things to happen in a hurry. And he wanted to *hear* that power. The average rider enjoyed being able to use his skills, balance, and coordination to wring the utmost in handling and performance from his machine—he

of bike, you'd parade down the road; on an R 60, you'd *ooze*.

The exhaust sound was in keeping with the looks of the bike. While the average rider would be busting his butt to lay money on an irresponsible accessory manufacturer for a set of open (or openable) megaphones for his street bike, the R 60 rider took great pride in knowing that he could ease up alongside a pedestrian walking down the road without getting even a single backward glance.

Perhaps a person afflicted with St. Vitus

rpm), and the inertia of the flywheel (once you got it spinning, it would resist valiantly all efforts to make it stop), made it well-nigh impossible to stall out the old model R 60 at a traffic light. Nor did you have to mess with the gearbox very often: the bike was perfectly willing to lug along in the wrong gear in town while you thought about other things. Of course, if you *did* want to change up through the gears smartly, then you might have a few problems, because the gearbox simply wouldn't be hurried. Many massive pieces had to

The 1967 R 60 delivered 32 hp; the new version churns out 46. The price you pay for this whopping increase is a narrower powerband.

move around in there, and it took a while.

The BMW would go through the corners, and it seldom left cylinder heads behind, but the steering geometry of the Earlesfork models left some with the feeling that the machine was going to flop over on its side right there in the middle of the corner unless the rider fed it some more throttle. Could you, while riding the old R 60 on twisty mountain roads, have imagined yourself aboard a roadracer giving 'em hell at Daytona? You would have needed a strong imagination.

What the old R 60 did best was go from one side of the country to the other side and back, effortlessly. It was a comfortable machine: the rider could take long trips on it without getting jarred to pieces. Compared with other brands, the R 60 just did not vibrate. And the factory had built the machines carefully, using overdesigned parts, so the bikes didn't break very often, and they didn't need constant adjustment. All you had to do was put in some gas, climb aboard, and take off unobtrusively for the other side of the continent.

The R 60 stood apart from the mainstream of motorcycling, and so—often—did its rider. He placed little value upon the handling and performance characteristics sought with fervor by riders of other brands; he was unwilling to put up with the common flaws of motorcycles that other riders took for granted; above all, he relished being inconspicuous while other riders were noisy extroverts. Once an R 60 rider, *always* an R 60 rider.

Now, in 1970, everything is changed. The BMW engineers have yanked the R 60 out of its hiding place on the edge of motorcycling and planted it squarely in the middle of the action.

Look at the photographs of the machine. The old unobtrusiveness is gone; the new R 60 is very definitely *there*, and it gets noticed, particularly when wearing white paint. Our first impression was one of shock. Several other riders reacted the same way. One said, "It looks like they shoved a VW engine into a motorcycle frame." Another rider studied the bike for a while and commented, "If the Jolly Green Giant picked up an R 69 by its wheels and squeezed from both ends, that's what you'd get."

The machine looks massive. It swallows up shorter riders, and it will look big beneath larger riders, too. The lines of the original R 60 have been intensified almost—but not quite—to grotesquerie. The motorcycle is unmistakably German, easily associated with pickelhauber helmets

and Teutonic castles, and the Kaiser's pre-WWI officers would have created the same effect in parades had they been mounted on the new R 60 as they did on their magnificent horses. This R 60 is a serious machine, not to be taken lightly.

From the side, the slabsided oversize gas tank jumps out and hits you in the eye. It is out of proportion; in their desire to give you 250 miles of riding between filling stations, the design engineers went overboard and designed the tank about three inches too deep.

The engine cases are larger and bulkier than before, and they extend up beneath the bottom of the tank; this strikes a jarring note to the rider who prefers to see airspace between the bottom of the tank and the top of the engine.

When you've gotten past the gas tank and the engine cases, your eye follows the well-proportioned and gracefully-upswept exhaust pipe and muffler. Then you notice

the painted fenders—a narrow sport fender up front and the deeply-valenced rear fender—with their tasteful pinstriping. All of the details, with the exception of the garish turn signals and hangers, are carefully done and understated. After a while, when the initial shock has worn off, you realize that the lines of this bike are even simpler than those of the previous R 60. As is often the case with simple but unusual designs, the looks of the bike grow on you, and before the end of the test we found ourselves wishing we owned it.

We climbed aboard the machine for the first time with a touch of apprehension. We were in for another shock. When you look at the bike from the saddle, it seems to change into a different motorcycle altogether. The gas tank is now perfectly proportioned; it seems long and slender and inviting. The layout of the handlebars, controls, instruments, and headlight is clean, businesslike, and elegant. From the saddle,

the R 60 still seems big, but it is no longer an intimidating machine.

To start the engine, you simply tickle the carbs and then touch the starter-button near the right handlebar-grip. The clutch pull is easy, but the clutch on the test bike engaged very quickly, and we had to be careful when slipping it to get the wheels rolling. You do need to slip the clutch a bit, because the gearing is rather tall, and the engine doesn't really come to life below 4200 rpm. Gone is the variable-sensitivity twistgrip and gone is the low-rpm lugging ability of the engine. This new R 60 will not haul you unthinkingly around town like a Farmall tractor; you've got to pay attention to what you're doing.

Below 10 mph, the bike feels unstable; torque reactions generated when you rotate the twistgrip at those creeping speeds cause the bike to lean slightly to the right. Not enough to put you into the bushes: just enough to unsettle you slightly.

Above 10 mph, the bike stops playing games, and then it is all yours. We were so amazed at the responsiveness in handling that we spent 15 minutes riding along at 20 mph, throwing the machine over to the left and then the right and then the left. The bike heeled over and recovered exactly as we asked it to—far more readily than most other bikes its size. In fact, we began to wonder whether it would get squirrelly at higher speeds.

If you wind the machine up tight in low gear and then shift into second, the shift lever says, "Click," the transmission says, "CLUNK," the rear wheel dances around while the flywheel makes up its mind how fast to spin, and WHAM! the bike tries to run out from under you. Not much like the old R 60, which delivered 32 hp; the new version churns out 46. The 1967 R 60 that we tested did the quarter mile in 16.2 seconds, going through the traps at 79 mph. The top speed was 88 mph. Our Technical Editor took the 1970 R 60 down the strip in 15.2 seconds, with a best speed of 85.38 mph. The top speed of this machine is around 97 mph.

The price you pay for this whopping increase in performance is a narrower powerband. You don't want to ride the bike with the engine turning less than 4200 rpm; below that speed, it takes the engine too long to get up a head of steam when you turn on the throttle. But above 4200, the machine is right with you. The engine seemed happiest when turning 6600, right at the redline. Even though the odometer had only 600 miles on it, everything felt free and easy and still eager, and an eye had to

> The R 60 somehow manages to feel light and responsive, yet rock-steady, all at the same time. The machine goes where you aim it.

be kept on the tach to keep from overrevving the engine. The old R 60 would go long distances at 65-70 mph; the new model feels as if it would run all day long at 85-90. The only thing lacking is a five-speed gearbox; the machine works okay with four, but with the narrower power-band it could use a bit more overlap in the gearing, and a lower first gear.

As you charge along the highways, you can glance at the handlebar mirror and see everything behind you; there's not a bit of quiver. The magnificent saddle will shiver just a bit at 3500 rpm, and aside from that, it just doesn't want to know about vibrations. The handlebar grips (which are hard and uncomfortable) transmit just enough vibration so you can feel it, and that's not much at all. The gas tank shakes a bit more, but not enough to generate knee discomfort. The footpeg rubbers, which are large and seemingly luxurious, must be made out of the wrong materials, because more vibration can be felt through them than from any other source. Although the Japanese have done some good work in the last few years to get the vibes out of their bikes, the R 60 still has the edge.

We need not have worried about the bike's being squirrelly at high speeds. The faster it went, the more controllable the machine felt. With the mechanical steering-damper unscrewed, the R 60 somehow manages to feel light and responsive, yet rock-steady, all at the same time. You flick it over in a corner, and it's all there, solid and stable. If you want to make small corrections to your line through the corner, just shift your weight a small amount, or turn the bars a touch, and the machine goes where you aim it.

Something was wrong with the suspension. The front forks are advertised as having 8½ inches of travel. While stopped, I could pull the front brake and work the forks up and down and get about five inches of travel; nothing felt as if it were binding. On the road, the bike would eat up small bumps without even bothering to let you know about them. Hitting a medi-

Continued on page 137

BMW R 60/5 600cc STREET

Price, suggested retail	East Coast, POE $1548
Tire, front	3.25 in. x 19 in., Continental Rib
rear	4.00 in. x 18 in., Universal
Brake, front	7.8 in. x 1.2 in.
rear	7.8 in. x 1.2 in.
Brake drum swept area	58.8 sq. in.
Specific brake loading	9.7 lb/sq. in., at test weight
Engine type	Horizontal opposed four-stroke twin
Bore and stroke	2.89 in. x 2.78 in., 73.5mm x 70.6mm
Piston displacement	36.6 cu. in., 599cc
Compression ratio	9:1
Carburetion	(2) 26mm Bing
Ignition	Battery and coil
Bhp @ rpm	46 @ 6600
Mph/1000 rpm, top gear	15.6
Fuel capacity	6¼ gal.
Lighting	12v, 180 watts
Battery	12v, 15ah
Gear ratios, overall	(1) 13.1 (2) 8.7 (3) 6.3 (4) 5.0
Wheelbase	54.6 in.
Seat height	32 in., with rider
Ground clearance	6½ in., with rider
Curb weight	438 lbs., with ½-tank of gas
Test weight	573 lbs., with rider
Instruments	Speedometer, tachometer, odometer
0-60 mph	6.9 seconds
Standing start ¼ mile	15.20 seconds, 85.38 mph
Top speed	97 mph

BMW R69 *Continued from page* 98

and virtually service-free drive system.

Much can be said about the rest of the BMW and most of it in the same vein. Two electrical systems operate independently and with high reliability: a Bosch magneto ignition and a Bosch 6-volt dc lighting system. The throttle mechanism has a gear-driven cam and chain that offers progressive opening—more opening for the same radial twist at the high end of the range. The BMW's front brakes feature twin-cam actuation, but the stock linings are too hard to effectively pull the big machine down from speed. We prefer brakes that are progressive to the point of lockup, given a squeeze that's near the limits of what's humanly possible. You can't lock the BMW's front brakes on dry pavement, although their action is very smooth, and reasonably strong. Real earholers might want to fit stickier linings in front. The rear, foot-operated brake has an elaborate lever and rod linkage that minimizes snatchiness on bumpy downhill grades, and that brake *can* be locked with reasonable pressure.

Behind BMW's "on the move" push lies the completion of their all-new all-motorcycle producion facility. Previously, the bikes were beginning to get edged out by the cars with which BMW has been so successful in recent years. Now the motorcycle people have their own quarters, their own engineers and research team, and a much more independent management. We can probably look for some more aggressive selling and a more rapid development pace for the bike division in the future.

Our R 69 US test bike went the distance with flying colors. The new forks are a great engineering success, and a definite improvement for high-speed riding on rough, winding roads. A suggestion in the sales literature that they would be useful for off-the-road riding is a trifle absurd, for nobody we know is going to go trail riding on a 440 pound motorcycle with less than six inches of ground clearance. The brand new BMW R69 US remains what it has long been, a superbly crafted, carefully developed, highly reliable touring machine. And for long distance, high-speed touring, there is no better motorcycle on earth. ◉

Continued from page 123

As for torque reaction from the before-and-after crank and flywheel—you just don't notice it except when blipping the throttle from idle at a stop light. Incidentally you can now get full throttle with one twist of the wrist. The old BMWs took two grabs.

The best fun on those backroads was driving with some would-be Juan Fangio. Most often he would be driving a BMW 2002 TI, the company's sportiest sports-sedan that can't be bought in this country because of exhaust-emission laws. Usually the driver was familiar with the road as if it served as his daily playground. When he would see me coming up in the rearview mirror, the game was on. That's a very agile little car, with a top speed of well over 100 mph. Because the roadway was so narrow and because he would do apex-to-apex cornering, I often had to hang on his rear, waiting for an opening. If a straightaway came into view, I could zap him easily. The R75 surges forward with great elan in midrange. Another place I could get by was steep upgrade turns. Grades don't seem to have much effect on the R75's throttle response, but they slow up the cars. Must be power-to-weight ratio. I never lost any of those races—though it probably proves nothing more than that I'm a hazard to public safety. Cornering and accelaration—two new trump cards for BMW and two good ones.

In the day of superbikes with multi-cylinder and cush-mounted engines, smoothness has taken on new meaning. BMW's finely balanced flat-twin engines have always set the standard against which other bikes were measured, but now the gap is closing. Vibration was absolutely never a problem, never an irritant on the R75. The engine still bolts directly to the frame and you can still get a clear image through the rearview mirror at 80 mph. Yes, BMW is moving to bigger, somewhat harsher engines and the multis spread out power pulses so evenly that their dynamic imbalance is virtually negated. I would still give the BMW a slight edge, but happily for big-bore motorcycling, vibration seems to be disappearing altogether as a factor in choosing a ride.

Bavaria's Mad Ludwig passionately pursued his mission of building castles. The Wright Brothers thought men could fly and Henry Ford thought a cheap car could be built for everyone. BMW thinks a flat twin is the answer for the next generation of high output, high performance street bikes. They have moved their indexing needle away from the touring-utility end of the scale well into the street-sport zone. At $1700, the R75 is an expensive but beautifully crafted motorcycle. If it wants for style, it certainly doesn't want for riding effectiveness. BMW's engineers have their mission. Who knows? They might very well be right. ◉

BMW *Continued from page* 136

um-size bump, the suspension would work smoothly, with no loss of control or shock to the rider. When we hit a big bump, our tail would leave the saddle. This didn't worry us, because when we rejoined the bike we were still heading in the same direction as when we parted company. Still, it was puzzling. Somehow our Tech. Editor figured a way to ride the bike and keep one hand on the slider leg when he hit big bumps and flew up off the machine, to see how far the suspension was compressing. He found that he would get about an inch of fork travel before the fork springs had compressed all they were going to. He rode a stretch of pavement where the tar joints were raised about an inch above the surface of the concrete, and the forks wouldn't compress at all on those joints, so the machine would hobby-horse and snap his neck with regularity. This gets to be a drag, and he returned with a stiff neck and a headache. Unfortunately we were unable to tell whether the problem was caused by faulty design of the suspension, or whether only the test bike had a malfunction in one of its suspension parts.

The brakes worked well enough to suit the solo rider; we got on them hard just once: when a taxi stopped suddenly in the middle of a turnpike so that it could make up its mind whether or not to leave at a particular exit. But we wouldn't want to have to make a panic stop while riding two-up.

Aside from the problem with the suspension, we ended up liking the new R 60. But we are not the oldline BMW rider, and we are curious about how they—as a group—are reacting to the bike. Have they changed their values along with the radical changes in the machine, and will they stay with the brand? Or is an entirely different group of riders buying the new model? If you bought or ordered an R 60 this year, and you feel like satisfying our curiosity, please drop us a note and tell us what kind of rider you are: BMW traditionalist, or another breed of cat. BMW has made its move in from the periphery: was it the right move? ◉

LATE FLASH

After we returned the R 60/5 to Butler and Smith, they took apart the forks and discovered that a bent fender brace had caused one slider leg to bind. We took to the road again, and now the BMW kept both wheels on the asphalt, no matter what. But the forks were still sending too many jolts to the rider's shoulders and spine. To try to find out why, we dropped the front wheel and pulled the fork springs. Because BMW's manufacturing tolerances are so tight, the forks weren't broken in at 1100 miles, and were not yet working freely. Probably after another 2000 miles, they will deliver the outstanding handling and comfort that has been the cause of most of BMW's solid reputation. ◉

BAVARIAN BEAUTY

BMW has the reputation for smooth, effortless power . . . Charles Deane finds out why

MM ROAD TEST

▶ **Motorists' eyes take on a glazed expression as you burble quietly past . . . you stop at the traffic lights and a window is wound down alongside . . . "Great bike that, I remember Georg—you know, Georg Meier. He won the TT in 1939 on one of them!"**

And that is your introduction to the BMW—not so much a motorcycle, more a tradition.

The horizontally opposed transverse twin has been running since time immemorial, and when you ride a BMW you almost without thinking assume an air of superiority over the common-or-garden Mini, Minx or Cortina owner.

Not for you the smouldering little family saloon or rattling, gauntlets near ankle-straps, backside in air, coffee-bar racer . . . you are a BMW owner!

What is it that makes the BMW motorcycle so superior? Is it the price? At £800 plus it could be part of the answer, but it is really only one of a number of reasons why the Be-em is seen in the eyes of the majority as the ultimate in two-wheeled transport.

We collected our BMW R60/5 from Chas. Coombe of Bath Road, Slough, Buckinghamshire, who is a main agent for these Bavarian beasties. It had just over 2000 miles on the clock and to us was just another motorcycle to ride and test.

Chas. Coombe is an expert on these machines and similar to us, after years of stripping down motors, replacing clutches and grinding in valves, has a jaundiced eye about anything mechanical.

"They're good machines," he said, "but they do have their problems the same as any other bike. The only trouble is the cost in putting them right . . . For example, a pair of front forks costs .£157 to replace, a battery for the latest models costs £14, and if the sealed transistor electrics pack goes that sets you back £18 10s. 0d. a time. Not funny if you've spent your last penny on buying the machine. You have to have money to be able to run a BMW, just like running an expensive car."

Anyway, after nervously signing the note saying we would return to owner in good condition, we were introduced to the latest model from the Bavarian Motor Works.

On the right handlebar was the throttle twistgrip, front brake lever, and combined starter/flashing indicator switch and button. On the left handlebar was the clutch, dipswitch/horn and headlight flasher/button.

The ignition/light key was set in the headlight nacelle, just in front of the speedometer, revcounter combined with oil, generator and main beam warning lights.

The rear brake pedal was on the right and the gear lever—one down, three up—on the left. Apart from the electric starter, there is also the standard kick-start mechanism on the left with the unusual BMW sideways action.

"The toolkit's in the tray under the seat," said Chas., "and mind how you take her off the centre stand, she's a bit top heavy."

"OK.," I smiled nervously and promptly almost dropped the Be-em on to one of its expensive-looking cylinder heads.

A 29-in. inside leg straddled the comfortable looking dual-seat and surprisingly both feet could be placed firmly on the ground.

Fuel taps, one each side of the large five-gallon tank were turned on, the twin carbs tickled, the ignition key pushed home and then a single prod on the starter button brought the motor to life.

A blip of the throttle and I almost fell over again as the torsional reaction of the motor forced the bike over. "That's something you'll have to get used to, especially when changing down gear," said Chas.

Remembering previous experience of a certain R69S, I smiled, pulled in the clutch, selected first gear and departed quietly from the Chas. Coombe premises.

Normally when riding some-

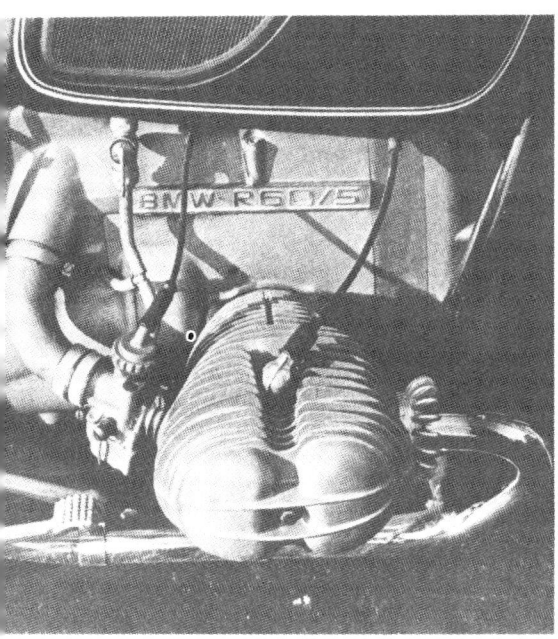

Forty bhp at 6200 rpm from the very tidy BMW 60/5

Silence is golden and the large silencers certainly keep it that way

body else's machine, first gear always grates, clashes and clonks before you ride away red-faced, gritting your teeth behind a sickly smile. But that first BMW gearchange was the sweetest, quietest I've ever made.

The clutch was light and very smooth and the gear went home without the slightest tap . . . but it wasn't to last! At 20 mph I changed into second gear—clonk! At 30 mph I changed into third—clonk! And at 40 mph I changed into fourth—clonk!

In fact, I clonked gears for almost all of the 600 miles we covered with the BMW on test. It wasn't through lack of trying . . . I counted slowly to three in between changes—still clonk! I tried rushing the changes—heavy clonk!

Complaint

At times I was worried that the gearbox would be damaged, but it came to no grief and was obviously robust enough to stand the impacts of gear changing. However, in this day and age one would think that BMW would do something to remedy the cause of the trouble.

Apart from this one complaint, there was very little else to criticise on the machine.

At tickover the motor was extremely quiet and the machine oscillated slightly when standing still. But, once on the move, it could be trickled along at walking pace in first gear without any snatching of the transmission or oscillation felt through the frame or steering.

Acceleration was reasonably brisk for a touring-type bike, although with the sluggish gearchange, the BMW doesn't com-

pare with the really fast sportsters on this count.

One point where it does score heavily against the sportsters when accelerating is the noise factor. Silence is golden as far as the Bavarian bike builders are concerned and even with the throttle right against the stop the Be-em never raised its exhaust note above a deep, throaty grumble. The large air cleaner, with long manifolds to the twin carbs, also kept the intake noise to the minimum.

The riding position of this machine is very good. The seat is extremely comfortable and the miles fly by effortlessly at the steady 70 mph legal limit.

You simply sit in the "armchair" comfort of the bike and every control is within reach without so much as having to bat an eyelid.

Only with a passenger on the pillion, when the rider had to move further towards the fuel tank, was the problem of the air intakes to the carbs discovered. They rubbed against the rider's shins and the feet had to be turned awkwardly to use both brake and gear pedals. The pillion footrests were also too close to the rider's and there came the occasional complaint: "You're treading on my foot!"

One of the marvellous things about the BMW is its lack of vibration. As the engine began to rev towards its maximum of 6200 rpm it became almost turbine-like and one could actually see rearwards in the handlebar mirror without any blurring—something which could be said for very few other machines.

The gear ratios were suitably spaced for a tourer and with a

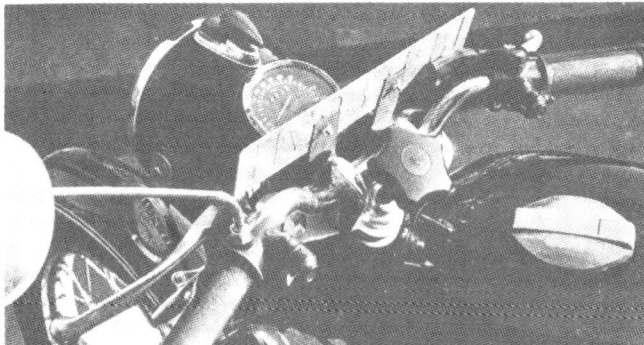

The handlebar layout showing neat controls and hidden rev-counter

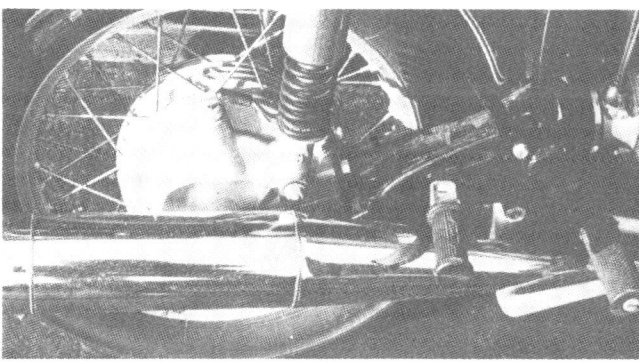

Shaft drive means cleanliness. Note neat suspension leg adjuster

The very effective twin-leading-shoe front brake. Note alloy rim

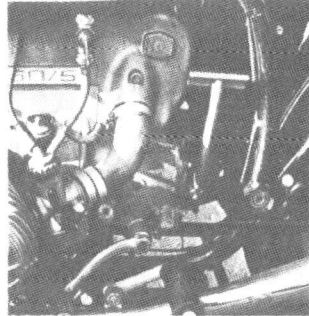

The only sign of oil on the bike came from the gearbox cover

ROAD IMPRESSIONS TEST

BMW 60/5

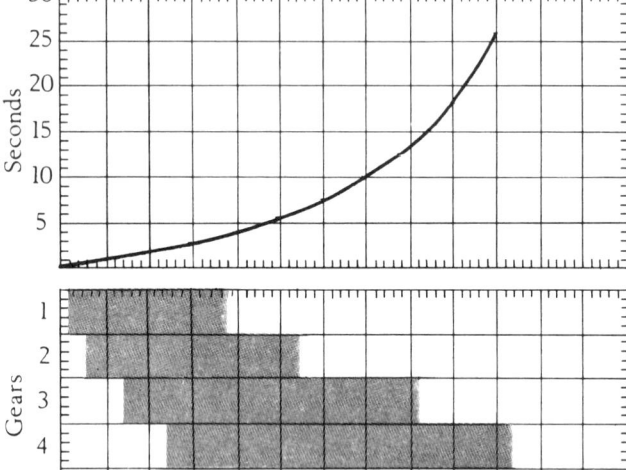

Miles Per Hour

fuel consumption (average figure)   **52 mpg**
braking from 30 mph   **28 ft.**

SPECIFICATION

Engine: Horizontally opposed twin cylinder ohv. Bore and stroke 73.5 × 70.6 mm, giving 599 cc. Compression ratio 9.2:1. Wet sump lubrication. Claimed power output 40 bhp DIN at 6400 rpm, 46 bhp SAE at 6600 rpm. Twin Bing 26 mm slide type carburettors.

Transmission: Four-speed cross-over gearbox driven through a single plate, diaphragm-spring clutch mounted on engine flywheel. Final drive by shaft and crown wheel and pinion. Gear ratios 2.835, 1.875, 1.364 and 1.091:1; layshaft reduction 1.375:1; final drive reduction 3.36:1.

Electrics: Bosch 12 volt AC DC lighting and coil ignition, from 200-watt alternator and battery. Electric starter and flashing indicators standard.

Wheels: Light alloy rims, front 3.25 × 19, rear 4.00 × 18, front brake twin-leading-shoe, rear single-leading-shoe. Friction area 2 × 107 sq. cm per brake.

Suspension: Front, telescopic forks; rear, swinging arm with adjustable dampers.

Dimensions: Wheelbase 54.5 in., seat height 33.5 in., width 29.1 in., kerb weight 463 lb., fuel tank capacity 5.3 gal.

Price: £826 8s. 3d. inc. duty, etc.

Importers: BMW House, 361 Chiswick High Road, W.4.

---

very wide spread of power from the 600 cc twin, the bike could almost be ridden to a standstill in top gear without transmission snatch. The lowest usable speeds in the gears are shown in the graph alongside.

Fuel consumption for the R60/5, which included motorway cruising, about-town riding and a couple of fast trips to the coast, averaged out at 52 mpg.

The handling of the new range of BMWs is impeccable. At low or high speeds the bike always feels perfectly under control and in spite of its fairly high centre of gravity it can be swung through bends, nadgery or otherwise, almost like a lightweight.

The only disconcerting thing was the torsional reaction of the motor as you blipped the throttle when changing down gear. The bike would dip or twitch slightly and at first was a little worrying, but it's a peculiarity of the machine which one soon gets used to in the first couple of hours riding.

Braking from any speed can only be described as superb on the R60/5. The twin-leading-shoe front brake is smooth and progressive in operation and, although it could be used to the point of making the front tyre squeal on the road, there was never any fear of it locking the wheel unexpectedly.

The rear unit was equally as progressive, but on the test machine developed an annoying squeak.

Design-wise the new range of BMWs have undergone quite a number of mechanical changes from the earlier models. For example: the push-rods to operate the overhead-valve gear are now set below the barrels and not above. This is supposed to improve lubrication of the camshaft as well as help oil return from the cylinder heads.

Also, an electric starter is now a standard fitting and this is enclosed in the casing above the crankcase.

This casing has given the motor a very chunky look and is a great improvement when it comes to cleaning the unit.

A powerful 200-watt generator supplies the 12-volt electrical system and lighting is another excellent feature of the BMW. The 45/40 headlamp has an asymmetric dipped beam which provides a sharp cut-off and avoids dazzle for oncoming vehicles.

The rearlight is large and also combines a stoplight which is operated by both front and rear brakes. Large and effective flashing indicators are fitted as standard and for the first time we've encountered a handlebar control switch for indicators which is positive enough in use to avoid the problems of switching on and off when wearing heavy gloves without overswitching.

One minor complaint on the instrumentation of the BMW is the combined speedometer and rev-counter. The rev-counter occupies the lower section of the speedometer and is so small that it is virtually impossible to read. Not only this, but it is located directly behind the steering damper knob and cannot be seen with the rider sitting in normal riding position.

One of the items which we feel could also be usefully fitted as standard is a good, solid pair of crashbars. It's not all that unusual for even the most experienced motorcyclist to take a tumble on a greasy or icy road and the one disadvantage of the horizontal twin is the vulnerability of the cylinders.

It has been known for the complete head, barrel, etc, to be wiped off a BMW in a spill and at the least to have the rocker covers cracked.

Avon Fairings are we know making a special fairing for the new range of BMWs which incorporates a very firm crashbar moulded into the fairing.

For anybody contemplating having one of these bikes, we would definitely recommend that a crashbar is fitted.

Finally, there is only one other item which must receive comment and that is the general finish of the machine. It is all that one would expect for the money—the paintwork is mirror-smooth, the chromium-plating excellent, and although it is difficult to tell at first glance, the mudguards are double-skin glass-fibre and consequently are not prone to rusting.

Unfortunately, they *can* be broken and the cost of replacement is a very expensive £12 10s. 0d.

That then is the BMW R60/5; expensive, very select and one motorcycle which has earned a formidable reputation. It has its faults, but the rest of the machine compensates—that's if you can afford to own one!

CYCLE WORLD
R O A D   T E S T

BMW R 75/5

Drastically redesigned? Kind of. Superbike performance? Kind of. Rolls Royce of Motorcycles? Definitely.

THE GERMAN MIND is orderly. It is precise. German craftsmanship is second to none in the entire world. And, appropriately, Germans are somewhat slow to change their ways of doing things—even when the change would be an improvement over a well established practice. But the Germans at Bayerische Motoren Werke, A.G., in Munich changed their motorcycle drastically in only a year's time. Well, kind of drastically.

While the hottest bikes in the BMW line were never noted for ripping up asphalt at the drag strip, the new 750 R75/5 will. It's a Superbike. Kind of. But it's not a Superbike in

character. It still retains that stodgy look and feel which is the source of revulsion to hotbloods and the font of joy to traveling men who want to get from Point A To Point B, a far piece away, with absolutely no hassle. The tradition goes on uninterrupted, and the many design changes to the R75/5, in spite of some disregard to the human engineering factor, will make sure it goes on, better and faster.

The engine retains its horizontally opposed configuration, but the cast iron cylinder barrels are gone and have been replaced by light alloy units with a perlitic cast-in liner. The liner is formed by a special process to give increased wearing qualities and near ideal heat dissipation to the outer barrel. Fin area has been increased by 10 percent, which, combined with the superior heat transfer qualities of the barrels, results in a 40-degree reduction in oil temperature.

Cylinder head design has been improved somewhat by setting the valves at a narrower angle (63 degrees instead of the 80 degrees previously used). This makes the combustion chambers more compact. Also improved is the method of attaching the head to the cylinder. Four through-bolts screw directly into the crankcase, and two additional bolts connect each barrel and head together to assure a gas-tight seal at high temperatures and pressures. Torque is supplied more evenly around the mating surfaces, which means that lower poundage can be used to achieve the same sealing qualities.

In the /5 series engines, the camshaft has been moved from above the crankshaft to below it for a couple of reasons. Perhaps the most important of these is that its present location allows the cylinders to be placed higher, thus precluding the possibility of dragging the rocker box covers when cornering

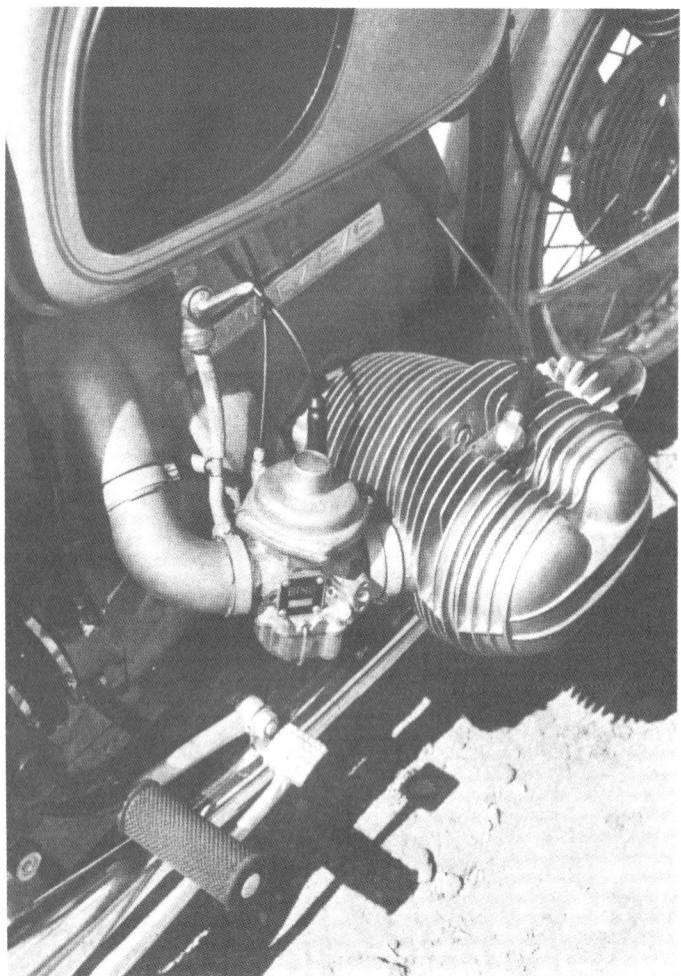

valve in the intake manifold, where a vacuum is present, assuring the proverbial cleanliness of BMW engines.

Carburetion on the R75/5 is accomplished by using two Bing 32-mm constant pressure carburetors. They depend on manifold vacuum, engine speed, and the opening of a butterfly valve to control the raising of the slide, which is connected to a tapered pin. Raising the slide increases the cross section of the ring and allows fuel to emerge from the atomizer jet, but only as fast as the engine can use it.

Hence, it is impossible to flood a properly adjusted carburetor of this type by "blipping" the throttle too vigorously. Fresh air is admitted to the carburetors through an anti-turbulence chamber which houses a large, paper-element air filter. It is conceivable that the restrictions posed by such a "rat-maze" could have an adverse effect on performance, but BMW felt that silent running (from squelching the intake roar) was more important. And a power output of 57 bhp figures out to 76 bhp per liter, which is quite good. Our only objection to the carburetors is their proximity to the rider's shins. There just wasn't any way to keep that sensitive part of one's anatomy far enough away to prevent a painful knock, short of planting one's posterior on the passenger's portion of the saddle. And if you're carrying a passenger, be prepared to suffer.

To gild the lily, BMW installed an electric starter, presumably for the American market. The unit develops a healthy 0.5 hp and is capable of spinning the engine over rapidly, even in sub-freezing temperatures. It is housed on top of the engine, and the resulting increase in engine height makes the engine look bigger than it should to some onlookers. A repeat lock prevents the starter from being actuated once the engine is running, saving the flywheel gear teeth and the starter gear from damage.

Electrical chores are handled admirably by a crankshaft-mounted 12-V, 200-watt, three-phase Bosch alternator. Even at idle, when the charging control light goes off, there is sufficient power to begin charging the battery. AC current from the alternator is rectified to DC by diodes, and a mechanical contractor is used as a voltage regulator.

Featuring modern, thin-plate construction, the battery is rated at a healthy 18 amp/hr. and provides a cold start current of 65 amps.

One of the most vehement criticisms of earlier BMWs was the clutch/transmission unit. An inordinately heavy flywheel was used in an effort to keep the engine as smooth as possible. But, in order to allow the constant-mesh transmission to shift noiselessly, an excessive delay was necessary for the engine to slow down enough for the flywheel surface and clutch surface to reach approximately the same speed. Our last test BMW, a 1968 R 6OUS (CW July, 1968), was notoriously noisy and cumbersome in shifting because of the aforementioned flywheel, which made it necessary to wait a few seconds before attempting a shift. Happily, BMW has seen fit to reduce the weight of the flywheel proportionately with the increased size of the engine, so smooth, rapid shifts were the rule rather than the exception on this machine. But it still is noisy.

The automotive-type, single-disc dry clutch is a model of perfection. Clutch lever pressure is very light, and the assuredness with which the clutch takes up the drive is astounding. The last thing one would expect from a BMW is a "wheelie" when one is banging a shift into second gear. But that's what we got. Scaareee! Even after several runs at the drag strip, the clutch needed little adjustment and continued its job with very little initial slippage. The clutch unit is spline-coupled to the gearbox, as in previous models.

Closer gear ratios are featured in the redesigned transmis-

hard with today's improved tires, which allow greater lean angles than ever before possible. Another advantage is better lubrication to the cam lobes and followers.

Defying the BMW tradition of having no chains in their twin-cylinder motorcycles, the /5 series all use an automotive-type, silent-running duplex chain to drive the camshaft. A plastic-coated tensioner blade acts as a vibration damper, and the flywheel end carries the new Eaton system oil pump.

A totally new crankshaft is employed. It is now a one-piece forging with exceptional bending and flexing resistance. Bearing dimensions are the same as on BMW's 2.8-liter automobile engine—that is, hefty. Following automotive practice, the main bearings are now of the plain, three-layer variety, using bronze, lead and indium.

Pistons and rings have been changed, too, with a thin, chromium-plated top ring, a shouldered ring in the middle and an equal chamfer ring at the bottom for positive oil control. These thinner rings have less tendency to "flutter" at high engine speeds.

Plain bearings have a greater load-carrying capacity than roller bearings of the same size, but they require a copious supply of oil to carry away the extra heat generated in performing their task. This is accomplished by the use of an Eaton-type oil pump which is a four-lobed eccentric rotor revolving in a five-chambered housing. At 6000 rpm, the pump circulates 212 gal. of oil per hour through the engine. This means that the entire contents of the oil sump passes through the bearings some 355 times every hour.

A large-capacity oil filter is used and features a full-flow pressure-relief valve. The pressure regulating valve is placed downstream from the filter so that only filtered oil may pass back into the engine. Crankcase breathing is accomplished through an anti-turbulence chamber and then to a diaphragm

sion which also aid in smooth shifting. Gear pinion teeth arc wider to cope with the increased power of the engine, and an all-new Palloid-pattern crown wheel is featured. A vibration damper on the mainshaft, a taper dog engagement and an eccentric selector fork are notable features.

Final drive remains basically unchanged. A drive shaft running in an oil bath is enclosed within the right-hand swinging arm member. A universal joint is used at the transmission output shaft to compensate for the swinging arm's up-and-down movements. Changes in length of the drive shaft are compensated for by curved, helical teeth in an internally splined coupling shaft.

Also new is the main frame which has been reduced some 10 lb. in weight over the previous models. Taper-drawn oval tubes were introduced to the motorcycle industry some 30 years ago by BMW, and are once again used in the /5 series frames. The relatively low-slung oval tube backbone intersects the twin tubes of the cradle just behind the steering head, and the complete assembly is reinforced by long welded seams and gusset plates to form an exceptionally rigid unit in all planes.

Slight flexibility in the longitudinal plane, a desired feature, is still present and the lightweight rear end structure which supports the dual seat carries bolt-on mountings for the upper ends of the suspension struts. Weight of the frame is now a light 29 lb.

The telescopic front fork, first developed by BMW in 1933 and adapted to their production models in 1935, was replaced in 1954 by the Earles, leading-link fork. This fork possessed excellent suspension characteristics with surprisingly fast reaction to road irregularities. But the leading-link front fork had a serious disadvantage in that it had heavy steering as a result of the large mass of the main fork stanchions which lay well ahead of the pivot axis of the steering. A low-frequency

wobble was apt to occur at low speeds, while at high speeds a large castor angle and a hydraulic steering damper were necessary to tame the fork reactions.

Although an amazing 8.4 in. of fork travel is claimed for the new telescopics, the fork spring length is so short that the forks lose almost half their travel when the machine is moved off the center stand. Add the weight of even one rider and they collapse even further, leaving only about 3.5 in. of travel available for impact. And the travel for the rebound stroke is, in our estimation, mostly wasted. Under normal riding conditions, the forks would not bottom, but under heavy braking they did with a resounding thump. A longer spring with perhaps a bit higher poundage rating would improve the front suspension immeasurably.

Rebound damping, on the other hand, was considered nearly ideal, and the fork legs feature lengthy fork leg sides to increase the wearing properties. Careful location of the sliding tubes offer what is claimed to be a reaction superior to the leading-link unit in encountering road irregularities. An additional benefit is a weight reduction of six pounds over the Earles-type fork.

At the rear of the machine, the suspension units are excellent and feature a three-way, spring-rate adjustment by means of a lever. Rear suspension travel has been increased from 4.1 in. to 4.9 in.

Pre-loaded taper roller bearings support the swinging arm member and are easily adjusted with the aid of a torque wrench.

Redesigned brakes add to the overall newness of the machine. Although they are slightly smaller in swept area than the previous units, a slightly larger diameter imparts a feeling of security to the rider when braking down from 80 mph or so in a panic-stop situation. Strong, straight spokes connect the hubs to newly designed alloy rims, with a reduced section size and an increase in strength. Tire sizes of 3.25-19 front and 4.00-18 rear provide the required amount of stopping and going traction. Fiberglass fenders add to the reduction in overall weight, with the front fender brace doing double-duty as a fork brace.

Big it looks and big it is. With a curb weight of 457 lb. the BMW is certainly no lightweight, but it doesn't pretend to be. An illusion of largeness is created by the curiously humped fuel tank, which would be much more attractive if the top were flatter. Finish is up to traditional BMW standards. Welds are almost mathematically perfect, and paintwork is outstanding. Our test bike was finished in the famous German

Rennsilber and never failed to catch an envious glance at every corner. German chrome needs no comment.

Everything seemed to fit perfectly with beautifully matched engine castings, cylinders, cylinder heads and rocker box covers. Allen screws abound on the machine, and the most complete tool kit we've seen contains almost everything needed to perform any work short of an overhaul. The toolbox is located in a heavy plastic tray under the seat, with ample room inside for spare light bulbs, road maps and a set of marbles or two.

The seat is one of the most comfortable we've seen, and the passenger portion seems almost orthopedic. It couldn't be better, and can be locked to protect the tool kit.

An increasingly rarer item is also found beneath the seat: a tire pump that actually works! Another nice touch is the beautiful cast-aluminum turn signals, and spring (not split) lockwashers abound everywhere.

Riding the R75/5 is quite an experience. Vibration is felt only when accelerating hard at low engine rpm, particularly in high from 40 to 50 mph. But this becomes practically negligible at higher engine speeds. Of course, the torque reaction from the longitudinally mounted crankshaft is still present to a marked degree when blipping the throttle, and the rear end tends to rise markedly under hard acceleration and sink under deceleration. But handling and general road manners are very good. We liked the mechanical and exhaust silence which has been synonymous with BMW for decades, and high speed handling qualities make it possible to dive into turns much faster than one would think. Pushing hard through a turn is easy, but it's hard to forget that you're riding a big machine.

Defects are few in number, in our estimation, but are inexcusable when one considers that BMW took the time to design a new machine. As we have mentioned, the position of the carburetors made stop-and-go riding painful to the shins. The problem is more pronounced with a passenger aboard because this forces the rider to sit more forward on the seat. Regarding the carburetor's function, we would prefer to have smaller (physically), slide-type carburetors to keep our shins from looking like those of a hockey player. Another minor complaint arose from the positioning of the turn signal switch. It was difficult to operate without shifting one's grip on the throttle, which had very stiff return springs on our test machine.

Rubber handlebar grips are supposed to be comfortable, but the BMW's are not. They are hard and transmit vibration, causing a tingling sensation in the hands after riding for 50 miles or so.

Instrumentation is very complete with the speedometer and tachometer being contained in the same instrument. Although the speedometer was reasonably accurate, it tended to fluctuate slightly at certain speeds. But the tachometer looked as though it had an acute case of Saint Vitus's dance at normal highway speeds. Neutral indicator, oil pressure and high beam indicator lights are all located within the single instrument, and a large green light on the top, left-hand side of the headlamp blinks when a turn signal is flashing.

Performance is certainly up to what is expected of a Superbike. A standing quarter-mile of 13.89 with a terminal speed of 91.27 mph is nothing to be sneezed at coming from such a docile, long-winded machine. And a top speed of 108.23 mph with the engine not fully broken-in is quite good. It will run all day at 80 to 90 mph. Overall gas mileage worked out to a figure of 42 mpg, which could improve as the engine loosens up.

In spite of its drawbacks, the BMW must still hold claim to the reputation, "The Rolls Royce of Motorcycles." ◙

BMW R 75/5

SPECIFICATIONS

List price .... $1848 POE
Suspension, front .... telescopic fork
Suspension, rear .... swinging arm
Tire, front .... 3.25 x 19
Tire, rear .... 4.00 x 18
Brake, front, diameter x width, in. ... 7.9 x 1.2
Brake, rear, diameter x width, in. .... 7.9 x 1.2
Total brake swept area, sq. in. 59.5
Brake loading, lb./sq. in. 9.86
Engine, type .... ohv opposed Twin
Bore x stroke, in., mm ... 3.22 x 2.77, 82 x 70.6
Piston displacement, cu. in., cc 45.2, 74.5
Compression ratio 9.0:1
Carburetion .. (2) 32mm Bing constant velocity
Ignition .... battery and coil
Claimed bhp @ rpm .... 57 @ 6400
Oil system .... gear pump, wet sump
Oil capacity, pt. 4.75
Fuel capacity, U.S. gal. 6.3
Recommended fuel .... premium
Starting system .... electric, kick
Lighting system .... battery, alternator
Air filtration .... paper element
Clutch .... single-plate, dry
Primary drive .... none
Final drive .... (2.91) shaft and bevel gear
Gear ratios, overall:1
    5th .... none
    4th 4.36
    3rd 5.45
    2nd 7.50
    1st 11.35
Wheelbase, in. 54.5
Seat height, in. 33.5
Seat width, in. 11.5
Handlebar width, in. 30.0
Footpeg height, in. 10.5
Ground clearance, in. 7.1
Curb weight (w/half-tank fuel), lb. 457
Weight bias, front/rear, percent 45.5/54.5
Test weight (fuel and rider), lb. 587

TEST CONDITIONS

Air temperature, degrees F 82
Humidity, percent 66
Barometric pressure, in. Hg. 28.90
Altitude above mean sea level, ft. 350
Wind velocity, mph 6-8
Strip alignment, relative wind:

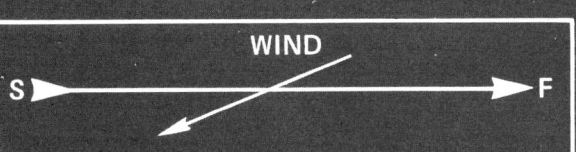

PERFORMANCE

Top speed (actual @ 6455 rpm), mph ... 108.23
Computed top speed in gears (@ 7000 rpm), mph:
    5th .... none
    4th 119
    3rd 96
    2nd 70
    1st 46
Mph/1000 rpm, top gear 17.1
Engine revolutions/mile, top gear 3510
Piston speed (@ 7000 rpm), ft./min. 3231
Fuel consumption, mpg 42
Speedometer error:
    50 mph indicated, actually 46.30
    60 mph indicated, actually 56.32
    70 mph indicated, actually 66.42
Braking distance:
    from 30 mph, ft. 27.5
    from 60 mph, ft. 130.7
Acceleration, zero to:
    30 mph, sec. 2.3
    40 mph, sec. 3.0
    50 mph, sec. 4.5
    60 mph, sec. 5.6
    70 mph, sec. 7.1
    80 mph, sec. 10.0
    90 mph, sec. 13.8
    100 mph, sec. 19.0
Standing one-eighth mile, sec. 9.75
    terminal speed, mph 80.00
Standing one-quarter mile, sec. 13.89
    terminal speed, mph 91.27

ACCELERATION / ENGINE AND ROAD SPEEDS / RPM X 100

SS¼

SS⅛

TIME IN SECONDS

Iron fist in a velvet glove

AN EVALUATION OF THE £1,120 R75/5 BMW

WHEN it came to testing the R75/5 I approached the event with unconcealed joy. I was being given the chance to try the latest model from a factory whose products I have ridden these last dozen years. Even in the most optimistic mood I think it's going to be some years before I can seriously consider owning an R75/5, for with a price tag of £1,121 it has been made clear that this machine is not for ordinary mortals. Oh yes, the average rider might, just, be able to afford one if he wants it more than anything else in the world. But this is not how BMW Concessionaires, who import the BMW range into this country, see their future market. Their sales approach has been geared to appeal to the affluent business man or professional man, one who perhaps is not particularly young but has enough money to run a good car *and* buy an R75/5 for fun. Are they on target with such a sales approach? It means they have to create a whole new market among a class of people whose enthusiasm, if ever they were motorcycling enthusiasts, has lain dormant for many years. The whole success of the operation is geared to motorcycling becoming respectable. And more than respectable: it means that someone has to take motorcycling by the scruff of the neck and make it fashionable. It is, I think, too big an operation for one producer, but he can perhaps achieve limited success with clever advertising and, with any luck, the rest of the high-priced machine makers, observing success, may follow. You might ask where this leaves the practical riders who ride a machine for pleasure but who are more affected by economic considerations? Where indeed . . .

How successful has the BMW marketing operation been to date? It is early days yet, but even at over £1,000 the R75 *is* being sold and with the increase in the number of dealers throughout the country it can be expected that the new BMWs will be seen in increasing numbers. To show that BMW's "affluent rider" marketing policy is not all that far off the mark I can instance one dealer who has sold over a dozen of the new models, and *all* for cash. But with upwards of a dozen dealers selling the new machines how long before the early sales potential is exhausted? There must be a limit, even in these affluent times, to the amount of *new* riders prepared to spend £1,121 on a motorcycle. When that limit is reached will the BMW then be offered to established riders at a less crippling price?

Contrary to what one or two national newspapers have reported, BMWs are not being marketed in this country for the first time in 30 years. The blame for these reports must lie with a slightly misleading Press handout that said, in part, that "for the first time in 30 years a *marketing organization* was being created". BMWs were first offered to the British public some years after the war, in 1950.

Up to 1954 riders could buy models with telescopic front forks and plunger rear suspension. In 1955 the models were extensively redesigned and the R50, R60 and R69 was imported with Earles-type front forks and swinging-arm rear suspension. These lasted until last year, although an upgrading of power in 1961 saw the R69S replace the R69. Naturally the machines all had horizontally opposed twin-cylinder engines and shaft drive (except the R25/6/7 single-cylinder series).

BMW TEST

The "new" BMWs are titled R50/5 (498 c.c.), R60/5 (599 c.c.) and R75/5 (745 c.c.). They are identical one with another in most respects with common-to-all crankshafts. The difference in engine size is merely one of bore, with different cylinder barrels and pistons to increase displacement. The price range is from £1,121 down to £857. For the extra £160 one gets a slightly bigger barrel and piston, constant vacuum carburettors and an electric starter.

Being a BMW owner gives a tester certain advantages when it comes to testing the R75. I have had more than the usual opportunity to meet other R75 owners, and an occasional chance also to look inside the engine. The first of these was positively frightening, for I called on a dealer friend just as he removed the head of a 75. "The owner is complaining that it is making noises," he said. Which wasn't surprising as we found that the arrow on the piston that should be pointing to the front was reversed and one of the valves was making contact. It is almost reassuring, when I think about it, to find that even BMWs have quality control problems. As far as I know, this has only happened on the one occasion.

All my thoughts about the whys and wherefores were banished the moment I sat on the R75/5. A wretched bus journey across to Slough had left me frozen and a cup of coffee from Charlie Coombes, whose shop had serviced the 75, had only slightly eased the chill. It was a raw January day. Just the kind of day not to be getting the best from a high-powered motorcycle. I left Charlie's shop and almost immediately swung on to the nearby M4. Those first few yards recaptured the memory of all the joy I had on a similar model last year in the Isle of Man. It really was as smooth as I remembered, and as quiet. Ouch, I didn't remember those carburettors digging in my shins, though! This was to remain the only riding problem that I had during the test. BMWs have seemingly been so concerned with getting the much criticized constant vacuum carburettors right that they have failed to notice that the unit is so large that it encroaches uncomfortably on the rider's leg space. Riders with large feet will have no problem but "normal"-sized riders will find that the carburettor tops will cause painful pressure on the shins. It is a problem that is confined to the R75/5 for the two smaller models have conventional Bing slide-type carburettors, and even without riding the R60/5 it was clear that there was ample clearance for the rider's legs on those models. I am told that there is now an R75/5S in Germany and this has reverted to the old-type carburettors. It is, one hopes, only a matter of time before all the 750s are so fitted.

Pointing the R75 towards London, I shivered as the cold found gaps in my nylon suit. I had never really warmed up after the bus journey and even my hands had started cold. As the machine became warm I allowed the revs to rise. At 70 it was a "floating carpet". There was not enough vibration to disturb the mirror on the end of its stalk, what little exhaust noise there was was caught on the wind and whisked away over the frozen countryside and all that I could hear was a faint drone as the engine revs rose.

Almost imperceptively speed would rise if a careful eye was not kept on the speedometer. The tachometer is unhappily situated at the bottom of the speedometer and is too small and obscured by the cables. No matter if the speedometer showed 70, 80 or 90 m.p.h. the only effect on the rider was a steady increase in wind pressure. As the BMW got into its stride along the M4 so my enjoyment rose. I was sure, from that moment, that here was the ideal touring mount. It is not as rapid from 0 to 60 as almost all its rivals but BMWs claim that the 57 b.h.p. engine will propel it to 60 m.p.h. in 6.1 seconds, which should satisfy all but the most ardent traffic lights dragster. The touring rider is not concerned with such matters. He wants a machine that will go and keep going no matter how hard it is ridden. This machine would, I am sure, cruise at anything up to 110 m.p.h. for as long as the rider can stand the sheer physical stress of riding at that speed. This, of course, is an important and recognized factor in sustained high-speed touring, and where the BMW scores off most of its more dashing rivals is that it makes such light work of high speed. No matter what speed the rider chooses to cruise at, he is not going to be subjected to vibration of the kind that leaves him numb with fatigue at the end of a day's riding. Vibration on the R75 is such that one has to grip the petrol tank tightly with the knees to feel it at all, the fingers are unaffected by that tingling sensation that so many high-speed mounts develop the moment they are given their head and, probably most important of all, the high-speed rider never has to concern himself for a moment with the thought that something might come undone or fracture. It's a fat lot of use averaging 100 m.p.h. from Brussels to Munich if one's luggage has been distributed among the population on the way.

Those first few miles along the motor-way did wonders for me. By the time that I was purring over the Hammersmith flyover I was not only warming-up but positively glowing.

It was a different sort of machine that was needed for the rest of the journey into London. No matter how fast or potent a machine is, in London it is soon reduced to the speed of the rest of the traffic and from then on only good manners count. All too often a bike is perfect

on the open road but becomes an over-heated, spluttering monster when out of its element. I would have been sur-prised had the BMW deteriorated in this way. It didn't, for with its efficient cool-ing and low centre of gravity it was as happy in a traffic jam as a machine of this size is capable of being. The bonded single plate diaphragm clutch has changed little from that on the earlier models and it will take any amount of

abuse, although in any event little abuse is needed, for the R75/5 will purr along at just about nil m.p.h. in bottom gear with the clutch out, leaping forward at a touch of the throttle.

The gearbox is that which was fitted to the R69US and is a slightly modified ver-sion of the older type. The modifica-tions have had the result of making gear-changes easier than before and this gearbox is quite the best I have tried on a BMW. This does not, perhaps, agree with the assessment of most who have written about the R75/5 but it is one of the benefits of being experienced in BMWs. As most BMW owners will tell you, it can take anything up to six months to learn to change gear properly and generally learn to enjoy the machine. Until then no one can be blamed for dis-missing the BMW gearbox as the worst in the world. It is if used the wrong way. It can take a long time to learn the technique and if that sort of time is not available how can the writer be blamed for failing to appreciate that there *is* a technique? The R75's box was a beauty, all changes could be accomplished silently, and it was entirely positive. If anyone tells you otherwise I would be prepared to prove them wrong. But there is one essential to silent gear-changes that the R75 lacked and that is that the throttle should cut the engine immediately upon closure. On our 75 it occasionally failed to do this completely and one was often faced with a 1,500

BMW TEST

r.p.m. tickover at traffic lights. It would be easy to lay the blame at the door of the vacuum carburettors but I was more inclined to suspect the cables. The book tells us that they are nylon sheathed, others, who claim they know, say that it isn't really nylon but a similar substance. Whatever it is all the cables were originally stiff and unyielding and only began to feel like a BMW's should after extensive work with an oil can. If the covers were nylon this shouldn't be necessary but a considerable improvement was the result of such work and the reliability of the tickover was helped. It was still not perfect, though. One thing that I did like about the cables was that all exposed ends are rubber sheathed. The rider should rarely be troubled by water in these cables. (Although when one thinks about it if they *are* nylon water is said to improve them!)

Any owner of the older-style BMWs can point to certain features he would like to see improved. On the new models it is gratifying to see that most of these points have received attention. Take the handling. The longer one rides a BMW (or any other machine, for that matter) the more one grows used to its faults. Some riders I know have learned to go very quickly indeed on the old Earles-fork models and I am bound to say that I was rarely troubled by its, shall we say, quaintness. Then I tried the R75/5. And this is how a BMW should be!

The frame is little changed at the front, with the twin duplex cradle arrangement retained, with a bracing bar from below the head to just in front of the point where the twin tubes curve at the top to meet the still massive single top tube. Where there is a change is in the rear swinging arm. Gone is the isolated rear unit tacked on the rear. Instead a bolted-on rear sub-section has its suspension units running from the top to the U swinging arm section in triangulation. One's first reaction is that there must be a considerable weight saving here but, having held both frames alongside each other, I now doubt if the saving is as much as 10 lb. I cannot say that I am too impressed with the rear sub-frame. Perhaps I have become used to BMW *over-engineering* but it seems the least robust

part of the machine. Two pressed steel plates serve to anchor the silencer and carry the pillion footrests. These I like not at all for they are quite out of character.

Suspension changes

The considerable changes to the suspension of the BMW have had two results. They have tightened up the handling to a considerable degree, raising it right out of the touring class. If ever BMWs take production racing seriously, the new-style handling will be a boon. The second effect of the changes has been to make the machine, inevitably, firmer to ride. It was possible, on the old models, to ignore all but the largest obstructions. On the latest versions, even though the telescopic front forks are said to have 8½in travel, road shocks are now transmitted to the rider just as they are on any other good-quality machine. A third, small but to some important, result of the suspension changes is that fitting a side-car is not encouraged. I have heard of one or two unions between the /5 series and sidecars but have not, as yet, heard of any really successful marriages.

Looks

How do you rate the look of the new models? Opinion among owners is mixed. Some prefer the sportier look of the new one but some, perhaps the majority, feel the whole machine looks unnecessarily bulky. Clearly the culprit is the engine. Few object to the 5½-gallon tank for most riders prefer a tank that will take them more than 100 miles on a fill-up. It's the engine that's the problem. Did it have to use up *all* the space? Obviously the electric starter had to go somewhere and its home in a large housing above the engine is very roomy. BMWs have turned the engine upside down on the new models. Most people know this by now but we will just do a quick recap in case there are any who have missed it. The basic problem with BMWs over the years has been its oiling system. The big-end eye was splash lubricated from "thrower plates". These were dished plates mounted on the outside of the crankshaft bobweighs and they threw, by centrifugal force, oil into the big-end. Which was all very well but for the

presence of a dreaded substance known as sludge. The centrifugal force that threw the oil *out* of the thrower plates also threw foreign bodies in the oil *into* the plates. Opinion has always differed on the source of these bodies and their effect on the engine but they clearly either come from the oil or the petrol, with present opinion tending to blame the lead in the petrol. Whatever the cause, the result has been big-end failure at comparatively low mileages, say, anything from 35,000 to 50,000 (although some bikes have gone twice that mileage); due to the thrower plates becoming filled with sludge and subsequently starving the roller bearing big-ends of oil. The alternative for BMW owners has been to strip the engine before the plates were full (usually at about 30,000 miles) and thus preserve the life of the crankshaft. It is rather a performance and many owners decide that it would be cheaper to replace the crankshaft when it goes.

High-pressure lubrication

The latest engines have an Eaton wet-sump high-pressure (about 80 lb sq. in) lubrication system. A rotary pump draws oil through a micro-mesh paper filter and delivers clean oil to all essential points. The crankshaft now has plain bearings and these have the great merit of being replaceable without the need for complete dismantling of the engine. It is ironic that such a measure should be adopted when the need, in theory anyway, has lessened, for engine life should be greatly increased because of the new oiling system. The camshaft now is at the bottom of the engine, driven by a spring-tensioned chain. While this is claimed to improve the oiling system, and it has had the effect of tidying up the cylinders on top, it has created its own problems underneath for the push-rod tubes are now rather inaccessible and few owners will keep them as well as they used to when they were on top for the world to see. The contact-breaker points are mounted on the end of the camshaft with the three-phase alternator mounted immediately above, on the end of the crankshaft. Above that the silicone diode rectifiers use up the remaining space inside the front engine cover. BMW electrics have long benefited from a dry, accessible place to live and the new models have retained this benefit, although the contents of the engine housing have been altered. All electrical connections are now tab connectors, replacing the old grub screw-held fittings. A great improvement. Two six-volt coils are mounted beneath the petrol tank with

BMW TEST

the starter relay and voltage regulator.

The bulky look of the engine unit is not helped by the increase in depth of the gearbox housing. The gearbox itself requires no extra space but the housing has been increased in size to accommodate the air filter. These in turn feed to the carburettors by plastic tubes. The whole arrangement is bulky and unsightly and most certainly not an improvement on the old system. As for the plastic air tubes—too awful for words.

To return to the engine. Compression ratio is highish, for BMW, at 9 to 1, with the familiar rocker covers being retained to protect the valve-gear. Alloy barrels with cast-iron sleeves molecularly bonded to them replace the old iron barrels. They save weight and improve cooling but marginally increase noise. The entire engine unit is tilted backward slightly to line the universal coupling at the rear with the rear drive, thus giving a straight run to the shaft. As the cranked coupling worked satisfactorily on the old models it seems to me that they have spoilt the line unnecessarily, although the increased power available might have presented problems. It is interesting that the handbook only recommends the use of multigrade oil for sub-freezing temperatures. Above that it suggests a good HD oil of SAE 30 or 40. Will this revive the old controversy over what is HD oil? Some say that any good oil is correct while others say that by HD they mean diesel engine oil. Certainly VW recommend HD and many VW agents use oil of Castrol CR or Shell Rotella type. If this *is* the type of oil they mean, it is a rare garage that carries it on the forecourt.

Electrically, the R75/5 is an excellent motorcycle. The 180/200w 12-volt three-phase alternator supplies ample power for all needs and the starter motor rarely required more than the merest touch of the button. The 45/40w headlight is as good as any motorcycle light I have used and the flashing indicators are better than any. They were the only indicators that I have found completely satisfactory during the day. The horn, too, was first class but the Bosch horn fitted to BMWs always has been and I doubt if this 12-volt version is better than a good six-volt as fitted to the older models. Brake lights are fitted to the front and rear brakes and a headlamp flasher is built into the left-hand dipswitch. The electrical switches were the only parts of the R75 electrical system that were below par. Identical-looking switches are fitted to each handlebar control. The right-hand one is the starter and flashing indicator control and the left-hand one is for the horn, dipswitch and headlamp flasher. It was the left one that gave trouble, failing to unflash when it was flashed and showing a marked reluctance to supply a dipped beam in a hurry. Other riders, too, have complained of the same thing. The battery remains in its familiar place under the seat, allthough it has grown,

not surprisingly, to twice its former width.

One of the biggest surprises about the R75/5 is to find it is now one of the, if not the, lightest 750s on the market, weighing in at 419 lb dry, which is exactly the same as the R60/5. Considerable weight saving has been effected somewhere as there is more engine, a bigger seat and bigger petrol tank than the old models, yet it weighs some 26 lb less than the R69S. Some, but not much, of the weight is from the frame. Plastic doubtless helps in this and the plastic mudguards front and rear contribute their share. One is somehow instinctively against plastic mudguards, or plastic anything else, on a BMW yet, provided it does the job better than metal, why should one object? Certainly the only criticism that could be levelled at the mudguards on the '75 was not that plastic was used but that not *enough* plastic was used, especially at the rear. For on wet days mudguarding is less than adequate and pillion riders get a steady stream of muddy water directed at their backs. The rear guard could, with benefit, be a good three inches longer at both ends.

I had no complaints at all with the general controls. The very comfortable dualseat was ample enough for two and wide enough, without forcing one's legs too far apart. The European-style bars were just perfect. I like my bars just as they were on the R75, not too wide and so placed that I am leaning slightly into the wind. The Magura controls were, as always, excellent with the exception of the cold-starting lever. This was mounted on the left-hand side of the gearbox housing and when used brought into life a "starting" carburettor. It was not intended to be progressive and when the engine was warm should have been opened completely. Perhaps we were unlucky with our one but it would not reopen without help from the rider. I soon discovered that it wasn't needed anyway for the engine always fired at the touch of the button without the aid of the starter carburettor. It was warm enough to use almost immediately and the only time it let me down was one wet afternoon as I came out of the Olympia Show. Pressing the starter button brought only the sound of rushing electricity, which was not surprising as some cad had pinched my plug covers! He couldn't have done it in a better place for I dashed back into Olympia and borrowed two off the BMW stand! What the thief doesn't know is that he has pinched a pair of the worst plug covers around. Even on the new one I fitted a spark could be seen jumping from the metal body to the cylinder fins if it was held ¼in away. I do hope whoever has them finds that out on a wet night in the middle of Dartmoor!

To complete a rundown on the cycle parts. The dualseat is lockable and hinges when unlocked to reveal a sumptuous tool tray. This holds a comprehensive tool kit and a puncture outfit

and still leaves room to spare. They have, thankfully, spared the fabulous connectorless BMW pump, which is locked away under the seat. The same key serves as a steering-lock key. Some steering locks are scant deterrent to a determined thief. If you loose your key with the steering locked on this machine only an electric drill will get you out of trouble! The other key necessary with a BMW is that for the ignition. It is one of the few components which is interchangeable with the old models and serves as ignition key and light switch.

The brakes have changed little from the old model with the same 2 l/s 8in front and single l/s 8in rear that have given such good service over the years. The front brake was capable of stopping the R69S in 21 feet 10 years ago without the help of the rear, so who needs discs? The trouble is that the Germans will use such hard linings. On our test model the brakes had still not bedded down with 1,800 miles on the clock. They were improving all the time and would perhaps be very good in another 1,000 miles, but while we had it they needed considerable pressure to stop effectively. Then it all happened at once. The effect in the wet was akin to someone poking a stick in the wheel and had it not been for the excellence of the Metzler C6 tyres I could have well come unstuck once or twice. I have never used better tyres than the Metzlers that are used on the R75. A 3.25 × 19in front and fat 4.10 × 18in rear combined to make this one of the best handling wet-weather machines I have ever ridden. And did we have some wet weather during the test! Not that you will find me complaining about rain in January. My view is that as long as it is raining the roads are clear of snow and ice.

I can't say that I was too enthusiastic about the exposed rear suspension springs but I gather that the factory will be offering rubber gaiters to cover them before long. I think that I prefer that mod that Charles Lock of MLG did to his R60/5. All he did was fit a set of old R60 front fork shrouds. A simple and effective solution.

Look closely at any R75/5 and you will, like as not, observe severe blueing of the exhaust pipes. Ours had and so had most of the others I have seen. Something like Honda's double-skin system might be worthwhile. The silencers are cranked to encourage moisture to run back rather than stay inside and rot their innards. It is early days yet to judge how effective this is but I'll bet it won't be long before enthusiasts this side of the water find a way to fit the popular stainless steel ones that the old models often display. No one is going to be very keen on paying £20 for the genuine article if it does need regular replacement. It might even make it easier to fit panniers neatly.

It is possible to be quite critical of the R75/5 just by sitting down and looking at it, and rightly so, for anyone contemplating spending over £1,000 on a motorcycle is entitled to ask: "Is it worth it?" Consequently our detail analysis has been more searching than usual. All things considered, the machine has stood up to it well. The only basic design fault that one would like to see altered is that business of the intrusion of the carburettor into the rider's leg space and if, as we believe, this is being revised then our only real criticism of the R75/5 as a motorcycle *to ride* is settled.

When we talk of the BMW as a motorcycle to ride we come to the whole crux of the matter. For it is here that it shows itself to be one of the world's best motorcycles. It is marginally less mechanically quiet than earlier BMWs, with the alloy cylinders acting as a sounding board for the tappets and the timing chain just about audible as it follows its simple path. The engine is still considerably quieter than any other made today. The same goes for the exhaust note. BMWs always have been renowned for first-class silencing and the latest /5 series compare in every way with the old models. The silencing is so good that, if one wished, full-bore standing starts can be made in bottom gear with hardly a second glance from passers-by. On tickover the exhaust note has a "squeak" reminiscent of the old Gold Star (and later Commando) note, but much less obtrusive. Used fairly hard and in varying conditions the R75/5 returned just over 50 m.p.g. Full-bore motorway going would reduce this considerably. Even at 40 m.p.g. the 5½-gallon petrol tank gives a range of over 200 miles with a half-gallon reserve. The twin petrol taps are positive and easy to use with a heavily-gloved hand. BMWs, traditionally conservative in performance claims, say that the R75/5 will do 110 m.p.h. It will, I am sure, not only reach that figure but surpass it in favourable conditions. In the chilly winter conditions of the test the opportunities, and the inclination, to find this out were rare and we are sure readers will forgive us if we tell them that on a sunny June day we will take it to Silverstone and play racers but in the winter—no thanks.

Compared with the R69S there is no increase in vibration and, if anything, flexibility has been improved. The whole machine makes so little fuss about its searing starts that, short of a series of drag races up the High Street, it is difficult to judge just how well the acceleration of the '75 compares with that of its rivals. Without figures to back me up, I would imagine that it now compares with a good 650 twin but it would probably still lag behind, for the first few hundred miles, most of the other 750 "superbikes". Riders will not buy an R75/5 for its performance, though, but because it will go very quickly with the minimum of effort, and will keep going. Some years ago a good friend of mine described his R69S as having "an iron fist in a velvet glove". I think that the R75/5 can lay claim to that title, too.

To return to the question: "Is the R75/5 worth the money?" As long as I have ridden a BMW other owners have been on the defensive about the price. They have always pointed out how much cheaper they are in Germany. For example, the R75/5 sells, we are told, for £575 to German buyers (even after the recent 10 per cent price increase that added over £100 over here) and for about the same in the United States. Why, then, is it so expensive over here? This question is not made easier to answer by M.R.W.'s comment last month that the Laverda sells for £630 in Italy, yet only rises to just over £800 once it reaches these shores. Surely both are subject to the same taxes and import duty? The high selling price of the BMW is reflected in the cost of its spares, but some of the items seem unnaturally pricey; for example, a battery costs £18 and the plastic-front mudguard £17. Higher up the tree, if one is unlucky enough to shunt a pair of front forks, new ones will set you back something like £145. Not the sort of prices that will endear R75/5 owners to insurance companies.

So, with all these costs to consider, is a BMW R75/5 worth the money? Who can answer such a question? If you were to ask *me* I would answer, reluctantly, "No", but if you were to follow with the question "Would I *buy* one", I would unhesitatingly reply "Yes, if I could afford it". Illogical? Maybe I would buy an R75/5 (with the important qualification that something would *have* to be done about those carburettors) because it gives me exactly the sort of motorcycling that I enjoy best.   B. P.

BMW ROAD TEST (Cont'd) . . . . .
Continued from page 128
will find the electric starter neatly tucked away inside the casting. This is the reason why you don't see many wires or pieces of machinery hanging outside the engine itself. Everything is neatly tucked away.

The starter made the fire-up procedure on those cold mornings a simple matter. Turn the key on, flip up the choke, push the button, and the engine fired instantly, and every time. One thing we did find out very quickly was that the BMW is a very cold-blooded machine until it is allowed to warm up for a few minutes. Perhaps this is a good thing, though, because it will discourage anybody from leaping on and charging off before the oil temperature has had a chance to come up a bit.

There are two areas we have not touched on as yet. One is the brakes, and the other is the rear shaft drive system. There is little we can say about the shaft drive system that has not been said before. It is quiet, maintenance free, and absolutely smooth. Although it is an all-new design, it is still based on the earlier machines, which we might add, have proven to be excellent examples of what smoothness is all about. So much for that.

The brakes, however, are another matter entirely. Naturally, with an increase in performance, the rider would expect an increase in braking power. The power of the new BMW brakes is most impressive. We possibly may be tempted to use the word staggering, but in this case, we don't think this would really be true. Almost, but not quite. The truth of the matter is, the rider, if he really wants to, can lock up both wheels when the machine is absolutely flat out. You cannot ask for any more brakes than that. Also, we found that repeated hard usage did not seem to diminish the braking power one iota. As any rider knows, after he has been around motorcycles for a bit, the careful use of the front brake is mandatory if he is to remain scab free for any period of time. Because of the BMW's powerful front brake, we never found it necessary to use more than two fingers when slowing down, regardless of speed. This will give the reader some idea as to the actual power exerted by the front binder when applied.

We could go on for hours extolling the virtues of the new BMW. We don't feel this is necessary, however, for by now the reader has a pretty good idea about our feelings in the matter, and if road riding is your bag, one ride on a new BMW will tell you more than a thousand words ever could. It's a fabulous piece of machinery and should provide the owner with years of reliable service, and more than just average performance. ●

TWO POINTS OF VIEW

BMW R75/5
by Dave Minton

WE HAD LEFT WALES AND ITS SLY skein of tarmac. Alan Aspel on the 600 held West over the border, while I, with more time on my hands, looked South.

Except for a spell of 50 miles or so earlier on, we both stayed at the bars of the model we gravitated towards. Alan on the 600, me on the 750. One of the principal reasons being owed to my larger feet — they were less troubled by the big carburetters and foot control arrangement than were Alan's. However fast the rider of a smaller engined motorcycle may travel, the ride of a man on an accompanying bigger model will be an easier one due solely to the advantages of power. To hold the R75/5 Alan had been scratching. I had not, but I wanted to. We parted and I did.

At smack on 6300 rpm in top we tramped along the concrete. I tucked all my ragged edges in, but that was it, no more speed was, or could be forthcoming, for even now, the biggest flat twin was over the top. Not in danger mind, simply at its utmost power delivery. So it went on. Miles sped past, many, many of them. I checked my mirror, as I had been doing continually throughout the weekend, and just caught a flash of white. Omigod! I froze. Eighteen months at least. What's a

patrolman doing there? How did he get there? Panic!

To slow was utterly pointless. He knew. I knew. He knew I knew, and I knew he knew. We both knew we both knew, and anyway, by now we were off the trunk road. He followed for another mile or so, then as we came into the boundaries of a large country town pulled ahead and The Official Hand squeezed my speed's life out.

He walked back towards me from his full-faired Saint (Trophy). "You know there's a 70 limit in this country, don't you?"

Heavy and insensitive carburetters on the 750 completely changed the character of the machine from that of the 600. Low engine speed, surging and stiff throttle control, combined with the physical problems of foot control location behind oversize carburetters almost destroyed the agility of the R75/5.

"Yes." (Dammit. Must remember to keep my mouth shut at speed in future. It's all dry and sticky. Bet he thinks it's fear).

"Do you know what you were doing, then?"

"Well, er, yes." (Can't admit to 105/110 for twenty miles. Haven't got the gall).

to discover what a BMW would do, and to study its reaction to speed. I learned that on one exceptionally poorly surfaced curve the BMW had taken it in its magnificent stride at full whack, he had almost lost his Saint and crossed the central reservation in his attempt to tail on. "It was all over the bloody place.' We talked on for half an hour. He knew his 'bikes, that chap.

Whatever the rights, wrongs, morals and what-have-you to be learned from that episode, and admittedly there are quite a few, the patrolman's comments concerning his machine's comparative performance were singularly revealing. As a range, Triumph motorcycles offer better roadholding than any other single, yet complete, marque in the world. Their cornering ability is outstandingly good, of that there can be no argument. His Saint was, in fact, a Trophy, which is no more than single carburetter Bonneville, and moreover, equipped with streamlining of a sort. It was a motorway special.

Whereas I knew not that he was doing so, he was chasing hard to keep up, but found it beyond his machine. What fast cornering I enjoyed nearly brought him off, despite his great skill as an experienced, and professional, motorcyclist. I have thought hard on that, and have only had my enormous admiration for BMW added to by the experience.

Ride a Bee Emm up the road and back and you will wonder what all the fuss is about. Give it an easy time over a journey, and you might like it, but you will not truly appreciate it. On the other hand, if you try to beat it to death with the throttle cable over 500 miles of varying roads, including some mountain ones, then, ah, then, you will get inside, and know that superfine, bold spirit. That is exactly why Alan and I went to Wales. We knew that the new flat twins had something special to offer; we had to find out.

The new BMWs have no more in common with the old range of Earles fork models, than has the present range of BSAs with the old A10 series. Gone are the ball race engine bearings, dynamo, magneto, Earles forks, anchored rear suspension boxes, camshaft lubrication problems and, to an extent, clonky gearchanges, frame pliability, and the need for an hydraulic steering damper.

To my mind, the most outstanding performance aspect of the whole bike is its roadholding, and handling ability. Without any prior discussion on the matter, Alan and I agreed after one day's riding in Mid and North Wales, that we had never ridden so far, so fast, so close to the ground, so often. It was not very long before we discovered that every bend was an event to be celebrated. Direction changing was a cinch. The only effort needed was a slight pull on the inner handlebar end to pick it up ready for the next corner. Once into it,

"Pretty fast."

"Pretty fast?"

"Very fast."

"That's better."

Then he studied the Bee Emm. "Hmm." (Bike interest? Hope? Anything's better than waiting for it).

"A BMW actually. 750. New model. I'm just on my way back from a weekend in Wales." (Hope, hope).

"I know what it is, and I know where you are from. I've been trying to keep up all the way from (and he named a large town 25 miles back along the road). That,"

and he pointed to his white, blue-piped, ticking, oil smeared, sighing 650, "will do 100 mph, and that," he pointed to the BMW, "was much, faster, very, very much faster than it."

"Oh."

"As a matter of fact, it was impossible around some of those bends as well as the straights.' He smiled a little. Just the corner of his eyes, but it was enough. And he hadn't gone for his black book either. Waves of saggy relief flowed through me.

As things turned out, he had ridden over 15 miles beyond his patrol boundary just

Continued on next page

the machine stuck to its line apparently immovable, but the feeling was deceptive, for the 750 could be hurled into another direction change, or nudged over to another line by half an inch, equally easily and safely.

The excellent Metzeler covers must take some of the credit. They appeared to be modelled on non-triangular racing lines, especially the back one, which had a well rounded tread spreading beyond the rim width. The front was more conventional. They were not perfect, however, because on wet roads, each wheel moved twice, independently of the other, which was not as bad as it sounds. The movements were small, and at medium and low speeds, so were nothing to do with aquaplaning – plus the fact that we were travelling around corners at much higher speeds than we generally would in the wet, due to the incredible stability of the machines.

The odd thing is that an amount of frame flexing took place. Below 60, the movement manifested itself in the steering head area and then disappeared completely until 85 plus cornering came in, and then the rear end lazed gently. Do not be under a misapprehension, though. More rigidly framed machines exist in plenty, but faster cornering machines do not. The movement was small, and utterly safe. I suspect that the back shifting was caused by the soft suspension coming under attack from the transverse torque reaction business during moments when it was also under the duress of handling bumps and speed and cornering. On top of that the flywheel effect was too much. The front might have been the tyre, but I doubt it, or it could have been over-soft springs reacting against drastic line chopping wrenches, which I suspect, for the factory now shim them to reduce the over-generous 8½ inch fork travel. At both ends, damping was perfect and just as well matched to each other.

The heads would not ground – and how we tried! Before they did, the footrests grounded. So often did my feet touch, that to stop my boot soles chamfering further, I rode with the balls of my feet on the rests. The pegs were not low by any means. That they grounded so often is simply a reflection on the uncanny roadholding ability of the BMW.

Fade-free brakes

IN THE SAME CATEGORY COMES braking. I ride on the brakes, rather than the gearbox. I prefer it, especially with a torquey motor like the Bee Emm. I would rate the front one as the only brake comparable to a Honda Four's. Although a nine inch tls unit, apparent servo effect is almost nil, and panic stops require panic strength grip. At low speeds the action is soft and easy; at high speeds, rocklike. As with most German linings, they required a little warming first thing in the morning to

BMW R75/5

gain maximum efficiency. Fading was, at least in my hands on the road, impossible. Heat, if anything, added to their stopping power. The long, soft fork action, coupled to the powerful front brake, made early hard stops unusually busy ones, but after a short period, was forgotten.

One of my greatest pleasures on riding a BMW is to revel in the luxury (necessity?) of shaft drive. Silent, reliable, clean, cheap to maintain, good looking, superior in performance, and long lasting. Low engine speed riding was improved immensely by its firm power transmission, while at speed, its main attribute lay in the assurance it provided. Only on a fast over-run were the bevel gears audible, and then they whined as proudly as a Riley Kestrel's used to. From the flexible plastic convolution

Finish was good, but not to the same quality for quality's sake that made the earlier range so famous. You can see the welding seams now.

between the gearbox and pivoted fork came the *only* oil seepage on the machine, and that was nothing more than a one inch dusty tearstain on the plastic itself.

The engine? Well, I don't know what to say. Sheer perfection at every turn. Starting was instant, tick-over faultless, powerband immense, operation silent (except for a wide set valve and rocker gap), cleanliness absolute, performance breathless, and manners royal.

The kick starter pedal was completely ignored, and deemed unnecessary. Electric starting was utterly reliable. From tickover speeds (900 rpm) upwards the power was there to be used, and indeed was, large lumps of it punching out at no higher than 2000 rpm, with fast satisfyingly acceleration resulting from such a low engine speed throttle tweak. I stated that the R69S we

tested two years ago in May was a Grand Turismo of a motorcycle. The R75/5 is even more so. The engine simply contributes to this of course, but it is nevertheless possibly the most important part of an express tourer. Faster motorcycles do exist, but I'll wager there is not one that would cover 500 miles in less time, and certainly not one that would do it with less rider fatigue.

Happiest cruising speed of the 750 appeared to be about 90 mph and, as this was only 5200 rpm, as well as having an easy time of it, the engine was just over its maximum torque development period – so was well within its power band, ensuring a consistent speed, instantly able to accelerate, should it be necessary.

Through the gears, the maximum speeds were 1st (11.31:1, 7000 rpm) 47 mph; 2nd, (7.47, 7000) 72 mph; 3rd, (5.44, 7000) 80 mph; top (4.36, 6300) 110 mph. Unlike so many claimed speeds this one was accurate. Timed on a stop-watch the speedometer was only three mph out at 90, so the speedometer was registering well over the maximum claimed of 109 mph, and this in a two-piece suit, and slightly crouching stance. 27 mph in top gear ambled the engine over at no more than 1700 rpm. It would pull even less, down to 1300 before showing any sign of protest, and that was only mild. Acceleration was utterly deceptive; silent as a lake, but shocking when provoked.

BMW still produce the best riding position, along with Ducati. Rather Vincentish, and so good as not to be a compromise, but the perfect/proper/only roadster set-up. I would have preferred handlebars an inch longer either side, simply to keep my hands wider than my shoulders; I find it more comfortable that way, but even so, the narrow bars were excellent. Switch placing was ideal, and suggested to me that the BMW has come from a factory of motorcyclists. Each button and knob falls to the thumb without any searching. The dipper and flasher activators are mounted vertically on either bar side. Starter and horn buttons are in the same switch bodies. The flashers were extremely bright; at night perhaps too much so, but it helped in strong sunlight.

The seat foam was too soft, allowing me to sit through it, and rest on the steel pan. I preferred the old, sprung base R69S construction.

Whether or not you have £1121 to spend on a motorcycle will doubtless influence your estimate of its worth. Import duty kills it, that and shipping costs, and British distribution costs. In Germany the big BMWs are no more expensive than our own 'bikes are in this country. If you can afford it, get one now and for the next few years know good motorcycling at its ultimate, for there is certainly nothing else like a BMW in this world.

TWO POINTS OF VIEW
BMW R60/5
by Alan Aspel

Correct rear suspension setting was imperative. The Editor required minimum spring strength on the 600; the Assistant Editor medium setting on the 750. A change of riders set the 600 yawing badly at speed, although the 750 still behaved well.

WAY, WAY BACK IN THE DAYS OF my 'teens, when National Service was not so much a threat to the freedom, as to the Tony Curtis hairstyle, my obsession for that which was dear to the Good Way of Life and thus totally unreachable was a permanent joke among friends. Jane Russell was the pinnacle (or pinnacles) of eroticism; a Campagnolo "double-clanger" (I was a competing cyclist at the time) was the ultimate in pedalling hardware; and something called a BMW used to whisper its way around the neighbourhood, black, white-lined and excrutiatingly elegant.

There was something else called a Black Shadow which, apparently, was to be desired in the world of powered two-wheelers, but of that I knew only that there was one to be seen if you happened to be standing on a certain corner at a particular time of the evening on a special day of the week when Superman thundered past, wearing a flat hat, arrogant expression and a jacket which, I was told, was worn by barbers.

But it was the BMW which remained in my mind. The mysticism, the aloofness, the utter superiority. Awestricken, I once spoke to the man who was able to ride this machine. I swear that he was almost human.

Although I was later to buy a Black Shadow, I could never quite shake off that feeling of inferiority which the Bee Emm imposed, and would retaliate in the only manner I knew – sheer, crude, unabashed performance which could make this aristo-cratic creation disappear from my mirror and, temporarily, my mind.

Habits – and complexes – die hard, and it was still with a touching of the forelock that I greeted the /5 series. True to style, it was in the penthouse of one of London's most exclusive hotels that we were formally introduced – which is precisely the style in which BMW Concessionnaires GB Ltd. have gone about their marketing. Not for them, the greaser, the rocker or the old-fashioned ton-upper. Without a trace of shame, they are aiming straight for the executive weary of tedium in a weekend traffic jam; the business/professional man Looking for Freedom in the most respectable manner; and for the hyperenthusiast who happens to have something like £1000, give or take a hundred, lying around in loose cash.

The market is, quite plainly, limited. Among the people I know, or know of, perhaps only five could afford to go to their local dealer with the ready. Of those five, only two would seriously consider such a buy, for they are already committed to what they think to be the ultimate machinery. But by directing their sales approach at the "grey-haired teenager" (their term, not mine), BMW *must* hit the target. Motorcycling has, in the past two of three years, become so downright respectable that I sometimes think about giving it all up. If we don't stop sounding our aitches there is a real danger of our world being inhabited by refugees from the golf club; men who would wear their over-trousers *inside* their boots.

PR exercise

WE WERE MORE THAN USUALLY anxious to ride one of these flat twins, but, in order that Dave Minton and I could jointly sample the pleasures in one of our now customary long, fast rides, we demerred with a request that we had a 600 and a 750 at the same time.

The telephone rang. It was Douglass Austin of Smee's, BMW's public relations agency. There was an R75/5 awaiting us at Charlie Coombes's shop at Slough, if we would care to borrow it for a week. Thanks all the same, we said, but we'd rather wait for the pair so that we could . . . . They quite understood our problem, but there *was* an R75/5 available if we simply wanted to borrow it for a week.

Which was how I came to have two bites of that glossy, black cherry.

As far as I'm concerned, first impressions don't last, despite what They say. First impressions (apart from the illuminated £ sign that blurs the vision) are, or were, of a bulky machine, stocky, muscley – and a stylist's dream away from the earlier models. After 1954, the teleforks gave way to the Earles-type – which always seem to provoke a BM owner to a stance of instant

Continued on next page

Continued from previous page

defence. Mere mention of them is sufficient to bring forth a series of ' Oh, yes, buts. . .". I'm not sure why.

The Americans – where lies the most lucrative market – first received the benefits of the restyling, and it was only in the colour ads in the US magazines that we saw the changes. The American sales line, by the way, is "The Silent Minority". Even in that great and garish country, the appeal is to the discriminating rather than the hairy. We sat around and waited, and they eventually arrived.

Once under way, the big BMW changed character completely. Big machine it is, should you be gazing at it from the seat of a car or the saddle of a lesser motorcycle (*all* motorcycles are lesser, in the mind of a BM man), but the centre of gravity is so low that it is child's play to manoeuvre, both in traffic and on the open road – as we were later to discover, to our enormous joy.

The very least one could expect, incidentally, especially for that kind of cash transaction, is electric starting. How civilised, to simply set things in motion by the touch of a button.

So different is the BMW from anything else that one has to, in many instances, rethink instinctive actions and reactions. Dave Minton and I, for example, ride at a similar pace, one which we find mutually satisfying when we travel together, since neither (generally) has to hang around for the other. While Dave uses his brakes on the approach to a bend, going round in a high gear and accelerating away, I change down before a curve, drive round and change up once on the straight. I found it necessary to alter my riding to suit the engine – or engine layout – characteristics, more especially in the wet. Engine braking on a "conventional" machine does little to change one's line of approach, unless it's overdone, of course; to do so on the R75 could have an unnerving effect and on a wet road could, quite conceivably, cause an accident of a rather different nature!

The riding position is as good as could be asked for. Short, only slightly raised 'bars give a leaning-into-the-wind stance which is, after all, very right and proper, if the 'bike is to be used in its correct manner. Which makes me wonder why the American machines feature high-rise 'bars. Perhaps, for one reason or another, the wind seldom blows hard on an American rider . . .? It was, I imagined, my untidy riding position which caused me not to notice the carburetters as much as I had been told I would; but it was plain that they could be offensive if they wanted to, and they bore the wax of my overtrousers when the machine was returned.

Lack of vibration

VIBRATION IS NOT SOMETHING which concerns BMW riders. It happens, certainly; it would be a remarkable

machine which didn't – but to a lesser extent with a flat twin than with any other. There is no vibration barrier, through which one has to drive in order to leave it behind and retain one's teeth. At high speed there is a small degree of high-frequency vibration; and at tick-over there is something quite unique. Not a vibration, but a series of individual, quite distinctive tugs in alternate, opposite directions as the pistons casually travel the length of their bore. So slow is idling, by the way, that it fails to register on the tachometer. My suggestion is a stethoscope.

Such vibration as there is can only – as far as I was concerned – be felt through the hands, barely discernibly. It was impossible to feel by means of knees on the tank, since the carburetters prevented my short legs from gripping it. And it was difficult to know at what revolutions the engine was turning because the tachometer, which is embraced in the speedometer instrument, was obscured by criss-crossing clutch and front brake cables.

The first opportunity of town-type riding came as I left the motorway. Brakes had not been tried, neither had road-holding. The answers came, thick and fast. I'd been warned that braking might not be as good as I might expect, since German linings are almost as hard as the drum itself. Linings are as those fitted to Porsche cars, so if you should see a

Fuel consumption, especially on the 750, was the best yet experienced on a fast ridden big 'bike. Although, in fairness to the others, they had not the advantage of a smaller engined machine with them during testing.

startled Porsche driver approaching a hazard, you'll know the reason why. Braking on the R75 (not the model which Dave Minton later borrowed) was so good that the poorer stopping power of the R60/5 was accentuated. Although the 'bike had only something like 2000 miles on the clock, the linings had bedded down comfortably. So comfortably bedded, in fact, that to awaken them in the morning could have surprising results, as they grabbed at any passing piece of brake drum and caused the tyres to squeak in protest.

And, speaking of tyres . . I have a natural distrust of anything which isn't stamped "Made in England", gives me at *least* 23% more grip (than what?), or doesn't have precisely the right tread pattern. Which made the Metzelers that much more impressive. The rear had the old-style racing profile (over-rounded) and the pair were as good as anything I've met elsewhere. Just once, in the wet, on a fast and uncomfortably tight right-hander, the front stepped out a fraction – but it was mud, and not lack of grip, which brought that about. In the dry, they just couldn't be faulted. Which is just as well, when one is rushing about on £1200-worth of someone else's machinery.

Comment from non-BMW riders about gearboxes usually brings forth the same defensive attitude that fork-type remarks encourage. Accusations that the gearbox makes more noise than the power unit are answered by the retort that, in fact, it is perfectly possible to make a silent change, once the art is mastered. Art it certainly is, for I found that, by the end of my first week with the R75, I was finding it much easier to keep the "ker-lunk" to a minimum. But, while other gearboxes may be quieter in operation, none is more positive than that of the BMW. There is a certain knowledge that, once a gear is in, it's *in*, to stay.

Nothing is perfect, and the only serious fault I could honestly find with the BMs – both of them – was the lighting. In every other respect, the electrical system is first-rate, with the alternator providing sufficient for every demand, most especially the electrical starting. On one occasion I arrived home very late one evening and, rather than manoeuvre the 'bike into the garage, threw a cover over it. A frost sharpened the next morning but the 750 still fired, first prod of the button – and without the choke. In fact, it would refuse to start with the choke, although not, apparently, running rich.

But the headlight I found to be insufficient for cruising on unlit roads within the 'bike's performance limits. Indeed, one evening in a Berkshire backwater, I had the most difficult task in identifying road-edges, although, in fairness, the road was curvaceous enough to have tried the most brilliant of white lights. There seemed to be a lack of concentration in the beam; plenty of spread, but not quite enough immediately in front, where it was most needed.

Other electrical equipment was above reproach. The direction indicators (everything by Bosch) were on a par with a motorcar's, and horn, although not of the rather arrogant kind I had anticipated, got people jumping out of the way when they had failed to notice a large, almost silent machine bearing down on them.

Commuting, albeit the commuting which Dave and I do each day of the week at 80 miles apiece, is not always the best manner in which to appreciate a machine, despite the advantages of knowing a stretch of road so well that relative qualities can be more easily gauged. There is no substitute for a long, winding, undulating ride . . . as we kept telling each other. But to where? Nothing can be worse than aimlessness, when at any moment you could decide that enough was enough, and that it looked like rain anyway so why don't we stop at *that* pub rather than the next one. So we talked about it, looked at maps and said that, since we'd been to the West Country any number of times, the North, Scotland, South Wales and just about anywhere else in National Rallies, how about North Wales? They had a couple of hills there, so legend had it; distance was just right for a two-day trip. All that we overlooked was the fact that Wales is "dry" on Sundays and that, should we fancy the proverbial swift half, we'd find Welsh pubs as barren as Inverness on a flag day – unless we were resident.

Comparative daintiness

IT'S SILLY. I KNOW IT'S SILLY. How could a pair of carburetters completely change the character of a machine, alter riding position, inspire confidence, improve brake leverage and gear changing and, above all, create an impression of comparative daintiness? I'd become accustomed to the "big" 750, its mannerisms, its handling, the positioning of my feet to avoid those carburetters. So how was it, when I knew perfectly well that only bore was smaller, that I felt to be on a diminutive machine? Suddenly everything becomes more manageable, more convenient, more relaxing. Another bit of silliness was the fact that the R60/5 had a silver tank. I liked that.

Stroke is identical at 70.6 mm, but the 82 mm bore on the bigger 'bike is reduced to 73.5 for the 600, putting on another 200 rpm and thus lifting the rev

---

IT ALL, ALWAYS, BOILS DOWN TO THE SAME OLD QUESTION: WOULD I BUY ONE? WITHOUT HESITATION – BUT IT WOULD BE THE R60/5. SWEETER, DECEPTIVELY "SMALLER" AND LIGHTER, WITHOUT THE COMPLICATIONS OF THOSE CONSTANT VACUUM CARBURETTERS . . .

---

ceiling to 6600 for maximum output of 46 bhp. Maximum permissible engine speed is quoted as 7000 rpm for both machines, the larger of which produces 57 bhp – a thoroughly respectable figure in this age of the "Superbike". (Which gives me the opportunity of saying that we wish, how we wish, that that dreadful cliché would lose itself along with the uptights, cool-losing and mind-blowing. Ask a Vincent owner if he thinks of a Commando as a Superbike . . .).

The Big Minton on the R75/5 was as happy as a pig in . . . its own environment, while the Small Aspel astride the R60/5 bore a smile of unusually broad dimensions.

Which is where I was going to recite the Ballad of North Wales and tell of how we threaded our way along A5; how R75 had occasionally to ease off for R60; how 600 had, occasionally, to really scratch to stay with 750 – but only because of greater accelerative power of the big 'un; how the hills of Shropshire stretched, grew, broadened, cast off their foliage and became the mountains of Wales; how those two beautiful machines hummed and droned and whined their way around those superbly-surfaced roads, unspoiled by heavy traffic, free of congestion,

devoid of the horrors of suburbia; but most of all, absolutely most of all, I could have told you of the way in which BMWs make their way around corners.

With the riding of the BMs, we have, on MCI, now featured all the current er . . . I *mustn't* say superbikes . . luxury, expensive, sportsters and tourers. I didn't get to ride the Guzzi Ambassador (must be losing my touch), which is probably the BMW's nearest rival, but have enjoyed – immensely – the other machinery made available to us. Nothing, absolutely nothing, ever took bends like the Bee Emm. Our progress along a serpentine, lakeside road, surfaced with black velvet, moved me to comment that it was "poetry in motion". I've never put a machine down so far, so fast, so often. Tarmac seemingly skims past the nostrils, boots chamfer, knees seem in imminent danger of wearing to a point. Those forks with an 8¼ inch stroke, rear dampers set on medium, that snatch-free shaft drive, that smooth, smooth engine . . . .

That's what motorcycling's all about; that kind of sheer, unadultereated, almost sensual pleasure.

Space is our greatest enemy in this magazine business. There's so much to say, so little room in which to say it – and we must get the ads in.

It all, always, boils down to the same old question: would I buy one? Without hesitation – but it would be the R60/5. Sweeter, deceptively "smaller" and lighter, without the complications of those constant vacuum carburetters, their diaphragms and relative heaviness in operation. There is, I hear, an R75/5S in Germany with ordinary old slide carbs. Now *that* should be all right.

Yes, he'd buy one, he says blandly, conveniently overlooking details like wife, children, mortgage, gas bills and rates. With a price tag like £958 I'd need a second mortgage. But I suppose I could sell the house, send my wife out to work, put the children in a home, ignore the final demands. Even then, I'd want the price tattooed across my forehead so that all the world might know I was a man of discrimination.

See page 158 for specifications.

SPECIFICATION:R70/5 SPECIFICATION:R60/5

Engine:

Horizontally opposed twin cylinder four-stroke. Capacity, 745 cc. Bore and stroke, 82 x 70 mm. Compression, 9.0:1. Valve operation, pushrod. Camshaft location, below crankshaft. Maximum power, 57 bhp at 6400 rpm. Maximum torque, 43 lbs/ft at 5000 rpm.

Carburetters:

Two Bing butterfly valve, diaphragm controlled, constant velocity, vacuum instruments. Diameter, 32 mm. Single paper air filter common to both carbs.

Electrics:

Generator, crankshaft mounted, 180/270 w Bosch three phase alternator. Energy transferred through slip ring. Battery, 12 v 15 ah. Starter motor, 12 v .5 hp engaging through centrifugally energised pinion to toothed flywheel rim. Ignition, single contact breaker operating at twice engine speed, and twin compensated 6v ht coils. (Ensures easy starting due to 12v current through coils, but once running, current reduced to 6v). Headlamp, 6.3 in, 45/40 w.

Transmission:

Final drive, shaft, contained within RH pivoted fork leg with universal coupling, and driving through palloid spiral bevel gears in rear wheel housing. Clutch, dry single plate, diaphragm spring controlled. Gear ratios: 1st, 11.31:1; 7.47; 5.44; top, 4.36. Selection, LH foot pedal, up-for-up.

Lubrication:

Engine oil grade, recommended, SAE 40 for high speed and 86°F plus, or SAE 30, 32-86°F. Capacity, 4.75 pints held in wet sump. Pump, Eaton type hypo-trochoid (Eccentric four lobe gear) working at 80 lbs sq. in. pressure. Consumption approximately 500 mpp throughout test.

Fuel:

Tank material, steel. Capacity, 5 galls inc. ½ gall reserve. Consumption, 45 mpg during test. Commuting, 52 mpg. Four star petrol used throughout test.

Frame:

Tubular steel, oval section, full double loop cradle. Rear sub-frame bolted on.

Suspension:

Front, telefork, two-way hydraulically damped. Travel, 8½ in. Rear, pivoted fork, two-way hydraulically damped, three-way adjustable for load by incorporated pegs. Travel 5 in.

Wheels:

Front: 19 in. Tyre, 3.25 in Metzeler interrupted rib. Brake, 7.9 in diam. Linings, 1.2 in wide. Rear: 18 in. Tyre, 4.00 in Metzeler, semi-racing interrupted rib pattern with circumferential buttressing. Brake, 7.9 in sls.

Dimensions and performance:

Engine width, 29 in. Seat height, 33.5 in. Clearance with average rider, and fuel, 6.5 in. Weight, including complete road equipment and full tanks, 463 lbs.

Price: £1121.

Engine:

Capacity, 599 cc. Bore and stroke, 73.5 x 70.6 mm. Maximum power, 46 bhp at 6600 rpm. Maximum torque, 35.4 lbs/ft at 5000 rpm. Compression, 9.2:1.

Carburetters:

Two Bing, barrel slide type. Diameter, 26 mm.

Transmission:

Gear ratios: 1st, 13.0:1; 9.47; 6.28; top, 5.04.

Fuel:

Consumption, 44 mpg during test ride. Commuting, 50 mpg.

Price: £958.

The paint and overall finish are superb, and all detail and trim work is tastefully executed.

THE SECOND TIME IS A CHARM

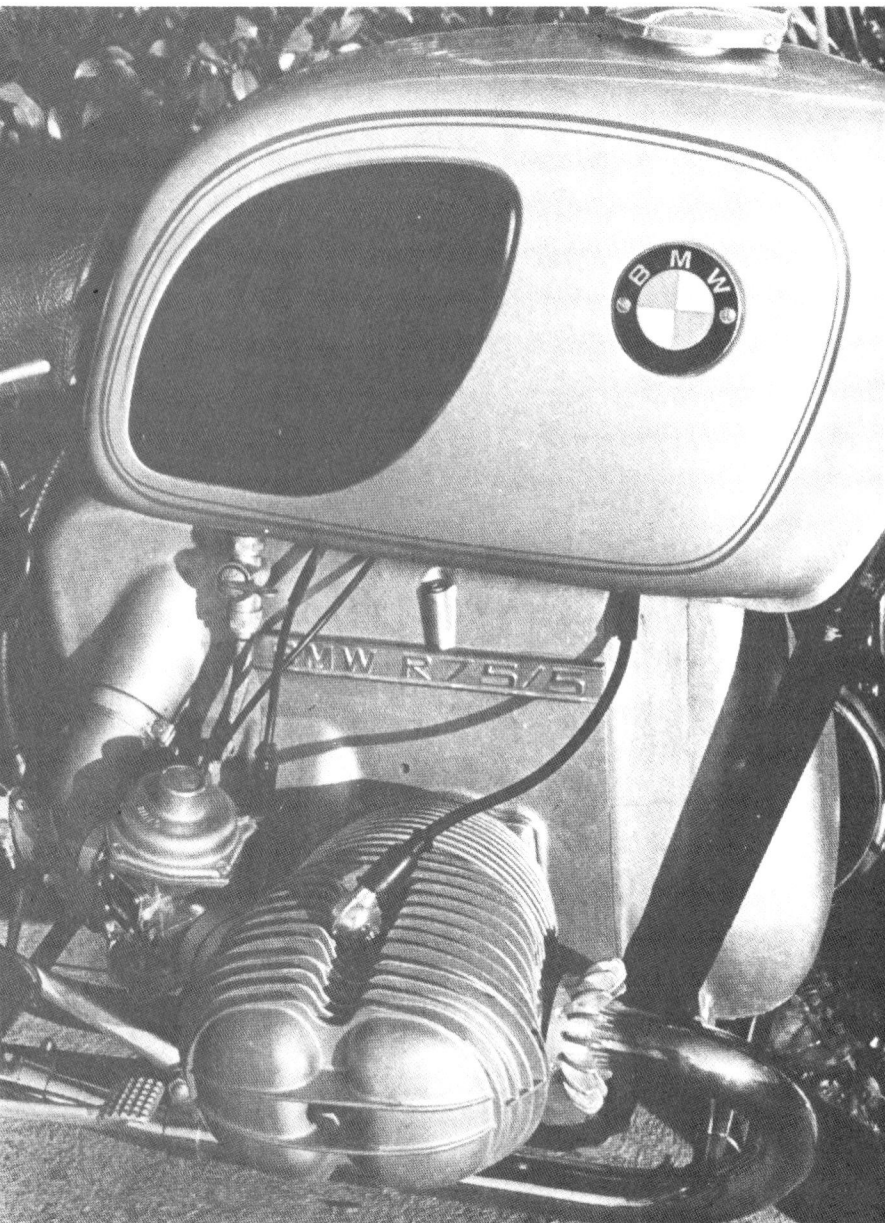

Last Year Cycle Guide **Road Tested the R-75/5 and Reported a Few Flaws. BMW has Corrected the Problems this Year.**

It has been about a year since we first road tested the then new R-75/5. The overall impressions left by this new opposed twin cylinder shaft driven machine were pleasant, but there were a few disconcerting problems.

Last year, the bike didn't handle as well as we had expected. Some BMW executives were very disturbed when we said the machine wiggled, but that's exactly what it did. I was raked over the coals on several occasions by some BMW people. They said in the thousands of miles of testing, they had never encountered the difficulties Cycle Guide had outlined in the road test.

Nevertheless, we stuck to our posi-

tion. Later, another publication ran into the same situation and reported the same findings.

Another problem was the carburetion, but we are very happy to report this has been corrected and the power plant will sit there ticking over all day. After riding it hard for 100 miles, the engine will seem as snappy and responsive as it did at the outset.

Very few motorcycles can make this claim. This didn't happen overnight. The considerably wide power range, the amount of horsepower available, overall quality and reliability are the result of years of research and development.

We found people had mixed emotions about the styling. While certainly

no one can fault the overall finish, people either liked the appearance or disliked it intensely. Personal feelings about styling aside, we found after riding the BMW for a while, its superb quality quickly spoils you.

The only fault with the entire machine's quality is the terrible chrome plating job on the mufflers. Not just bad, but terrible. It's been a long time since we've seen plating this poor. The rest of the bike was fine. We only hope the test bike's chrome was an exception.

Paint work is absolutely first-class and the fiberglass work on the fenders is outstanding. Few would believe the mud guards are constructed of cloth and resin until they feel the material beneath the fenders. Even there, the finish is smooth, indicating above average fiberglass work.

From a technical standpoint, the new R-75 has some interesting fea-

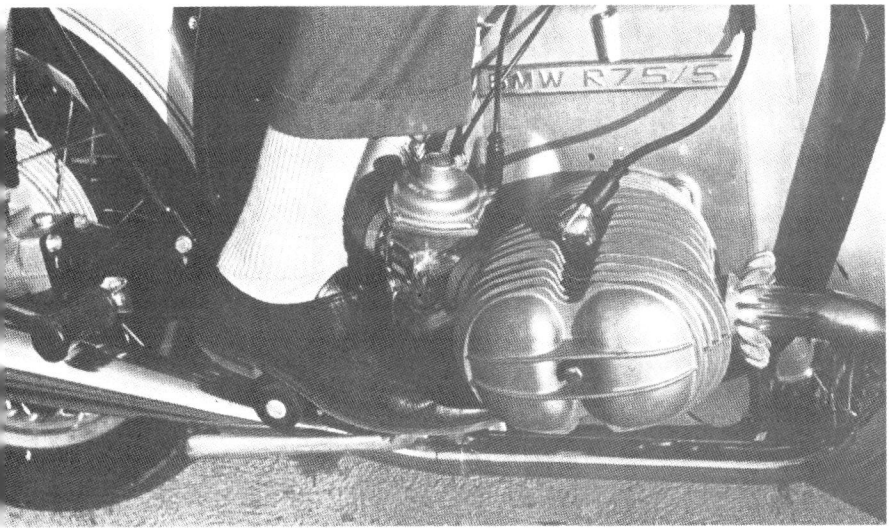

With the rider's feet tucked in behind the cylinders, the BMW provides a built-in footwarmer for cold weather.

It seems that the carburetion difficulties have been finally worked out. The 750 starts quickly using the richening device.

tures. From the outside the engine package looks bulky and heavy but, amazingly, it's not.

The factory's designers enclosed all the accessories normally found outside of the engine, such as starter and air filter, thus making it appear bulky. The large aluminum casting atop the crankcases houses these two and permits the engine to breathe lots of clean air. An engine as large as the R-75's needs a great deal of air and the big enclosed air filter meets this requirement. Because it is sheltered from the elements, filter life is considerably prolonged.

When BMW developed their new design package last year, they felt it necessary to raise the cylinders. We're not really sure why. Our only assumption is that this allows the rider to go into a sharper corner before the cases contact the pavement.

The self-starter found on the new models spoils you very quickly. In cold weather, we made several attempts before the engine finally caught. Once warm, the engine fires instantly with the touch of the starter button.

We also found that with use, the bike seemed to start easier. Perhaps we were just getting accustomed to the bike's little idiosyncrasies. All motorcycles are individuals and few machines share identical starting procedures.

We definitely disliked the transmission unit. The bike tested last year had a very noisy shifting setup. This year's model was worse. Even when running at 100 mph and shifting from third gear into fourth, there was a loud, obnoxious klunk. You always get this klunking sound whether shifting up or down.

While there certainly is no harm

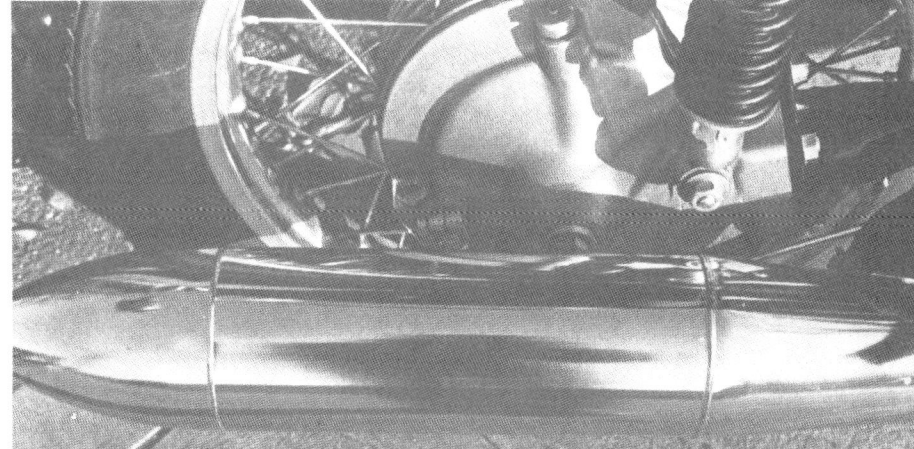

We were surprised to see the poor chrome work on the mufflers. The rest of the brightwork looked just fine.

being done to the engine, it's unnerving. Even though BMW lightened and improved the flywheel to facilitate smoother shifts, the process is still far too noisy. In heavy traffic, we received some embarrassingly odd looks from motorists and from motorcyclists.

BMW's single-plate dry clutch is smooth and very light. It engages quickly, but you will immediately learn to compensate for this. Because the engine has tremendous torque capabilities, it's never necessary to rev the engine up before releasing the clutch for fast starts.

For a large machine, the R-75 has more than enough torque output at low speed. This makes the BMW considerably easier to ride than some of

its counterparts. We found that riding with or without a passenger, this machine never really seemed to notice the difference. The R-75 always put out plenty of power.

We certainly wish the factory would slow down the throttle action in the first 1/8 to 3/16 of a turn. Under 3,000 rpm, the engine runs roughly, but once over this figure, it smooths out quickly and the rider never really needs to check the tachometer to know when to downshift. The vibration under 3,000, however, is severe enough to let the rider know he should shift unless he is completely numb and has no feeling in the seat of his pants.

This bike really shines on the freeway. Last year we couldn't say this, but the new model is a different story. After finishing last year's test, we had an opportunity to ride a BMW with two people on the freeway. We discovered that some of the handling

keep your feet and shins toasty. In warm weather, this heat is not objectionable. It was just an added extra in case the air gets brisk.

A few people had complained the foot position was uncomfortable but we didn't agree. Whether it is comfortable or uncomfortable for you will mostly depend on your build. There is no question that the rider's feet are tucked in close to the engine, but it doesn't take more than five minutes to become accustomed to this.

We were very surprised by the BMW's fast quarter-mile time. Consistent ETs in the mid 13.70's were common and a quarter mile top speed of 90.68 was the best we could achieve. Top speed never dropped below 89. Flat out, the R-75 would run a hair over 106 mph which is certainly fast enough for anyone. The motorcycle has sufficient horsepower and torque available to pull a taller gear. We believe that suitably geared, the R-75/5 would easily run 120.

You'll find the dual seat a really fine item for those long two-up trips. The adjustable rear shocks smooth out the rough spots.

Under the seat you'll find a tray containing the complete tool kit. You'll find the tire pump here also.

problems we experienced riding solo disappeared. The factory must have also discovered the problem because they raised the front end slightly which altered the front end geometry a bit. It now seems that last year's BMW front end was a borderline situation and when a second person rode the motorcycle, it changed chassis geometry just enough to cancel this uncomfortable, unstable sensation.

The forks have also received some attention. It seemed last year's machine had the annoying tendency to feel as though the fork tubes were locking in the lower stanchions. In essence, this amounted to riding a motorcycle with a rigid set of forks. Happily, this has been corrected.

Our '71 model displayed none of the earlier uncomfortable sensations. It's a delightful road bike in every sense of the term. If you're a freeway flyer, the R-75 will prove to be a great source of enjoyment. It now handles the way a BMW owner would expect it to.

We were impressed by the amount

of horsepower available over such a wide range. It has plenty of torque to handle riding two up long mountain grades or whistling down the road at 100 miles per hour. The more miles put on the motorcycle, the better it seemed to run. This is traditional for BMW and runs true to form with our test of other BMW models. They really seem to run best when they get about 10,000 miles.

We discovered one interesting thing the first cold morning we rode the freeway. Normally, at 67 to 75 miles per hour, one's feet tend to get a bit chilly. Not so with the BMW. Since your feet are tucked behind the cylinders, the barrels act as radiators to

At any speed, the one constant feature is the bike's smoothness and lack of noise, both from an exhaust and a mechanical standpoint. One reason the engine is so quiet is because the air filter is tucked inside the engine, eliminating the normal induction noise found on most motorcycles. This is just a small facet but we mention it to show what lengths the factory has gone to quiet their top-of-the-line model.

Should any panic situation arise, you quickly discover the BMW brakes are more than up to doing their job. The stoppers are quite good and, like the engine, the load won't make much difference. We found that in most circumstances, no more than two fingers were ever necessary on the front brake to bring the machine down to a safe stop quickly from 60 or 70 mph. The rear binder is equally effective. It's nice to know that the BMW is not only fast, but can be stopped quickly.

For the economy minded, you'll find you should be getting about 45 miles to the gallon, a respectable figure for a 750 with the R-75's performance capabilities.

It's obvious the factory has spent a lot of time studying people to determine what kind of engineering they would like to see on a quality motorcycle. Everything from the handlebars to the seat and footpegs scored the highest marks with us.

We particularly liked the seat. It's possible to ride this motorcycle for a long time without squirming or trying to find a more comfortable spot. If you like long-distance riding, you'll definitely appreciate the six-gallon gas tank. Under normal conditions, you should get around 250 to 275 miles per tank.

Now that BMW has corrected last year's errors, we feel BMW's new product is one of the best buys available for the road rider. If you thrill to the call of the open road, the R75/5 will put a lot of miles between breakfast and dinner and make every passing mile an enjoyable and different experience.

—*Bob Braverman*

BMW R75/5

ENGINE

Type	horizontally opposed twin cylinder 4-cycle
Bore and stroke	82 × 70.6
Displacement	745cc
Compression Ratio	9.0:1
Rated max. horsepower	57 @ 6,400 rpm
Rated max. torque	43.3 @ 5,000 rpm
Ignition	alternator/battery
Carburetion	twin constant velocity 32 mm concentrics
Lubrication	wet sump pressure fed

DIMENSIONS

Length	82.7 in.
Seat height	33.5 in.
Wheelbase	54.5 in.
Ground Clearance	6.5 in.
Dry weight	419 lbs.

WHEELS AND BRAKES

Front tire size	3.25 × 19 in.
Front brake type	double leading shoe, internal expanding
Rear tire size	4.00 × 18 in.
Rear brake type	internal expanding

TRANSMISSION

Type	constant mesh 4-speed
Cluth	dry, single plate diaphragm
Internal gear ratios	1st, 3.896:1; 2nd, 2.578:1 3rd, 1.875:1; 4th, 1.50:1
Final ratio	2.91:1
Countershaft gear	11T
Rear wheel	32T

GENERAL

Air Filtration	dry paper
Battery type	12V-15AH

CAPACITIES

Fuel tank	6.25 gal.
Fuel reserve	.5 gal.
Oil sump	4.7 pts. (w/filter)

FRAME AND SUSPENSION

Front suspension	telescopic double damping
Rear suspension	adjustable spring over shock
Frame type	tubular double cradle
Steering damper type	friction

COLORS

Black and Silver

DISTRIBUTORS

EAST: Butler & Smith, Inc., Walnut Street and Hudson Avenue, Norwood, N.J. 07648.
WEST: Flanders Company, 340 S. Fair Oaks Avenue, Pasadena, Calif. 91101.
CANADA: BMW Motorcycle Distributors, Willowdale, Ontario.

A middleweight BMW: The R60/5 on the road

AND really, where else? The massive reserves of strength in all the parts, the durable finish, the lack of any troublesome chain; all these cut down the time spent tinkering in the garage. It's not a heavy machine: nor is it large and unwieldy. It sits quietly chuffing on the stand and shakes gently. And so it does on the road: it chuffs quietly along at no great pace, and shakes gently the while. Neither it nor its rider is really in a hurry, yet ground is covered quietly and quickly.

If you want performance, the R60/5 is not for you. It is possible to wind it up to about 100 m.p.h., but this requires some patience, and if you wish to out accelerate the eager spridgets from traffic lights you will have to be very slick with your gear changing. There is a fair amount of power available, but the peaky power band conspires with the undistinguished gearchange to foil any really effective use of it. You don't win at the bottom end of the rev. range. The R60 pinks spitefully on anything less than the most highly rated 5-star petrol if any speed below 35 is attempted in top. Third (or second) is the town gear, and a fine wide speed range it has too. These comments are the result of conscious, and deliberate experiments, but once one relaxes (relapses?) into the BMW's rhythm, there is a marked degree of flexibility: perhaps the quiet and gentlemanly progress subconsciously gears down the twitch of the throttle wrist? It certainly seems like it. This BMW is the first comparatively smooth machine that was invariably travelling *slower* than I had thought before checking the headlamp-mounted speedometer.

Lack of effective acceleration (bearing in mind the 600 c.c.s and 40 + h.p.) was a distinct deterrent to overtaking into oncoming traffic in the drenching dusks of my week of road-testing. It was a question of change down (in agony to try to avoid the "crunch"), full throttle, and a good little wait if the car in front was doing over 60: but oh! the softness of those beautifully effective silencers. I'd willingly lose 5 b.h.p. from my Honda 4 for a similar soft note from those four pipes. I see, rereading the last sentences, that I have been rather unkind and to redress the balance will point out that a pillion passenger makes no visible difference to performance: it's that gearchange that kills it.

The transmission, taken as a whole, is exemplary. The final drive is much stronger than that of the earlier R69S, and the drive line has a fine solid feel to it. Shock absorption has not been neglected, and its effects are occasionally noticeable. The clutch is really light and pleasant to use. The drive is taken up very smoothly,

● **The latest BMWs are very alike—apart from engine capacity and power. It may be instructive, therefore, to read this report in conjunction with that on the R75/5 published last month.**

and the basic design is evidently "right". Much development has gone into the improved transmission for the new series of BMWs, and some odd difficulties were overcome on the way. The gearchange mechanism itself has a powerful indexing plunger to "help" the rider, in addition to more massive and sturdy cogs. The ratios are nicely spaced and the gearchange is positive. It would take a determined man either to overchange or to miss a gear, but I can recommend a good religion if quiet gearchanging is required.

The seat/footrest/handlebar positions are beautifully set out: everything is to hand, the knees fit naturally into the tank rubbers, the gearchange pedal is in just the right place, and there is a slight inclination to lean forward—not enough to make the wrists ache at low speeds, but enough to breast an 80 m.p.h. wind in comfort. The seat itself is comfortable, but a little hard. It has a convex surface that does not indent easily, so that in heavy rain the water soaks everywhere underneath the rider's and passenger's garments. The passenger has an ordinary leather grab-strap to hang onto, and two neatly chromed handles to clutch. In fact the passenger would be most comfortable as long as she had praeter-

naturally short legs. The pillion footrests are ludicrously poorly placed. They are far too far forward, and far too high. As a result the passenger is bent double, cramped onto a mere tithe of that vast seat, and subjugated to a tap-dance on her toes by the heels of the driver—who in his turn becomes very irritated. *This* BMW is a solo, unless the couple have a jointly equable temperament: and steel-tipped boots.

Here we have the nub of the matter: this is no refined R69S: this is a semi-touring, semi-sporting machine, and the compromises jump up and clamour for attention after a day or so. Take the handling, for example. This BMW is really good. The braking too—this machine really stops well. The road holding and the steering are equally good. A friction damper is fitted but is quite unnecessary. The R60 weighs a good 450 lb, but feels far lighter: it is great fun laying it down on a fine line through some twisting Hampshire road. It holds line well, doesn't lose the back end over bumps, and nothing grounds before the stands finally touch. Changing line is light work which belies the high centre of gravity. The new BMW telescopic forks are really strong, and have that rarity, a tough fork brace to increase torsional rigidity still further. The spring rates are a little strong for a really comfortable ride, but they pay off in precise handling. The rear suspension units have—sadly—lost their full enclosure, but retain

It is an "honest" machine
but definitely for a certain class of rider

the hand adjustment for spring preload. This small detail is worth a lot: on how many other machines do people actually change preload for passengers; and again when they get off? Like winkers, you never really know how you did without them before you had them. The Metzeler

the chatter of tappets. Charles Coombe assured me that all the clearances were correct, as he had just done them before loaning me the machine.

You may have wondered where we could find a BMW R60 in its natural state, out of captivity? Many of our

the machine on which I have had the pleasure of riding for a week, and we offer him our sincere thanks.

To return to the BMW: I soon became accustomed to the sound of half-a-dozen domented tricoteuse knitting madly over my toes. The intake silencing is good,

tyres were excellent on the wet roads with which I was cursed, and never gave any cause for concern. The silencers, cranked in that distinctive manner, are the final payoff from the new and livelier image. The ground clearance is materially increased by this cranking of the exhaust system, and here is the culprit for the cramped pillion rider. The footrests are above the raised section of the silencers. The balance pipe between the two exhaust systems runs across the front of the engine unit, and no doubt increases the rigidity of the exhaust system. The engine itself was described in detail in the January (1970) issue of *Motorcycle Sport*, where I gave a full technical description of the new R 50/60/75 range. One thing I was not prepared for was

readers will know that Charles Coombe and David Dickinson both used to work for MLGs: not long ago MLGs turned wholly to cars, but well before this, Dickinson had set up in Tintern (Mon), and Coombe in Slough in a little shop on the A4 Bath Road near the link to the M4 motorway. Specializing in BMWs, and also selling MZs in the last few months, his trade has built up rapidly and considerable numbers of BMWs have flowed through his shop to his customers from England, America and elsewhere. Indeed, the flow is such that it has been impossible to hold machines in stock, as they are sold as rapidly as they can be obtained. Mr. Coombe has an R60/5 of his own, and has occasionally let it out on road test or evaluation. This is

and the massive air filter is housed in the hump on the engine cases over the gearbox. The carburettors are 26 mm Bings, of typically Mikuni/Amal appearance and standard design. They are provided with large float bowl ticklers, but no choke. This was a distinct cause of annoyance. The BeeEm is a cold blooded beast, and wakes up slowly; starting by the electric starter is easy, but keeping the fire alight long enough to let it tick-over and warm the cockles of its heart was a distinct bind. After a few minutes it would take some throttle, but only when good and warm. Perhaps the omission of a choke is to aid the cause of rebore specialists? All that tickler petrol washing oil off the bores . . . The aspiration through those Bings is fairly efficient: I managed over 50 m.p.g. in mixed riding, and am not famed for leisurely progress. The fuel tank takes full advantage of the available space, and takes a good five gallons without feeling bulky—or indeed looking it The oil reservoirs are similarly generous, and have a welcome feature in the use of Allen socket headed bolts as plugs. Allen bolts are used fairly widely on this machine, and help to sustain the general air of effective and ample design

The angle at which it is set would ensure a sharp cartwheel if it were to dig in. You have been warned. In my turn, I was told of another point to watch. The steering column lock is in an awkward position, and if the key (which does *not* double as an ignition key) is left in after the steering has been unlocked, the fork leg clouts it firmly, and bends it or breaks it off in the lock. Again, you have been warned: this would be doubly frustrating as the steering lock key also

take care to plug it in correctly! Setting the timing is a straightforward task, and requires only the removal of the bulbous front engine cover. The overall accessibility is exemplary. The massive aluminium housings for the winkers are quite impressive, and the wide spacing of the winker bulbs themselves is a distinct safety factor. The only fault that I encountered in a week's riding was a failure of one of the winker bulbs, confirming that vibration is still a real

and engineering to the level of detailed examination. The driver's footrests are adjustable—always a welcome feature— and yet quite strong enough to survive the odd clout when off the road. I am now able to understand how the riders of BMWs manage to get through the ISDT so well: men of iron they may be, but their machines certainly give them every assistance other than a light weight. The ground clearance is splendid; as is quite obvious in the photographs. The stands are good and hold the machine stably on most reasonably firm surfaces. The prop stand has one invidious feature: it is quite invisible under the left cylinder head when the machine is resting on it, and as it holds the BMW at only a modest angle, is easily forgotten.

unlocks the seat for access to the tool kit in its tray over the rear mudguard, and thus you would be barred from any attempts to put matters aright. You would be unsuccessful anyway, as the removal of such broken keys is a far from easy task.

The electrical equipment is very good on the whole: I have a personal dislike of the grinding, wheezing starter motor, but no complaints about its effectiveness. The headlight is a bit short on range, but gives a fine allround view for lower speeds when things nearer at hand are of greatest interest. The ignition pack is fully encapsulated, and contains the usual transistors, etc. It also costs over £18, and *if* the reverse polarity protection is as poor as I have seen elsewhere,

factor as it failed at a continuous cruising speed of about 6,000 r.p.m. in third while breasting a water-bearing gale. The indicator switch really works easily and well with or without heavy gloves, and the horn has a deep and mellow note that definitely frightened several cats and dogs in my path. A major advance over the horns fitted to many motorcycles.

The rev-counter and speedometer needles were prone to violent oscillations at a marked change in speed, and took their time settling down after rapid acceleration. The rev-meter is so small and badly placed that it was of little value. I hope this is corrected soon, as the BMW could easily be over-revved by riders who have not yet obtained an automatic rev-watching reflex. The BMW vibrates quite a lot, and my passenger was in no doubt of this! It remains a low-frequency shake, however, and never reaches the spine-tingling pitch too often cursed in other machines.

Strangely, the vibration from an R69/S that I compared with the R60/5 was less. The older machine had more guts, revved more easily, and had distinctly more torque than the R60/5: the brakes were not as good, however.

The design of the new BMW brakes departs only a little from the older models'. The self-adjusting system of cable to one brake arm and leading to the other works as well as ever, and a new lining material certainly provides a good consistent "bite". The self-servo action is at an effective compromise, and gives a nice feel to the action. Stopping the BMW was never a problem. Starting it was, however. The classic BMW pegged key was a real brute to get into the socket, and I now have six or seven blood blisters on my hands from it: perhaps further comment would be unwise.

An odd observation: the twin flat cylinders keep one's feet warm, but not dry: the high placing of the cylinders conspires to convert the lightest rain into a series of thin streams of water from the fins. The fins themselves slow down the air flow, so one gains no real benefit from travelling faster. I got very wet though my boots, which have proved more than adequate in other circumstances.

The BMW is really designed to last, and the massive solidity of all about it is very appealing. I am really puzzled as to how to give it an overall rating. It is a solid product but the money for it seems overmuch: but compare it with the Guzzi V7, which is far more impressive (but has poor performance)—and it looks about right once more. Performance is limited, but 80 m.p.h. cruising is possible for very long distances without fatigue.

It is "light", and certainly handles well, but seems to have sold its superb touring heritage for a cramped redesign of sporting pretensions. To be honest, I don't really know what to make of it. I would *not* recommend performance oriented riders to get it, even though the top speed is there and usable: subjectively it just doesn't deliver. For tourists: yes, but keep away from 3-star or lower petrol, or you will have even less tractability without pinking. At last a picture emerges: a country with good petrol, long distances, and solo riders with a lot of money. America again.

And in Europe, France. And so it hath come to pass, that there they have sold a multitude.

I am grateful for having had the chance to assess the BMW on its home ground: roads and by ways in mixed weathers. It is supremely practical, and that new sporting handling is a delight. I give no judgement: it is an honest machine, but definitely for a certain class of rider. Can one say more?
M. R. W.

BY BOB PIERCE

I WON'T DENY IT. I was still afraid of my newly acquired BMW—my first motorcycle. And there I was, ready to roll on a 2600-mile trip from my home in suburban Chicago to San Francisco.

My bike was a '67 R50 with 8000 miles on it. It had a windshield, luggage rack and a motor that was tight and sweet to listen to.

To add to my fears, it was raining, hard and steady. It was October—Saturday, Oct. 11—one of the Midwest's most reliable months.

GREEN IN THE SADDLE

I was a green rider. Three weeks and less than 150 miles of saddle time. And I was still spooked from my mad, maiden ride when I hooked a shock-absorber on a car bumper and flattened myself on the trunk of a very hard Buick.

I was turning in a small parking lot when it happened. I goosed the throttle when I meant to retard it! I had a thigh bruise like a pie pan and a morbid memory of how it feels to be shot out of a cannon.

Two questions kept me skittish: 1) With no rain-riding experience, how hairy was my first day in a deluge with 75 lb. of gear apt to be? 2) With no hill-city experience what were the odds I'd roll downhill backwards at the first stoplight on San Francisco's vertical streets?

Think I'm kidding? I was so chicken I almost turned back a mile from home. It's stupid to tell this, but the damn bike fell over on me just waiting at a stoplight!

I put my supporting foot on a gob of grease. My angle of rest and the gutter gradient did the rest. I started to slide. With my weight, 75 lb. of gear and 420 lb. of BMW committed to that foot, I went down on my back like Fido playing "dead dog." Witnesses just looked puzzled. Was I showing off, or did I always get off a bike that way?

Embarrassment was one thing. Picking the loaded bike up was something else! My first two tries were ball-busters. Then I got smart. I placed my feet just right, squatted down, straightened my back and came up with my legs like a piano mover. Up she came like a trunk full of pig iron, fighting me all the way. I prayed I'd never have to lift her again.

I walked the bike around the corner, started her up and slowly circled three or four blocks wondering whether this trip was really necessary.

When my cool came back I sloshed on to a rendezvous with Route 66, the old Chicago-to-L.A. highway Tex Benecke used to rave about.

TRAVEL GEAR

My gear included a great little Eureka Drawtite tent and an Eddie Bauer arctic sleeping bag. October nights in the western highlands can get pretty frigid.

I got the sleeping bag into a heavy plastic duffle bag with other gear. I laid the duffle bag across the passenger half of the saddle and kept its width less than the handlebars so nothing could snag me from the side. Two medium suitcases rode the luggage rack with the tent bag on top of them.

Main support for the load was a 10-ft. web belt. I passed the belt under the front of my saddle to the middle of its length. Then I laid the two resultant 5-ft. lengths over the load about a foot apart and buckled them under the trailing edge of the luggage rack.

For lateral stability I used my bungy cords from one side of the rack to the other over the suitcases and tent.

I carried a quart of top-off oil in a plastic bottle, new inner tube and clutch cable, extra shoes, flashlight, lock and chain, etc., in canvas saddlebags. A bungy cord tie-down on each side kept the bags from shifting position under way.

A piece of canvas 30 by 48 in. made a rain cover for the load and provided a secure, accessible place to stow sweaters, jacket and rain gear where they could be grabbed as needed. Two bungy cords from the passenger safety strap over the covered load to the trailing edge of the luggage rack kept the cover snug all the way.

A shaving kit fastened to the handlebar with a single bungy was convenient for carrying sunglasses, tire and plug gauges, extra plugs, pen, electric razor, etc.

FIGHTING A HEAVY LOAD

Most of the load weight was ahead of the center of the rear wheel. I experienced no instability on the road. But the two times I had to right the bike from the dead-dog position—man, I can tell you 75 extra lb. on top can make the righting of a BMW one hell of a strain!

The heavy load also made it impossible for me to rock the bike up on the center stand. I struggled with this problem on and off for two days before I left home. Finally, I tried rolling the back wheel up on a short piece of 2 by 4 before pulling her back for the vault on the stand. It worked! The added impetus of rolling off the block put her on the stand easily every time. I carried a short length of 2 by 4 anyway as a crankcase prop in case of a flat up front.

I also carried a small square of half-inch plywood, about 6 by 6 in. For beer and bladder stops on unpaved ground, I centered the kickstand on it to keep the stand from sinking and pulling the bike down.

Beating southwest toward St. Louis against the sting of raindrops was exhila-rating. The faster I rode, the harder the sting, like rice thrown in your face at a wedding. Beak and cheeks got numb after a time and I ignored them.

Plowing along like a water skier in high speed traffic, I envied the motorists the nicety of their hard-working wind-shield wipers. Looking at the world through rain-spattered glasses is a tricky business.

I found the eyes are clever though at looking between the rain drops. Also, that a slight downward tilt of the head stretches the droplets, reduces their density and improves the view.

For the hell of it, I tried it without the goggles. But my eyelids went crazy trying to keep my eyeballs dry. I yanked the goggles down again.

"RAIN GEAR STINKS..."

Trip notebook entry for that day: "Rain gear stinks. Should have tried it out before leaving home. Thought tucking tail of poncho under crotch would keep pants dry. Nylon pant sleeves no

Ilustrations by Jim Crawford

good on a bike. Rain pants—get some! . . . With arch straps to keep pant legs down over boot tops!"

I was soaked from the waist down all the way to Granite City, Ill. (outskirts of St. Louis), some 6 hr./300 miles down the road. It was dark when I got there. The rain picked up force as I stopped at the end of the 66 lead-off ramp. My throttle hand was numb in a cold, mushy glove and I over-accelerated in a right-hand turn. Instantly, the drive-wheel bolted on the bias and

dumped me in the middle of a busy four-lane leading into town.

I was lucky. Oncoming cars and trucks stopped, lighting my purple face in the downpour as I "oooofed" through the weight-lifting act once more and slowly forced the bike to its wheels.

A farmer in a pickup offered to tote the bike to a garage if it was damaged. The BMW was fine, but his offer was encouraging. I had expected people to be indifferent, if not a little hostile, toward cyclists. I was wrong. For 2600 miles people were not only considerate, many were honestly intrigued with my undertaking.

Minutes later while I was still trying to get the flooded motor to start,

another pickup stopped. The driver was half boiled. He got out in the rain in his shirt sleeves and offered to truck me and the bike to town—or better still, goddammit, leave the bike there and solve my problem by buying me a drink. His wife had just left him and he was planning to spend the weekend on a barstool getting even with her.

I stayed at the Sun Motel that first night in Granite City. I was a soggy mess. Good rain pants, and I would have stayed dry. My full Bell helmet over-lapped the poncho collar just right. For all that dousing, no water shipped in at the neck.

Hope for a dry second day dissolved when I looked out the window Sunday

Travels Of An Old Dude

Going West, Or East,
Or Anywhere Is The Classic
Adventure, The Road Rider
Syndrome That Appeared
Long Before Bronson. Do You
Wonder Whether You Have What It Takes
To Take Off? Don't. All You Need Is
Time, A Few Weeks In The Saddle,
And A Good Bike Underneath You.

Travels Of An Old Dude

morning. My BMW was shimmering with the steady splatter of water. A good breakfast cheered me up, but half an hour of the starting game with flooded carburetors modified my outlook.

Once the bike got flooded I always had a struggle. Both times the bike went over with me I had a hell of a time bringing her back to life and now my ignorance of the right technique held me up again. When she popped it was the last kick I had left.

Missouri is like a roller coaster. I was elated as I sailed up and down over the wet, autumnal countryside. At Rolla, a happy, hairy haggle of hippies laughingly wagged thumbs and hailed me with pleasantries as I waved and burbled by. They looked biblically wretched huddled under papers and ponchos in the deluge like they were waiting for Noah to steam up in the Ark.

I stopped at several stores, but no rain suits. If it had not been for the chill of October at 65 mph I might have gotten used to wet laundry.

BRONSON RUBS OFF

Five or six times that day I forgot completely about my clammy underwear. I was a kid again. Local girls, joyriding two or more in a car, were hailing me like Bronson. They would catch up slowly, then shout and wave as they passed. I began to enjoy these interludes with Miss America. She kept right on popping up every day of my journey.

Notebook entry: "Winds stronger crossing Missouri today. Mayflower van passed me on a gusty hilltop. Combination of wind force and suction yanked the bike hard, set up hell of a wobble. Was I startled? Better believe it. Wonder if suction hasn't swallowed a rider here and there when wind force and passing clearance are just right?"

It was dark and still raining when I pulled into the "Glo Motel" in Springfield, Mo. I was wetter than a gym sock on the shower room floor. I peeled to the skin, then discovered the room had no hangers—and no phone to ask for some. How could I get all my dripping gear up in front of the wall heater?

I sat naked on a cold plastic chair and thought about it. The bungy cords! The ceiling was blocked with 18-in. acoustical tiles laid loose on a metal gridwork. I poked the bungy hooks up over the metal cross sections and created a great floating "mobile" of soggy jockey shorts, gloves, sweaters, shirt, sox, jacket, T-shirt, pants and boots—all floating mystically in the rising warmth of the heater. Talk about beautiful! I felt like you know Who on the seventh day.

NO RAIN, NO START

No rain! Monday morning was dreary but dry. But I couldn't get the bike to start. For two hours I tried this, tried that, waited for the carbs to drain—stupid! I had called two bike shops but didn't expect help for another 30 min. when Clyde Jenkins, owner of a '47 BMW R50, drove up in a station wagon and solved my problem.

Clyde, a friendly mechanic about my age, 48, had watched me pumping the kicker from the stoplight at the corner. He showed me how to open the throttle wide and pump the kicker to drain the carbs. He also showed me the proper throttle setting to start. I hadn't been cracking it enough! Jumping her from not enough gas to too much seems like I should have stumbled into the right proportion more often.

Clyde said he rode his old BMW every weekend. "Like to get out there and move. She loves it when I hold her needle right on 80!"

Ate a fishburger and a cheeseburger at McDonald's before leaving Springfield. Repeated the order at McDonald's in Joplin and had a big steak dinner at the Standard Truck Stop in Tulsa. I wasn't exercising, but it took plenty of calories to keep my wind-swept torso warm.

Now that the rain was over the first store I stopped at, Adran's in Joplin, had rain suits. For $6, I bought overall-type pants with a jacket. I tried one on and kept it on all day as a windbreaker. Thirty-five to 40 degrees is cold on a motorcycle.

Notebook entries: "Checked tires in Joplin. Both down about 5 lb. Bike toppled over against the gas pump. Damm little wing stand no good with a load ... Lucky I abandoned original plan to go west on I-80. Joplin weatherman says Nebraska and Colorado have a foot of snow!"

CLEAR LENSES FOR NIGHT

It was dark when I got to Tulsa on the Oklahoma Turnpike, but I decided to push on to Oklahoma City—more turnpike for 88 miles. It was vervy rocketing through the night, splitting the cold, brittle air. But something was wrong with my lights. It took me about 5 min. to realize I still had my green goggles on. I switched to clear lenses—what a difference!

I slept warm and well that night in my tent and sleeping bag at the Oklahoma City KOA (Kampgrounds of America) for $2.50, which included clean washroom, shower, store, all you need.

Tuesday rolled up cold and sunny. According to the *Amarillo Globe-Times* it was the coldest October 14 since 1914: 31 degrees. I wore everything I had with the rain suit over it, but I still got stiff with the chill before I made the 270-mile hop to Amarillo.

Like all cold-weather BMW riders, I found tucking the feet under those way-out cylinders gives heat. I could feel it through my boots even at 60 mph.

I passed the same bunch of hippy hitchhikers I saw back at Rolla, Mo. They were dancing at an intersection in Erick, Okla., "Home of Roger Miller—King of the Road." Persistence pays. Here they were, traveling for nothing and ahead of me.

Notebook entry: "Nose burn getting bad. Need to fix nose shield flap onto goggles or something. Hate to see a beak plastered with Noxema."

A cowboy in a gas station told me the weather for Wednesday would be warmer, in the 60's. Great! But I still half expected to get caught in a snow storm before I got through New Mexico and Arizona.

Had a great Mexican dinner in Amarillo. Huge platter of enchiladas, tacos, frijoles, rice and dos botellas of Carta Blanca, the great Mexican beer. I found KOA Amarillo, but the rate was $3 and several motel signs were begging me to stop for $4. So I chickened out on camping and took a warm room and bath.

Another perfect day! It was great to be alive that Wednesday morning as I loaded the bike in the warm, rising sun. I was looking forward to the rugged beauty of the real West now—New Mexico, Arizona and California.

Before leaving Amarillo I stopped at a BSA shop on 66 for an oil change. I wanted DA-40 but the shop sold Oilzum. The shop owner said it was great. The poop on the can goes further than that: "Oilzum is the choice of champions. If motors could speak we wouldn't need to advertise." Who could argue with bullshit like that?

THE BURGLAR ALARM

A BSA rider from New Orleans told me about a cheap burglar alarm while I was changing my oil. "You see them in variety stores for 98 cents. They're made in Hong Kong. Little battery/buzzer to tack up next to doors and windows. If the door is opened it pulls a string and sets the buzzer off. Well, I rigged one up for my bike. Lift the kickstand and it would go off. Used it at a motel in Mobile one night. I parked the bike in front of my room. There was no front window so, to be sure I could hear the buzzer, I left my door open about half an inch. During the night someone took my pants off the chair with $45 in them."

There was an abrupt change from Panhandle flatness to rugged, mountain terrain just before the New Mexico border. From that point on it was a ride on a magic carpet. The serenely beautiful desert/mountain West has always grabbed me. Absorbing mile after mile

of New Mexico's scenic vastness by motorcycle was pure delight. The only, only way to go!

Notebook entries: "Going up, getting colder. Tucumcari 4089 ft. Santa Rosa 4800 ft. Terrific guacamole salad, enchilada dinner and sopaipillas with honey at Jo & Mary's Cafe in Santa Rosa. Mary said there was snow at upcoming Cline's Corners last Sunday, but it had melted . . .

"Finally learned when to shift down to third climbing grades. Know I must have been lugging slightly through Missouri hills. She really perks up in third."

It was still early when I reached Albuquerque, so I chased the falling sun on into Grants, N.M. I got there at dusk and put up at the Milan Motel; no campground signs anywhere.

The sunny mountain air was intoxicating as I crossed the road Thursday morning for bacon and eggs at the Busy Bee Cafe. Shapely young waitress was friendly, but she had a large cold. She said 200 tourists were stranded in Grants for two weeks by a record snowfall a couple of years back. About this time of year, too.

I ate a little faster than usual. I knew a new storm front was expected from the west in 24 hours. I began to fight a fateful feeling I would get snowbound somewhere in northern Arizona and be forced off the road.

COLD IN THE MOUNTAINS

As I rolled on into Arizona there was lots of sun, but ominous cloud dreadnaughts began floating over the horizon toward me in alarming numbers. As I climbed toward Flagstaff it grew very cold. I put on every rag I had including the rain suit. A goose-down jump suit is the only thing for cold-weather biking—this trip convinced me!

The heady, pine-scented air of the Flagstaff pinnacle was delicious to sense, even being blasted at me at 65-75 mph.

The descent from Flagstaff to Winslow was sensational. I kept her between 75 and 80 all the way down. The only

thing that passed me was a California chopper with a Hell's Angel on it. We flipped hands at each other as he slid by. He was bald, fiftyish; taking the cold, cold wind in a T-shirt and "uniform" vest.

I passed him later on the outskirts of Winslow when he stopped to put a jacket on. This helped. I didn't feel quite as fragile anymore.

I made Kingman, Ariz., about 5 p.m. after dropping down, down still farther from Winslow, like an endless bobsled ride. Talk about grandeur—the memory of those limitless vistas I was treated to that day is still sharp in my mind!

I had a cheese omelette at a cafe I picked because of a parking place in front of the window. I just got served when the manager drew the shades to signify he was closed to additional customers. This bugged me some because I made it a habit to keep my eye on the bike and the gear. I finally subdued my middle-class, up-tight temptation to run out and put the chain on it.

I cruised out to the Kingman KOA on the east side of town. For $2.50 I had a hot shower and a smooth tent site. It was a great night for desert starlight and sound, sound sleep.

I got off at 9 a.m. Friday morning. Decided not to eat till I got to California. Needles was just 61 miles away. As it turned out I rolled through Needles and didn't stop till Amoy, a tiny oasis on the great desert floor. As I left the cafe, Bob Stone of Barstow asked about my trip. He's a trail rider, 100-cc Yamaha.

CATCHING NEUTRAL

Luckily, I thought to ask him about the trouble I was having slipping into neutral at stoplights. Catching neutral and getting the approval of the little green light on my speedometer was a sometime thing, 1 out of 10 maybe—like catching a greased pig.

"Hell no, don't bother with neutral at stoplights," Bob said. "You won't hurt the clutch by holding her in. Just keep the bike primed and ready to go. Then get off pronto to keep the cars from climbing your back!"

(Editor's note: holding the clutch in may be the most expedient answer when you can't grab neutral at a stoplight. However, it's tiring, and poses a possible problem should the clutch begin grabbing or the clutch cable let go, thus jetting you off into traffic against a red light. A much more acceptable solution to find a recalcitrant neutral is to slip into it, just before the bike comes to a complete stop.)

He also directed me to the best place in Barstow for good, cold beer: the "Noisy Nag."

A desert headwind became so fierce after Amoy I could only make 50 mph comfortably in third gear! It blasted me pretty good all the way to Boron.

After pie and coffee in Boron, the bike started, but pooped out in 100 yd. She ran another block and pooped again. I pulled off the road, put her on the center stand and dug out the repair manual.

I was checking one of the float bowls when Dale Robertson, a young diesel

An Old Dude

mechanic, reined up beside me on a new 650 Triumph. Together we looked things over. The plugs were dry; we had a spark, so the trouble was in the fuel system.

After 30 min. we had the bike running, but roughly. Dale led the way to a small garage where LaVerne Hall and Jimbo Baghosin were tuning a hot rod. LaVerne dropped everything and tackled my problem. Throttle cable and idling screw adjustments were the answer. For the second time—just like I had rubbed a lamp or something—a fellow cyclist had materialized at my side when I needed help. Payment? Forget it. My Boron friends wouldn't take a cent. The motorcycling fraternity is one hell of a club!

I spent the night in a Boron motel and pursued my westward way on Highway 58 (I left 66 at Barstow) Saturday morning. I fought stiff headwinds all the way to Tehachapi—I mean fourth gear was useless, especially on the way up the Tehachapi Mountains. The R-50 is a great little bike, but it's no wind-beater.

"AMERICANA"

It was another dream world glissade down the other side of the mountains into the vast San Joaquin Valley, with miles of cotton and sorghum fields. I passed a hippy-decorated house in Bakersfield bearing a large signboard invitation to "SLEEP WITH HANK!"

I switched to Highway 99 there and followed it north to 46, about 16 miles. Going west again on 46 I stopped beside a field of ripe, fluffy cotton near Wasco to relax and soak up some of the warm, sunny atmosphere. I topped off the oil level. It was novel having a whole field of Handiwipes to wipe the dipstick.

Thirty-one miles west of Wasco I turned northwest on 33 to Coalinga. From there it was a sinuous ride up and over the Diablo Range on 198 to San Lucas and Highway 101. These low coastal mountains have a weird, dessicated look in the winter months. An unrelieved carpeting of short, beige grasses rides every undulation to the horizon. I had the Kafkaesque feeling of a lone trespasser on some huge, dead golf course.

Sudden relief from this sense of unreality came near lonely Priest Station, a two-or-three-building spot.

I was rounding a downgrade curve at 70 mph when a white-tailed buck and doe raced out of a thicket to my right, headed for a point in the road just ahead of me. The fields on both sides were fenced with barbed wire. The buck spied me first, aborting his take-off over the right-hand fence. He wheeled and returned to the thicket.

But the delicate doe was committed to the air. She cleared the fence, landed 15 ft. in front of me, covered the road in three bounds and sailed over the fence to my left vanishing like a comet. My brakes made all the difference. The doe's timing was deadly. If my brakes had failed I would have checked out with the wrong "deer" on my lap.

A homemade sign below Priest Station told me "JUSUS LIES!"

At San Lucas I turned north on 101. I had another great Mexican meal at a most unlikely place in Soledad—the Greyhound Bus Station.

At Salinas I took a side road seven miles west to the coast and my favorite highway of all the highways I have ever been on: California 1, the famous beach route that rides the glittering Pacific shoreline the length of the State.

I wanted to camp at Sunset Beach State Park, but the camp was full. I settled for the beautiful seaside KOA at Watsonville for $3.

I woke in my tent early Sunday morning to a stimulating message on the camp p.a. system: "Good morning you knockabout foresters, you highway pioneers. Breakfast has been in progress for 15 min. Come on, Mr. Sims. How are you, Lt. Governor? The flapjacks are hot and we've got real maple syrup. Come and get 'em!"

A ROBIN HOOD IDYLL

A free breakfast! This KOA was on the ball. I was ravenous. I stepped out of the tent—into Sherwood Forest. Everybody I met had a green Robin Hood hat on.

The first one I talked to was standing at a urinal in the shower house. Over his shoulder he told me I was in the midst of an International Travel Trailer Association campout . . . no green hat, no hot pancakes!

Back in the tent, rolling my sleeping bag, I heard girlish voices. I looked out. I was surrounded by pretty, pajama-clad girls of the grammar school set—six of them. They appeared like genies out of a bottle to invite me to a pancake breakfast in the trailer next door.

My host at this memorable breakfast was Hal Sower of San Carlos, a friendly physicist about my age. His daughter, Mary Beth, was 10 that day. He was treating her and her friends to a birthday campout.

Hal filled me with pancakes and told me about his work developing laser beams for optical surgery. When my mouth was available for talking again I told him about my trip and the virtues of the BMW.

My ride from Watsonville to San Francisco that sun-fulled Sunday was

too much! Really. My joy-of-living level has never run higher than during the two or three leisurely hours I soared over the shimmering edge of the Pacific from Watsonville to the Golden Gate.

Down to the surf, up to a craggy promontory, down to the sea again. Fields of lettuce, spinach and artichokes, some running right to the sandy lip of the sea. And pumpkin patches full of fat, golden globes and happy San Franciscans parading up and down the rows to make their selections.

There's a high point just south of Pacifica that provides a thrilling, tortuous climb to a spectacular view of the ocean.

SOULFUL ROAD

The Sunday parade of choppers and stock bikes streaming out of San Francisco that afternoon was tonic to my cycling soul. A greater road for a Sunday ride I never expect to find.

I stopped at Broadmoor for gas and a San Francisco map. And then I was there, fighting my way through the after-game traffic at Kezar Stadium. It was time to try some of those steep-hill stoplights that had been bugging me.

I rode north from the Stadium/Golden Gate Park area to Balboa Blvd. where I turned east and headed for the hilly heart of town. Hillside lights along the way weren't giving me any trouble. In fact, my hill-holding confidence was growing fast. I surmounted Knob Hill, awed, but capably enough, and went on to conquer the high-flying roadway to the base of Coit Tower.

I was satisfied. Nothing to it but the added pleasure of cycling over steep-hilled, exciting terrain.

I glided down to Fisherman's Wharf. I was reflecting on my eight-day accomplishment when I saw a 350 Honda with Japanese plates and a mountain of luggage. The rider, Kohei Iwamoto, was easy to identify in a full leather suit. He was eating at a lunch counter and writing postcards to his friends in Yokohama.

Kohei told me he was on the last lap of a 31,000-mile around-the-world trip—Yokohama, Russia, Europe, United States, Hawaii, Yokohama. He was then on his 215th day and due to sail that week for Hawaii on the President Cleveland.

I commented on his high-wide baggage load. "Big baggage, big tire," he said. He pointed to his 4.00-18 on the drive wheel. I asked about the 350's performance on so long a journey. "Thirty-one thousand miles," he said, "no trouble."

So there you are—2600 miles or 31,000 on bikes as different in size, design, price as the R50 BMW and the 350 Honda—the range of motorcycle adventure is whatever you want to make it.